Transient Psychosis:

Diagnosis, Management and Evaluation

Transient Psychosis:
Diagnosis, Management and Evaluation

Edited by

Joe P. Tupin, M.D.
Professor and Chairman,
Department of Psychiatry,
University of California,
Davis Medical Center,
Sacramento, California

Uriel Halbreich, M.D.
Associate Professor and Director,
Division of Biological Psychiatry,
Albert Einstein College of Medicine
of Yeshiva University,
Bronx, New York

Jesus J. Pena, J.D., M.P.A.
Senior Vice-President,
Saint Michael's Medical Center,
Newark, New Jersey

BRUNNER/MAZEL, *Publishers* • New York

Library of Congress Cataloging in Publication Data
Main entry under title:

Transient psychosis.

  Includes bibliographical references and index.
  1. Psychoses. I. Tupin, Joe P., 1934-
II. Halbreich, Uriel, 1945-   . III. Pena, Jesus J.
[DNLM: 1. Psychotic disorders. WM 200 T772]
RC512.T73 1984   616.89   83-23965
ISBN 0-87630-353-X

Published by
BRUNNER/MAZEL, INC.
19 Union Square
New York, New York 10003

MANUFACTURED IN THE UNITED STATES OF AMERICA

Contents

Contributors

FARUK S. ABUZZAHAB, SR., M.D.,
PH.D.
*Clinical Professor, Departments of
Psychiatry, Pharmacology, and
Family Practice and Community
Health, University of Minnesota,
Minneapolis, Minnesota*

DAN BLAZER, M.D., PH.D.
*Associate Professor of Psychiatry;
Head, Division of Social and
Community Psychiatry, Duke
University Medical Center, Durham,
North Carolina*

HARVEY BLUESTONE, M.D.
*Director, Department of Psychiatry,
Bronx-Lebanon Hospital Center;
Professor of Psychiatry, Albert
Einstein College of Medicine, Bronx,
New York*

RONALD CAMPBELL, M.D.
*Resident in Psychiatry, Department
of Psychiatry, University of
California-Davis Medical Center,
Sacramento, California*

RANDALL CHRISTENSON, M.D.
*Staff Psychiatrist, Pine Rest
Christian Hospital, Grand Rapids,
Michigan*

PATRICK T. DONLON, M.D.
*Clinical Professor, Department of
Psychiatry, University of California
at Davis, Davis, California*

JEAN ENDICOTT, Ph.D.
*Director, Research Assessment and
Training Unit, New York State
Psychiatric Institute, and Professor
of Clinical Psychology, Department
of Psychiatry, College of Physicians
and Surgeons, Columbia University,
New York, New York*

MARC GALANTER, M.D.
*Director, Division of Alcoholism and
Drug Abuse; Associate Professor,
Department of Psychiatry, Albert
Einstein College of Medicine, Bronx,
New York*

ALAN J. GELENBERG, M.D.
*Associate Professor of Psychiatry,
Harvard Medical School; Chief,
Special Studies Clinic, Erich
Lindemann Mental Health Center,
and Massachusetts General Hospital,
Boston, Massachusetts*

SUSANNA GOLDSTEIN, M.D.
*Research Psychiatrist, Albert
Einstein College of Medicine, Bronx,
New York*

EFRAIN A. GOMEZ, M.D.
Associate Professor of Psychiatry,
Baylor College of Medicine, Houston,
Texas

URIEL HALBREICH, M.D.
Director, Division of Biological
Psychiatry, and Associate Professor,
Psychiatry, Albert Einstein College
of Medicine, Bronx, New York

LEO E. HOLLISTER, M.D.
Senior Medical Investigator, VA
Medical Center; and Professor of
Medicine, Psychiatry and
Pharmacology, Stanford University
School of Medicine, Palo Alto,
California

DAVID JANOWSKY, M.D.
Professor of Psychiatry, University of
California at San Diego, La Jolla,
California

ANTHONY L. LaBRUZZA, M.D.
Assistant Professor of Psychiatry,
Yale University, New Haven,
Connecticut

GABRIEL V. LAURY, M.D.
Psychiatry Service, VA Hospital,
Montrose, New York; Department of
Psychiatry, New York Medical
College, Valhalla, New York

JONATHAN LISANSKY, M.D.
Assistant Professor of Psychiatry,
University of New Mexico School of
Medicine; Chief, Division of Consult
Liaison Psychiatry, V A Hospital,
Albuquerque, New Mexico

JOHN MELELLA, M.S.W.
Chief of the Forensic Psychiatry
Clinic, Bronx-Lebanon Hospital
Center, Bronx, New York

MENACHEM MELINEK, M.D.
Associate Director, Department of
Psychiatry, Bronx-Lebanon Hospital
Center; and Assistant Professor,
Department of Psychiatry, Albert
Einstein College of Medicine, Bronx,
New York

DEBORAH Y. MUTH, M.S.W.
Program Manager, Borderline Day
Treatment Program, University of
California-Davis Medical Center,
Sacramento, California

ALBERTA J. NASSI, PH.D.
Assistant Clinical Professor and
Clinical Director, Borderline Day
Treatment Program, Department of
Psychiatry, University of California-
Davis Medical Center, Sacramento,
California

JESUS J. PENA, J.D., M.P.A.,
Senior Vice-President, Saint
Michael's Medical Center, Newark,
New Jersey

S. CRAIG RISCH. M.D.
Department of Psychiatry,
University of California at San
Diego, La Jolla, California

PEDRO RUIZ, M.D.
Professor of Psychiatry, Baylor
College of Medicine, Houston, Texas

CHARLES B. SCHAFFER, M.D.
Assistant Professor and Director,
Inpatient Psychiatry Unit,
Department of Psychiatry,
University of California at Davis,
Sacramento, California

DANIEL S.P. SCHUBERT, M.D.,
Ph.D.
Director, Research Department of
Psychiatry, Cleveland Metropolitan
General Hospital and Case Western
Reserve University School of
Medicine, Cleveland, Ohio

RICK J. STRASSMAN, M.D.
Clinical Research Fellow,
Department of Psychiatry,
University of California at San
Diego, La Jolla, California

JOE P. TUPIN, M.D.
Professor and Chairman, Department
of Psychiatry, University of
California at Davis, Davis,
California; and Chief of Psychiatry,
University of California-Davis
Medical Center, Sacramento,
California

NICHOLAS WALSH, M.D.
Fellow, Division of Alcoholism and
Drug Abuse, Department of
Psychiatry, Albert Einstein College
of Medicine, Bronx, New York

Introduction

The term "transient psychosis" does not appear in official psychiatric literature. It is a term, however, widely used by mental health professionals for a number of decades—important and interesting because it emphasizes that all psychoses are not chronic. Indeed, the prognosis may be good and the duration limited. At the same time, it suggests that, under certain circumstances, even short-term psychiatric events can have psychotic elements and thus represent a major disruption of individual functioning.

This concept is a critical one. If one reviews the literature over the last 50 to 80 years, it is characterized by a slow recognition of the different kinds of psychoses. Careful clinical observations, correlated with treatment response, outcome of family history, and other significant criteria, have identified psychoses caused by physical conditions, delirium, changes in mood and the continually perplexing schizophrenia. However, brief psychotic episodes have little literary documentation.

DSM-III (1) refers to "brief reactive psychosis," a designation which captures the essence of the term used in this book. Several major characteristics (lack of chronicity of the psychosis, return to a previous level of mental functioning, and short duration) are compatible with the concept of brief reactive psychosis; the main variation is one of degree. On page 200, the DSM-III stresses the severity of the precipitating event, citing it as one which would "evoke significant symptoms of distress in almost anyone." While this observation or requirement for the diagnosis of brief reactive psychosis is significant, it fails to recognize that transient psychosis can be a consequence of stressors which fall short of this level of severity. Indeed, it is implicit throughout this book that an inverse relationship may exist between the severity of the stressor and the level of preexisting psychopathology, suggesting that severe personality disorders predispose individuals to episodes of transient psychosis. The stressors may in fact be minimal to mentally healthy individuals and *not* evoke significant symptoms of distress. As a result of this complexity

—treating an acute psychosis coexisting with a chronic personality disorder—several of the following chapters describe both short- and long-term management to develop optimum therapeutic intervention.

This posture stresses the diverse etiology, both intrinsic and extrinsic, of the individual. In addition to preexisting personality disorders and external stressors, drugs, drug withdrawal, or other medical conditions may play a role in initiating a transient psychosis. Many but not all of these will meet the criteria for brief reactive psychosis.

Particularly exempt from this diagnostic arena are medical and drug-related conditions, which should be carefully considered whenever a clinician is confronted with short-term psychotic episodes, as outlined in following chapters. The editors wish to highlight how important such diagnoses and constant reevaluation are to insuring appropriate treatment. It is hoped readers will recognize the complexity inherent in this type of psychosis and not be led into simplistic diagnostic conclusions and automatic treatments.

The audience who will most benefit from this material are those actively involved in clinical treatment of the severely mentally ill: working in psychiatric emergency settings, acute admission wards, walk-in clinics, and inpatient psychiatric units. Also, those clinicians involved in drug and alcohol programs, day hospitals, or other specialized settings for the long-term care of patients with personality disorders will frequently be exposed to patients exhibiting transient psychoses. In addition to psychiatrists, psychologists, nurses and social workers, mental health administrators, who have long recognized this group of patients as high users of mental health services, will benefit from information regarding long-term outpatient care, preventing costly admission to inpatient services or emergency room visits.

In summary, transient psychotic episodes may be caused by a variety of external or internal stressors, the severity of which may depend on preexisting vulnerability caused by an underlying personality disorder. Because of this coinciding acute and chronic problem, both short- and long-term treatment programs are indicated, and specific interventions range from psychotherapeutic to medical and psychopharmacologic.

This book is the first attempt to bring together writings on transient psychosis as diverse as the following: narcissistic and borderline personality disorders, substance abuse, and emergency care. We value the opportunity to present it and hope the working clinician will find it useful.

ACKNOWLEDGMENTS

The editing of a book with as large a number of contributors as this one requires a great deal of coordination with regard to people's differences and people's styles.

The editors would like to thank the contributors for their patience and their cooperation in responding to the demands made upon them.

In addition, we would also like to thank Ms. Christine Baumgartner, Ms. Susan Lulek and Ms. Karen Silver for their invaluable assistance in coordinating the work necessary to ensure the successful completion of this book, and Ms. Betty Garrison for her work in verifying the references.

REFERENCE

1. *Diagnostic and Statistical Manual of Mental Disorders, Third Edition. (DSM-III).* Washington, D.C.: American Psychiatric Association. 1980.

PART I

Concept and Definition of Transient Psychosis

Chapter 1

Definition and Criteria for Diagnosis of Transient Psychosis

Uriel Halbreich, M.D., and
Jean Endicott, Ph.D.

DEFINITIONS:
LIMITATIONS OF DSM-III AND ICD-9

The term "transient psychosis" is usually used without defining the term or clarifying the concepts of the conditions under consideration. The term is used to cover a wide variety of conditions. The features most commonly mentioned by authors who do attempt to describe or define the concept are (a) a relatively abrupt onset of delusions, hallucinations, marked incoherence or confusion, or grossly bizarre or disorganized behavior in the absence of a prolonged prodromal period, and (b) relatively brief duration of the psychosis.

The variety of conditions covered under this umbrella includes disorders ranging from acute exacerbation of schizophrenic symptoms or manic episodes to micro-periods of psychotic symptoms of less than a day's duration in an otherwise well-functioning and healthy individual.

Although there is a tendency on the part of clinicians and investigators to limit the duration of the psychotic episode to a few days or weeks, time covered is often unspecified and may range up to a month or so. Many of the conditions discussed by various authors are covered by other terms in DSM-III (1). The lack of diagnostic specificity limits the value of the term for both research and clinical purposes, and is one of the reasons why the long-term prognosis, treatment response, and familial aggregation of "transient psychosis" are unknown.

How has the concept of transient psychosis been reflected in the official nomenclature? In DSM-II (2) clinicians had a very limited number of diagnoses to use for patients who had psychotic features. For the most part they could be defined as schizophrenic, manic, psychotic-depressive, acute or chronic organic brain syndrome, or paranoid state. There were no criteria for conditions that tended to be brief or to have atypical clinical features.

In DSM-III, a clinician still has a limited choice of diagnoses available. Figure 1 shows the diagnostic decision tree used for differential diagnosis of psychotic features. As can be seen, after ruling out organic mental disorder, malingering, and factitious disorder, there is provision for five different major categories for conditions that last longer than two weeks—major affective disorders, schizoaffective disorder, schizophrenia, schizophreniform disorder, paranoid disorders). DSM-III contains a diagnostic category called "brief reactive psychosis" in which the five major types of disorder have been ruled out, the psychotic reaction lasts less than two weeks, and onset follows "profoundly upsetting environmental states." In addition, there is a diagnostic category called "atypical psychosis," which is a residual category described as suitable for use in cases in which there are psychotic symptoms that have occurred in the absence of a specific stress and do not meet criteria for specific psychotic conditions. There is no mention of a time duration criterion for atypical psychosis.

Of course, a clinician can always use the category "diagnosis deferred." This could be done with the assumption that he or she would be able to specify the condition once additional information was obtained or once the disorder developed into a more classical clinical picture, either by duration or by symptomatology. If the psychosis resolves rapidly and no information relevant to the differential diagnosis is forthcoming, the clinician is expected to choose from among the listed DSM-III diagnoses. It is in cases such as this that brief reactive psychosis or atypical psychosis might be used.

If one is interested in formulating clinical guidelines for patients who have brief periods of psychotic symptoms or in initiating research studies of these disorders, DSM-III has several limitations. First, there is the implication that one cannot have (or make the diagnosis of) a major affective disorder or paranoid disorder if the episode is less than two weeks' duration, with or without psychotic features. Second, while the term "atypical psychosis" is used to describe conditions that last less than two weeks which occur in the absence of profound stress, it also covers conditions that may last much longer than two weeks. Consequently, the clinical concept of transient psychosis does not have a place within the official nomenclature of DSM-III.

The World Health Organization (WHO) Nomenclature—International Classification of Diseases, Ninth Edition (ICD-9) (3) is even less specific concerning the transient psychoses. It includes an entity called "transient organic psychotic condition," with subcategories "acute confusional state," "subacute confusional state," "other," and "unspecified." These conditions are generally reversible. The acute states last hours or days. The subacute states last for several weeks or longer. No specific time limit is defined. The distinction between acute and subacute states appears in the definitions of other psychotic states, like paranoid state, but again without any clear definition of time.

Similarly, no time specification is given for the ICD-9 category "nonorganic psychoses," which are largely or entirely attributable to recent life experience. They include depressive and excitative reactions, reactive confusion, acute paranoid reaction, and psychogenic paranoid psychosis that is "more protracted." Other unspecified reactive psychosis includes hysterical and psychogenic psychoses and psychogenic stupor; unspecified psychosis is "to be used only as a last resort, when no other term can be used." As in the DSM-III, a clear clinical concept of transient psychosis (apart from the organic type) is missing in ICD-9.

THE PROCESS OF DIFFERENTIAL DIAGNOSIS

There are stages in the use of the concept. In the first stage, usually in the emergency room, one is confronted with a patient with an acute psychotic reaction which has been ongoing for a short period of time; the eventual duration of the period of psychosis is, of course, unknown. The second stage is after-the-fact, when the psychotic period is over. The potential sources of information available to the diagnostician during these two stages may differ considerably. After the psychosis is over,

Figure 1

DIFFERENTIAL DIAGNOSIS OF PSYCHOTIC FEATURES

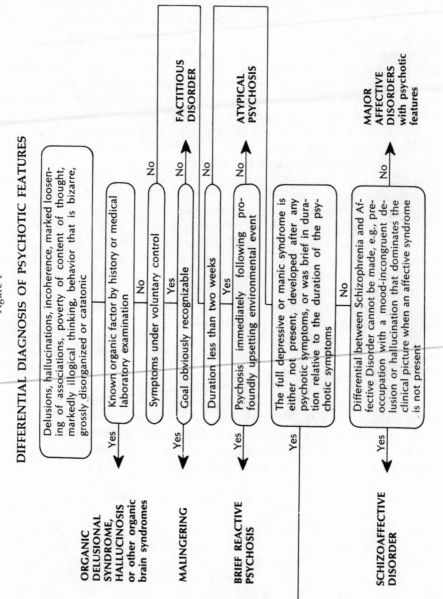

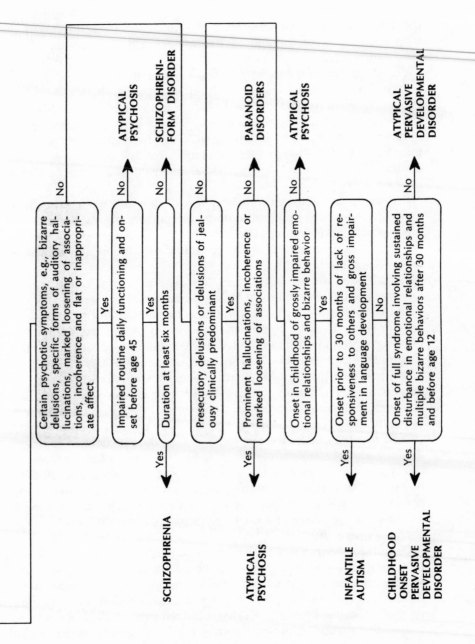

the differential diagnostic problems present during the acute stage are more easily resolved through questioning either the patient himself or family members.

The diagnosis of transient psychosis is usually made after-the-fact (i.e., when the clinician knows the duration of the psychotic condition). However, when it is made after-the-fact or in the light of prior history, it is difficult to identify specific cross-sectional phenomena characteristic of these very brief psychotic periods, although frequently certain symptoms are reported—psychomotor agitation, confusion, relatively vivid delusions and hallucinations, behavioral disorganization, and catatonic-like behavior.

Because of the transient or brief nature of the phenomena, the diagnosis often depends upon self-reports or reports of others. Frequently, the psychotic or disorganized behavior has not been viewed by a mental health professional and there has been no direct opportunity to assess reality-testing at the time.

We advocate the use of the term "transient psychosis" descriptively to cover periods characterized by psychotic symptoms which last less than two weeks. We further advocate that the term "idiopathic transient psychosis" be used for those periods which at present are not known to be accounted for by other, underlying conditions. A major part of the differential diagnosis should focus on whether or not the current condition and past history of the patient suggest some condition such as organic brain syndrome, affective disorder, or schizophrenia, or prior episodes of psychotic features not otherwise differentiated. As shown in Figure 2, the term "transient psychosis" can be used descriptively to cover a number of possible conditions. So far, the best defined common denominator of transient psychoses is the time dimension. For sake of clarity, the two-week cutoff point is proposed. One should remember, however, that this is an arbitrary point. With further knowledge of the nature, history, etiology, pathogenesis, pathophysiology, and treatment response of the various transient psychoses, the time dimension may change or diversify.

Once the time frame is established or suggested for a given case, the first group of transient psychoses to be considered is the organic transient psychoses. The categorization of an episode into this group is done if there is evidence from history, physical examination, or laboratory tests of a specific organic factor that is judged to be etiologically related to the disturbance. A positive answer results in specific management and treatment according to the causative organic factors.

If the evaluation yields negative results, one should evaluate whether

Figure 2

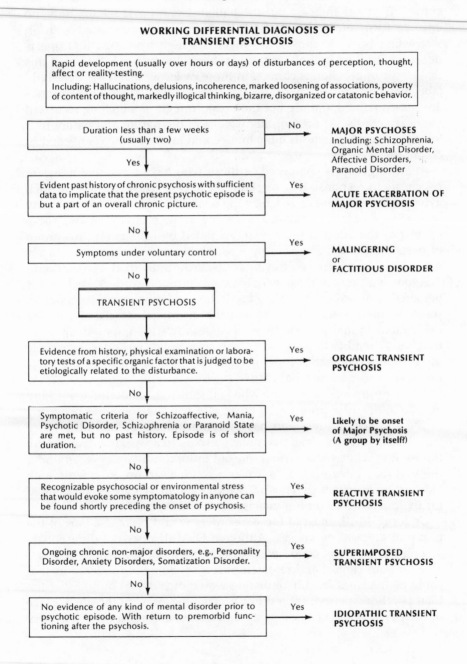

**WORKING DIFFERENTIAL DIAGNOSIS OF
TRANSIENT PSYCHOSIS**

Rapid development (usually over hours or days) of disturbances of perception, thought, affect or reality-testing.

Including: Hallucinations, delusions, incoherence, marked loosening of associations, poverty of content of thought, markedly illogical thinking, bizarre, disorganized or catatonic behavior.

Duration less than a few weeks (usually two) — No → **MAJOR PSYCHOSES** Including: Schizophrenia, Organic Mental Disorder, Affective Disorders, Paranoid Disorder

Yes ↓

Evident past history of chronic psychosis with sufficient data to implicate that the present psychotic episode is but a part of an overall chronic picture. — Yes → **ACUTE EXACERBATION OF MAJOR PSYCHOSIS**

No ↓

Symptoms under voluntary control — Yes → **MALINGERING** or **FACTITIOUS DISORDER**

No ↓

TRANSIENT PSYCHOSIS

↓

Evidence from history, physical examination or laboratory tests of a specific organic factor that is judged to be etiologically related to the disturbance. — Yes → **ORGANIC TRANSIENT PSYCHOSIS**

No ↓

Symptomatic criteria for Schizoaffective, Mania, Psychotic Disorder, Schizophrenia or Paranoid State are met, but no past history. Episode is of short duration. — Yes → **Likely to be onset of Major Psychosis (A group by itself?)**

No ↓

Recognizable psychosocial or environmental stress that would evoke some symptomatology in anyone can be found shortly preceding the onset of psychosis. — Yes → **REACTIVE TRANSIENT PSYCHOSIS**

No ↓

Ongoing chronic non-major disorders, e.g., Personality Disorder, Anxiety Disorders, Somatization Disorder. — Yes → **SUPERIMPOSED TRANSIENT PSYCHOSIS**

No ↓

No evidence of any kind of mental disorder prior to psychotic episode. With return to premorbid functioning after the psychosis. — Yes → **IDIOPATHIC TRANSIENT PSYCHOSIS** the patient meets the symptomatic criteria for one of the major psychoses. If that is the case but the patient has no past history and the episode turns out to be of short duration, one is presented with an interesting issue. In most cases there is a high likelihood that one is dealing with the onset of a major psychosis; the future will show if this diagnostic impression is correct. In these cases, a "diagnosis deferred" label may be justified. There are cases, however, in which such episodes are self-contained and are not the breakthrough of a lifelong recurrent major psychosis. At present, knowledge of the nature and pathophysiology of these episodes is quite limited and more research is needed to clarify these issues.

Another group is composed of those who have a reactive transient psychosis in response to a recognizable severe stress. In making such a diagnosis, one should recognize the relativity of "stress." The severity of a stress should be evaluated according to the background and social context of the affected individual. As noted by Jaspers (4), this group of psychoses is characterized by most observers as being emphatically meaningful, associated with events outside the individual, and transient.

A fourth group are those with ongoing chronic disorders, such as the personality disorders, including borderline and schizotypal personality, some of the anxiety disorders, and the disorders associated with somatization. In many cases, these episodes of "superimposed transient psychosis" tend to be very brief "micropsychotic" episodes, especially in borderline and schizotypal personalities. These episodes are quite prevalent and may also be reactive to stress.

A fifth group would be those who had shown no evidence of any kind of mental disorder prior to the onset of a psychotic episode occurring in the absence of stress and have returned to the premorbid level of functioning after the brief psychotic episode. In a working diagnosis of transient psychosis, one would rule out those conditions covered under the first four categories. This leaves a residual group of patients with "idiopathic transient psychosis," which eventually may be subdivided for the purposes of clinical management and research.

Under DSM-III, most of these disorders would become a part of the group of atypical psychoses. Although DSM-III does not differentiate among this group of conditions, further differentiation would be desirable for both clinical and research purposes. Some of the features that could be the basis for differentiation would include: (a) duration of the total psychotic period; (b) level of functioning prior to the appearance of the psychosis; (c) clinical symptomatology; and (d) level of recovery after the psychosis is over. Another clinical feature based on past history is whether this is the first episode or is a recurrence of a short transient episode of the same nature.

Special consideration in the understanding of transient psychoses should be given to social and cultural factors in the pathogenesis and clinical manifestation of the psychotic episode. In some societies, many of the transient psychoses may be culture-bound entities, such as *susto*, *latah, amok, negi negi,* Koro trance, or *windigo*. These are characterized by the abrupt onset of psychotic symptoms, which should be viewed in the context of the background and religious beliefs of the social group to which the psychotic individual belongs (5; see Chapter 3). These entities are sometimes referred to as "hysterical psychosis" (6,7,8). The phenomenology is often rapidly changing, including paranoid, religious, and hypochondriacal delusions, the episode is of brief duration, and the disorder usually has a good prognosis.

CLINICAL IMPLICATIONS OF DIAGNOSIS

When a comprehensive workup of a patient results in a working diagnosis of transient psychosis, it should have an immediate influence on the clinical treatment and disposition. Many times it calls for an intensive treatment without hospitalization, if the conditions in the emergency room permit immediate treatment or if the disposition can be delayed. If the patient must be hospitalized, a psychiatric intensive care facility is preferable, provided that the conceptual framework does not lead to an extended observation before a decision is made. The management and treatment of transient psychosis are discussed in detail elsewhere in this volume.

Even though at present most episodes of transient psychosis are managed in a similar fashion—primarily with rapid administration of neuroleptics—the differentiation of various transient psychoses is far from being an intellectual exercise. It may have substantial practical implications for research, as well as day-to-day clinical work.

REFERENCES

1. *Diagnostic and Statistical Manual of Mental Disorders, Third Edition. (DSM-III).* Washington, D.C.: American Psychiatric Association, 1980.
2. *Diagnostic and Statistical Manual of Mental Disorders, Second Edition. (DSM-II).* Washington, D.C.: American Psychiatric Association, 1968.
3. World Health Organization: *Manual of the International Classification of Diseases. Injuries and Causes of Death, 9th Revision.* Geneva: WHO, 1977.

4. Jaspers, K.: *General Psychopathology*. Manchester: Manchester University Press, 1963.
5. Yap, P.M.: Classification of the cultural-bound reactive syndromes. *Aust. N. Z. J. Psychiat.*, 1: 172-179, 1967.
6. Hirsch, S.J. and Hollander, M.H.: Hysterical psychosis: Clarification of the concept. *Am. J. Psychiat.*, 125: 909-915, 1969.
7. Kiev, A.: Transcultural Psychiatry. *New York: The Free Press, 1972.*
8. Langness, L.L.: Hysterical psychosis: The cross-cultural evidence. *Am. J. Psychiat.*, 124: 143-152, 1967.

Chapter 2

Borderline States and Psychosis

Joe P. Tupin, M.D.

INTRODUCTION

There is conceptual, diagnostic, etiologic, treatment, and prognostic confusion about a group of patients loosely described as "borderline." In fact, even the terminology is confusing. Each of the following has been used: borderline syndrome (1); borderline personality organization (2); borderline personality disorder (3-5); borderline schizophrenia (6); and schizotypal personality disorder (7-9). Klein (10) has suggested that the same patient group might best be called atypical affective disorders.

Controversy has developed over whether this is a single (2) or multicategorical concept (9,11), and whether it is related to schizophrenia, the major affective disorders, neurosis, or character pathology. There is also debate about the etiology of the borderline states—whether they arise from psychologic, genetic, or organic factors, or a combination of all (11). Finally, some experts have argued that the borderline concept reflects degree of pathology rather than a distinct syndrome.

Much of the literature has focused on the psychologic characteristics of these patients, with an emphasis on the structural aspects of personality organization. Splitting, projective identification, ego defects, object relationships, and early childhood mothering patterns have been particularly important to these authors (12-15).

The increasing frequency with which this diagnostic category is used is reminiscent of the "discovery" of manic-depressive illness following the introduction of lithium in the late 1960s. This disorder has, of course, proved to be far more complex than originally believed. It seems prudent, therefore, to view this newly emerging area carefully from a phenomenologic perspective, as well as from other perspectives, if order is to be brought out of controversy.

Minimal attention has been given to the description of psychotic episodes in the borderline states, although Liebowitz (16) and Rieder (17) have reviewed the relationship to schizophrenia and affective illness. Attention has been largely directed toward psychotherapeutic intervention with reports on the results of hospitalization, day hospitals, group psychotherapy, behavior modification, and psychopharmacology (10,18-22).

In this presentation, I will attempt to identify the major diagnostic characteristics of the borderline states and then proceed to conceptual and etiologic considerations and the nature of the psychoses.

TERMINOLOGY

Gunderson (22) has explained the terminology used to describe the borderline states as follows:

Borderline personality organization: This term, used by Kernberg, suggests a broad and inclusive concept, possibly covering a variety of subgroups identified both by behavior and etiologic considerations. Kernberg's emphasis is not only on the behavior but on the psychologic coherence and the patient's response to psychotherapy. The disorder described seems to lie in a conceptual space between neurosis and schizophrenia ("psychosis"). In this model, neurosis includes neurotic character disorders.

Borderline syndrome: This term, used by Grinker and his colleagues (1), is, again, relatively broad, including several subtypes, lying between neurosis and schizophrenia, possibly having some overlap with affective disorders. There are four subtypes: Group 1 emphasizes poor relationships, inappropriate negative behavior, poor grooming, and rage outbursts. Group 2 patients are inconsistent, with movement toward others through repulsion characterized by negative affect, social isolation, loneliness, depression, and self-destructive behavior. The as-if patients of Deutsch (23), who have given up their search for identity, are in Group 3. Group 4 patients have predominant depressive symptoms and search for the lost symbolic relation with a mother figure.

Borderline personality disorder: This is a still more restricted term as used by Gunderson and Singer (3), and Gunderson and Kolb (24). It originated with Knight (4) and Frosch (5) and emphasizes the descriptive and phenomenologic elements, with some potential overlap with schizophrenia. Descriptive terms focus on low achievement, impulsiveness, manipulative suicide, heightened affectiveness, mild psychotic experiences, high socialization, and disturbed close relationships. Within each of these broad categories there are several specific descriptors. Emphasis has been placed on comparative and empirical studies to develop these categories.

This term is included in DSM-III, which lists the following characteristics: impulsiveness, unpredictability, unstable and intense interpersonal relationships, inappropriately intense anger, poor control of anger, identity disturbance, affective instability, intolerance of being alone, physically self-damaging acts, and feelings of boredom.

Borderline schizophrenia: Here, other terms, including schizotypal personality disorder, latent schizophrenia, and pseudoneurotic schizophrenia, all emphasize the schizophrenic aspects of this group of patients. Particular emphasis is placed on the existence of cognitive disturbances, which separates this population from both traditional schizoid personality disturbance and borderline personality disorder. Spitzer et al. (9) have been persistent advocates of this separation and of the inclusion of both schizotypal personality disorder and borderline personality disorder in DSM-III. Patients in both groups are characterized by oddities of thinking, perception, speech, and behavior; they may exhibit magical thinking, ideas of reference, social isolation, and recurrent illusions, among other characteristics. Kety et al. (6) have used this term, including it in their schizophrenic spectrum disorders.

Atypical affective disorders: Klein (10) has suggested that since depression is a common component in descriptions of these patients who are often responsive to antidepressants, their underlying disturbance may actually be affective illness. Others have shared this view, including Stone (11) and Liebowitz (16), who suggest a close relationship to primary affective disorders.

In summary, experts seem to differ on the exact conceptual nature of this syndrome and its diagnostic limits. They do seem to agree that it is a distinct entity, however, and that it lies outside the traditional concepts of neurosis and psychosis, particularly schizophrenia. All point to the personality instability and the common descriptive factors, which are more shared than not, and to the brief psychotic episodes that punctuate the course of the illness.

COURSE AND PROGNOSIS

In this area, issues seem considerably more uncertain. Of the few follow-up studies, the most carefully done is that of Carpenter and Gunderson (25) in which a group of schizophrenics from the International Pilot Study of Schizophrenia (26) and a group of "psychotic border" borderline patients were followed using explicit criteria. The most impressive finding of this study was that at five-year follow-up there was little difference between the two groups; the single exception was somewhat higher social functioning on the part of the borderline patients—largely through maintenance of their previous level, whereas the schizophrenics' social functioning seemed to deteriorate. Outcome criteria included duration of hospitalization, frequency of social contacts, quality of social contacts, useful employment, quality of useful work, absence of symptoms, ability to meet own basic needs, fullness of life, and overall level of function. One point bears emphasis: According to their histories, the borderline patients had been symptomatic for at least three to five years before the index hospitalization.

The findings of this study suggest that the borderline syndrome, whatever it is, is fairly stable over time, and, when compared to schizophrenia, shares many of the same outcome characteristics. Goldstein and Jones (27) have focused on adolescent and familial precursors of borderline conditions, and their findings also reveal the longstanding chronic nature of the condition.

On the other hand, Masterson and Costello (28) report more optimistic findings in their follow-up study of borderline adolescents treated in a psychoanalytically-based program during the late 1960s and early 1970s. The program consisted of an inpatient stay of at least one year—to effect physical separation from the parents as well as control acute acting-out behavior—and continuing outpatient psychotherapy upon discharge. Therapy—both on the ward and off—was designed to resolve the acute abandonment depression (which the authors theorize manifests in adolescence as a result of the increased conflict between separation and continued parental approval, when parents reward only regressive, symbiotic behavior), as well as to help overcome the developmental arrest of the adolescents.

Mean follow-up was 3.9 years and results showed that although 42% of the adolescents remained severely impaired at follow-up, 58% had maintained improved functioning—some dramatically, others only minimally. While the authors' goal was to further facilitate understanding of the borderline syndrome rather than compare it to other diagnostic entities, they too determined several prognostic criteria: "the degree of early life stress; the level of early ego development; the mastery of early developmental tasks; and the effectiveness of early social relationships (object relations)" (p. 254). Also, the results of their study show the specific model of treatment—hospitalization for at least one year combined with continuing outpatient care—"exerts a strong influence" on adolescent borderlines' adult functioning.

PSYCHOMETRIC DATA

A review article by Margaret Singer (29) states that:

> . . . there is rather clearcut agreement about test patterns of persons who should be diagnosed as borderline, namely those persons who show ordinary reasoning and communication on highly structured test situations—but who on projective techniques, such as the Rorschach, where structure is low, demonstrate flamboyantly deviant reasoning and thought processes (p. 193).

She also states that borderline responses are often filled with primary process association and "schizophrenic thinking; frequently the unstructured responses are elaborated, idiosyncratic, and show peculiar reasoning." These patients oversimplify secondary elaborations. Their separate perceptions tend to become intermingled and related simply because the responses are close together.

In summary, the borderline patient does well with structured test situations and poorly with unstructured ones. The defects are characterized by a variety of cognitive, perceptual, and affective disturbances.

PSYCHOSIS

Gunderson (30) describes characteristics of the psychoses associated with borderline states in some detail. Generally, such episodes are considered to be brief, often precipitated by some specific stress, and characterized by depersonalization, depression, paranoia, and, to a lesser extent, derealization, with both auditory and visual hallucinations reported occasionally. Delusions are most often associated with depressive content, with themes of worthlessness, hopelessness, or guilt. Ideas of reference are also reported.

Generally, the patient feels uncomfortable about the psychotic experience. In the series reported, there were virtually no nihilistic or religious delusions, delusions of thought insertion, interference, or broadcasting. Derealization is somewhat more common in schizophrenics.

Borderline patients are slightly more likely to report psychotic experiences from marijuana or alcohol, but this is not helpful in differentiating this condition from other diagnostic groups. Generally, the psychoses are not described as bizarre or grandiose.

The description of borderline personality contained in DSM-III (31) suggests that brief reactive psychosis, as well as major depression, may be complications of the syndrome. Brief reactive psychosis is described as the "sudden onset of a psychotic disorder of at least a few hours but no more than two weeks' duration, with eventual return to premorbid level of functioning . . . immediately following a recognizable psychosocial stressor . . ." (p. 200). Confusion and emotional turmoil manifested by rapid shifts from one dysphoric affect to another are common. Behavior may be bizarre, with posturing, outlandish dress, and the like. Speech may be inarticulate and repetitive, with volatile and inappropriate affect; transient hallucinations and delusions may be seen; and confabulation is not uncommon. DSM-III further notes that another diagnostic group, the histrionic personality, may decompensate under stress, to give a psychotic picture where histrionic features predominate. This had been called hysterical psychosis. It seems unlikely that these psychotic episodes are descriptively the same as schizophrenia or bipolar illness. Underlying genetic or psychologic factors may be overlapping, however, and depression is commonly noted in these patients.

RELATION TO OTHER SYNDROMES

A number of authors have noted the coexistence of borderline conditions with a variety of specific personality disorder patterns. DSM-III makes this point, as does Rinsley (12), among others. Hysterical personality disorders, recently reviewed by Blacker and Tupin (32), have a continuum of severity from good to bad prognoses, suggesting a borderline aspect in this condition.

Other studies (32, 33) have generally found the borderline group separately identifiable when compared to various neurotic, personality disordered, schizophrenic, and adjustment reactive patients.

CONCEPTUAL ISSUES

In the conceptual area, one can address a number of questions regarding etiology, description, and relationship to other syndromes. I would like to focus primarily on the latter: how this condition relates to other syndromes, and what implications for diagnosis, etiology, and treatment can be drawn from these relationships.

Most writers have emphasized the fact that borderline states lie on the borderline; that is, between neuroses—including character neuroses—and psychoses, specifically schizophrenia. This notion of a continuum has been advanced by a number of researchers and is central to the thinking of Kernberg (33) and others, although they also emphasize the categorical independence of the borderline state.

Other investigators have emphasized the likelihood of subtypes along a spectrum between schizophrenia and the affective disorders, with varying degrees of disability and intensity of symptoms. Typical of this thinking is the work by Stone (11) and Spitzer et al. (9). Stone suggests at least nine subtypes, ranging across a two-dimensional continuum between low and high severity and between pure schizophrenia and pure manic-depressive disorder. These nine subtypes are drawn from the literature and his own research.

Spitzer et al. (9), on the other hand, suggest only two subtypes: borderline states, which reflect a personality disorder, and the schizotypal, considered to be more related to chronic schizophrenia. Kety at al. (6) clearly identify a subgroup called borderline schizophrenia, which they believe is genetically related to chronic schizophrenia. Their work suggests, however, that patients with acute schizophrenia do not share the same genetic loading. This observation is used by Stone to suggest another subdivision of the borderline category—those patients who have a genetic vulnerability and those who do not. Symptomatology may be continuous, however.

Three interesting conceptual models are illustrated in the Figures 1,

Figure 1. Structural diagnosis of borderline*

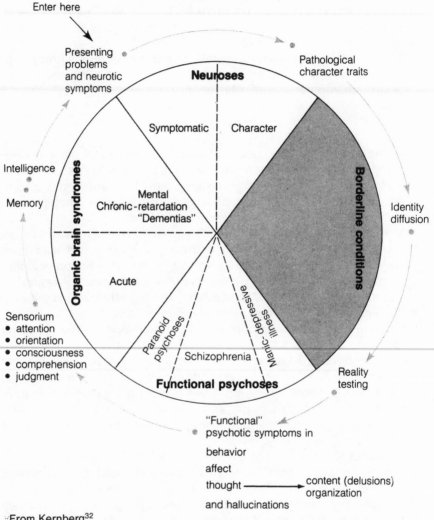

*From Kernberg[32]

2, and 3. Obviously, these represent three distinct models, with Gunderson and Stone attempting to reconcile various sources of data, and Kernberg showing a more "pure" schema of psychopathology.

I would like to suggest a fourth model, which would set primary affective disease and schizophrenia apart from the borderline syndrome and emphasize their genetic-biologic origins. However, it would not exclude the possibility that there are patients who have the genetic loading for primary affective disease or schizophrenia, but manifest only part of the complete syndrome, making them latent, atypical, or borderline. Such mild versions or formes frustes of these major functional psychoses are likely to exist since we see similar mild variations of other genetic conditions. This suggestion has already been advanced by Stone. He emphasizes the frequency with which family members of identified borderline patients can be diagnosed as having either schizophrenia or major affective illness. Moreover, a given individual might share all or part of the genetic material for both of these conditions, thus giving a true schizoaffective picture—a third borderline, genetically determined condition. These three categories, which may be overlapping to some

Figure 2. The borderline: Interrelationships among overlapping diagnostic categories[1]

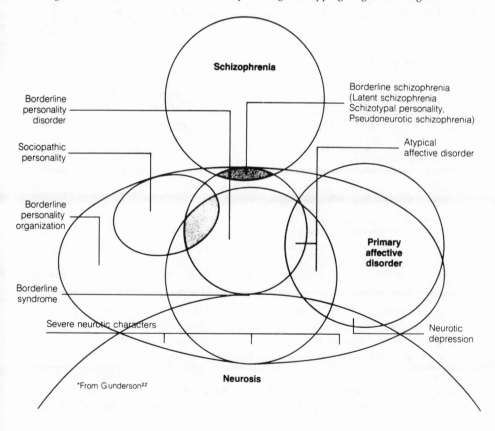

Figure 3. The borderline syndrome*

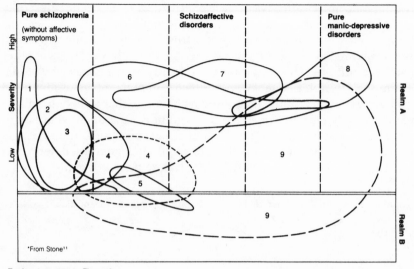

Explanatory note to Figure 3

The universe of severe emotional disorders has been divided into two realms:
A. the realm including the severe and mild forms of schizophrenia and manic-depressive disorders, arranged as a continuum of phenotypes from schizophrenia (without affective symptoms), through the evenly mixed schizoaffective disorders, to the pure affective disorders
B. the realm of disorders in which no hereditary predisposition to schizophrenia or MDP is discernible

Onto this universe are mapped a number of regions relating to various borderline types:
Region 1 Zilboorg's ambulatory schizophrenia
Region 2 Schmideberg's borderline
Region 3 borderline schizophrenia of Kety and Rosenthal
Region 4 borderline of Robert Knight
Region 5 Helene Deutsch's as-if personality
Region 6 pseudoneurotic schizophrenia of Hoch and Polatin
Region 7 schizoaffective as used by Kasanin
Region 8 hysteroid dysphoria of Donald Klein
Region 9 borderline in Kernberg's usage

Note that Regions 4, 5, and 9 overlap both realms, since they correspond to patient groups, some of whom have genetic loading for schizophrenia or MPD, and some of whom do not.

extent, are similar to the schizotypal group of Spitzer et al., the borderline schizophrenia of Kety et al., and Klein's atypical affective disturbance.

If one views personality organization as distinct from neurosis, there is a group of patients with severe, extreme personality disorders that have many of the characteristics of borderline personality disorder. Personality disorder is not likely to have a single dimension of intensity but rather to distribute along a continuum of pathology. In this view, borderline personalities would represent severe personality disturbances of various explicit types, with common severe adaptive behavior problems, poor prognosis, and psychotic episodes. These patients also differ in some characteristics, since psychologic development has allowed each individual to pursue a different developmental course. Thus, when the borderline patient is functioning at his or her best, he or she may exhibit characteristics more typical of the histrionic personality, antisocial personality, narcissistic personality, obsessive compulsive personality, etc. In other words, borderline personality disorder would be a kind of end-stage personality disturbance. The commonality of these patients, the borderline element, would seem to arise very early—related perhaps to a combination of constitutional elements and the mothering encounter. The subsequent development probably depends on family psychopathology and consultations.

In summary, I would suggest that there exist two groups of borderline patients: one involving the milder form of the apparently genetically determined psychoses, schizophrenia, and primary affective disorders; the other arising from defects in early psychosocial development, which, because children develop along different pathways, are manifested in varying symptom patterns. Of course, since the presence of a genetic disturbance does not preclude a psychologically determined personality disorder, nor vice versa, there must be some patients whose disorders overlap these two apparently independent domains. Moreover, a psychosis may require different therapeutic interventions depending on whether it is reactive or genetically determined.

Future etiologic and therapeutic studies must, I think, consider the implications of this conceptual model, which, in the richness of its psychopathology, must lead us toward a multidimensional therapeutic strategy.

REFERENCES

1. Grinker, R. R., Werble, B., and Drye, R.: *The Borderline Syndrome: A Behavorial Study of Ego Functions.* New York: Basic Books, 1968.
2. Kernberg, O.: *Borderline Conditions and Pathological Narcissism.* New York: Aronson, 1975.
3. Gunderson, J. G., and Singer, M. T.: Defining borderline patients: An overview. *Am. J. Psychiat.,* 132: 1-10, 1975.
4. Knight, R.: Borderline states. *Bul. Menninger Clinic,* 17: 1-12, 1953.
5. Frosch, J.: The psychotic character: Clinical psychiatric considerations. *Psychiat. Quart.,* 38: 1-15, 1964.
6. Kety, S. S., Rosenthal, D., Wender, P. H., and Schulsinger, F.: The types and prevalence of mental illness in the biological and adoptive families of adopted schizophrenics. In: D. Rosenthal and S. S. Kety (Eds.), *The Transmission of Schizophrenia.* New York: Pergamon, 1968, pp. 345-362.

7. Rado, S.: Theory and therapy: The theory of schizotypal organization and its application to the treatment of decompensated schizotypal behavior. In S. Rado (Ed.), *Psychoanalysis of Behavior*. New York: Grune & Stratton, 1962, pp. 127-140.
8. Meehl, P. E.: Schizotaxia, schizotypy, schizophrenia. *Am. Psychologist*, 17: 827-838, 1962.
9. Spitzer, R. L., Endicott, J., and Gibbon, M.: Crossing the border into borderline personality and borderline schizophrenia: Development of criteria. *Arch. Gen. Psychiat.*, 36: 17-24, 1979.
10. Klein, D. F.: Psychopharmacological treatment and delineation of borderline disorders. In: P. Hartocollis (Ed.), *Borderline Personality Disorders*. New York: International Universities Press, 1977, pp. 365-384.
11. Stone, M. G.: The borderline syndrome: Evolution of the term, genetic aspects and prognosis. *Am. J. Psychother.*, 31: 345-365, 1977.
12. Rinsley, D. B. An object-relations view of borderline personality. In: P. Hartocollis (Ed.), *Borderline Personality Disorders*. New York: International Universities Press, 1977, pp. 47-70.
13. Mahler, M. S., and Kaplan, L.: Developmental aspects in the assessment of narcissistic and so-called borderline personalities. In: P. Hartocollis (Ed.), *Borderline Personality Disorders*. New York: International Universities Press, 1977, pp. 71-86.
14. Fairbairn, W. R. D.: A revised psychopathology of the psychoses and psychoneuroses. In: *An Object-Relations Theory of the Personality*. New York: Basic Books, 1954, pp. 28-58.
15. Bion, W. R.: Emotional turbulence. In: P. Hartocollis (Ed.), *Borderline Personality Disorders*. New York: International Universities Press, 1977, pp. 3-13.
16. Liebowitz, M. R.: Is borderline a distinct entity? *Schizophrenia Bul.*, 5: 23-38, 1979.
17. Rieder, R. O.: Borderline schizophrenia: Evidence of its validity. *Schizophrenia Bul.*, 5: 39-46, 1979.
18. Adler, G.: Hospital management of borderline patients and its relation to psychotherapy. In: P. Hartocollis (Ed.), *Borderline Personality Disorders*. New York: International Universities Press, 1977, pp. 307-324.
19. Crafoord, C.: Day hospital treatment for borderline patients: The institution as transitional object. In: P. Hartocollis (Ed.), *Borderline Personality Disorders*. New York: International Universities Press, 1977, pp. 385-398.
20. Horwitz, L.: Group psychotherapy of the borderline patient. In: P. Hartocollis (Ed.), *Borderline Personality Disorders*. New York: International Universities Press, 1977, pp. 399-422.
21. Hunt, H. F.: Behavioral perspectives in treatment of borderline patients, In: P. Hartocollis (Ed.), *Borderline Personality Disorders*. New York: International Universities Press, 1977, pp. 325-344.
22. Gunderson, J. G.: The relatedness of borderline and schizophrenic disorders. *Schizophrenia Bul.*, 5: 17-22, 1979.
23. Deutsch, H.: Some forms of emotional disturbance and their relationships to schizophrenia. *Psychoanalytic Quart.*, 7: 467, 1938.
24. Gunderson J. G., and Kolb, J.E.: Discriminating features of borderline patients. *Am. J. Psychiat.*, 135: 792-795, 1978.
25. Carpenter, W. T., Jr., and Gunderson, J. G.: Five year follow-up comparison of borderline and schizophrenic patients. *Comprehensive Psychiat.*, 18: 567-571, 1977.
26. Carpenter, W. T., Jr., Partko, J. J., Langsner, C. A., and Strauss, J. S.: Another view of schizophrenia subtypes: A report from the International Pilot Study of Schizophrenia. *Arch. Gen. Psychiat.*, 33: 508-516, 1976.
27. Goldstein M.J., and Jones, J.E.: Adolescent and familial precursors of borderline and schizophrenic conditions. In: P. Hartocollis (Ed.), *Borderline Personality Disorders*. New York: International Universities Press, 1977, pp. 213-230.

28. Masterson, J. F., with Costello, J. L.: *From Borderline Adolescent to Functioning Adult: The Test of Time*. New York: Brunner/Mazel, 1980.
29. Singer, M. T.: The borderline diagnosis and psychological test: Review and research. In: P. Hartocollis (Ed.), *Borderline Personality Disorders*. New York: International Universities Press, 1977, pp. 193-212.
30. Gunderson, J. G.: Characteristics of borderlines. In: P. Hartocollis (Ed.), *Borderline Personality Disorders*. New York: International Universities Press, 1977, pp. 173-192.
31. *Diagnostic and Statistical Manual of Mental Disorders, Third Edition. (DSM-III)*. Washington, D.C.: American Psychiatric Association, 1980.
32. Blacker, K. H., and Tupin, J. P. Hysteria and hysterical structure: Developmental and social theories. In: M. Horowitz (Ed.), *The Hysterical Personality*. New York: Aronson, 1977, pp. 95-141.
33. Perry, J. C., and Klerman, G. L.: Clinical features of the borderline personality disorder *Am. J. Psychiat.*, 137: 165-173, 1980.
34. Kernberg, O.: The structural diagnosis of borderline personality organization. In: P. Hartocollis (Ed.), *Borderline Personality Disorders*. New York: International Universities Press, 1977, pp. 87-122.

PART II

Etiological Factors in Transient Psychosis

Chapter 3

Cultural Factors in the Symptomatology of Transient Psychosis

*Pedro Ruiz, M.D., and
Efrain A. Gomez, M.D.*

INTRODUCTION

Brief reactive psychosis, according to DSM-III, is "a psychotic disorder of at least a few hours' but no more than two weeks' duration, with eventual return to premorbid level of functioning. The psychotic symptoms appear immediately following a recognizable psychosocial stressor that would evoke significant symptoms of distress in almost anyone. The precipitant event may be any major stress, such as the loss of a loved one or the psychological trauma of combat" (1, p. 200). This diagnostic category leaves much to be desired concerning etiological factors or treatment approaches.

While DSM-III suggests that the precipitant event should represent a major stress, such as the loss of a loved one or the psychological trauma of combat, the importance of cultural factors in the genesis and manifestations of brief reactive psychosis is not mentioned. For a long time, it has been known that cultural and religious beliefs have been shown to affect the individual's mental and physical health, as well as the ways in which symptoms are manifested. Psychotic reactions such as *latah*, *susto, amok, negi negi,* and *windigo* do not easily fit within the standard psychiatric nomenclature devised by Western societies, and are inadequately explained by traditional formulations used by professionals.

The recently increased migration to the United States from Southeast Asia, the Caribbean, and Latin American countries gives us an opportunity to rethink the influence of culture on symptom formation. Yap (2) tentatively places the so-called culture-bound reactive syndromes in four categories as follows:

1) primary fear reactions which may produce malignant anxiety, *latah, susto,* and psychogenic "magical death";
2) "hypereridism" or morbid rage reactions such as *amok* and *negi negi*;
3) specific culturally related nosophobias, e.g., "Koro trance" dissociations; and
4) possession syndromes, including *windigo* psychosis.

Fernandez Marina (3) has also described among Puerto Rican patients a hyperkinetic reaction of sudden onset, violent behavior, and uncommunicativeness which he termed the Puerto Rican Syndrome.

The symptomatologic manifestations seen in these culture-related mental disorders can help us to understand the difficulties involved in trying to reduce them to Western psychiatric categories. The basis of some mental disorders is undoubtedly biologic in nature, and in this respect the disorders are comparable regardless of geography and culture. The same cannot be said of the historic psychosocial process called *disease.* Disease has idiosyncratic manifestations—particular, unique and different in various parts of the world. This may sound obvious, but even investigators committed to transcultural psychiatric research have not been able to rid themselves of a pervasive ethnocentricity and have often tried to reduce cultural differences—which they considered pathoplastic modifications—to universal pathogenic processes.

The wish to unify all mental pathology under one system is understandable, but this aspiration should not blind us to the necessity of considering social and cultural factors in every case we study. Furthermore, it would be ideal to study these disorders not from the outside, but from inside their culture of origin. This would encourage a multi-dimensional understanding of etiology, pathogenesis, clinical course, treatment, and prevention.

For example, in the past, an overrepresentation of schizophrenia has been described among immigrant patients, with the result that most of them have been treated with neuroleptics, electroconvulsive therapy, and other biologically oriented treatments. However, when the stress to which these individuals are reacting is relieved, manifestations of bizarre behavior return to a socially acceptable form without disintegration of the personality. In this instance, and many others, reliance on Western models for psychiatric diagnosis, which for the most part ignore sociocultural factors, may contribute to incorrect diagnosis and treatment. This usually happens when the therapist has not been exposed to training cases which include patients from different cultures. Different world views provide different explanations for psychopathologic disturbances; within the framework of a shared world view, "atypical" behaviors become more understandable as culturally patterned responses to culturally patterned stresses.

CULTURAL VALUES AND PSYCHODYNAMIC ISSUES IN SYMPTOM FORMATION

Successful cultural adaptation depends on the way that individuals handle different kinds of stresses through the use of their personality resources, as well as culturally determined ways of dealing with them. Along these lines, Weidman and Sussex (4), using a peasant society as a reference, see the relationship between culture and the individual as a conceptual model. In such societies a tradition of inquiry into the matter of magic provides some means of understanding about the kind of danger the individual is exposed to, as well as his or her individual responses.

Silverman (5) has also observed the existence of a general apprehensiveness in these societies, as well as insecurity not only about the forces in nature, but also about what the future holds for them; under these conditions, the individual's ability to control his environment, as well as the forces of nature, is of paramount importance. In this context, security is provided by the group and lies within the group; cooperation and harmony by every member of the group are necessary to meet the threats coming from a perceived hostile environment. The cultural values and a shared world view determine the nature of the universe to which people must adapt and within which different types and degrees of dangers must be handled.

Langness (6) and Rubel (7) have implied that a certain way of looking at the world may help the individual to "encapsulate" his community within himself, as the only island of safety in a perceived hostile world. Safety depends upon the approval of others and an adequate individual performance within the system, whether it be in terms of suppressing aggression or of behaving in certain acceptable ways.

The role of helplessness in *susto* (fear) is a good example. As used throughout Latin America, *susto* appears to communicate an individual's inability to fulfill adequately the expectations of the society in which the individual lives and has lived. *Susto* functions as a culturally and socially sanctioned avenue of escape for an individual suffering from intraculturally induced stress. It is more common in women and children because their roles are quite restricted and they have fewer acceptable ways to reduce stress than men in the societies in which it exists.

As developing societies begin to experience the effects of change, one tends to observe an increase in the witchcraft and sorcery practices. It has also been pointed out that an increase in the incidence of transient psychosis occurs in the early days of cultural change. As cultural changes continue, more people have new grounds for testing old beliefs, for doubting them, and maybe for eventually abandoning them (8).

All these studies suggest the manner in which cultural values and a shared view of the world determine the nature of the universe to which groups of people must adapt. What is stressful for some may not be stressful for others; for instance, it is hard for Westerners to understand the tremendous shame involved in "loss of face" for a Japanese individual. In some Eastern societies, "loss of face" involves not only fear of public reprobation, but also threats of total annihilation.

In the face of extraordinary stress, individuals use defenses beyond those of repression, denial, introjection, and projection, which may serve them well in coping with ordinary stress. When faced with extraordinary stress, the world view and belief in sorcerers and witches may lead individuals to behave in ways not sanctioned by society. If the cognitive system includes the belief that loss of personal control can be caused by spirits, dissociation might be a good way to relieve anxiety. While in a state of dissociation, the individual may engage in a culturally prohibited behavior. Dissociation is not considered pathological if culture or religion sanction it. The dividing line between what is considered normal behavior and what is not resides in the loss of control by the individual over his environment.

In this respect, it is important to underscore the ability of the individual to quickly reintegrate after a major psychological disintegration. This is characteristic of many of the so-called culture-bound reactive syndromes. A psychodynamic understanding of these culture-bound reactive syndromes is only possible when this understanding is based on a shared world view, common language and common expectations, thus making possible a meaningful communication. Although the psychocultural aspects of the disease processes are related to biological factors, they are not reducible to the latter. Furthermore, when exploring sociocultural factors, one usually finds intriguing and puzzling problems, arising from specific belief systems concerning illness and health. These belief systems are also important in understanding the formation and content of symptoms. The way the patient perceives, experiences and interprets the world around him is rooted in the customs and traditions of his culture, one of which is child-rearing practices. Every culture prescribes and sanctions ways of dealing with developmental and environmental crisis. A Western-centered psychodynamic formulation is usually ineffective and sometimes offensive to a patient from a non-Western world.

PHENOMENOLOGICAL ISSUES

Although by definition the diagnosis of brief or transient reactive psychosis is not made if the psychotic symptoms persist for more than two weeks, in formulating a differential diagnosis one should keep in mind mental disorders and schizophreniform disorders, such as organic mental disorders, schizophrenia, paranoid disorders, affective disorders, hysterical psychosis and atypical psychosis. Let us review these disorders within this clinical context.

Schizophreniform Disorders

Schizophreniform disorders by definition require a duration of more than two weeks. However, several factors may contribute to a difficult differential diagnosis: the frequently identifiable precipitating psychosocial stressor, the tendency toward acute onset and quick resolution, the emotional turmoil and confusion, the tendency to recover to premorbid levels of functioning, and the absence of an increase in the prevalence of schizophrenia among family members.

Organic Mental Disorders

Organic mental disorders, particularly those involving delirium, organic delusional syndromes, and intoxications, can be distinguished from transient psychosis on the basis of history, physical examination (including a thorough neurological examination), mental status examination, and laboratory tests. The results of these approaches usually reveal specific organic factors judged to be etiologically related to this disturbance.

Schizophrenia

Onset, course with evidence of deterioration from a previous level of functioning, a duration of more than six months, and relevant family history are distinguishing characteristics of schizophrenia. In general, third world psychiatric disorders have been said to present themselves in a rather undifferentiated way, only gradually revealing a distinct underlying pathology (9). Specifically, transient culture-bound psychosis can be differentiated from bad prognosis schizophrenia, in that good prognosis in schizophrenia is characterized by an older age of onset, the presence of clear precipitating features, little personality deterioration, and a history of affective and cultural components in the symptomatology. It is interesting to note that relatives of schizophrenic patients emphasize the presence of delusions as evidence of illness, while relatives of individuals suffering with brief psychotic reactions due to cultural factors consider the presence of aberrant behavior, usually of an agressive nature, rather than the delusions or hallucinations, as being abnormal. Furthermore, the meaning of delusions and hallucinations from the perspective of the individual's culture and life experiences is apparent to an astute observer, without having to resort to psychodynamic explanations.

Paranoid Disorders

Paranoid disorders, although considered separate from schizophrenia, are often viewed as schizophrenia by many professionals in the field. The paranoid delusions seen in brief psychotic reactions as a result of cultural factors do not stem for a suspicious, paranoid, premorbid personality; furthermore, the content of the persecutory beliefs tend usually to be accepted as valid by the patient's relatives and friends. In general, the patient's beliefs are not altered by medications, and if the individual is considered abnormal by members of his or her family, it is not because of his/her beliefs, but rather because of his/her actions.

Affective Disorders

Bipolar and major depressive episodes may follow a major psychosocial stressor; however, the diagnosis of a major affective disorder should be made when the clinical picture meets the criteria for this disorder, without regard to whether or not it is associated with a psychosocial stressor. Patients with transient psychosis are less likely to demonstrate flight of ideas, major subjective distress, or overt hypomania. In expressing religious delusions, patients may say that they have a special relationship with God, that they have a religious mission, but they do not see themselves as specially chosen. Belief in the validity of their relationship with God is shared by relatives, who frequently express similar beliefs. If one is not alert to this situation, this belief could be seen as a manifestation of grandiosity, thus resulting in a diagnosis of mania.

Grandiose delusions appear to be particularly associated with migration from rural to urban areas. The beliefs expressed by these patients are consistent with their predominant mood, but they are not dependent on it. Sometimes they even persist after treatment. Reactive psychosis has been characterized by Jaspers (10) as being emphatically meaningful, as being caused by events outside the individual, and as having a transient course and a paranoid content. After recovery, the patient usually recognizes that he has been ill; however, he may perceive the psychotic experience not as an illness, but as an abnormal state, usally precipitated by malevolent supernatural forces. Rather than delusions which are associated with an alteration of the personality structure, their beliefs are delusional-like ideas arising from recognizable, preceding affects and life experiences.

Hysterical Psychosis

The term hysterical psychosis, which includes many of the culture-bound reactive syndromes, is recognized in different countries under different names. These syndromes, which usually have a problem-solving effect for the individual, are exaggerated caricatures of culturally sanctioned communications (11). The essential diagnostic feature of hysterical psychosis is the presence of an overwhelming environmental stressor. The clinical picture is characterized by an acute and dramatic onset which is related to a profoundly disturbing event. The content of the delusions, hallucinations, and depersonalizations is culturally determined. In many cases, it has been observed that after the resolution of an episode of transient psychosis, a depressive component does appear.

Culture-bound acute psychotic syndromes have been best described by psychiatrists practicing in the Caribbean and African countries

(12,13,14). Nosologically, there is a spectrum ranging from a florid psychotic picture to psychotic-like states. Recognized as a separate entity during the nineteenth century in Europe, they appear to have been absorbed into the group of the schizophrenias under the influence of Bleuler.

These psychoses are characterized by rapidly changing phenomenology, including paranoid, religious, and hypochondriacal delusions. They are often precipitated by social factors, have a short course, and show a good prognosis. In French-speaking countries, such atypical reactions have been described under the name of *bouffées délirantes* (15,16); their precipitant causes are sometimes tied to the experience of migration. When they occur in the Caribbean countries, individuals usually present a good premorbid personality and have a single delusional theme, usually having to do with witchcraft. These ideas are usually maintained even after these patients have been discharged from the hospital. These patients recover rapidly, whatever the treatment. Similar mental disorders have been described in several underdeveloped countries.

It is of interest to note that in the nineteenth century, immigrants coming to the United States from predominantly rural countries frequently developed acute psychotic reactions characterized by anxiety and delusions about magical influences and persecution. In general, the content of these psychotic reactions was meaningful in the context of the patients' past experiences (17).

On the basis of cross-cultural evidence (18), it has been observed that hysterical psychosis may occur in cultures where child-rearing practices and social experiences are such that hysterical personality is not frequently observed. In this regard, even Freud (19) suggested that hysterical psychosis was due to a failure in repression, occurring in response to a current stress. Finally, in regard to the expressions of hysterical psychosis, Easser and Lesser (20) proposed the division of hysterical manifestations into two types: 1) hysterical personality, for the better integrated patients; and 2) hysteroid, for the borderline patients.

Atypical Psychosis

This is a residual category for cases in which the only disturbance is psychotic symptoms characterized by unusual features such as monosymptomatic delusions and persistent auditory hallucinations. This type of psychosis may be associated with the menstrual cycle or postpartum, and does not meet the criteria for other forms of psychosis. Sometimes there are no observable precipitating events in this type of psychosis.

DISCUSSION

Patients experiencing acute psychotic reactions usually have a good premorbid personality and recognizable sociocultural stressors. The onset of the psychosis is acute, its course is short, and its prognosis is good. The symptoms usually have a problem-solving orientation and generally are exaggerations of religious or culturally sanctioned manifestations. Since religious and magic beliefs are important factors in developing societies, by emphasizing the university of man, a substitute satisfaction is offered for failure to assimilate to the dominant society. To some extent, folk healers do this by using the culture and traditions of the patient in the process of healing. For instance, *curanderism* (folk healing), which is commonly practiced in Central America, particularly in Mexico, has its roots in a well established belief system. Its practice is also rooted in customs and traditions. It conceptualizes health and illness in personalistic or supernaturalistic terms.

Western scientific medicine emphasizes what illness is, namely the result of abnormal structural or functional changes of organs and system; on the other hand, people who believe in folk medicine are not interested in what an illness is, but rather in what an illness means. It is important that therapists learn the cultural background of their patients, even if the patients live in countries like the United States in which cultural backgrounds are given little importance. It is extremely unlikely that individuals totally discard their past. Instead of disowning their traditional beliefs, the patients can be encouraged to integrate them into their new lifestyle. When there is a synergistic correlation between the therapist's culture and the culture of his patient, and when therapists try to understand the patient's world view, there is a greater potential for improvement and cure. Puzzling symptoms can then be understood within the context of cultural belief systems.

It appears that the best way to avoid culturally determined errors in the diagnosis and treatment of transient psychosis is to develop curiosity about the patient's culture and traditions, as well as self-awareness of one's biases and blind spots. To the extent that therapists are able to understand how their patients perceive the world around them, how they feel about it, and how they interpret it, they will be able to better help the patients, and therefore the outcome of the treatment will most probably be a successful one. In spite of culturally determined differences in the manifestations of personality styles, defense mechanisms, modes of gratification and stereotypes, the inquisitive therapist who is aware of his own limitations in treating patients from different cultures and ethnic backgrounds need not refer them to someone else. Through empathy, introspection and knowledge, he can enter and share the patients' world view, as well as communicate meaningfully with them.

Psychiatry should draw equally from the nomothetic and idiographic sciences. That is to say, sometimes therapists will search for general laws that could be applied to a particular case; at other times they will study a particular case in its own right, paying attention to values and characteristics which are unique and not generalizable. A nomothetic psychiatric approach is ecumenic and can be best applied to the biological aspects of psychiatry; on the other hand, an idiographic psychiatric approach is more useful in understanding behavior and culture. Therefore, an integrated approach will best help us to understand the biological and the sociocultural aspects of psychopathology, as well as its interpretation, treatment, and prevention.

A CASE ILLUSTRATION

A few years ago, we had the opportunity to study the case of a 21-year-old Peruvian Indian woman who was exposed to two different culturally related treatment approaches. The illness in question was manifested by restlessness, loss of sleep, frequent headaches, and anorexia. She also admitted hearing voices which commanded her to undress and behave like a bitch in heat. This condition developed suddenly after a frightening sexual experience which took place at her village in the foothills of the Andes of Peru. Prior to this experience, the patient in question was in excellent general health. In terms of her cultural background, she was of Indian peasant stock and lived a restricted life; she was not allowed by her family to leave the village in order to work as a domestic, as customarily happens in this region of Peru. Her family and the people of the village had a strong telluric orientation which was demonstrated in customs, traditions, and folklore. For instance, they believed in the extraction of the soul from the body caused by an angry earth as a punishment for transgressions committed against nature.

In this case, a psychiatrist was first consulted and a diagnosis was made of agitated depression. The patient was treated with antianxiety and antidepressant medications; however, non-compliance led to failure with this approach. Later on, a *curandero* (folk healer) was consulted and he diagnosed her as suffering from *susto*. It was explained to her that this condition emanated from her soul's being extracted from her body by the angry spirit of the mountain. He further explained to her that her soul had to be restored to her body at the site where the sexual transgression took place. There, the *curandero* proceeded to call her name five times while massaging her forehead with a mixture of wild flowers. Following this treatment exercise, the flowers were left at a crossroads so that a passerby would take away the disease with him. A few days later, she fully recovered from all her symptomatology.

CONCLUSION

In this study, we have attempted to define the concept of "transient psychosis," taking into consideration the current diagnostic nomenclature (DSM-III), as well as the relationship existing between culture and symptom formation. From another angle, we have reviewed the role of cultural values in psychodynamic determination and symptom formation. Particular attention was paid within this context to the coping styles of Western and non-Western societies. Later on, we analyzed, from a phenomenological point of view, relevant clinical data which could assist in making a differential diagnosis between "transient" psychosis and other significantly related mental disorders, such as schizophreniform disorders, organic mental disorders, schizophrenia, paranoid disorders, affective disorders, hysterical psychosis, and atypical psychosis. In addition, we discussed the importance of understanding illnesses from the point of view of the patients' perceptions, and how this has a direct impact on treatment outcome. Finally, we presented a clinical case as a point of illustration of the relationship between cultural background, illness and treatment. It is hoped that this study will inspire therapists in the field to be better trained in the realm of transcultural and cross-cultural psychiatry, and thus be better equipped to treat patients from different ethnic and cultural backgrounds.

REFERENCES

1. *Diagnostic and Statistical Manual of Mental Disorders, Third Edition. (DSM-III)*. Washington, D. C.: American Psychiatric Association, 1980.
2. Yap, P.M.: Classification of the culture-bound reactive syndromes. *Austral. N. Z. J. Psychiat.*, 1: 172-179, 1967.
3. Fernandez Marina, R.: The Puerto Rican Syndrome: Its dynamics and cultural determinants. *Psychiat.*, 24: 79-82, 1961.
4. Weidman, H.H., and Sussex, J.N.: Cultural values and ego functioning in relation to the atypical culture-bound reactive syndromes. *Int. J. Soc. Psychiat.*, 17:83-100, 1971.
5. Silverman, S.F.: Agricultural organizaton, social structure, and values in Italy: Amoral familism reconsidered. *Am. Anthropologist*, 70: 1-20, 1968.
6. Langness, L.L.: Hysterical psychosis in the New Guinea highlands: A Bena Bena example. *Psychiat.*, 28: 258-277, 1965.
7. Rubel, A.J.: The epidemiology of a folk illness: Susto in Hispanic America. *Ethnology*, 3: 268-283, 1964.

8. Wittkower, E., and Weidman, H.H.: Magic, witchcraft and sorcery in relation to mental health and mental disorder. In: N. Petrilowitsch and H. Flegel (Eds.), *Social Psychiatry*. Basel and New York: S. Karger, 1969, pp. 169-184.

9. Lambo, T.A.: The role of cultural factors in paranoid psychosis among the Yoruba tribe. *J. Ment. Sci.*, 101: 239-266, 1955.

10. Jaspers, K.: *General Psychopathology*. Manchester: Manchester University Press, 1963.

11. Hirsch, S.J., and Hollender, M.H.: Hysterical psychosis: Clarification of the concept. *Am. J. Psychiat.*, 125: 909-915, 1969.

12. Royes, K.: The incidence and features of psychoses in a Caribbean community. In: *Proceedings of the Third World Congress of Psychiatry*, Montreal, 1961, pp. 1121-1125.

13. Bustamente, J.A.: La reaccion psychotique aigrie, la transculturacion, le sous-developpement et les changements sociaux. *Psychopathologie Africaine*, 5: 223-233, 1969.

14. Kiev, A.: *Transcultural Psychiatry*. New York: The Free Press, 1972.

15. Collomb, H.: Les bouffées délirantes en psychiatrie Africaine. *Psychopathologie Africaine*, 1: 167-239, 1965.

16. Constant, J.: Les bouffées délirantes en Guadeloupe: Essai d'analyse semiologique, psychopathologique et culturelle à propos de 112 observations. *Psychopathologie Africaine*, 8: 169-199, 1972.

17. Ranney, M.H.: On insane foreigners. *Am. J. Insanity*, 7: 53-63, 1950.

18. Langness, L.L.: Hysterical psychosis: The cross-cultural evidence. *Am. J. Psychiat.*, 124: 143-152, 1967.

19. Freud, S.: Further remarks on the defense neuro-psychoses. *Standard Edition*, Vol. III. London: Hogarth Press, 1962, pp. 159-174.

20. Easser, B.R., and Lesser, S.R.: Hysterical personality: A re-evaluation. *Psychoanalytic Quart.*, 34: 390-405, 1965.

Chapter 4

Medical Illness as a Cause for Psychosis

Anthony L. LaBruzza, M.D.

This chapter addresses the issue of medical illness presenting with psychiatric symptoms, particularly transient psychotic states. The discussion is directed toward a multidisciplinary audience of mental health professionals and will focus on practical guidelines for the detection of medical illness during the initial psychiatric interview. An exhaustive review of the myriad medical conditions which can masquerade as psychiatric disorder is beyond the scope of this presentation. It is hoped that after reading this chapter the reader will be more alert to the possibility of underlying medical pathology as a cause for the patient's symptoms and have a clearer rationale for when to consult a physician or psychiatrist.

Many psychiatric symptoms such as anxiety, depression, bizarre thoughts, and strange behavior are nonspecific and occur in both psychiatric and medical disorders. In certain cases disturbances of mood, thought, perception, and behavior are the first and, for some time, only manifestation of underlying physical illness. For example, severe depression may herald the discovery of carcinoma of the pancreas or other retroperitoneal carcinomas by several weeks or months.

As the next section of this chapter will show, a significant percentage of people who present for psychiatric evaluation will, upon investigation, be found to have an underlying medical illness which is responsible for their symptoms. It is important, therefore, that the evaluating clinician, no matter what his or her professional discipline, think in terms of differential diagnosis of psychiatric and medical disorders, so that significant medical illness is not missed. Clinical diagnosis not only guides treatment decisions but also significantly determines the final disposition of the patient (1, 2). An early and accurate diagnosis will allow for rapid, definitive, and potentially life-saving treatment measures.

STUDIES OF PHYSICAL ILLNESS IN PSYCHIATRIC PATIENTS

Elsewhere the author (3, 4) has reviewed a number of studies in which psychiatric patients were investigated for medical illness. Table 1 summarizes the key findings of fifteen such studies done between 1936 and 1980.

Malzberg's *Mortality Among Patients with Mental Disease* (5), published in 1934, brought professional attention to the high physical morbidity and mortality rates among psychiatric patients. Two years later Comroe (6) reported his follow-up of 100 patients diagnosed as neurotic, in which he discovered 24% to be medically ill. Phillips (7) in 1937 studied 164 consecutive psychiatric admissions; he found 45% of these psychiatric patients to be medically ill and considered 39 patients (24%) to have medical conditions with a "direct" relationship to their psychiatric complaints. Subsequent studies of psychiatric inpatients by Marshall (8), Herridge (9), Slater and Glithero (10), Johnson (11), Maguire and Granville-Grossman (12), Burke (13), and Hall et al. (14) supported Phillips' finding of a high rate of medical illness among psychiatric inpatients, with a range of 33.5% to 80% physical morbidity in these studies. In addition, 5% to 46% of psychiatric inpatients studied were reported to have medical illnesses which caused or exacerbated their psychiatric complaints.

In a similar way research about outpatients confirmed Comroe's original finding of high physical morbidity among psychiatric outpatients. In their reports Davies (15), Eastwood (16), Burke (17), Hall et al. (18), and Koranyi (19, 20) found that 43% to 51% of psychiatric outpatients whom they investigated were medically ill, and in 7.7% to 36% of cases

TABLE 1
Studies of Psychiatric Patients with Medical Illness

Senior Author	Year	Number of Patients	% With Any Medical Illness	% With Medical Illness Directly Related to Psychiatric Symptoms
Comroe (6)	1936	100 OPT	24	—
Phillips (7)	1937	164 INPT	45	24
Marhall (8)	1949	175 INPT	44	22 (contributory)
Herridge (9)	1960	209 INPT	50	5 (causative)
Davies (15)	1965	72 OPT	51	36 (probably related)
Slater (10)	1965	73 INPT (hysterics)	56	30 (causative)
Johnson (11)	1968	250 INPT	—	12 (causative)
Maguire (12)	1968	200 INPT	33.5	—
Koranyi (19)	1972	100 OPT	49	20
Burke (13)	1972	202 INPT	43	—
Eastwood (16)	1975	124 OPT	"high"	—
Burke (17)	1978	133 OPT (Day Hospital)	50	—
Hall (18)	1978	658 OPT	—	9.1 (causative)
Koranyi (20)	1979	2,090 OPT	43	7.7 (causative)
Hall (14)	1980	100 INPT	80	46 (caused or exacerbated)

the medical illness caused or was related to the psychiatric symptoms. Odegard's 1952 report (21) from Scandinavia further drew attention to the "excess mortality of the insane."

Taking a somewhat different approach to diagnosis, Goodwin et al. (22) studied patients whom physicians tend to dislike. In a medical clinic he asked four physicians to rate a group of 22 patients according to how well they knew the patient, how well they liked the patient, how cooperative the patient was, how well the patient was doing medically, and any traits that made the patient dislikeable. Goodwin found that "dislike was significantly correlated with the patient's degree of organicity . . . (the) most disliked patients contained all patients with signs of organic brain damage and all suicidal patients." Explanations given by the physicians for their dislike of these patients revealed that they did not recognize the patients' psychiatric status.

In another provocative study Slater and Glithero (10) reported the outcome of 85 patients diagnosed as having conversion hysteria and followed up an average of nine years after the initial diagnosis was made. Of the original 85 patients, upon follow-up four had committed suicide and eight had died of natural causes. The remaining 73 patients fell into three groups. The first group consisted of 19 patients for whom the diagnosis of hysteria was coupled with an organic diagnosis. The second group totaled 22 patients in whom an organic basis for the original symptoms was eventually found. Finally, a third group of 32 patients showed no evidence of organic disease, but in this group two had developed unambiguous schizophrenia, and eight suffered from cyclothymic depression.

In the largest outpatient study reported, Koranyi (20) made the important observation that medical illness often went unrecognized by the clinician who referred the patient to his psychiatric clinic. In fact, 46% of the 902 patients whom Koranyi discovered to have significant medical illness were undiagnosed by the referring sources. The high physical morbidity of Koranyi's 2,090 patients may be related to the fact that they were predominantly of poor social class. By far the most common medical illnesses among this clinic population were cardiovascular disease, central nervous system disease (excluding neoplasms), and endocrine, nutritional and metabolic disorders. These conditions were followed much less commonly by gastrointestinal illness, pulmonary disease, genitourinary disease, hematopoietic disorders, neoplasms, infectious and parasitic diseases, adverse drug reactions, skin and subcutaneous tissue disease, and musculoskeletal and connective tissue disease. It is noteworthy that diabetes mellitus was 2.5 times more prevalent among this clinic population than in the general population and often presented as erectile impotence with accompanying marital difficulties.

In another large study of 658 psychiatric outpatients Hall et al. (18) made similar observations:

> The most frequent presentations were of depression, confusion, anxiety, and speech or memory disorders. The presence of visual hallucinations was believed to indicate medical etiology until proven otherwise. . . . Cardiovascular and endocrine disorders were the most frequent causes of psychiatric symptoms, followed by infection, pulmonary disease, gastrointestinal disorders, hematopoietic disease, CNS disease, and malignancy.

In this study 20% of patients with a medically induced psychiatric disorder experienced *visual* hallucinations, distortions, or illusions, as compared to only 0.5% of patients with nonmedically related psychiatric complaints who reported unusual visual symptoms. Hall also concluded that "the tandem use of a symptom checklist and biochemical screening provides a system helpful in defining those patients who require intensive medical investigation" (18). Those patients with four or more positive responses on a medical review of systems symptom checklist showed significant laboratory evidence of medical disease.

ORGANIC MENTAL DISORDERS

Psychiatry has traditionally drawn a distinction between *organic* and *functional* disorders. Organic brain syndromes are defined as mental disorders characterized by a constellation of psychological or behavioral signs and symptoms which are caused by or associated with impaired brain tissue functioning (e.g., intoxication, delirium, dementia). The term *organic mental disorder* is used in DSM-III (23) to designate a particular organic brain syndrome in which the etiology is known or presumed (e.g., alcohol amnestic syndrome). Although all psychological processes are believed to depend on brain tissue functioning, the functional disorders are considered not to be attributable to specific organic factors; for example, adjustment disorders are felt primarily to be responses to psychosocial stressors. Functional disorders such as schizophrenia, mania, and paranoid states have not been demonstrated to be due to the presence of a specific etiologic organic factor.

An analogy with another organ system such as the cardiovascular system may further clarify the issue. When heart tissue fails to function properly, there occurs a constellation of signs and symptoms which comprise the syndrome of heart failure. In a like manner, when brain tissue fails to function properly there occurs a number of signs and symptoms which constitute a syndrome of brain failure, i.e., an organic brain syndrome. The clinical presentations of organic brain syndromes are quite variable and depend on the nature and localization of the underlying pathophysiological process, as well as the premorbid personality of the involved individual. The most commonly occurring organic brain syndromes are delirium, dementia, intoxication, and withdrawal. A summary of the DSM-III classification of organic mental disorders is found in Table 2.

As mentioned previously, psychiatric symptoms such as anxiety, depression, hallucinations, delusions, altered perceptions, and bizarre behavior are nonspecific and occur in both functional and organic mental disorders. It is difficult to know whether such symptoms result directly from brain tissue dysfunction or are a reaction to the cognitive deficits and psychological alterations which are essential features of the organic mental disorders. For instance, if cognitive impairments are perceived as significant losses which lower self-esteem, then emotional reactions of anxiety, irritability, shame, depression, and even suicide may ensue.

TABLE 2
DSM-III Classification of Organic Mental Disorders*

I. *Organic Brain Syndromes* (OBS)—psychological or behavioral abnormality associated with dysfunction of the brain, without reference to etiology.
  A. *Delirium*—clouding of consciousness; difficulty shifting, focusing and sustaining attention; disturbance of sleep-wakefulness cycle and psychomotor activity; disorientation; memory impairment; perceptual disturbance; incoherent speech; rapid onset; fluctuating course.
  B. *Dementia*—loss of intellectual abilities, e.g., memory, judgment, abstract thinking and higher cortical functions, severe enough to impair social and occupational functioning.
  C. *Organic Amnestic Syndrome*—impaired short- and long-term memory without clouding of consciousness or dementia.
  D. *Organic Delusional Syndrome*—delusions are the prominent feature without delirium, dementia or prominent hallucinations.
  E. *Organic Hallucinosis*—persistent or recurrent hallucinations in a normal state of consciousness and attributable to a specific organic factor.
  F. *Organic Affective Syndrome*—a disturbance of mood resembling a manic or major depressive episode due to a specific organic factor without delirium, dementia or prominent delusions or hallucinations.
  G. *Organic Personality Syndrome*—marked change in personality such as emotional lability, poor impulse control, apathy, suspiciousness or paranoia, due to a specific organic factor but not due to any other OBS.
  H. *Intoxication*—maladaptive behavior and a substance-specific syndrome due to recent use and presence in the body of a substance.
  I. *Withdrawal*—a substance-specific syndrome that occurs after stopping or reducing intake of a substance which was previously regularly used by an individual to produce an intoxicated state.
II. *Organic Mental Disorders*—organic brain syndromes in which etiology is known or presumed.
  A. *Primary Degenerative Dementia*—dementia of insidious onset with uniformly progressive deteriorating course; senile or presenile onset; exclusion of all other specific causes of dementia.
  B. *Multi-infarct Dementia*—dementia with stepwise deteriorating course with "patchy" distribution of deficits, focal neurological signs and symptoms, and evidence of significant cerebrovascular disease.
  C. *Substance-induced Dementia*—dementia caused by the direct effects of a substance on the central nervous system.
III. *Substance Use Disorders*—behavior associated with taking various substances that affect the central nervous system.
  A. *Substance Abuse*—a pattern of pathological use of the substance for at least one month with impairment of social or occupational functioning.
  B. *Dependence*—tolerance or withdrawal. (Tolerance: the need for markedly increased amounts of the substance to achieve the desired effect, or markedly diminished effect with regular use of the same amount.)

*Adapted from DSM-III [23]

Compulsive individuals may react to organic impairment with fear of loss of control and may try to compensate by excessive orderliness or obsessive symptomatology. Some people become circumstantial in their speech or confabulate to conceal memory deficits. Chronically suspicious persons, especially those who develop hearing loss, may become frankly paranoid with delusional beliefs (24). Impaired judgment may lead to inappropriate behavior or impulsive sexual, aggressive, exhibitionistic, or acquisitive acts. In general, the features associated with an organic mental syndrome in a given individual reflect both the premorbid personality of that individual and the nature of severity of the organic impairment. One can have a marked emotional reaction, however, to a relatively mild organic deficit.

The causes of organic brain syndromes are legion, and detailed discussion may be found in a textbook of medicine. For purposes of this chapter a commonsense overview will be presented and further elaborated in the next section. Dysfunction of brain tissue may occur because of a *primary* condition within the brain itself or be *secondary* to conditions arising outside the central nervous system. A number of diseases such as Alzheimer's, Pick's, Huntington's, and Parkinson's disease cause loss or degeneration of neurons in the substance of the brain. Trauma, infections and tumors may also damage brain tissue. In epilepsy there are abnormal electrical discharges of neurons within the brain. Vascular disorders such as subarachnoid hemorrhage adversely affect brain tissue function. There are also disorders of the cerebrospinal fluid system, as in normal pressure hydrocephalus, which cause organic deficits.

The brain depends on the rest of the body for its nourishment and internal environment. If an inadequate supply of blood reaches the brain or if that blood is deficient in oxygen or glucose, the brain cannot function properly. Endocrine and metabolic disturbances, infections with fever and sepsis, and electrolyte and acid-base imbalances may provide an improper internal environment for brain tissue functioning. Similarly, drugs, alcohol, poisons, heavy metals and other toxins may impair brain tissue directly or impair other organs which the brain depends on for adequate functioning. Certain nutrients, such as vitamin B_{12}, folate, and thiamine, are also essential for the operation of the central nervous system.

ASSESSING DELIRIUM AND ACUTE PSYCHOSIS

Generally acute psychosis and delirium should be considered medical emergencies. As mentioned above, the organically impaired patient may become quite agitated or explosive, exhibit poor judgment and impulse control, and consequently be at risk for harming himself or others. In some instances the organic factor which produces the psychotic or delirious state may constitute a life-threatening medical illness. It follows that the first concern of the clinician in assessing the acutely psychotic or delirious patient is to rule out a life-threatening medical condition. Having ruled out potentially fatal conditions, the evaluator next turns his attention to other serious illnesses which, though not imminently life-threatening, need prompt medical attention.

Anderson (25, 26) has identified seven not uncommon medical causes of delirium and acute psychosis which are potentially fatal. These include:

1) Cerebrovascular accident
2) Hypertensive encephalopathy
3) Hypoglycemia
4) Hypoxic and hypoperfusion states
5) Meningitis and encephalitis
6) Poisoning (e.g., with tricyclic antidepressants)
7) Wernicke-Korsakoff syndrome

Other life-endangering conditions which might be added to Anderson's list are diabetic ketoacidosis and nonketotic hyperosmolar states, hyperthermia, acute adrenal insufficiency, and thyroid storm. Once these dangerous conditions have been ruled out, Anderson advises that three other serious medical problems be specifically considered: namely, electrolyte and acid-base disturbances, systemic infections, and subdural hematoma.

Having ruled out these life-threatening or serious medical illnesses, the clinician should next consider whether the clinical picture before him could best be explained in terms of an idiosyncratic drug reaction, a drug-toxic state, or a drug-withdrawal state. Because drug use and abuse are so prevalent in our society, drug-induced mental disturbances are commonly seen in psychiatric emergency rooms. On clinical grounds one can distinguish four relatively common types of drug-induced psychotic states or deliria (4, 27):

1) Adrenergic delirium (due to excess sympathetic nervous system activity)
2) Anticholinergic delirium (due to parasympathetic nervous system blockade)

3) Hallucinogen-induced delirium (with or without sympathetic excess)

4) Phencyclidine (PCP)-induced delirium

Adrenergic delirium may present with a paranoid schizophreniform reaction, hypomania with emotional lability, or stereotypy. The paranoid reaction due to amphetamine toxicity is virtually indistinguishable cross-sectionally from a paranoid schizophrenic episode. Fear and anxiety are usually prominent in cases of sympathetic hyperactivity. On physical examination the pulse is rapid, the pupils are large and reactive, the skin is sweaty and pale, blood pressure is elevated, and there is usually tremor or motor restlessness. In addition, there may be dizziness, weakness, palpitations, agitation, a throbbing headache, rapid breathing, and urinary frequency. Some common causes of adrenergic delirium include the use of psychostimulants such as amphetamines or cocaine; withdrawal from alcohol, barbiturates, and sedative-hypnotics (e.g., Valium); and hypoglycemia and hyperthyroidism.

A particular type of adrenergic delirium which is both common and life-threatening is the delirium tremens (DTs) of alcohol withdrawal. Delirium tremens rarely occurs in patients under 30 or in the absence of at least three years of chronic alcohol abuse. It is associated with a mortality rate of 10% to 25%, depending on the physical health of the patient. Serious alcohol withdrawal is characterized by the signs of adrenergic delirium described above and particularly by *tremor of the upper extremities*. If DTs are to occur, they usually do so within one to three days after the patient ceases or reduces alcohol consumption. In addition to the tremor there are disorientation, hyperactivity, fever, marked wakefulness, and terrifying hallucinations, which may be visual, tactile, olfactory or auditory. Patients may complain of the floor moving beneath their feet, of frightening animals such as snakes, or of bugs crawling on their skin (formication).

Another medical emergency associated with chronic alcoholism is the Wernicke-Korsakoff syndrome, which is due to poor nutrition, in particular to the deficiency of thiamine. Wernicke's encephalopathy has sudden onset and consists of ophthalmoplegia and ataxia followed by mental disturbance. The ophthalmoplegia is characterized by nystagmus and a paresis of the external recti muscles of the eyeball with resulting lateral gaze palsy and convergent squint. The ataxia takes the form of a wide-based gait, falling, and inability to walk or stand. The mental disturbance is a global confusional state with impairment of memory and perception and confabulation. The patient is unable to learn new material such as the name of the doctor and he may fall asleep in mid-sentence. This syndrome is a medical emergency and must be treated with thiamine 50 mg IM or IV immediately and 50 mg IM daily until a normal diet is resumed.

Anticholinergic delirium may present with bizarre mental or neuro-logical symptoms, psychomotor agitation, short-term memory impair-ment, clouding of consciousness, and hallucinations, especially visual hallucinations. On physcial examination there are dry mucous mem-branes, a rapid weak pulse often with palpitations, widely dilated and sluggishly reactive pupils, blurred vision, hot dry flushed skin, fever, constipation, urinary retention, hyperreflexia, and diminished bowel sounds. There may also be marked thirst, difficulty swallowing, pho-tophobia, elevated blood pressure, excitement, confusion, disorienta-tion, muscular incoordination, gait and speech difficulties, and hyper-thermia due to inability to sweat, especially in hot weather. Among the more than 600 substances known to have anticholinergic properties are medications such as tricyclic antidepressants, antipsychotics, anti-histamines, antispasmodics, antiparkinsonian drugs, ophthalmic solu-tions, belladonna alkaloids such as atropine and scopolamine, and over-the-counter preparations such as sleeping pills, cold remedies, motion sickness preparations, and cough medicines. There have been recent reports (28, 29) of abuse of anticholinergic compounds, particularly tri-hexyphenidyl (Artane), for their euphoriant effects.

Hallucinogen-induced delirium generally presents with hallucina-tions, sensory (especially visual) distortions or illusions, alterations in mood usually toward euphoria, and depersonalization or derealization. Occasionally there are acute panic reactions or "bad trips." Hallucino-gens such as STP, mescaline and nutmeg have sympathomimetic prop-erties and may present additionally with signs of adrenergic delirium, whereas LSD and psilocybin (indole-type hallucinogens) do not present with signs of sympathetic nervous system excess.

Because phencyclidine is a common drug of abuse with unusual prop-erties (30), the PCP-induced delirium will be considered separately. PCP may act as a depressant, a stimulant, an anesthetic, or a hallucinogen, depending on the dosage, route of administration, and species of the drug. The low-dose syndrome occurs after ingestion, usually by smok-ing, of 5 to 10 mg of PCP. There may be mild agitation, a blank stare, confusion, combativeness, anxiety, disorientation, misperceptions, par-anoia, a tendency toward violence, unpredictable behavior, or a schizo-phreniform psychosis. Physical signs include rapid pulse and respiratory rate, mild-to-moderate hypertension, normal or constricted pupils, horizontal and vertical nystagmus, excessive drooling and salivation, spitting, gait ataxia, hyperreflexia, muscular rigidity, analgesia, and vomiting. Moderate doses (10 to 20 mg) of PCP may produce a stuporous state with open eyes and repetitive, purposeless movements. High doses of 100 mg or more of PCP generally produce a coma. Overdosage with PCP can also result in seizures, respiratory depression, and death.

Having ruled out the above drug-related psychoses, the clinician continues to proceed systematically with the differential diagnosis, seeking the possible underlying organic cause of the presenting clinical picture. Table 3 summarizes various medical conditions which can produce delirium, dementia or psychosis.

TABLE 3
Disorders Causing Delirium, Dementia or Psychosis*

I. *Primary Brain Dysfunction*
   A. Parenchymatous Disease of the CNS
         Alzheimer's disease
         Huntington's Chorea
         Parkinsonism
         Pick's disease
         Wilson's disease
   B. Epilepsy and Postictal States
   C. Brain Tumors—Primary and Metastatic
   D. Trauma
         Concussions
         Open and closed head injuries
   E. Infections and Postinfectious States
         Brain abscess (bacterial, fungal, gummatous, cysticercosis)
         Encephalitis (e.g., herpes)
         Jakob-Creutzfeldt disease (slow virus)
         Meningitis (bacterial, fungal, tubercular)
         Neurosyphilis
   F. Vascular
         Aneurysm
         Atherosclerosis
         Cerebrovascular accident (stroke)
         Cerebral emboli
         Collagen-vascular disease
         Hypertension and hypertensive encephalopathy
         Subarachnoid hemorrhage
         Subdural hematoma
   G. Normal Pressure Hydrocephalus
II. *Secondary Brain Dysfunction*
   A. Systemic Infections with Fever and Sepsis

B. Hypoxic and Hypoperfusion States
        Anemia
        Cardiac arrhythmias
        Cardiac failure
        CO_2 narcosis
        Hypotension
        Pumonary dysfunction
        Severe blood loss
C. Exogenous Drugs, Toxins and Poisons
        Alcohol (intoxication and withdrawal)
        Amantadine
        Amphetamines
        Anticonvulsants
        Antihistamines
        Antihypertensives
        Antiparkinsonian drugs
        Atropine
        Baclofen
        Barbiturates (intoxication and withdrawal)
        Benzodiazepines (intoxication and withdrawal)
        Bromides

        Cannabis
        Cimetidine (Tagamet)
        Cocaine

        Digitalis
        Disulfiran (Antabuse)
        Diuretics (electrolyte disturbance)
        Glutethimide
        Hallucinogens (LSD, PCP, etc.)
        Heavy metals (lead, manganese, mercury, thallium, etc.)
        Insecticides (organophosphate)
        Insulin
        Isoniazid

        L-dopa

        Methaqualone
        Methyldopa
        Meperidine
        Meprobamate
        Nutmeg
        Opiates

        Phenothiazines
        Phenylpropranolamine
        Propranolol

*Sources for Table 3 are references 2, 23, 25, 27

GUIDELINES FOR IDENTIFYING PATIENTS AT HIGH RISK FOR MEDICAL ILLNESS

The first section of this chapter reviewed the evidence that a significant percentage of patients who present for psychiatric evaluation have an underlying, frequently unrecognized medical illness which accounts for their psychiatric disturbance. As a result of these research findings the author argues that evaluating clinicians ought to rule out organic etiology as part of the initial evaluation. The process of detecting physical illness usually requires the skills of a physician who is familiar with medical illness and has access to laboratory and other specialized tests. There is much information, however, that the nonmedical clinician can gather in an initial interview that will alert him/her to the possibility of underlying medical illness and the need for psychiatric or medical consultation. The following guidelines are derived from the author's clinical experience and review of the literature.

1) The clinician needs to have a high index of suspicion for medical illness as a possible underlying cause for psychiatric disturbance.
2) Age of onset of symptoms is an aid to diagnosis. Schizophrenia rarely begins after 40 years of age. Manic-depressive illness has a mean age of onset in the early 30s. A first episode of acute psychosis in a person over 40 is most likely organic in origin.
3) Rapidity of onset of psychosis suggests an organic etiology. An acute psychosis of rapid onset may follow the ingestion of drugs such as LSD, PCP and other substances or may be a toxic or side effect of a medically prescribed drug. The psychosis of temporal lobe epilepsy is usually characterized by rapid onset and rapid clearing. Schizophrenic psychosis is generally preceded by a prolonged prodromal period.
4) A careful personal and family history of medical illness should be obtained. Certain medical and psychiatric conditions have a hereditary basis. Uncommon inherited disorders such as Wilson's disease and Huntington's chorea may first present with psychiatric symptoms, including psychosis.
5) A change in mental status in a patient with a diagnosed medical illness is often due to a complication of the medical illness or to the medications used to treat the illness.
   Example: An insulin-dependent diabetic man was brought to the emergency room by the police for confused, agitated, and threatening behavior. His blood glucose was low and his symptoms cleared when he was given glucose.
6) *Visual* hallucinations, distortions or illusions ought to be considered organically based until proven otherwise.

7) Paranoid symptoms, especially in the elderly, are often linked to hearing loss (24).

8) The clinician should pay attention to feelings of dislike for a patient. In Goodwin's study (22) the most disliked patients were suicidal or had organic brain syndromes.

9) A previous history of functional psychotic episodes does not render immunity to organic psychosis. In fact, psychiatric patients as a rule are more likely than usual to have medical illnesses.

   Example: A middle-aged man with a history of frequent schizophrenic episodes and multiple admissions to a state psychiatric hospital was brought by police to a general hospital emergency room for confusion and bizarre behavior. The patient was well-known to the police and the general hospital staff and was reflexively sent to the state psychiatric hospital for admission. At the state hospital he was discovered to have a fever of 105°F and he died within an hour of admission.

10) Certain readily observed physical signs and symptoms are important indicators of organic illness. A fever may be a clue to a systemic infection or meningitis. A rapid pulse may be seen with infections, hypoglycemia, hypoperfusion, anemia, and hyperthyroidism among many other conditions. Hypertensive encephalopathy is suggested by markedly elevated blood pressure, whereas in hypoperfusion states blood pressure tends to be low. Headache and a stiff neck may be signs of meningitis or intracranial hemorrhage. Pupillary size may be a clue to a drug-induced delirium. Markedly dry skin suggests dehydration, especially in the elderly, or the possibility of an anticholinergic delirium. Needle marks on the skin suggest drug abuse. A confused alcoholic with nystagmus, ophthalmoplegia, and ataxia is likely to be suffering from Wernicke-Korsakoff syndrome and needs parenteral thiamine to prevent permanent neurological damage. A thorough physical examination ought to be performed by a physician whenever an organic etiology is suspected.

11) Erectile impotence may be the first sign of diabetes mellitus and requires a medical workup.

12) Hall (18) recommended the use of a medical review of systems checklist and biochemical screening to identify patients requiring intensive medical investigation. In Hall's study those patients with four or more positive responses on the medical symptom checklist showed significant laboratory evidence of physical disease.

13) Slater's follow-up study (10) of conversion hysteria demonstrated that the majority of patients so diagnosed went on to develop medical illness within a nine-year period. Hence the diagnosis of conversion hysteria should be made with extreme caution.

14) It is important to inquire about every substance that a patient ingests, injects, or otherwise puts into his/her body. Many people fail to report or deny the use of over-the-counter medications, laxatives, suppositories, illicit drugs, fad diets, exposure to fumes and industrial toxins or insecticides, or alcohol abuse. *Example:* The wife of a distinguished college professor presented to the emergency room with complaints of severe anxiety and visual hallucinations. Although she and her husband denied alcohol abuse, she developed full-blown delirium tremens after admission to the hospital.

15) Finally, a careful mental status examination needs to be performed and will often yield clues to an organic illness. Fluctuating level of consciousness, inability to sustain attention, memory deficits and disorientation to time, person, or place are highly suggestive of an organic delirium.

Chedru and Geschwind (31) suggest that handwriting impairment or dysgraphia is the most sensitive indicator of an impairment of consciousness. In 33 out of 34 acutely confused patients whom they investigated, handwriting was impaired in its motor, spatial or linguistic aspects. Letters were clumsily drawn, strokes were reduplicated in letters such as M and W, letters were improperly aligned, strokes did not follow the usual upward and downward orientation, and spelling errors were frequent. Handwriting improved as the confusional state cleared.

Keller and Manschreck (32) critically reviewed the standard tests of higher intellectual functioning and found the following mental status examination items to be most useful, reliable and valid in detecting organicity: orientation to time, place and person; ability to recall remote personal and recent general events; ability to recall three objects after two minutes or to repeat a simple sentence; and fund of general information such as the ability to recall past Presidents of the United States, major cities, celebrities or current events.

Isaacs and Kennie (33) recommended use of the *set test* as an aid to diagnosing dementia in the elderly. A simple mnemonic for remembering this test is the word FACT. The patient is asked to name ten Fruits, ten Animals, ten Colors and ten Towns, scoring one point for each correct answer with a maximum score of 40 points. Patients scoring 14 or less are likely to be demented and need further medical evaluation. A score from 15 to 24 has a low association with dementia, and a score of 25 to 40 essentially rules out dementia.

A more specialized screening test for organic impairment is the Bender-Gestalt Visual Motor Test (34). This test is usually performed by a trained psychologist and is quite accurate in detecting or ruling out organicity.

Finally, a valuable test that can be easily learned and used by mental health clinicians is the "Mini Mental State Examination." Folstein et al. (35) developed this test as a rapid, reliable and valid method for testing the higher cognitive functions and distinguishing dementia from functional disorders. Because of its clinical usefulness this test is reproduced in Table 4.

TABLE 4
The Mini Mental State Examination*

Part I:
a. What is the year, season, date, day of the week, month?   (5 points)
b. Where are we: country, state, city or town, hospital, floor of building?
                                                                       (5 points)
c. The examiner names three objects, taking one second to say each. The patient is asked to repeat all three objects after the examiner has said them.
                                                                       (3 points)
d. Serial sevens. One point for each correct answer. Stop after 5 answers. *Or,* Spell the word "world" backwards.   (5 points)
e. Recall the three objects named in (c).   (3 points)
Part II:
a. The patient is shown a pencil and a watch and asked to name them.
                                                                       (2 points)
b. The patient is asked to repeat: "No ifs, ands, or buts."   (1 point)
c. The patient is handed a sheet of paper and asked to carry out a three stage command: "Take this paper in your right hand, fold it in half, and put it on the floor."   (3 points)
d. The patient is shown a sign which reads "Close your eyes" and is asked to read and obey the sign.   (1 point)
e. The patient is asked to write a sentence.   (1 point)
f. The patient is asked to copy a Bender-Gestalt figure.   (1 point)

Interpretation of results of Mini Mental State Exam: Demented patients averaged 9.7 points out of 30. Cognitively impaired depressed patients scored an average of 19 out of 30 points. Uncomplicated depressed patients averaged 25 out of 30 points. The average score for normal subjects was 27.6 out of 30. Scores of 12 or less out of 30 indicate a high probability of organic illness.
*Adapted from Folstein et al. (35).

REFERENCES

1. Baxter, S., Chodorkoff, B., and Underhill, R.: Psychiatric emergencies: Dispositional determinants and the validity of the decision to admit. *Am. J. Psychiat.*, 124: 1542-1546, 1968.
2. Slaby, A. E.: Emergency psychiatry: An update. *Hospital and Community Psychiatry*, 32, 10: 687-698, 1981.
3. LaBruzza, A. L.: Detection of medical illness during psychiatric evaluation.*J. Psychiatric Treatment and Evaluation*, 2: 115-117, 1980.
4. LaBruzza, A. L.: Physical illness presenting as psychiatric disorder: Guidelines for differential diagnosis. *J. Operational Psychiatry*,12, 1: 24-31, 1981.
5. Malzberg, B.: *Mortality Among Patients With Mental Disease.* Utica, NY: New York State Hospital Press, 1934.
6. Comroe, B. I.: Follow-up study of 100 diagnosed as neurosis. *J. Nerv. Ment. Dis.*, 83: 679-684, 1936.
7. Phillips, R.J.: Physical disorder in 164 consecutive admissions to a mental hospital: The incidence and significance. *Brit. Med. J.*, 2: 363-366, August 21, 1937.
8. Marshall, H.: Incidence of physical disorders among psychiatric inpatients. *Brit. Med. J.*, 11: 468-470, August 17, 1949.
9. Herridge, C. F.: Physical disorders in psychiatric illness: A study of 209 consecutive admissions. *Lancet*, 2: 949-951, 1960.
10. Slater, E. T., and Glithero, E.: A follow-up of patients diagnosed as suffering from "hysteria." *J. Psychosom. Res.*, 9: 9-13, 1965.
11. Johnson, D.A.W.: The evaluation of routine physical examination in psychiatric cases. *Practitioner*, 200: 686-691, 1968.
12. Maguire, G.P., and Granville-Grossman, K. L.: Physical illness in psychiatric patients. *Brit. J. Psychiat.*, 115: 1365-1369, 1968.
13. Burke, A. W.: Physical illness in psychiatric hospital patients in Jamaica. *Brit. J. Psychiat.*, 121: 321-322, 1972.
14. Hall, R. C. W., Gardner, E. R., Stickney S. K., et al.: Physical illness manifesting as psychiatric disease: II. Analysis of a state hospital inpatient population. *Arch. Gen. Psychiat.* 37: 989-995, 1980.
15. Davies, D. W.: Physical illness in psychiatric out-patients. *Brit. J. Psychiat.* 111: 27-33, 1965.
16. Eastwood, M. R.: *The Relation Between Mental and Physical Illness.* Toronto: University of Toronto Press, 1976.
17. Burke, A. W.: Physical disorders among day hospital patients. *Brit. J. Psychiat.*, 133: 22-27, 1978.
18. Hall, R. C. W., Popkin, M. K., Devaul, R. A., et al.: Physical illness presenting as psychiatric disease. *Arch. Gen. Psychiat.*, 35: 1315-1320, 1978.
19. Koranyi, E. K.: Physical health and illness in a psychiatric outpatient department population. *Canadian Psychiatric Association Journal*, 17: 109-116, (suppl), 1972.
20. Koranyi, E.K.: Morbidity and rate of undiagnosed physical illness in a psychiatric clinic population. *Arch. Gen. Psychiat.*, 36: 414-419, 1979.
21. Odegard, O.: The excess mortality of the insane. *Acta Psychiatrica et Neurologica Scandinavica*, 27: 353-367, 1952.
22. Goodwin, J. M., Goodwin, J. S., and Kellner, R.: Psychiatric symptoms in disliked medical patients. *JAMA*, 241: 1117, 1979.
23. *Diagnostic and Statistical Manual of Mental Disorders, Third Edition, (DSM-III).* Washington, D.C.: American Psychiatric Association, 1980.
24. Zimbardo, P. G., Anderson, S. M., and Kabat, L. G.,: Induced hearing deficit generates experimental paranoia. *Science*, 212: 1529-1531, June 26, 1981.

25. Anderson, W. H.: Differential diagnosis of acute psychosis. In: T. C. Manschreck (Ed.), *Psychiatric Medicine Update: MGH Review for Physicians*. New York: Elsevier North Holland, 1979.
26. Anderson, W. H. and Kuehnle, J. C.: Strategies for the treatment of acute psychosis. *JAMA*, 229: 1884-1889, 1974.
27. DiSclafani, A., Hall, R. C.W., and Gardner, E. R.: Drug induced psychosis: Emergency diagnosis and management. *Psychosomatics*, 22, 10: 845-855, October 1981.
28. Rubinstein, J. S.: Antiparkinson drug abuse: Eight case reports. *Hospital and Community Psychiatry*, 30: 32-37, 1979.
29. Bluhm, R. E., and Koller, W. C.: Anticholinergic abuse—when to suspect it, what to do about it. *Drug Therapy*, 11: 150-155, January 1981.
30. National Institute on Drug Abuse: *Drug Clinical Notes*, Diagnosis and treatment of phencyclidine (PCP) toxicity. October 1979, U. S. Government Printing Office 1979: 311-246/1136.
31. Chedru, F., and Geschwind, N.: Writing disturbances in acute confusional states. *Neuropsychologia*, 10: 343-353, 1972.
32. Keller, M. B., and Manschreck, T. C.: The bedside mental status examination—reliability and validity. *Comprehensive Psychiatry*, 22: 500-510 1981.
33. Isaacs, B., and Kennie, A.: The set test as an aid to the detection of dementia in old people. *Brit. J. Psychiat.*, 123: 467-470, 1973.
34. Bender, L.: A visual-motor gestalt test and its clinical use. *Am. Orthopsychiatric Assoc. Monograph*, No. 3, 1938.
35. Folstein, M. F., Folstein, S. E., and McHugh, P. R.: Mini-mental state—a practical method for grading the cognitive state of patients for the clinician. *J. Psychiatric Res.*, 12: 189-198, 1975.

Chapter 5

Hormone-related
Transient Psychoses

Susanna Goldstein, M.D.,
and Uriel Halbreich, M.D.

The emotional disturbances to be discussed in this chapter are characterized by a demonstrated (or at least hypothesized) hormonal change or disturbance.

This heterogenous group can be divided into three main subgroups:

(a) primary endocrine diseases with eventual psychiatric manifestations;

(b) major physiological hormonal changes throughout the life-cycle accompanied by an increased frequency of psychological disturbances; and

(c) an iatrogenic subgroup of psychiatric disorders subsequent to hormonal treatment.

There is a growing appreciation of the interaction between central nervous system functioning and endocrinology, of the importance of psychological influences on endocrine regulation, and of the influence of hormones on behavior in man. Nevertheless, a difficult question is faced: What sort of evidence would confirm or refute the hypothesis that an abnormality or change in a particular hormone causes mental disorder? In most cases the form of mental disorder is not specific to the endocrine status and is not directly related to the severity of the endocrine disorder, the dosage of hormonal treatment, or the magnitude of hormonal change. Not all persons affected by hormonal imbalance or change will demonstrate psychiatric disturbances. Moreover, the psychiatric disorder often persists after the endocrine balance has been restored. Therefore, the demonstration of endocrine abnormalities or differences between subjects having a certain psychiatric disorder and those who do not supports the hypothesis of endocrine cause but is not sufficient for its establishment. Conversely, a failure to demonstrate the abnormality or difference will not rule out hormonal etiology.

Keeping those reservations in mind, let us proceed now to the first group: definite endocrine disorder followed by mental symptoms. Although psychiatric abnormalities associated with endocrine disease have been noted for centuries, there has been a remarkable paucity of work using modern methods of psychiatric diagnosis and comparative-qualitative assessment of psychopathology. Thus we rely, in many instances, on clinical impressions gleaned from case studies and requiring further rigorous research with modern methods for firmer data and analysis.

THYROID DYSFUNCTION

The thyroid hormones interact with a great number of metabolic processes, influencing the concentration and activity of numerous enzymes; metabolism of substrates, vitamins and minerals; secretion and degradation rates of virtually all other hormones and the response of target tissue. As a result, no tissue or organ system escapes the adverse effect of thyroid hormone dysregulation.

Thyrotoxicosis

The term *thyrotoxicosis* refers to the biochemical and physiologic complex resulting from stimulation of tissues with an excess of thyroid hormone. Alterations of nervous function are an almost invariable element of thyrotoxicosis and are most commonly seen as nervousness, emotional lability, hyperkinesia, restlessness (1), shortening of attention span and a need to be moving around and doing things, despite a feeling of fatigue (2). Patients lose their tempers easily and have crying spells, but usually without depressive affect (3). In rare cases, severe psychotic disturbances may occur.

Acute organic brain syndromes often accompany "thyroid storms" and show a picture of typical delirium, usually with fever. These syndromes are a grave medical emergency and warrant urgent intervention. Because of the ample evidence of hyperthyroidism which accompanies their development, diagnostic confusion is unlikely. In a rare patient, an "apathetic hyperthyroidism" can progress to stupor and coma and can cause diagnostic difficulties.

Psychoses with affective and schizophrenic features are sometimes indistinguishable from the corresponding functional psychosis. A presentation with manic features is far more usual than a depressive syndrome. The schizophreniform manifestations can mimic all types of schizophrenia (paranoid, disorganized, or catatonic) and in some studies have been found to outnumber affective psychoses.

There is no specific "thyroid psychosis," but the hyperthyroidism may lend a distinctive coloring to the syndrome—a distinctly manic component in an otherwise typically schizophrenic picture or a profound agitation in a depression. Paranoid features are common across the spectrum. The distinction between an affective and schizophrenic syndrome is often very hard to draw and a mixture of organic features is common (4).

Pathological fluctuations in thyroid activity were suspected to have a role in the onset of mania in manic-depressive disease but no such correlation has been demonstrated (5).

The acute psychosis may be first manifested during treatment with antithyroid drugs, presenting either as an acute organic brain syndrome or as a schizophreniform psychosis (6). It is suggested that the psychosis may be precipitated not only by the rapid alteration from severe excess to normal (7) or hypothyroid levels, but also by the rapid increase to severe deficiency to an euthyroid state. The acute organic syndromes usually subside rapidly as the thyrotoxicosis comes under control, but the affective or schizophreniform types may be more extended and have a varied course.

Hypothyroidism

A deficiency of thyroid hormone beginning in fetal life or at birth results in retention of infantile characteristics of the brain, hypoplasia of cortical neurons, retarded myelination, and decreased vascularity (8).

If the deficiency is not corrected in early infancy, irreversible damage with severe mental retardation results. The characteristic features of a deficiency of thyroid hormone beginning in adulthood are a general slowing of intellectual functions, loss of initiative, memory defects, lethargy and somnolence. In some patients the mental symptoms are the initial indicator of hypothyroidism (9).

There is no specific myxedema psychosis (10); the only unifying feature is a frequent paranoid quality. The commonest form, sometimes called "myxedema madness," is an acute or subacute organic brain syndrome with features of delirium, florid delusions, and hallucinations (2). It has been suggested that these patients have specific visual hallucinations of small animals (11), confusion, and impaired consciousness. Auditory hallucinations are common, most often accusatory and threatening in nature. The course may fluctuate. A chronic organic brain syndrome or dementia may progress insidiously and may reach an advanced stage by the time the condition is diagnosed. Hypothyroidism is an important and sometimes overlooked consideration in the evaluation of causes of intellectual impairment, particularly in the geriatric population.

Hypothyroid psychoses with depressive features are often severe, with agitation (12) or bizarre hypochondriasis, and may prove particularly resistant to treatment until the underlying myxedema is diagnosed and corrected. Myxedema should always be an important differential diagnosis in cases of intractable depression.

Hypothyroid schizophreniform psychoses are characterized by mental slowing and prominent paranoid features. Organic mental features are usually found both in schizophrenic form and depressive types when carefully sought.

There is some evidence to suggest that hypothyroidism may be etiologically related to rapid mood cycles (13).

The treatment of myxedema is usually rewarding. Purely organic psychoses of less than two years' duration respond best to thyroid replacement alone (14). Patients with longstanding dementia may be left with intellectual or memory defects even after correction of the hypothyroidism. Psychotic disorders with mainly depressive or schizophrenic features have variable outcomes and may require additional treatment in the form of antidepressant or antipsychotic medications.

In some cases (15) there is a deterioration of mental status soon after starting thyroid replacement. The patients may become agitated, suspicious and frankly psychotic. In a review of these cases, the psychopathological features were noted to meet the DSM-III criteria for organic affective syndrome, manic type. The syndrome appears four to seven days after initiation of aggressive thyroid replacement and lasts one or two weeks. It usually resolves without sequelae. The most useful predictor for the occurrence of the syndrome is pretreatment psychopathology.

PARATHYROID DISORDERS

Parathyroid hormone is involved in the regulation of circulating calcium and in the metabolism of organic phosphate. Increased amounts of hormone result in hypercalcemia and its accompanying hypophosphatemia, while deficiency of the hormone leads to hypocalcemia and hypophosphatemia.

Hyperparathyroidism

In the great majority of hyperparathyroid patients, the physical features are predominant but mental symptoms are also common. In a small group of patients, the first pathological manifestations are mental, the commonest change being anergia, sometimes associated with irritability and occasional explosive outbursts. Organic mental symptoms were reported in 12% of patients in one series (16) and were chiefly in the form of memory impairment and mental slowing (17, 18, 19)

Psychosis appears to be rare in hyperparathyroidism, although it may occur in association with a "parathyroid crisis" as an acute organic mental syndrome characterized by spells of confusion, hallucinations, and aggressive behavior. In less acute cases, confusion and intellectual impairment may lead to misdiagnosis of dementia (20). There are also very rare psychotic states with mainly schizophrenic features (thought disorder and paranoia), but these appear to be probably coincidental. The mental disorder associated with hyperparathyroidism is thought of as wholly reversible, the duration of symptoms notwithstanding, and resolution coincides with decrease in serum levels of calcium. Sometimes a short-lived psychiatric disturbance characterized by catatonia, acute agitation or confusion sets in within a few days of parathyroidectomy (21, 22). There are cases in which the parathyroidectomy is an unintentional complication of thyroidectomy. It is not clear whether the syndrome is a distinct entity definable as "post-parathyroidectomy psychosis" or, rather, a general postoperative reaction.

Hypoparathyroidism

Hypoparathyroidism may be frequently accompanied by various psychiatric manifestations (23); most frequent are the organic mental disorders. Acute symptoms most often occur following surgical removal of the gland. Conversely, in cases of idiopathic hyperparathyroidism, a chronic insidious course is common, with patients having difficulty in concentration, emotional lability and intellectual impairment.

Another common change is "pseudoneurosis": depression, nervousness, irritability, frequent crying spells, social withdrawal, anxiety or panic attacks. This "pseudoneurosis" is frequently symptomatically indistinguishable from "idiopathic" neurosis. Hypoparathyroid psychotic disorders with schizophrenic or manic-depressive features are rare (23). The acute syndromes resolve promptly, as opposed to the chronic intellectual impairments. The "pseudoneurotic" symptoms also usually resolve, although a secondary neurotic disorder often becomes chronically established and must be treated appropriately.

CORTICOSTEROID HORMONE DISORDERS

Cushing's Syndrome

Cushing's syndrome is a state of sustained increased level of cortisol and (usually) of adrenal androgens. This entity actually includes a group of endocrinopathies resulting from adrenal cortical disorders, namely, excessive secretion of ACTH or corticotrophic-releasing factor (CRE).

Since Cushing's original description of this characteristic clinical picture in 1932, there have been some descriptions of isolated cases of Cushing's syndrome occurring in association with psychosis (24). The psychiatric manifestations can be severe (25, 26); they are strikingly prevalent and are occasionally the presenting symptoms. There is no single characteristic psychiatric picture and the gamut of symptoms covers a large part of the known psychiatric phenomena. Depression of some degree, often though not invariably associated with retardation, is the feature most frequently encountered (24). Apathy and retardation, which can be severe, bordering on stupor, may be replaced by irritability, agitation, anxiety, restlessness, hyperactivity, crying spells, and grossly disturbed uncooperative behavior. Both retardation and irritability states alternate in the same patient at different times. Marked fluctuations in the severity of the patient's condition are also typical. The depressive psychosis of Cushing's syndrome patients often involves delusions, hallucinations, and overt paranoid ideation. A schizophrenia-like psychosis, though unusual, may occur (27).

Adequate treatment of Cushing's syndrome usually relieves the physical, metabolic, and mental disturbances.

Addison's Disease

Addison's disease is the result of low output of adrenal steroids—cortisol, aldosterone, corticosterone, and androgens.

Mild psychiatric abnormalities are present almost without exception in Addison's Disease patients. The commonest of these are depression and apathy, with loss of drive and initiative. The patient may also show fluctuations of mood and episodes of marked anxiety and irritability. In many cases, there is impairment of memory. The severity of the symptoms correlates directly with that of the endocrine disorder. Addisonian crises are often heralded by increasing irritability, apprehension, and episodes of panic, proceeding to an acute organic brain syndrome with impaired consciousness and stupor.

Psychosis associated with Addison's disease was once claimed to be exclusively paranoid in nature (28, 29, 30), but a more recent survey of cases indicates that it can vary in type and appear with either paranoid or affective features (depressive, manic or both). It can also mimic undifferentiated schizophrenia or other organic psychoses (31). These overtly psychotic manifestations are relatively rare compared to the higher frequency of psychosis with Cushing's disease. They are fluctuating, evanescent and connected with somatic complications of the Addisonian syndrome. However, at least one case of Addison's disease has been reported in which a long-term psychotic syndrome made its appearance during an adequately treated period, when hormonal levels were within normal limits (32).

Adequate replacement therapy is successful in alleviating both the mental and physical signs of Addison's disease in most cases. ECT or neuroleptic medication has also been used in some cases (31, 32).

Corticosteroids and ACTH-induced Psychosis

Corticosteroids and ACTH, in therapeutic doses, may induce affective disturbances in many patients. Minor emotional symptoms such as irritability or euphoria with enhanced well-being are more frequent (33), but major psychotic disorders may also take place (34). Patients may have a stormy presentation of manic excitement with irritability and mood lability or psychotic symptomatology resembling acute paranoid schizophrenia. More infrequently, depression with apathy, crying spells, and suicidal behavior occur (35). Other psychotic manifestations are more heterogenous but are characterized by an underlying organic mental syndrome: confusion, clouded consciousness, disorientation, and memory disturbances. Auditory and visual hallucinations or paranoid ideation may appear. The content is often associated with the treatment situation. The same patient may manifest manic, schizophreniform, and organic symptomatology (36) sequentially (37).

The psychotic disorder associated with cortisone/ACTH administration may appear at any time during treatment—ranging from a few days to a few months. It has no constant relationship to dosage, although it is more likely to develop in patients on high doses. The duration varies extremely, from a few hours to months. There is at least one report that a persistent cyclical affective disorder may be induced by exogenous steroids (38).

Preexisting personality disorders, previous psychiatric disorder, or a history of previous steroid psychosis does not clearly increase the risk for the development of steroid psychosis during any given course of treatment (37, 39). However, this issue is still controversial (35).

Psychiatric side effects have been observed with various corticosteroid preparations and probably there is no substance that is superior to others in terms of its lack of psychiatric side effects. Moreover, there is a case report (40) which relates anabolic steroids, i.e., male hormones such as methandienone to the development of acute schizophreniform illness. The prognosis of steroid psychosis is usually good, with full remission following discontinuation or decrease of steroid dosage (35). Antidepressant or other psychotropic therapy is justified only in patients in which depression is persistent for at least two to three weeks after cessation of hormonal therapy.

PANCREATIC DISORDERS

Hypoglycemia

The most frequent cause of hypoglycemia is an insulin-secreting tumor of the pancreas. In acute hypoglycemia, which usually follows overdose of either insulin or oral hypoglycemic substances, the patient experiences malaise, anxiety, and panic and a detached feeling similar to depersonalization accompanied by hunger and restlessness. In untreated patients, epileptic seizures, periods of unconsciousness, and coma may follow (41).

Insulinomas more commonly lead to a subacute hypoglycemia, appearing as episodes of "unusual behavior" (42, 43, 44). The individual with subacute hypoglycemia may resemble one intoxicated by alcohol —apathetic or somnolent. The patient may be disoriented and confused; typically he is unaware of the changes in himself and may be negativistic.

In chronic hypoglycemia, which is rare and confined to patients with insulinoma, a change in personality develops slowly. Irritability, lability, apathy and even psychotic paranoid features may develop. Defects in memory and intellectual deterioration may proceed to moderate to severe dementia.

Patients with insulinomas not infrequently first come to medical attention because of the episodes of "odd behavior." These and the disturbances of consciousness may go on for months or years before diagnosis. The disease if protean and may mimic almost any psychiatric syndrome; the features and psychopathology of the attacks may vary from one occasion to another. The patient typically has amnesia for the attacks and may also not remember other periods.

The immediate outcome for most attacks is excellent, although symptoms may last for some hours after correction of blood sugar and prolonged coma may lead to permanent brain damage.

Diabetes Mellitus

Diabetes mellitus results from an absolute or relative deficiency of insulin production by the pancreas, which leads to disturbed carbohydrate metabolism and associated secondary changes in the metabolism of protein and lipids.

A few systematic surveys have been made of the emotional and mental changes in diabetes. The relationship exists on many levels. It is known that emotionally stressful experiences can lead to changes in blood glucose (46). Stress has often been blamed as an initial cause of the disease (47) and there is a prominent emotional effect on the course of an established diabetes (46). When a diabetic patient develops psychiatric disorders, it may at times be attributed to the disease itself. Episodes of diabetic coma or severe hypoglycemia can cause brain damage, as can the associated atherosclerosis (48, 49).

Multiple Adenomatosis

There are a few reports of multiple adenomatosis presenting as an acute psychosis (43, 45). Multiple endocrine adenomatosis is transmitted as a dominant autosomal trait and is characterized by adenomas in pancreatic islet cells and in the pituitary, adrenal and thyroid glands. In one case report the disease was presented as an acute depressive psychosis and was successfully treated by ECT (43). In another case report the multiple adenomatosis was presented with confusional episodes and violent behavior and mental retardation from early infancy, not explained by episodes of hypoglycemia alone (45). This patient's acute psychotic episodes disappeared following removal of an insulinoma.

PHYSIOLOGICAL HORMONAL CHANGES AND PSYCHOSIS

Puberty

Puberty is the transitional period between the juvenile state and adulthood, characterized by the occurrence of the adolescent growth spurt, appearance of secondary sexual characteristics and fertility, and profound psychological changes. The onset of puberty is a critical stage in a sequence of complex maturational changes.

Various behavioral changes in puberty have been described: lability of mood, increased aggression, increased interest in and concern about sexual functioning, etc. We are unaware of studies that systematically correlate normal behavioral changes during puberty with the very rapidly and markedly changing endocrine state.

The psychotic episodes related to these cyclical hormonal changes are called "periodic psychosis of puberty": a rare clinical entity described in a few case reports (50, 51, 52). In females it seems to constitute a distinct clinical entity with a syndrome of cyclic severe mental changes related to menses and starting with menarche. There are reports, however, that boys may also exhibit similar severe mental changes at puberty. The symptom cluster includes delusions, auditory and visual hallucinations, agitation and insomnia, emotional lability, bizarre posturing, staring spells and disorientation. The symptoms typically become apparent during the luteal phase of the menstrual cycle, several days before the onset of menses. Once bleeding occurs, the symptoms resolve within a few days, only to reappear during the next cycle. Initial onset of the symptoms is usually within the first few years after menarche. It is worthwhile mentioning that in some of the cases reported in boys, the cycles were also four weeks apart.

The validity of this syndrome has not been universally appreciated and it is not identified in DSM-III.

Paramenstrual Emotional Disorders

Both popular folklore and the scientific literature claim that many emotional and behavioral changes occur in conjunction with the menstrual cycle. Frequency of psychiatric crisis varies over the menstrual cycle. The paramenstruum (the several days before and the days of menstrual flow) has been shown to be associated with a higher frequency of psychiatric disturbance than the rest of the cycle, both in women with previously diagnosed psychiatric disorders such as depression and schizophrenia and in women with no known psychiatric disease (53-58).

There is disagreement as to whether the paramenstrual increase in psychotic symptoms in psychotic women is a result of the additive effect of the menstrual distress superimposed upon an existing psychotic process, or whether the menstrual distress is to be viewed as a more specific etiological agent. This last view may be supported by a differential increase of incidence of psychiatric crises during the paramenstruum; i.e., a significant paramenstrual increase of psychotic episodes among depressed, but not among schizophrenic women has been reported (58). The difference in pattern cannot be explained by a general increase of distress which should apply to all emotionally disturbed women.

In addition to the abundant literature concerning periodic worsening in the clinical status of psychotic women, there are several reports of periodic psychosis recurring in association with the menstrual cycle in women with no other psychiatric abnormalities (60).

The reported cases showed several characteristics in common: psychotic symptoms concomitant with the paramenstruum; more than three cyclic recurrences of similar psychoses; good remission during intervals and no residual signs when the psychotic episodes cease.

Williams (61) described the symptoms as characteristic of either the manic form of manic-depressive psychosis or the catatonic form of schizophrenia, with onset of minor somatic complaints followed by sudden changes in behavior with hallucinatory experiences, insomnia, restlessness, and confusion. In these cases the delirious features, autonomic symptoms, and unresponsiveness to high doses of medication (62) argue against the theory that they are manic-depressive or schizophrenic disorders triggered by or just coinciding with menstrual periods.

The case of recurrent cyclic premenstrual psychosis may be viewed as part of the group of premenstrual changes (PMC). The incidence of PMC is unclear due to differences of definitions, inaccurate reports due

to unawareness of therapists to the possibility of PMC, and method-
ological problems in research. The etiology of PMC is far from clear. The
biological hypotheses have implicated disturbances in water and sodium
retention (63), estrogen, progesterone (64), prolactin (65), the renin-an-
giotensin-aldosterone system (63, 66, 67), adrenal corticosteroids, central
catecholamines, central serotonin and central acetylcholine, endorphins
and other systems. An imbalance between several hormones, especially
estrogen and progesterone, has been suggested (68).

While an imbalance between neurotransmitters (norepinephrine and
acetylcholine) has been hypothesized in mental disorders with similar
syndromes (69), it might be assumed that changes in ovarian hormones
and several neurotransmitters are involved in interactive balances whose
impairment may be part of pathophysiology of the premenstrual
changes.

Many treatment modalities, based on etiologic hypotheses, have been
suggested. Regardless of the therapeutic agent, improvement has been
found in most uncontrolled studies, whereas the same therapeutic benefit was not demonstrated in controlled studies (70, 71). At present,
there is no definite treatment for the paramenstrual emotional disorders.

Postpartum Mental Disturbances

The puerperium is well established as a "high risk" period for development of more-or-less serious mental disturbances. Rates of incidence reported range from less than 1% up to 80% (72-74), with most
studies, including a recent prospective study, clustering at about one-
third (33%) of the women (75). It is clear that the incidence of psychiatric
illness in this period is much higher than expected in a matched group
of women. Maternity blues is a cross-cultural phenomenon and occurs
in cultures quite different from that of the West (76). Beyond these
epidemiological facts, there is disagreement on many points.

The first controversial point is whether there is one or several separate
entities under the rubric of postpartum disorder or whether the psychiatric disorders of the puerperium belong to one of the major categories, such as schizophrenia or affective disorders, precipitated by
psychological or endocrinological stress. The diagnostic issue is reflected
by the DSM-III. Postpartum psychoses that do not meet the criteria for
an organic mental disorder, schizophreniform disorder, paranoid disorder, or affective disorder should be included under atypical psychosis.
The nonpsychotic "milder" reactions are categorized respectively within
neurotic personality disorders. According to this view, which reflects

the prevailing opinion in the literature (77, 78), childbearing may act as a precipitating factor or trigger to almost any kind of mental disorder. On the other hand, other authors hold the opposite view: Hamilton (79) states with much conviction that "puerperal psychoses are unique in their etiology, in their organic components and in the subtile qualities of their psychodynamics." Brockington et al. (80) point to many and consistent differences between the symptomatology of puerperal psychosis and the comparison series of women with other psychoses. According to this view, there should be a nosological division for these psychoses.

Psychiatric disturbances subsequent to childbirth develop in a variety of patterns. The most common type is depression, which may appear during the third postpartum day in a mild, short-lived form—the so-called "postpartum blues." The main symptoms are depression, anxiety, and minimal confusion. This is the most common phenomenon, so common, in fact, as to be thought normal (73, 81). On the other end of the spectrum there are severe depressions with suicidal ideation, delusions, and hallucinations. Another form of postpartum psychosis is a manic syndrome (82). Postpartum manic patients are more likely to have Schneiderian delusions and hallucinations than are female patients who have mania other than in the postpartum period and they are less likely to have recurrent episodes of illness outside of the puerperium (82, 83).

The schizophrenia-like form of postpartum psychosis is distinguished (80) by an excess of manic-like symptoms such as elation, lability of mood, distractibility and increased activity, with fewer schizophrenic symptoms than control schizophrenic patients, but no fewer Schneiderian first rank symptoms. Sneddon and Kerry (84) named puerperal psychosis "spectrum psychosis," showing signs of affective, schizophrenic and organic features with rapid symptom changes. There seems to be yet another postpartum clinical phenomenon resembling a mild acute brain syndrome with attention deficits, poor recent memory, and clouding of consciousness (85, 86). This form seemed to be more frequent in the past when toxic and other obstetrical complications were more prevalent. According to Brockington et al. (80), the confusional component of puerperal psychosis is different from that found in acute organic brain syndrome and indicates only that these patients are more disorganized than other psychotics.

Theories concerning etiology range from psychosocial factors and intrapsychic conflicts to physiological factors, mainly focusing on the hormonal changes inherent in childbirth, which may act directly or indirectly, influencing the biogenic amines. The main endocrine changes are sudden withdrawal of hormones of fetoplacental origin and, during lactation, a continuous production of prolactin, a drop in the output of thyroxine relative to the pre-pregnancy level, and a decrease in cortisol with a tendency to "sluggish" pituitary response (88). Decrease in endorphin activity has been reported as well.

The fetoplacental hormones, LH, FSH, estrogen and progesterone, drop suddenly after delivery, but studies (89) failed to produce evidence of correlation of plasma levels of these hormones with mood and other clinical findings. The "sluggish" pituitary response to the lowered cortisol level may cause an increase in hypothalamic activity, which may spread to other hypothalamic functions with sleep disturbances and heightened sympathetic activity that can be perceived as increased anxiety (88).

According to some authors (87, 90, 91), patients who appeared clinically to have severe postpartum depression had low free plasma tryptophan concentrations similar to those found in depressive illness. This may be related to a more generalized disturbance in membrane transport which could impair the body's ability to regulate tryptophan concentration in the face of perturbing factors which occur at parturition.

There are very few controlled treatment studies but several anecdotal and impressionistic reports. Most "classical" biological and psychological treatment modalities were applied to postpartum emotional disturbances with varying success. The postpartum "blues" are short-lived and generally do not require other than supportive treatment. The more severe psychiatric disorders are treated by major and minor tranquilizers, antidepressants, and ECT as indicated, combined with psychosocial treatment programs such as conjoint mother-and-baby hospitalization (92). The use of lithium for postpartum mania is controversial (82). Other treatments are based on still unproven etiological theories.

Dalton (93), maintaining the common cause hypothesis for premenstrual and puerperal depression, finds that both have an excellent response to high daily dose progesterone. The beta-adrenergic blocking agent propranolol showed promising results in an uncontrolled open study (94). Hamilton (95) describes a 95% recovery rate with a treatment regimen which includes thyroid hormone. Generally, the long-term prognosis for postpartum mental illness was found to be correlated with the general psychiatric diagnosis (96). The more acute cases with predominant confusion, as well as the catatonic-like clinical picture, have a better prognosis (86, 97).

COMMENT

This review reflects considerable confusion in the literature concerning behaviorial symptoms associated with hormonal changes and disturbances. It is important to point out that many of the studies in this area were conducted a long time ago at a period when hormonal determinations were relatively inaccurate and the discrimination among various types of hormonal changes was inadequate—for example, the distinction between primary adrenal and primary pituitary hypersecretion. Moreover, most studies did not apply explicit diagnostic criteria for the psychiatric disturbances and used quite vague clinical definitions and descriptions.

At this point we can conclude that clinical experience supports the hypothesis that most, if not all, hormones are directly and indirectly associated with changes in mood and behavior. When severe enough, most endocrine disturbances lead to a final common behavioral pathway—delirium or dementia. However, even though it is impossible at this point to define specific "endocrine psychoses," there is some evidence that hormonal changes contribute to specific elements of psychopathology.

Future studies will hopefully define an association between endocrine and behavioral events. This knowledge would probably be of help in understanding some of the basic mechanisms of mental disturbances in addition to improving the diagnosis and treatment of mental disorders.

REFERENCES

1. Whybrow, P.C., Prange, A.J., and Treadway, C.R.: Mental changes accompanying thyroid gland dysfunction. *Arch. Gen. Psychiat.*, 20: 48-63, 1969.
2. Whybrow, P.C., and Hurwitz, T.: Psychological disturbances associated with endocrine disease and hormone therapy. In: E. J. Sachar (Ed.), *Hormones, Behavior and Psychopathology*. New York: Raven, 1976.
3. Artunkal, S., and Togrol, B.: Psychological studies in hyperthyroidism. In: M. P. Cameron, and M. O'Connor (Eds.), *Brain-Thyroid Relationship*. Boston: Little, Brown, 1964.
4. Bowers, M., and Singer, D.: Thyrotoxicosis and psychological state. *Psychosomatics*, 5: 322-324, 1964.
5. Checkley, S.A.: Thyrotoxicosis and the course of manic depressive illness. *Brit. J. Psychiat.*, 133: 219-223, 1978.
6. Brewer, C.: Psychosis due to acute hypothyroidism during the administration of carbimazole. *Brit. J. Psychiat.*, 115: 1181-1183, 1969.
7. Josephson, A.M., and Mackenzie, T.B.: Appearance of manic psychosis following rapid normalization of thyroid status. *Am. J. Psychiat.*, 136, 6: 846-847, 1979.

8. Radhey, L., Singhal, R.L., and Rastogi, Ram B.: Neurotransmitter mechanism during mental illness induced by alterations of thyroid function. *Adv. Pharmacol. Chemother.*, 15: 203-262, 1978.

9. Logothesis, J.: Psychotic behavior as the initial indicator of adult myxedema. *J. Nerv. Ment. Dis.*, 136: 561-568, 1963.

10. Easson, W.M.: Myxedema with psychosis. *Arch. Gen Psychiat.*, 14: 227-283, 1966.

11. Beck, H.G.: The hallucinations of myxedema. *Med. Times*, 54: 201-203, 1926.

12. Libow, L.S., and Durell, J.: Clinical studies on the relationship between psychosis and the regulation of thyroid gland activity. *Psychosomatic Medicine*, 27, 4: 377-382, 1965.

13. Extein, I., Pottash, A.L.C., and Gold, M.S.: Does subclinical hypothyroidism predispose to tricyclic induced rapid mood cycles? *J. Clin. Psychiat.*, 43, 7: 290-291, 1982.

14. Tonks, C.M.: Mental illnesses in hypothyroid patients. *Brit. J. Psychiat.*, 110: 706-710, 1964.

15. Josephson, A.M., and Mackenzie, T.B.: Thyroid-induced mania in hypothyroid patients. *Brit. J. Psychiat.*, 137: 222-228, 1980.

16. Peterson, P.: Psychiatric disorders in primary hyperparathyroidism. *J. Clin. Endocrinol. Metab.*, 28: 1491-1495, 1968.

17. Watson, L.: Clinical aspects of hyperparathyroidism. *Proc. R. Soc. Med.*, 61:1123, 1968.

18. Karpatis, G., and Frame, B.: Neuropsychiatric disorders in primary hyperparathyroidism. *Arch. Neurol.*, 10: 387-397, 1964.

19. Gatewood, J.W., Organ, C.H., and Mead, B.T.: Mental changes with hyperparathyroidism. *Am. J. Psychiat.*, 132: 129-132, 1975.

20. Argov, Z., Melamed, E., and Katz, S.: Hyperparathyroidism presenting with unusual neurologic features. *Eur. Neurol.*, 18: 338-370, 1979.

21. Mikkelsen, E., and Reider, A.: Post parathyroidectomy psychosis: Clinical and research implications. *J. Clin. Psychiat.*, 352-357, August 1979.

22. Green, J., and Swanson, I.: Psychosis in hypoparathyroidism with a report of five cases. *Ann. Intern. Med.*, 14: 1233-1236, 1942.

23. Denko, J.D., and Kaelbling, R.: The psychiatric aspects of hypoparathyroidism. *Acta Psychiatrica Scand.*, 164 (suppl.): 1-70, 1962.

24. Trethowan, W.H., and Cobb, S.: Neuropsychiatric aspects of Cushing's syndrome. *Arch. Neurol. Psych.*, 67: 283-309, 1952.

25. Spillane, J.D.: Nervous and mental disorders in Cushing's syndrome. *Brain*, 74: 72-94, 1951.

26. Michael, R.P., and Gibbon, J.L.: Interrelationships between the endocrine system and neuropsychiatry. *Int. Rev. Neurobiology*, 5: 243-302, 1963.

27. Hickman, J.W., Atkinson, R.P., Flint, L.D., and Hurxthal, L.M.: Transient schizophrenic reaction as a major symptom of Cushing's syndrome. *New Eng. J. Med.*, 264: 797-800, 1961.

28. Cleghorn, R.A.: Adrenal cortical in sufficiency: Psychological and neurological observations. *Canadian Med. Assn. J.*, 65: 449-454, 1951.

29. Smith, C.M.: Paranoid behaviour in Addison's disease. *Canadian Psychiat. Assn. J.*, 3: 145-154, 1958.

30. McCulloch, T.A.H., and Calverly, M.D.: Addison's disease with psychosis. *Canadian Med. Assn. J.*, 85: 31-33, 1964.

31. McFahrland, T.: Addison's disease and related psychoses. *Compreh. Psych.*, 4: 90-95, 1963.

32. Mattsyon, B.: Addison's disease and psychosis. *Acta Psychiatrica Scand.*, 255 (suppl.): 203-210, 1974.

33. Lidz, T., Carter, J.D., Lewis, B.I., and Surratt, C.: Effects of ACTH and cortisone on mood and mentation. *Psychosomatic Medicine*, 14, 5: 363-377, 1952.

34. Glaser, G.H.: Psychotic reactions induced by corticotropin (ACTH) and cortisone. *Psychosomatic Medicine*, 15, 4: 280-291, 1953.

35. Rome, H.P., and Braceland, F.J.: The psychological response to ACTH, cortisone, hydrocortisone and related steroid substances. *Am. J. Psychiat.*, 108: 641-651, 1952.

36. Kaufmann, M., Kahaner, K., Peselow, E.D., and Gershon, S.: Steroid psychoses: Case report and brief overview. *J. Clin. Psychiat.* 43, 2: 75-76, 1982.
37. Hall, R.C.W., Popkin, M.K., Stickney, S.K., and Gardner, E.R.: Presentation of the steroid psychoses. *J. Nerv. Ment. Dis.*, 167, 4: 229-235, 1979.
38. Pies, R.: Presistent bipolar illness after steroid administration. *Arch. Int. Med.*, 141: 1087, July 1981.
39. Carpenter, W.T., Strauss, J.S., and Bunney, W.E.: The psychobiology of cortisol metabolism: Clinical and theoretical implications. In: R.I. Shader, (Ed.), *Psychiatric Complications of Medical Drugs*. New York: Raven Press, 1972.
40. Annitto, J.W., and Layman, A.W.: Anabolic steroids and acute schizophrenic episode. *J. Clin. Psychiat.*, 41, 4: 143-144, April 1980.
41. Marks, V., and Rose, F.C.: Hypoglycemia. Oxford: Blackwell Scientific Publications, 1965.
42. Romano, J., and Coon, G.P.: Physiologic and psychologic studies in spontaneous hypoglycemia. *Psychosomatic Medicine*, 4: 283-300, 1942.
43. Carney, M.W.P., Weinbren, J., Jackson, F., and Purnell, G.V.: Multiple adenomatosis presenting with psychiatric manifestations. *Postgrad. Med. J.*, 47: 242-243, 1971.
44. Whitty, C.W.M., and Lishman, W.A.: Amnesia in cerebral disease. In: C.W.M. Whitty, and O.L. Zangwill (Eds.), *Amnesia*. Butterworths: London, 1966.
45. Fullerton, D.T., Lohrenz, F.N., and Holtey, W.J.: Successful electroconvulsive therapy in an adrenalectomized patient with endocrine adenomatosis. *Wisconsin Med. J.*, 66: 203, 1967.
46. Hinkle, L.E., and Wolf, S.: A summary of experimental evidence relating life stress to diabetes mellitus. *J. of the Mount Sinai Hospital*, 19: 537-570, 1952.
47. Trenting, T.F.: The role of emotional factors in the etiology and course of diabetes mellitus: A review of the recent literature. *Am. J. of the Medical Sciences*, 244: 93-109, 1962.
48. Ives, E.R.: Mental aberrations in diabetic patients. *Bul. of the Los Angeles Neurol. Soc.*, 28: 279-285, 1963.
49. Balle, R.N.: Brain damage in diabetes mellitus. *Brit. J. Psych.*, 122: 337-341, 1973.
50. Altschule, M.D., and Bren, J.: Periodic psychosis of puberty. *Am. J. Psychiat.*, 119: 1176-1178, 1963.
51. Jagdish, S. Teja: Single case study: Periodic psychosis of puberty. *J. Nerv. Ment. Dis.*, 162: 52-57, 1976.
52. Berlin, F.S., Bergey, G.K., and Money, J.: Periodic psychosis of puberty: A case report. *Am. J. Psych.*, 139: 119-120, 1982.
53. Janowsky, D.S., Gorney, R., and Castelnuovo-Tedesco, P.: Premenstrual-menstrual increases in psychiatric hospital admission rates. *Amer. J. Gyn.*, 103: 189, 1969.
54. Lederer, J.: Premenstrual kleptomania in a case of hypothyroidism and hyperfolliculinism. *Ann. Endoc.*, 24: 460-465, 1963.
55. Verghese, A.: The syndrome of premenstrual psychosis. *Indian J. Psychiat.*, 5: 160-163, 1963.
56. Dalton, K.: Menstruation and acute psychiatric illness. *Brit. Med. J.*, 1: 148-149, 1959.
57. Glass, S., Heninger, G., and Lansky, M.: Psychiatric emergency related to the menstrual cycle. *Am. J. Psychiat.*, 128: 705-711, 1971.
58. Abramovitz, E.S., Baker, A.B., and Fleisher, S.F.: Onset of depressive psychiatric crises and the menstrual cycle. *Am. J. Psychiat.*, 139, 4: 475-478, 1982.
59. Zola, P., Meyerson, T.A., Reznikoff, M., Thornton, J.C., and Concool, B.M.: Menstrual symptomatology and psychiatric admission. *J. Psychosom. Res.*, 23: 244-245, 1979.
60. Endo, M., Daigujl, M., Asano, Y., Yamashita, I., and Takahashi, S.: Periodic psychosis recurring in association with menstrual cycle. *J. Clin. Psychiat.*, 39: 456-466, 1978.
61. Williams, E.Y., and Weekes, L.R.: Premenstrual tension associated with psychotic episodes. *J. Nerv. Ment. Dis.*, 116: 321-329, 1952.
62. Felthous, A.R., Robinson, D.B., and Conroy, R.W.: Prevention of recurrent menstrual psychosis by an oral contraceptive. *Am. J. Psychiat.*, 137: 245-246, 1980.

63. Janowsky, D.S., Berens, S.C., and Davis, J.M.: Correlations between mood, weight, and electrolytes during the menstrual cycle: A review—angiotension-aldosterone hypothesis of premenstrual tension. *Psychosom. Med.*, 35, 2: 143-152, 1973.
64. Backstrom, T., and Mattsoon, B.: Correlation of symptoms in premenstrual tension to estrogen and progesterone concentrations in blood plasma. *Neuropsychobiology*, 1: 80-86, 1975.
65. Halbreich, U., Ben David, M., and Assael, M.: Serum-prolactin in women with premenstrual syndrome. *Lancet*, 2: 654-656, 1976.
66. Munday, M., Brush, M.G., and Taylor, R.W.: Progesterone and aldosterone levels in the premenstrual tension syndrome. *J. Endocrin.*, 73: 21, 1977.
67. O'Brien, P.M., Craven, D., and Selby, C.: Treatment of premenstrual syndrome by spironolactone. *Brit. J. Ob. Gyn.*, 86: 142-147, 1979.
68. Rausch, J.L., and Janowski, D.S.: Premenstrual tension: Etiology. In: R. Friedman, (Ed.), *Behavior and the Menstrual Cycle*. New York: Marcel Dekker, 1982, pp. 397-427.
69. Pradhan, S.M., and Bose, S.: Interactions among central neurotransmitters. In: M.A. Lipton, A. DiMascio, and K.F. Killan (Eds.), *Psychopharmacology: A Generation of Progress*. New York: Raven, 1978, pp. 271-281.
70. Smith, S.L.: Mood and the menstrual cycle. In: E.J. Sachar (Ed.), *Topics in Psychoendocrinology*. New York: Grune & Stratton, 1975, pp. 19-58.
71. Green, J.: Recent trends in the treatment of premenstrual syndrome: A Criteria and review. In: R.C. Friedman (Ed.), *Behaviour and the Menstrual Cycle*. New York: Marcel Dekker, 1982, pp. 367-395.
72. Pitt, B.: "Atypical" depression following childbirth. *Brit. J. Psychiat.*, 114: 1325, 1968.
73. Yalom, D.I., Lunde, D.T., Moos, R.H., and Hamburg, D.A.: "Post-partum blues" syndrome. *Arch. Gen. Psychiat.*, 18: 16-27, 1968.
74. Kendell, R.E., Wainwright S., Hailey, A., and Shannon, B.: Influence of childbirth on psychiatric morbidity. *Psychological Medicine*, 6: 297-302, 1976.
75. Cox, J.L., Connor, Y., and Kendell, R.E.: Prospective study of the psychiatric disorders of childbirth. *Brit. J. Psychiat.* 140: 111-117, 1982.
76. Harris, B.: Maternity blues (letter). *Brit. J. Psychiat.*, 136: 520-521, 1980.
77. Herzog, A., and Detre, T.: Psychotic reactions associated with childbirth. *Dis. Nerv. Syst.*, 37: 229-235, 1976.
78. Steiner, M., and Carroll, B.J.: The psychobiology of premenstrual dysphoria: Review of theories and treatments. *Psychoneuroendocrinology*, 2: 321-335, 1977.
79. Hamilton, J.A.: *Post-Partum Psychiatric Problems*. St. Louis: C.V. Mosby, 1962.
80. Brockington, J.F., Cernik, K.F., Schofield, E.M., Downing, A.R., Francis, A.F., and Keelan, C.: Puerperal psychosis. *Arch. Gen. Psychiat.*, 38: 829-833, 1981.
81. Pitt, B.: Maternity blues *Brit. J. Psychiat.*, 122: 431-433, 1973.
82. Kadrmas, A., Winokur, G., and Crowe, R.: Post-partum mania. *Brit. J. Psychiat.*, 135: 551-554, 1979.
83. Katonah, C.L.E.: Puerperal mental illness: Comparisons with non-puerperal controls. *Brit. J. Psychiat.*, 141: 447-452, 1982.
84. Sneddon, J., and Kerry, R.J.: Puerperal psychosis (letter). *Brit. J. Psychiat.*, 136: 520, 1980.
85. Kane, F.J., Harman, W.J., Jr., Keeler, M.H., and Ewing, J.A.: Emotional and cognitive disturbance in the early puerperium. *Brit. J. Psychiat.*, 114: 99-102, 1968.
86. Huhn, A., and Drenk, K.: Clinical classification and prognosis of post-partum psychosis. *Fortschr. Neurol. Psychiat.*, 41: 363-377, 1973.
87. Tulchinsky, D.: The post-partum period. In: D. Tulchinsky and K.J. Ryan (Eds.), *Maternal-Fetal Endocrinology*. Philadelphia: W.B. Saunders, 1980.
88. Hamilton, J.A.: Model utility in post-partum psychosis. *Psychopharmacology Bulletin*. 18, 3: 184-187, 1982.
89. Nott, P.N., Franklin, M., Armilage, C., and Gelder, M.D.: Hormonal changes and mood in the puerperium. *Brit. J. Psychiat.*, 128: 379-383, 1976.

90. Handley, S.L., Dunn, T.L., Baker, J.M., Cockshott, C., and Gould, S.E.: Mood changes in puerperium and plasma tryptophan and cortisol concentrations. *Brit. Med. J.*, 2: 18-22, 1977.

91. Stein, G., Milton F., Bebbington, P., Wood, K., and Coppen, A. Relationship between mood disturbances and free and total plasma trypotophan in postpartum women. *Brit. Med. J.*, 2: 457, 1976.

92. Lindsay, J.S.B.: Puerperal psychosis: A follow-up study of a joint mother and baby treatment programme. *Aust. N.Z. J. Psychiat.*, 9: 73-76, 1975.

93. Dalton, K.: Prospective study into puerperal depression. *Brit. J. Psychiat.*, 118: 689-692, 1971.

94. Steiner, M., Latz, A., Blum, J., Atsmon, A., and Wijsenbeek, H.: Propranolol versus cholorpromazine in the treatment of psychoses associated with childbearing. *Psychiat. Neurol. Neurochir. (Amst.)*, 76: 421-426, 1973.

95. Hamilton, J.A.: Puerperal psychosis. In: *Gynecology and Obstetrics, Vol. II*, chapter 24N, i-8. Hagerstown, MD: Harper & Row, 1977.

96. DaSilva, L., and Johnstone, E.C.: A follow-up of severe puerperal psychiatric illness. *Brit. J. Psychiat.*, 139: 346-354, 1981.

97. Hays, P.: Toxonomic map of the schizophrenias, with special reference to puerperal psychosis. *Brit. Med. J.*, 2: 715-719, 1978.

Chapter 6

Drug-induced Psychoses

Jonathan Lisansky, M.D.,
Rick J. Strassman, M.D.,
David Janowsky, M.D.,
and S. Craig Risch, M.D.

The purpose of this chapter is to provide guidelines for understanding the pathophysiology, phenomenology, assessment, and management of individuals with drug-induced transient psychotic episodes. In defining our focus we will elaborate upon psychotic reactions that range in time from several hours to several days. We will discuss only in passing those drug-induced reactions which last several weeks or more, or those causing significant confusion. Among the drugs we will consider which are etiologic of transient psychotic episodes are: 1) Hallucinogens (including LSD and mescaline); 2) phencyclidine; 3) psychostimulants; 4) anticholinergic agents; and 5) cannabinoids. We will also consider briefly the ability of several representative medically prescribed drugs, including L-dopa and the corticosteroids, to cause transient psychotic episodes.

HALLUCINOGENIC DRUGS

We will first consider the hallucinogens as prototypical of drug-induced transient psychotic states. The use of naturally occurring, exog-
enously administered substances for inducing altered states of
consciousness extends back to ancient times. Certain species of mushrooms were used as long ago as the time of the Vedas in India, around
5000 B.C. In the New World, mushrooms and certain cacti, barks, and
vines were employed for similar purposes by indigenous cultures. Abuse
of these agents apparently was fairly rare, perhaps because careful cultural, religious and social proscriptions determined a uniform manner
in which they were used, and the experiences one was expected to have
as a result of their use (1).

The "modern era" of use of mind-altering drugs for their experiential
value is often said to have begun with Albert Hofmann's accidental
ingestion of LSD-25 (lysergic acid diethylamide) in 1943 (2). However,
interest in mescaline and peyote was also briefly pursued at the turn of
the century (3). "Therapeutic" and "growth-enchancing" aspects of
these substances were widely pursued early on, spurred by such "auto-
experimenters" as Aldous Huxley (4), Timothy Leary (5), and Carlos
Castañeda (6). A great flurry of scientific activity with LSD and similarly
acting drugs occurred in the 1950s and 1960s, but was just as quickly
aborted in the late 1960s, as fears of their abuse potential and legislative
sanctions became prevalent.

Terminology and Definition

Psychedelic drugs, used here synonymously with the term hallucinogens, can be distinguished from other centrally-active drugs such as
psychostimulants, anticholinergic agents, and opiates that can also, under certain conditions, induce perceptual distortions, paranoid, and
other delusions, and other alterations of cognition, behavior, and affect.
Psychedelic drugs are capable, when pathologic effects are absent or
minimal, of "reliably inducing or compelling states of altered perception,
thought and feeling that are not of the type experienced otherwise except
in dreams, or at times of religious exaltation" (7).

Lysergic acid diethylamide-25 (LSD) is the prototypical psychedelic
compound, and is often the active ingredient in street psychedelics, even
those labeled as "mescaline" or "psilocybin." LSD is, as are psilocybin,

psilocin, diethyltryptamine (DET) and dimethyltryptamine (DMT), a member of the indolealkylamine class of drugs. Mescaline (one of the most active ingredients in peyote cactus) is a phenylethylamine, and "STP" (DOM; 2,5-dimethoxy-4-methylamphetamine) is a phenylisopropylamine.

On the basis of 1) subjective effects and neurophysiological actions; 2) cross-tolerance between compounds; and 3) response to selective antagonists, Martin and Sloan (8) have classified LSD, mescaline, psilocybin, and psilocin as "LSD-like." Differences among the various LSD-like drugs are primarily a matter of rate of onset, peripheral side effects, duration of action, and intensity of the experience. For example, LSD is relatively long lasting (eight to 12 hours, half-life about 12 hours), and more potent, with an average dose taken of 100-500 micrograms, than are mescaline, with an average dose taken of 200-500 mg and an average duration of action of six to eight hours, and psilocybin or psilocin, with an average duration of action of four to 12 hours and an effective dose of 10 to 50 mg.

Mechanism of Action

Serotonergic systems, especially in the midbrain raphe nuclei, or neurons projecting from those nuclei, have frequently been proposed as the primary source of psychedelic agents' hallucinogenic effects (9). These agents appear to preferentially inhibit serotonergic cell firing via binding to cell-body or dendritic 5-HT receptors, and to spare postsynaptic serotonergic receptors. As serotonin is primarily an inhibitory neurotransmitter, inhibition of these cells by LSD allows the next neuron in the chain to be freed from inhibition (10). Dopaminergic (DA) systems may also be involved in the central effects of psychedelics, with preliminary evidence indicating both agonist and antagonist effects of LSD on postsynaptic DA receptors (11).

Carbon-14 labeled LSD, given to animals, has shown LSD to be maximally concentrated in liver and kidney, and brain concentrations are maximal in hippocampus, basal ganglia, thalamic nuclei, and cerebral cortex. Most of LSD metabolites are excreted in the feces (12). Implanted cortical electrodes in humans have shown LSD-associated paroxysmal electrical activity in the hippocampal gyri, amygdaloid nuclei, and septum during perceptual changes, and these effects are reversed by chlorpromazine (13).

Physiologic and Behavioral Effects

The effects of an oral dose of LSD as low as 20-25 micrograms can be perceived within a few minutes, although with psilocybin and mescaline, onset of initial symptoms occur somewhat later, around 15-30 minutes.

Initial physical symptoms of psychedelic drug intoxication are sympathomimetic in nature. These may include dilation of the pupils (with retention of reactivity), nausea, flushing, chilliness, increased blood pressure and heart rate, tremor, hyperreflexia, piloerection, weakness, elevated body temperature, and dizziness (7). Psychological effects soon follow within 30 to 90 minutes, and include feelings of inner tension, affective lability, visual illusions and hallucinations, followed in frequency by auditory, and then other sensory changes, blending of sensory modalities (such as "seeing sound"—synesthesia), a slowing of subjective time, a sense of ego dissolution/detachment/fragmentation, recollection of long-forgotten memories, and an increased sense of meaningfulness for what is being experienced. Religious and mystical insights occasionally occur.

As the drug effects wear off, and if the experience has been regarded as generally positive, there is a calm yet energetic sense of detachment and control.

When doses are between one and 16 microgram/kilogram, the intensity of LSD's effects are proportional to dosage. Tolerance rapidly develops for psychedelic drugs, and at least three to four days are necessary for recovery of the prior sensitivity to drugs of this type. A withdrawal syndrome does not occur with abrupt cessation of LSD-like drugs. "Overdoses" of LSD are not directly fatal, and an LD-50 (lethal dose for 50% of the population) for the drug is not known for man. However, fatalities can indirectly occur from suicides during or after LSD use.

Adverse Reactions

The temporal relationship between the ingestion of a psychedelic drug and subsequent dysphoric or maladaptive symptoms is probably the most useful means of classifying psychedelic-induced adverse reactions.

The most common adverse acute reaction caused by psychedelic agents is a temporary episode of panic—the "bad trip"—which usually lasts less than 24 hours (14). Symptoms often include frightening illusions and/or hallucinations, usually of a visual and/or auditory nature, and overwhelming anxiety, to the point of panic. Aggression, with violent acting-out behavior, depression with suicidal ideation or gestures or attempts, and confusion and/or fearfulness to the point of paranoia may also occur, as may grand mal seizures (15).

Reactions which are somewhat more prolonged, but still can be considered transient, and which may require hospitalization, are often referred to as "LSD-psychoses," and include a heterogeneous population and group of symptoms (14,16,17). Although there are no hard and fast rules, some trends have been noted in retrospective analyses of those patients with LSD psychoses. As one might expect, there is a tendency for people with poorer premorbid adjustment, a history of psychiatric illness and/or treatment, a greater number of exposures to psychedelic drugs, and correlatively, a greater average total cumulative dosage taken over time, drug-taking in an unsupervised setting, a history of polydrug abuse, and a self-therapeutic and/or peer-pressure-submissive motive (18) for drug use to suffer from transient psychotic episodes after psychedelic drug ingestion. Symptomatically, these patients present with a wide variety of symptoms, reflecting the great diversity of their premorbid psychopathology (19). Formal thought disorder, hallucinations, illusions, violence, paranoid and other delusions, depression, regression, emotional lability, bizarre behavior, insomnia, hypomania, depersonalization, dissociative states, confusion, and apathy may occur.

In addition to the above psychotic phenomena, another psychedelic-induced mental state is the flashback experience. Flashbacks are intermittent phenomena, which may occur repeatedly for up to years, and which may be considered one of the most intriguing forms of "chronic" psychedelic drug-induced altered state. Using a general definition, they may be considered within the realm of transient psychotic episodes. Flashbacks may be defined as transient, spontaneous recurrences of a psychedelic drug effect, appearing after a period of normalcy, and following a psychedelic drug experience (20). Schick and Smith (21) divide these into 1) "perceptual," 2) "somatic," and 3) "emotional," depending upon which aspect of the experience seems to predominate.

The reported incidence of flashbacks varies from 20 to 50% of those patients who have had at least one psychedelic drug experience (20, 22). Individuals may not report that they have had or are having flashbacks. This may be due to the acceptance and tolerance of flashbacks, and/or because of the generally positive connotation these experiences have—i.e., that they are sometimes referred to as a "free trip."

The etiology of flashbacks is a topic of debate at the present time. Various theories have been proposed which may not necessarily be mutually exclusive, depending on the subject population. Although pre-disposing factors in the development of flashbacks have not been as well-documented, it does appear that a greater number of psychedelic drug experiences in subjects may increase the likelihood of flashback development. There is some consensus that perhaps those with adverse acute or chronic reactions may be more likely to develop and/or report such phenomena.

However, Matefy and co-workers (23) have shown that "flashbackers" show no significant psychopathological differences, as measured by the MMPI, or attentional processes as measured by the Embedded Figures Test, as compared to "non-flashbacking" drug users. Flashbackers have also been shown to score higher on a hypnotic suggestibility scale than non-flashbacking drug users. Matefy et al. (24) favor a "role-playing" model of flashbacks, whereby the phenomenon is described as a reaction learned during a state of high arousal resulting from drug use. Therefore, under other nonspecific high arousal states, a "psychedelic effect" is again experienced by means of conscious or unconscious association.

Other groups (25) suggest that flashbacks are a result of situationally induced exacerbation of pervasive personality characteristics (26). These characteristics would favor experiencing flashbacks in circumstances that tend to induce altered states of awareness (e.g., decreased sensory input, fatigue, fever, extreme relaxation, stress, etc.).

Psychodynamic formulations (22, 27), consider flashbacks as compa-rable to the conversion reactions/traumatic neuroses, where defensive functions of the ego are incapable of completely repressing memories and conflicts which were stimulated or exacerbated by the intense psy-chedelic drug-induced effects. In contrast, Rosenthal (28), in one of the earliest reports of flashback phenomena, proposed a physiological-neu-rochemical basis for flashbacks.

LSD as a Model of Schizophrenia

One of the major differential diagnoses confronting the clinician in the case of psychedelic-related psychoses is schizophrenia. In the early years of psychedelic drug research, there was hope that psychedelic drug-induced altered states of consciousness and psychotic episodes could provide a "model psychosis," whereby theoretical and clinical tools could be brought to bear on an easily induced, reproducible, and reversible state resembling schizophrenia (29). Several excellent reviews of this subject have appeared, beginning with Hollister's in 1962 (30). However, a variety of studies (31-33) have all confirmed that there are significant major differences between these two syndromes, especially when one is comparing acute psychedelic drug-induced states with the chronic forms of schizophrenia. There appears to be a greater similiarity between acute LSD-induced states and acute schizophrenia, but careful observation can still usually distinguish these two states. Thus, patients in the midst of a psychedelic drug intoxication show less flattening of affect than schizophrenics. Visual-perceptual alterations such as visual hallucinations or illusions generally predominate in intoxicated subjects, as compared to schizophrenics, where auditory perceptual changes are generally most common. Individuals with LSD-induced transient psychotic states tend to show less well-fixed delusional systems than schizophrenics, most likely due to the acknowledgment of the drug-induced nature of their experience.

In arriving at a decision concerning the etiology of a particular psychotic episode, the historical knowledge that a patient has taken a psychedelic drug is of obvious value in making the clinical diagnosis. Also, the absence or presence of a family history of schizophrenia is helpful, as is premorbid history.

Treatment and Course

Treatment of hallucinogenic-induced acute panic reactions should be directed towards allaying the patient's overwhelming anxiety. A quiet, comfortable room with a minimum of distractions should be available, and the patient should not be left alone. Most of these panicky individuals can be "talked down" by calmly discussing their fears and fantasies, offering orientation as necessary, reinforcing the concept that the experience is drug-induced and time-limited, and stressing that no permanent brain damage has been suffered.

For more severe episodes of agitation, minor tranquilizers such as diazepam should be used, given in oral or intravenous form. Chlordiazepoxide is preferable for intramuscular use, as its absorption by this route is more consistent than for diazepam. Usual doses range from 15 to 30 mg for diazepam or 50 to 100 mg for chlordiazepoxide, repeated every one to two hours as necessary to calm or sedate the patient (34).

Major tranquilizers should be reserved for only the most disturbed and agitated patients with panic reactions. Chlorpromazine was initially felt to be a specific LSD-antagonist (35), but paradoxical reactions (36) and the problems of hypotensive and anticholinergic crises when used to treat intoxication with DOM (STP), a highly anticholinergic psychedelic-like drug (37), would point towards using a less anticholinergic anti-psychotic drug such as haloperidol, 5-10 mg IM or 10-20 mg p.o.

Restraint and/or gastric lavage are generally to be avoided in a fright-ened, hallucinating patient, although where there is a concern of the patient hurting himself or others, or when other more potentially life-threatening drugs have been ingested, these procedures may be nec-essary.

Hospitalization is usually not necessary for the treatment of psyche-delic drug-induced panic reactions, but should be available. Once the acute reaction has subsided, usually within 12-24 hours, the patient should be sent home with someone responsible to monitor him for the next 12-24 hours. A follow-up appointment should be arranged in order to evaluate the need for further therapy (38). The prognosis is generally good for uncomplicated panic reactions, and many drug users will sub-sequently curtail the use of psychedelic drugs on their own.

The treatment of the "LSD-psychoses," as the previous discussion of these states would imply, varies with the salient symptomatology (38a). Tricyclic antidepressants, monoamine oxidase inhibitors, major tran-quilizers, lithium carbonate (39), ECT (40), and vitamin B3 (41) have been used with varying degrees of success. A period of drug-free ob-servation, lasting several days, using only minor tranquilizers as nec-essary, and then treating the resulting clinical picture as it comes more clearly into focus, would seem the most prudent means of clinical man-agement. The prognosis of these disorders is also quite variable in this group of patients. A two-to-six-year follow-up study of 15 patients with an "LSD psychosis" (42) revealed that approximately half did relatively well and half did poorly. There was a general trend for those with poorer premorbid adjustment and a more blunted, anergic clinical picture to do poorly. Patients with a more agitated, affective picture on admission tended to do better.

With regard to the management of flashbacks, treatment should be tempered by the fact that these are usually self-limiting and diminish in duration, intensity, and frequency with time. The individual often responds to assurance and education about the phenomena, but if their presence causes discomfort, the treatment should be similar to that of the acute panic reaction. Minor tranquilizers may be used acutely, in a judicious, time-limited, "as needed" basis. Behavior modification (43), ECT (40), diphenylhydantoin (44), psychotherapy (27), and other phar-macotherapeutic strategies have also been employed.

Patients should be advised that their flashbacks will most likely increase if psychedelic drugs are used again, as may also be the case with stimulants and/or marijuana. Persistently troublesome or increasing flashbacks indicate the need for a more thorough psychiatric and/or neurologic workup. The prognosis for flashbacks if the patient refrains from further use of mind-altering drugs is generally good.

TETRAHYDROCANNABINOL

Closely related to the effects of psychedelic drugs are the effects of ingestion of delta-9-tetrahydrocannabinol containing products of the marijuana or Cannabis sativa plant (45, 46). Of the several cannabis preparations, marijuana is prepared from the flowering tops and leaves of female plants, and in this country, it is usually smoked or eaten. Elsewhere, such as in India, it may be drunk as a tea called bhang. A more potent preparation of the upper leaves of the plant, which is usually smoked, is called gangha. Hashish is the resin of the flowering tops.

General Effects

General effects of cannabis intoxication often include euphoria, increased awareness of various sensations and stimuli, and excessive jocularity. There may be a distorted sense of time and space. Speech and thinking may seem amusingly disorganized and novel, and associations may be increased. Short-term memory and concentration are significantly impaired, as is the ability to perform complex psychomotor tasks such as driving. Increased appetite and drowsiness are common. Potentially more disturbing effects include depersonalization, agitation, restlessness, confusion, ideas of reference, paranoia, and panic.

Weil et al. (46) found that the effects of smoking marijuana were maximum 15 minutes after consumption. These diminished between 30 minutes and one hour, and they were largely dissipated three hours after the end of smoking. In 1970, Lemberger et al. (47) published studies in man on the disposition and metabolism of delta-9-tetrahydrocannabinol, the active ingredient of marijuana in man. They administered intravenous delta-9-tetrahydrocannabinol and found that its half-life was 56 hours, with metabolites still found in urine and feces after eight days. Dackis et al. (48) document the persistence of urinary cannaboid excretion during 21 days of supervised abstinence. Generally, a social dose of marijuana contains 3-8 mg of tetrahydrocannabinol. Higher doses in the range of 100-300 mg have been given in experimental settings.

Psychotoxic Effects

There have been a number of reports of adverse psychiatric reactions occurring in cannabis users. As with the hallucinogens, social and cultural setting, potency of the preparation, the route of ingestion, prior exposure, and prior emotional state are said to be important variables determining whether or not an adverse reaction will occur.

Four major types of adverse reactions which have been categorized may be summarized as: 1) acute panic or anxiety reactions; 2) acute toxic psychoses; 3) psychotic-like states in persons with a history of psychosis or use of hallucinogenic drugs; and 4) flashbacks.

Acute anxiety or panic reactions, often occurring in first-time marijuana users, are not unlike hallucinogen-induced panic reactions. Individuals experiencing these find the cannabis experience frightening instead of pleasing. A frequent and frightening thought is that a loss of control is occurring and/or that one is becoming insane, rather than having a transient drug-induced recreational experience.

Marijuana-induced anxiety or panic reactions commonly occur in obsessive-compulsive individuals who are afraid of losing control and who find the mild ego-distorting qualities of cannabis intoxication frightening. Individuals experiencing these reactions often present with a transient apprehensive and anxious state, which generally lasts one to four hours, and which is linked to the time of actual marijuana intoxication. The perceptions that one is losing one's mind, will never recover, or that the distortions experienced are a sign of underlying psychosis are common concomitants of the anxiety reaction.

In addition, an acute cannabis-induced toxic psychosis has been described by Talbott and others (49). Individuals with an acute toxic psychosis frequently become suspicious, acutely anxious, disoriented, confused and prone to act with very poor judgment. They may have feelings of depersonalization, suspiciousness, derealization, paranoia, and ideas of reference. Acute and severe transient paranoid states may occur. These episodes are relatively rare. Symptoms usually decrease or disappear as the cannabis effects wear off.

Furthermore, increases in psychotic symptoms in persons with a history of psychosis may also occur, consisting of an intensification of psychotic symptoms in patients with preexisting delusions or hallucinations. These effects occur relatively frequently in schizophrenics.

Making the diagnosis of adverse reactions to marijuana and other cannabis products depends upon obtaining a history of exposure, and the type of clinical presentation. Weil et al. (46) found conjunctival erythema and a mild increase in heart rate accompanying marijuana exposure. These signs may be of diagnostic usefulness. Interestingly, pupillary dilation is not a part of the cannabis response.

Treatment

Treatment of cannabis psychotoxicity depends upon the clinical presentation. Uncomplicated, acute panic reactions almost always subside within a few hours, and generally should be treated with firm and consistent calmness and reassurance. When severe agitation is present and reassurance is not helpful, administration of an antianxiety drug such as diazepam may be useful. Generally, antipsychotic drugs are not necessary or indicated in cannabis-induced anxiety reactions. If these are used, as with hallucinogens, one should avoid using those with relatively high anticholinergic properties, in order to avoid interactions with anticholinergic substances ingested or added to the marijuana preparation, such as PCP or scopolamine. Rarely, individuals with an acute panic or anxiety reaction will require hospitalization and observation until perception, orientation, and judgment are not acutely disturbed.

The treatment of cannabis-induced increases in psychotic symptoms in patients with preexisting schizophrenic episodes follows the general treatment of the underlying problem. Thought disorder, disturbances of affect, personality disturbances, delusions, and hallucinations should be treated with discontinuation of marijuana exposure and traditional treatment for the predominant type of disturbance. This may involve the use of psychotherapy, with or without the help of medications like antipsychotic drugs, minor tranquilizers, and/or lithium.

PHENCYCLIDINE

Phencyclidine (PCP) was first synthesized by Parke-Davis Laboratories in 1956 as an experimental anesthetic, named "Sernyl." In animal studies, PCP appeared to have remarkable analgesic properties, without causing sedation and without causing depression of the circulatory system or respiration. However, in its first clinical trial in 1958, Greifenstein and associates reported a significant incidence of postoperative delirium, agitation, and seizures; consequently, medical use of phencyclidine was aborted (50).

Phencyclidine was widely used in veterinary practice until 1979 when, because of epidemic illicit use, commercial manufacture was stopped.

However, chemicals for the synthesis of PCP are commercially available, and PCP and chemical variants of it are remarkably easy to synthesize; clandestine PCP laboratories have sprung up in urban centers all over the country, and illicit PCP use has remained epidemic.

Illicit PCP is commonly known as angel dust, Shermans, Supercools, Columbos, Wacs, crystal, goons, and other names, and the degree of its purity, as well as of its adulteration with other chemicals, varies widely. Often cigarettes are dipped into liquid PCP to make "tokes" that can be shared by several people. Alternatively, a powdered form may be sprinkled on marijuana and subsequently smoked. PCP has also been found in tablet form in varying sizes, colors, shapes, purities, and dosages.

Pharmacologic Properties

PCP is readily absorbed from virtually any route of administration. It is extremely lipophilic, and as a consequence quickly leaves the blood and is concentrated in adipose and brain tissue. It is metabolized by hydroxylation, and at least some of its hydroxymetabolites have biological activity approximately equal to the parent compound. Peak blood, brain, and adipose tissue concentrations occur approximately three hours after ingestion, with respective half-lives of one, two and four hours. Because of its high affinity for brain and adipose tissue, PCP can be found in these tissues long after it is undetectable in the blood. PCP also crosses the placenta and may be excreted in breast milk. Consequently, maternal ingestion represents a danger to a fetus or nursing infant. In animal studies, LD 50s for PCP have been estimated in the range of 33-85 mg/kg. Specific PCP receptors have been identified in rat brain preparations, although not much is known about their function (51).

As reviewed by Johnson (52), PCP affects all neurotransmitter systems studied to date. In particular, it is believed to potentiate central dopaminergic transmission. PCP has profound atropine-like effects at the muscarinic receptor, but also has anticholinesterase activity (53). Studies of the effect of PCP on central serotonergic activity have been contradictory. In animal studies, PCP is unique among the hallucinogens in being self-administered. It enhances the depressant effects of barbiturates and THC and potentiates the behavioral toxicity of amphetamines.

In general, PCP's toxicologic effects are dose-related but, nevertheless, extremely variable and unpredictable. Ayd (54) describes them as follows. For the 5-10 mg dose, the onset occurs in one to two hours, has a duration of four to eight hours, and is associated with ataxia, nystagmus, mood lability, hallucinations, vomiting, paresthesias, and analgesia. For the 10-20 mg dose, the onset occurs in one-half to one hour, has a duration of eight to 24 hours, and is associated with random movements, nystagmus, hyperreflexia and hypertension. For the 50 mg, with a duration up to four days, coma, hypertension, chills, seizures, and labored breathing are often observed; and for doses above 100 mg, respiratory depression, hypertensive crisis, cerebral bleeding, loss of deep tendon reflexes, impairment of liver and renal function, and lethality often occur.

Psychological Effects

PCP is believed to produce psychological but not physical dependence, and chronic users report tolerance to the psychological effects of PCP. Although not universally present, psychopathologic features frequently occur in PCP intoxication. These include schizophreniform psychosis, nystagmus and ataxia, memory loss, mutism, fragmented hallucinations and delusions, facial grimacing, difficulty estimating time, changes in body image, mood and behavioral lability, and paranoia and violence (55).

Luisada (56) describes three phases of the typical PCP psychosis: an initial phase lasting approximately five days, characterized by violent psychotic behavior; an intermediate phase of approximately five days consisting of relatively controlled behavior alternating with restlessness and unpredictability; and a final phase of approximately four days consisting of personality reintegration and disappearance of thought disorder and paranoia.

Psychiatrically, PCP intoxication may present in almost any manner, including mania, depression, schizophrenia or organic brain syndrome, and the symptomatology may be indistinguishable from these illnesses. Since PCP is rapidly cleared from the blood, blood and urine assays for PCP may be negative while brain and adipose tissue concentrations are at their highest concentrations. Furthermore, although there are a variety of assays for PCP in biological fluids, most are not sensitive enough to detect PCP more than six to eight hours after ingestion. However, Pitts and co-workers (57) have recently developed a capillary gas chromatograph-nitrogen detector method that can detect minute, but pharmacologically active concentrations of PCP in body fluids, and such methodology may significantly aid in the diagnosis of PCP intoxication. Because PCP intoxication is not easily diagnosed clinically or by most laboratory assays commonly available, diagnosis is frequently made by the patient's self-report or by history from family or police.

Treatment

Because of marked differences in dosages of PCP in illicit preparations, as well as its tendency to build up in body tissues, it is almost impossible for an abuser to regulate the dose or effects of PCP. Unfortunately, there is no specific, completely effective antidote for PCP intoxication, and medical management is essentially supportive. PCP abusers cannot readily be "talked down," as is common in the management of patients intoxicated with psychedelics. A reduction of sensory stimuli, accomplished by putting a patient in a quiet room or placing a blanket over the patient, is often helpful. However, the patient should be kept under close observation, as self-destructive and/or violent behavior and even suicide attempts are not infrequent.

Acidification of the urine with ammonium chloride or ascorbic acid, as well as increased fluid intake, will increase the urinary excretion of PCP, as well as concentrate it so as to help with the laboratory diagnosis. Since PCP is only slowly released from adipose and brain storage sites, urinary acidification should be continued for one month or more. Acidification of the plasma also markedly lowers PCP concentration in the cerebrospinal fluid, and will facilitate improvement in central nervous system function.

Propranolol (20-40 mg, three times a day) has been used as a sympatholytic antidote for PCP-induced hypertension and tachycardia. Since PCP has potent anticholinergic effects, any atropine-like delirium frequently develops. This may be managed with parenteral physostigmine (2-4 mg IM q 4 hours).

If pharmacotherapy for agitation or combativeness is necessary, diazepam (40-80 mg/day) or other benzodiazepines are the drugs of choice. If a neuroleptic is given—and the use of this modality is controversial—one should be chosen with low anticholinergic potency, such as haloperidol, so as not to further potentiate the anticholinergic effects of PCP.

Agitation and violent behavior are usually best managed by seclusion and restraints, but plasma CPK and urinary creatinine should be frequently monitored, since rhabdomyolysis may occur, with associated myoglobinurea and subsequent renal failure.

In conclusion, many clinicians believe that PCP is currently both the most prevalent and most dangerous drug of abuse in urban centers. Because of the wide variation in its clinical presentation, its ability to closely mimic many psychiatric disorders, and the difficulty in detecting it in biological fluids with current assay methodology, PCP intoxication may be very difficult to diagnose. For this reason, the clinician should be alert to the possibility of PCP abuse in his/her differential diagnosis, and should be equally knowledgeable about its management.

PSYCHOSTIMULANTS

A major cause of transient psychoses is the use of centrally active psychostimulants. A wide variety of drugs sold over the counter, prescribed, or acquired illicitly have central sympathomimetic properties (58). Some of these include methamphetamine, dextroamphetamine, methylphenidate, ephedrine, phentermine, phenmetrazine, fenfluramine, diethylpropiohydrochloride, cocaine, and phenylpropranolamine.

The sympathomimetic agents are structurally related to the endogenous catecholamines, including epinephrine, norepinephrine, phenylethylamine and dopamine, and mimic many of the properties of these agents. They cause a variety of peripheral and central sympathetic effects, such as mydriasis and tachycardia. In general, they are postulated to cause their effects by releasing central catecholamines, such as dopamine and/or norepinephrine, from central and peripheral presympathetic nerve endings. Effects may also occur due to inhibition of monoamine oxidase and/or stimulation of postsynaptic noradrenergic and/or dopaminergic receptors (58).

The psychologic effects of psychostimulants usually include behavioral activation, hyperalertness, talkativeness, increased thoughts, euphoria, emotional catharsis, improved concentration, insomnia, increased motor activity, and appetite suppression. Furthermore, upon cessation of their administration, a depressive anergic syndrome often occurs, lasting for several days, which may be associated with suicidal ideation, somnolence and irritability. Clinically, the psychostimulants are legitimately used in the treatment of depression in the elderly and in selected other cases for prevention of fatigue, obesity, narcolepsy, Stokes-Adams syndrome, childhood hyperkinetic syndrome, and hypotension, although some of the above uses are controversial.

In spite of many similarities, psychostimulants do differ from each other. For example, compared to amphetamine, methamphetamine has greater central nervous system potency; methylphenidate, on the other hand, is described as a "mild central nervous system stimulant with more effects on mental than motor activities" (58). Cocaine has behavioral and physiologic effects similar to amphetamine, but is absorbed more easily through mucous membranes, and has a plasma half-life of only approximately 30 minutes (58), as opposed to amphetamine and metamphetamine and methylphenidate, which have half-lives lasting four to eight hours, depending on urinary pH.

A number of studies suggest an association between centrally acting sympathomimetic drugs and psychiatric syndromes, including psychotic states. These syndromes occur when these compounds are responsibly prescribed and used as directed, when they are used for self-medicating purposes, and when they are used for recreational reasons and following an overdose.

Effects of Acutely Administered Low Doses of Psychostimulants

In individuals with preexisting psychotic symptoms, low doses of psychostimulants can activate these. For example, Janowsky et al. (59, 60) reported that in actively ill schizophrenic patients, in patients whose schizophrenia was in partial remission, and in manic patients with paranoid or grandiose delusions, giving small doses of methylphenidate, d- or 1-amphetamine caused an immediate and dramatic intensification of preexisting psychotic symptoms, lasting one to three hours. This psychosis activation was manifested by the patients' becoming more bizarre, more intensely delusional, more hallucinatory, and less insightful. Behavioral activation occurred simultaneously with the increased psychotic symptoms, manifested by increased interpersonal interactions, talkativeness and rapport. These patients showed none of the clouding of consciousness, amnesia, or disorientation consistent with a diagnosis of organic brain syndrome. In contrast, nonpsychotics and fully remitted schizophrenic patients showed only behavioral activation after methylphenidate infusion(59). The ability of d-amphetamine to activate psychotic symptoms in schizophrenics was also reported by Van Kammen et al. (61), who found that this compound reactivated psychotic symptoms in patients with remitted schizophrenia.

In contrast, however, 10-35% of schizophrenic patients who receive low doses of psychostimulants show temporary psychologic improvement (61); generally, the patients who improve have been the most symptomatic ones at baseline.

Effects of High Doses of Psychostimulants

Relatively high doses of virtually all centrally acting psychostimulants can produce psychotic symptoms in presumably nonschizophrenic individuals. Although manic episodes, organic brain syndromes, and catatonic episodes can occur with the intake of high doses of psychostimulants, the most common psychotic reaction occurring during psychostimulant administration is a paranoid state, very closely resembling paranoid schizophrenia (62-64).

In its most extreme form, this drug-induced paranoid psychosis consists of delusions of persecution, ideas of reference and influence, visual, auditory, olfactory and tactile hallucinations, increased aggressiveness, fear, anxiety, panic and agitation (usually in response to persecutory delusions), exaggerated, labile or flattened affect, loss of insight, increased sexuality, and a peculiar perseverative stereotyped behavior termed "punding," all occurring in the presence of a clear consciousness (64, 65).

Under the usual conditions of high-dose psychostimulant abuse, which involves repeated administration of the drug over several days, the psychotic symptoms unfold progressively, rather than abruptly. The pattern is similar to one reported in a prospective study by Griffith et al. (66-68), who administered high doses of d-amphetamine to six amphetamine abusers. Griffith's subjects initially showed behavioral activation, with talkativeness and, in some cases, a mild euphoria. As the cumulative dose of d-amphetamine reached 50 mg, most became depressed, quiet, clinging, hypochondriacal, and dysphoric. With further increases in dose, they progressed into a "prepsychotic" phase, in which they were sullen, suspicious, and uncommunicative, and had mild ideas of reference. Next, they developed a paranoid psychosis. They had evolution of a cold, distant, flattened affect, delusions of persecution, ideas of thought control and reference, fearfulness, and irritability. No formal thought disorder or hallucinations were noted. Similarly, Angrist et al. (69) gave comparable or higher doses of d- and l-amphetamine to psychostimulant abusers over a shorter period of time, and found a similar progression of symptoms. Their subjects developed olfactory, visual and auditory hallucinations, and perceived body distortions in themselves and in others. Some of their subjects also developed a typical schizophrenic thought disorder.

Others have noted that in the early-to-middle stages of an injection sequence or "run," a psychostimulant abuser is often preoccupied with minutiae and hidden meanings, is intensely curious and concerned with philosophic concepts, and may be hypersexual (65). The abuser may exhibit complex stereotypies, which manifest themselves as compulsive, repetitive grooming activities or manipulations of mechanical objects

(65), and in some ways resemble schizophrenic stereotypies. Ellingwood (65) noted that such perseverative, sterotyped behaviors occur most often in prepsychotic addicts who eventually become paranoid during the course of a "run." Hallucination development also is sequential and includes expression in auditory, visual, tactile, or olfactory modes (65). Hallucinations usually, but not always, are preceded by the development of paranoid symptoms, and often start as vague visual illusions or indistinct sounds which gradually become more vivid and specific. When amphetamine is discontinued, hallucinations of all sorts tend to be the first symptoms to disappear, suggesting that they are an effect of the high drug dose.

A somewhat different evolution of symptoms may result when high doses of a psychostimulant are given over a short period of time (minutes to hours). For example, Bell (63) aggressively administered intravenous methamphetamine, and most of his subjects rapidly became delusional, had visual and/or auditory hallucinations, and reexperienced prior psychostimulant-induced paranoid episodes, while maintaining a clear consciousness. In contrast to those in studies in which the amphetamine dose was increased more gradually (68, 70), Bell's subjects exhibited paranoid delusions and extreme behavioral activation, associated with euphoria, all occurring at the same time (63). These observations indicate that the behavior-activating effects and the psychotogenic effects of psychostimulants may co-exist and that they probably do not represent mutually exclusive phenomena.

The possibility exists that psychostimulant abusers need to be exposed to psychostimulants for a prolonged period of time to develop psychotic symptoms, and that when these have developed, such symptoms may occur more easily with subsequent exposures. These assertions are supported by studies (63), in which patients who had previously experienced drug-induced psychosis rapidly developed psychotic symptoms, while subjects with no previous history of psychosis did not often become psychotic.

Psychostimulant-induced Psychoses and Their Relation to Schizophrenia

There are a number of similarities and some subtle differences between psychostimulant-induced psychoses and schizophrenia. Those who suggest that a psychostimulant-induced psychotic state is not a model of schizophrenia note that these drug-induced psychoses may not show the specific affectual changes and associative disorders of schizophrenia and that schizophrenic thought disorder, described as "a splitting and loosening of associations, a concreteness in abstract thought, and an impairment in goal-directed thought" (71) is also not a prominent aspect. Angrist et al. (69), however, have documented that certain forms of schizophrenic thought disorder do indeed occur in nonschizophrenic cases of psychostimulant-induced psychoses, although these seem to be less prominent in amphetamine-induced psychosis than in schizophrenia.

It has been said that psychostimulant-induced psychoses are often associated with greater affective drive and affective lability than usually is noted in schizophrenics (69), although affective blunting has been observed. In this respect psychostimulant-induced psychoses often appear similar to acute schizophrenic, schizoaffective, or acute paranoid schizophrenic episodes.

Psychostimulant-induced psychoses do seem to differ from schizophrenia in that visual, olfactory, and tactile hallucinations seem more prominent (71). However, visual, olfactory, and tactile hallucinations can occur in schizophrenics, especially during acute episodes (29). Also, the presence of visual and olfactory hallucinations does not a priori suggest the existence of an organic brain syndrome.

Recently, a number of investigators tried to refine the diagnostic criteria for schizophrenia (72-75). The World Health Organization's international pilot study of schizophrenia has provided a highly discriminating cluster of 12 symptoms that strongly and specifically correlate with a diagnosis of schizophrenia (74). These are: 1) restricted affect; 2) poor insight; 3) hearing thoughts aloud; 4) waking early (negative correlation); 5) poor rapport; 6) depressed facies (negative correlation); 7) elation (negative correlation); 8) widespread delusions; 9) incoherent speech; 10) bizarre delusions; 11) unreliable information; and 12) nihilistic delusions.

Also, Schneider's first-rank criteria for schizophrenia (76), although not pathognomonic of schizophrenia, since they may occur in affective psychoses, are nevertheless very highly correlated with a diagnosis of schizophrenia. These criteria are: 1) audible thoughts; 2) voices speaking the patient's thoughts aloud; 3) voices arguing about or discussing the patient; 4) personalized delusional interpretations; 5) somatic passivity; 6) thought insertion; 7) thought withdrawal; and 8) thought broadcasting.

A review of case histories of psychostimulant-induced psychoses reported by a variety of investigators reveals that many of the World Health Organization's cluster of 12 symptoms and Schneider's first-rank criteria for schizophrenia can be found routinely in nonschizophrenic individuals experiencing drug-induced psychosis (62).

Although induction and activation of psychoses are prominent psychostimulant effects, these drugs also profoundly affect affective symptoms. Low doses of psychostimulants induce flight of ideas, elation, expansiveness, and emotional discharge; psychostimulant-induced psychoses often have a prominent affective component (71, 77, 78). Thus, psychostimulant-induced transient psychoses may be as "affective" as cognitive in nature, and may actually resemble mania during acute intoxication and depression after drug withdrawal.

Cocaine, because of its growing use, deserves specific consideration. As used in the 1980s, it is a relatively less common cause of transient psychoses. This may be because its duration of action is shorter, and it is quite expensive to buy large quantities. However, when it was more available at lower prices, cocaine-induced paranoid psychoses were relatively common. The initial effects of cocaine intoxication are euphoria and a heightened sense of concentration and strength, which are similar to those produced by amphetamine. Chronic cocaine abuse, however, can lead to insomnia and depression, which may progress to a frank psychotic state similar to the amphetamine-induced psychotic state described above. Hallucinations of bugs on, in, or under the skin are especially prone to occur with cocaine use.

Treatment

The treatment of high-dose sympathomimetic-induced psychotic states involves curtailing exposure to the offending agent and the cautious use of antipsychotic drugs (79). Remission of symptoms usually occurs in 24-48 hours, although a proportion of cases (10-20%) develop a chronic schizophrenic psychosis which may or may not reflect activation of an underlying tendency to this disorder. Ellinwood (80) warns against using a major tranquilizer with strong anticholinergic properties, since many street drugs such as PCP and STP are sold as stimulants and have anticholingeric effects. Furthermore, it is important to note that antipsychotic drugs slow the metabolism of amphetamines.

ANTICHOLINERGIC AGENTS

Known since antiquity, a variety of centrally acting anticholinergic substances have been popular for various recreational and ritualistic purposes because of the altered mental state they induce. Natural sources of centrally acting anticholinergic compounds include Amanita muscaria mushroom and Datura stramonium, also known as Jimson weed. Atropine and scopolamine are naturally occurring belladonna alkaloids which are classical anticholinergic agents. Numerous semisynthetic derivatives are also now available for medical use as antiparkinsonian agents, and such drugs are also present in over-the-counter soporific medications and in preparations used to decrease gastric motility, alleviate nasal congestion, and induce sleep. Furthermore, most tricyclic antidepressant drugs have central anticholinergic properties (58).

Anticholinergic substances may be taken orally, intravenously, or intramuscularly, absorbed in the form of eye drops or inhaled when mixed with tobacco. Furthermore, atropine and scopolamine may be absorbed after local application to mucous membranes (58). The onset of action of anticholinergic compounds is variable, depending upon the specific drug and the route of administration. Atropine, once present in the bloodstream, remains there only briefly, with the majority of it being excreted by the kidneys within the first 12 hours following ingestion.

Mechanism of Action

The mechanism of action of atropine and related anticholinergic substances in inducing central behavioral changes occurs via competitive inhibition of acetylcholine at central muscarinic receptor sites. As mentioned above, antipsychotic agents, tricyclic antidepressants and "street drugs" such as phencyclidine and "STP" may also antagonize central muscarinic receptors, and this effect may explain the occurrence of an anticholinergic toxic psychosis when these drugs are used.

The general physiologic effects of anticholinergic substances appear related in large part to the balance between muscarinic-cholinergic and adrenergic factors in regulating a variety of responses. Pupillary size, gastric motility, salivary gland secretion, vascular smooth muscle tone, heart rate and urinary bladder tone are all directly related to the relative predominance of cholinergic, relative to sympathetic, tone, with decreased cholinergic tone promoting an increase in pupil size, decreased gastric motility, decreased salivary gland secretion, and an increase in heart rate. Cholinergic tone may also be important in regulation of various central nervous system functions. It is clear that an abrupt decrease of acetylcholine activity by central blockade promotes disorientation, decreased memory and concentration, restlessness, visual hallucinations and illusions, and generalized confusion. These effects can be antagonized or reversed by maneuvers that increase central cholinergic activity.

Psychotogenic Effects

There are a number of characteristic features of the central anticholinergic syndrome. Orientation may, under some circumstances, be present, but usually is partially disordered or completely lacking. Concentration and immediate recall are likewise usually impaired. Hallucinations are common and may be visual, auditory, or tactile. Visual hallucinations are very common, and may be of various types—with bugs, animals, faces, and Lilliputian images being characteristic. Extreme agitation and confusion may dominate the clinical picture. Confusion may be so dramatic that the individual makes little or no sense and may be involved in purposeless activity, such as picking hallucinated objects off one's clothes. Thus, the fully developed syndrome is fairly easy to recognize. However, when isolated difficulty in thinking and/or agitation are the primary disturbances, the syndrome may be less easy to recognize and may present a diagnostic problem.

Associated physiologic effects of the central anticholinergic syndrome include dilated pupils, dry mouth, blurry vision due to paralysis of accommodation, urinary retention, increases in cardiac and respiratory rates, and possibly hypertension and hyperthermia, associated with inhibition of sweating. Gastric motility is usually decreased. Vasodilation of facial blood vessels contributes to an atypical appearance, referred to as the atropine flush. However, it is not uncommon to have a central anticholinergic syndrome unassociated with the above peripheral signs.

It is important to note that both amphetamines and anticholinergic agents cause mydriasis, tachycardia and hypertension. Amphetamines, unlike anticholinergics, however, will cause piloerection, salivation, and sweating (81).

The central anticholinergic syndrome may occur without exceeding recommended dosages of a given anticholinergic drug. It is more likely to occur in individuals taking morphine or other narcotics, and in those who are sleep-deprived or in physical pain. Also, it is more likely to occur in individuals over 60 years of age, especially if they are taking relatively high doses of the anticholinergic drug and/or have a prior history of confusion induced by sedatives. Similar observations have been made with respect to the tricyclic antidepressants.

The duration of the central anticholinergic syndrome varies with the type and relative amount of anticholinergic agent ingested, and with the route of administration. The onset may occur rapidly over a period of minutes to hours, and the effects may last from hours to days.

Treatment

General treatment for the central anticholinergic syndrome includes supportive measures, such as gastric lavage to limit intestinal absorption, administration of diazepam for sedation and for control of possible seizures in cases of extreme intoxication, and the use of cooling techniques in the case of hyperpyrexia. In uncomplicated cases, discontinuation of the offending agent, with careful observation and the judicious use of sedation, may be sufficient to treat the syndrome.

In cases in which rapid termination of the central anticholinergic syndrome is indicated, physostigmine 1-2 mg IV or IM given every two to four hours is indicated. To determine physostigmine efficacy, the physician should watch for clinical improvement and/or a breakthrough of peripheral parasympathetic signs. After physostigmine administration, confusion and delirium will usually clear for from one to four hours. Repeated administration of physostigmine over a period of days may be necessary in cases of prolonged central anticholinergic syndrome, since physostigmine is relatively short-acting.

DRUGS USED IN GENERAL MEDICAL PRACTICE

In addition to the above-mentioned drugs, a large number of drugs used in the general practice of medicine can cause transient psychotic episodes. These include antihypertensive agents, oral contraceptives, L-dopa, a variety of hormones including the glucocorticoids, antiarrhythmic drugs, and several antibiotics. We will now consider several representative examples of transient psychotic episodes caused by medically prescribed drugs.

L-dopa

L-dopa, a precursor of dopamine used extensively in the treatment of Parkinson's disease, has been reported to induce transient psychotic episodes. Goodwin has reviewed the literature on the behavioral side effects of L-dopa therapy, and has summarized the major psychiatric side effects of this agent (82). These include transient psychotic phenomena, activation of mania and induction of depression, and/or confusional states. With respect to L-dopa-induced depression, the described incidence has ranged in various studies from no depression to depression being the most frequently observed side effect of Parkinsonian patients treated with L-dopa. In one study, overactivity, restlessness, and agitation were reported in 3.6% of Parkinsonian patients treated with L-dopa, with hypomania reported in 1.6%, and hypersexuality in 0.9%. Similarly, two Parkinsonian patients have been reported in whom addition of the dopa decarboxylase inhibitor, carbidopa, caused a psychosis which included symptoms of mania, hypersexuality, agitation, and marked emotional lability. Also, Yamura-Tobias has noted L-dopa-induced activation of psychotic symptoms in chronic schizophrenic patients (83).

Murphy et al. (84) expanded the above clinical observations and reported that six of 22 bipolar depressed patients became less depressed after taking L-dopa. The other 16 patients became more angry, and the patients with psychotic depressive symptoms had an exaggeration of their delusions. Of nine of the 22 patients with a history of mania, eight became hypomanic on doses of three of more grams of L-dopa per day.

Thus, L-dopa seems to aggravate preexisting psychopathology, and patients with a previous history of affective disorder appear more susceptible to this exacerbation. Psychiatric side effects usually occur at therapeutic levels of 3-5 grams per day and are seen most frequently after several months of therapy, but may be seen much sooner. Psychologic side effects are generally reversible with a decrease in L-dopa dosage, and after such a decrease, it is sometimes possible to increase the dose more gradually to a therapeutic level and to continue to avoid psychologic side effects (85), L-dopa-induced depressions have been successfully treated with imipramine.

Corticosteroids and ACTH

Corticosteroids and ACTH, given in clinically recommended doses, have been noted to induce psychotic and affective symptoms. The incidence of the effects of these agents on affect has been variously reported as being between 40% and 80% (86). The most common mood change reported following corticosteroid therapy is euphoria (87), in which patients experience an enhanced sense of well-being and happiness. Less frequently, they may have a dramatic presentation of manic excitement, which may be difficult to distinguish clinically from an acute manic episode, and which may include irritability and mood lability.

Alternatively, they may present with psychotic symptoms similar to those occurring in acute paranoid schizophrenic episodes. Conversely, depression manifested by sadness, apathy, crying spells (86, 88) and even suicidal behavior may occur following corticosteroid administration.

The latency of the psychological responses to ACTH or cortisone is brief, with a mean elapsed time of 3.6 days before such changes are noted (86). Some of the earliest changes noted are lability of mood, increases in appetite, irritability, and frank euphoria. Patients who develop psychotic reactions tend to have been receiving higher doses of corticosteroids for longer periods of time. The dosages of corticosteroids reported associated with psychiatric effects have been extremely variable.

Psychiatric effects of corticosteroids and ACTH may be seen in virtually any patient receiving these drugs, and a previous psychiatric history or poor premorbid level of psychological function does not seem to be a determinant of the psychotoxic response to the medication (86, 89). Psychiatric side effects have been observed with other corticosteroids besides cortisone, and there is no reason to believe that one steroid preparation is superior to another in terms of its lack of psychiatric side effects.

Generally, psychiatric disturbances following corticosteroid therapy are manageable with a combination of supportive care and reduction in dosage of the offending drug. The psychiatric side effects of the corticosteroids and ACTH generally respond promptly to a lowering of the dosage of the drug involved and this applies to both nonpsychotic affective responses and to the psychoses (86). However, reduction in drug dosage must be accomplished cautiously, so as not to subject the patient to an iatrogenic adrenal insufficiency. Antidepressant therapy (i.e., ECT, tricyclic antidepressants) is probably not justified in cases of corticosteroid psychosis unless a depressive response to corticosteroid therapy persists longer than two or three weeks after cessation of therapy, or the depression is associated with suicidal activity. Also, consideration must be given as to whether or not the depression is a mood disorder or a realistic response to the exacerbation of the physical symptoms for which the steroid was given in the first place. Similarly, antipsychotic drug treatment may be necessary if psychotic symptoms do not rapidly dissipate upon drug withdrawal or when these symptoms represent a serious threat to the patient.

Antituberculosis Agents

Certain drugs used in the treatment of tuberculosis have been reported to alter affect. These drugs include iproniazid, which in one study, in doses of 4 mg/day, was reported to cause increased feelings of well-being and euphoria in one-half of the tuberculosis patients investigated. Mania, depression, and psychotic symptoms have been reported less frequently (90-92). Also, when iproniazid therapy was terminated, one-third of the patients who had received the drug for at least six months had terrifying dreams, nervousness, restlessness, and depression.

Cycloserine also has been found to affect mood states. Thirty male turberculosis patients treated with cycloserine (0.5 mg b.i.d.) had a 50% incidence of psychiatric side effects, with five having symptoms including hyperirritability and drowsiness; four having mood lability, hostility, depression, withdrawal, and suspiciousness; and six having psychosis (93).

Oral Contraceptives

Oral contraceptives and similar progestational agents have been reported to cause depression (94-99). More rarely, they have been associated with psychotic reactions both during treatment and on withdrawal (100). Treatment involves discontinuation of the offending agent and is otherwise symptomatic. It may include the use of appropriate antidepressant therapies.

Cardiovascular Medications

Antihypertensive agents are also associated with the induction of depressive syndromes, usually associated with anergy, sedation, and lethargy. Less commonly, schizophreniform psychoses may occur. Drugs which have been reported to cause such reactions include reserpine, alpha-methyldopa, propranolol, alprenolol, and possibly clonidine (101-109).

Cardiotropic medications have also been observed to cause psychiatric symptoms. Digitalis may cause psychiatric symptoms in up to 8% of patients treated. Hallucinations or delirium may occur (110-112). Similarly, aprindine used in the treatment of refractory supraventricular and ventricular arrhythmias may also cause psychotic reactions (113), as may lidocaine, which is well-known for its dose-related neurotoxicity. Confusion and delirium may be a prominent part of the clinical presentation of the above cardiac medications.

SUMMARY

In summary, a number of drugs can cause transient psychotic states. We have described in detail the ability of hallucinogenic drugs, phencyclidine, psychostimulants, marijuana, and anticholinergic agents to activate and/or to cause de novo transient psychotic episodes. In addition, we have reviewed briefly the psychotoxic effects of several drugs used in the general practice of medicine to induce similar transient psychotic episodes and/or alterations in mood. Since the above-mentioned drugs are ingested widely, knowledge of their psychotic effects and the treatment of these represents an important part of psychiatric practice.

REFERENCES

1. Stafford, P.: *Psychedelics Encyclopedia.* Berkeley, CA: And/Or Press, 1977.
2. Hofmann, A.: The discovery of LSD and subsequent investigations on naturally occurring hallucinogens. In: F. Ayd, and B. Blackwell (Eds.), *Discoveries in Biological Psychiatry.* Philadelphia: Lippincott, 1970.
3. Ellis, H.: Mescal, a new artificial paradise. *Contemp. Rev.,* 73: 130-141, 1898.
4. Huxley, A.: *Doors of Perception.* New York: Harper, 1954.
5. Leary, T.: The religious experience: Its prodction and interpretation. *The Psychedelic Review,* 1: 324-346, 1964.
6. Castaneda, C.: *The Teachings of Don Juan.* New York: Simon and Schuster, 1968.
7. Jaffe, T.: Drug addiction and drug abuse. In: A. Gilman and L. Goodman (Eds.), *The Pharmacological Basis of Therapeutics.* New York: Macmillan, 1980.
8. Martin, W., and Sloan, J.: Pharmacology and classification of LSD-like hallucinogens. In: W. Martin (Ed.), *Drug Addiction II: Amphetamine, Psychotogen and Marijuana Dependence. Handbuch der Experimentellen, Pharmakologie, vol. 45.* Berlin: Springer-Verlag, 1977.
9. Halaris, A., Rosenthal, M., De Nest, E., and Freedman, D.: The raphe neuronal system to serotonergic effects of LSD. *Neuropharmacology,* 21: 811-816, 1982.
10. Watson, S.: Hallucinogens and other psychotomimetics: Biological mechanisms. In: J. Barchas, P. Berger, R. Ciaranello, and G. Elliott (Eds.), *Psychopharmacology: From Theory to Practice.* New York: Oxford University Press, 1977.
11. DaPrada, M., Saner, A., Burkand, W., Bartholine, G., and Pletcher, A.: Lysergic acid diethylamide: Evidence for stimulation of cerebral dopamine receptors. *Brain Research,* 94: 67-73, 1975.
12. Renkel, M.: Pharmacodynamics of LSD and mescaline. *J. Nerv. Ment. Dis.,* 125: 424-427, 1957.
13. Monroe, R., Heath, R., Mickle, W., and Llewellyn, R.: Correlation of rhinencephalic electrograms with behavior. *EEG Clin. Neurophysiol.,* 9: 623-642, 1957.
14. Ungerleider, J.T., Fisher, D., Goldsmith, S., Fuller, M., and Forgy, E.: A statistical survey of adverse reactions to LSD in Los Angeles County. *Am. J. Psychiat.,* 125, 3: 352-357, 1968.

15. Fisher, D., and Ungerleider, J.T.: Grand mal seizures following ingestion of LSD. *California Medicine*, 106,3: 210-211, 1967.
16. Frosch, W., Robbins, E., and Stern, M.: Untoward reactions to LSD resulting in hospitalization. *New Eng. J. Med.* 273, 23: 1235-1239.
17. Robbins, E., Frosch, W., and Stein, M.: Further observations on untoward reactions of LSD. *Am. J. Psychiat.*, 124,3: 393-395, 1967.
18. Naditch, M.: Relation of motives for drug use and psychopathology in the development of acute diverse reactions to psychoactive drugs. *J. Abn. Psychology*, 84, 4: 374-385, 1975.
19. Cohen, S.: A classification of LSD complications. *Psychosomatics*, 7: 182-186, 1966.
20. Wesson, D., and Smith, D.: An analysis of psychedelic drug flashbacks. *Am. J. Drug Alcohol Abuse*, 3,3: 425-438, 1976.
21. Schick, J., and Smith, D.: Analysis of the LSD flashback. *J. Psychedelic Drugs*, 3,1: 13-19, 1970.
22. Horowitz, M.: Flashbacks: Recurrent intrusive images after the use of LSD. *Am. J. Psychiat.*, 126: 565-569, 1969.
23. Matefy, R., Hayes, C., and Hirsch, J.: Psychedelic drug flashbacks: Attentional deficits. *J. Abn. Psychology*, 88, 2: 212-215, 1979.
24. Matefy, R.: Role-play theory of psychedelic drug flashbacks. *J. Consult. Clin. Psychology*, 48: 551-553, 1980.
25. Heaton, R., and Victor, R.: Personality characteristics associated with psychedelic flashbacks in natural and experimental settings. *J. Abn. Psychology*, 85, 1: 83-90, 1976.
26. Naditch, M., and Fenwick, S.: LSD flashback and ego functioning. *J. Abn. Psychology*, 86, 4: 352-359, 1977.
27. Saidel, D., and Babineau, R.: Prolonged LSD flashbacks as conversion reactions. *J. Nerv. Ment. Dis.*, 163, 5: 352-355, 1976.
28. Rosenthal, S.: Persistent hallucinosis following repeated administration of hallucinogenic drugs. *Am. J. Psychiat.*, 121: 238-244, 1964.
29. Bowers, M.J., and Freedman, D.X.: "Psychedelic" experiences in acute psychoses. *Arch. Gen. Psychiat.*, 15: 240-248, 1966.
30. Hollister, L.E.: Drug-induced psychoses and schizophrenic reactions: A critical comparison. *Annals of the New York Academy of Sciences*, 96: 80-92, 1962.
31. Langs, R., and Ban, H.: LSD (LSD-25) and schizophrenic reactions. *J. Nerv. Ment. Dis.*, 147, 2: 163-172, 1968.
32. Hays, P., and Tilley, J.R.: The differences between LSD psychosis and schizophrenia. *Can. Psychiatric Assoc. J.*, 18: 331-333, 1973.
33. Young, B.G.: A phenomenological comparison of LSD and schizophrenic states. *Brit. J. Psychiatr.*, 124: 64-74, 1974.
34. Ungerleider, J.T., and Frank, I.: Management of acute panic reactions and flashbacks resulting from LSD ingestion. In: P.G. Bourne (Ed.), *Acute Drug Abuse Emergencies.* New York: Academic Press, 1976.
35. Abramson, H., Rolo, A., and Stache, J.: Lysergic acid diethylamide LSD (LSD-25) antagonists: Chlorpromazine. *Journal of Neuro-psychiatry*, 1: 307-310, 1959.
36. Schwartz, C.: Paradoxical responses to chlorpromazine with LSD. *Psychosomatics*, 8: 210-211, 1967.
37. Solursh, L., and Clement, W.: Use of diazepam in hallucinogenic drug crises. *JAMA*, 205, 9: 644-645, 1968.
38. Haddad, L.: Management of hallucinogen abuse. *American Family Practitioner*, 14, 1: 82-87, 1976.
38a. Ban, T.: Adverse effects of psychotomimetics: Proposition of a psychopharmacological classification. In: V. Raduco-Thomas (Ed.), *Pharmacology, Toxicology and Atrise of Psychotomimetics.* Quebec: Les Presses de L'Université de Laval, 1974, pp. 305-319.
39. Horowitz, H.: The use of lithium in the treatment of the drug-induced psychotic reaction. *Dis. Nerv. System*, 36: 159-163, 1975.

40. Muller, D.: ECT in LSD psychosis: A report of 3 cases. *Am. J. Psychiat.*, 128, 3: 131-132, 1971.
41. Hoffer, A.: LSD-induced psychosis and vitamin B-3. *Am. J. Psychiat.* 128, 9: 1155, 1972.
42. Bowers, M.B.: Psychoses precipitated by psychotomimetic drugs. *AGP*, 34: 832-835, 1977.
43. Matefy, R.: Behavior therapy to extinguish spontaneous recurrences of LSD effects: A case study. *J. Nerv. Ment. Dis.*, 156, 4: 226-231, 1973.
44. Thurlow, J., and Girvin, J.: Use of anti-epileptic medication in treating "flashbacks" from hallucinogenic drugs. *Calif. Med. Assoc. J.*, 105: 947-948, 1971.
45. Chopra, G.S., and Smith, J.W.: Psychotic reactions following cannabis use in East Indians. *Arch. Gen. Psychiat.*, 30: 24-27, 1974.
46. Weil, A.T., Zinberg, N., and Nelson, J.: Clinical and psychological effects of marihuana in man. *Science*, 162: 1234-1242, 1968.
47. Lemberger, L., Silberman, S., Axelrod, J., and Kopin, I.: Marihuana studies on the disposition and metabolism of delta-9-tetrahydrocannabinol in man. *Science*, 170: 18, 1970.
48. Dackis, C., Pottash, A.L.C., Annitto, W., and Gold, M.: Persistence of urinary marijuana levels after supervised abstinence. *Am. J. Psychiat.*, 139, 9: 1196-1199, 1982.
49. Talbott, J.A., and Teaque, J.W.: Marihuana psychosis. *JAMA*, 210, 2: 299-302, 1969.
50. Greifenstein, F.E., Devault, M., Yoshitake, J., and Gajewski, J.E.: A study of 1-aryl cyclo hexyl amines for anesthesia. *Anesthesia and Analgesic*, 37: 283-294, 1958.
51. Zukin, S.R., and Zukin, R.S.: Specific (3H) phencyclidine binding in rat central nervous system. *Proc. Natl. Acad. Sci. USA*, 76: 5372-5376, 1979.
52. Johnson, K.M.: Neurochemical pharmacology of phenocyclidine. In: R.C. Petersen, and R.C. Stillman (Eds.), *Phencyclidine (PCP) Abuse: An Appraisal.* NIDA Research Monograph, 21:44-52, 1978.
53. Becker, C.E.: Sernylon inhibition of private cholinesterases. *Clin. Chem. Abst.*, 41: 780-781, 1969.
54. Ayd, F.S.: Phencyclidine. *International Drug Therapy Newsletter*, 14, 5: 17-20, 1979.
55. Russ, C., and Wong, D.: Diagnosis and treatment of phencyclidine psychosis, clinical considerations. *J. Psychedelic Drugs*, 11, 4: 277-282, 1979.
56. Luisada, P.V.: The phencyclidine psychosis—phenomenology and treatment. In: R.C. Petersen and R.C. Stillman (Eds.), *Phencyclidine (PCP) Abuse: An Appraisal.* NIDA Research Monograph, 21: 241-253, 1978.
57. Pitts, F.N., Yago, L.S., Aniline, O., and Pits, A.F.: Capillary GC-nitrogen detector measurement of phencyclidine (PCP) ketamine and other arylcycloalkylamines in the picogram range. *J. Chromotography*, 193: 157-159, 1980.
58. Goodman, L.S., and Gilman, A.: *The Pharmacological Basis of Therapeutics*, 5th edition. New York: Macmillan, 1975.
59. Janowsky, D.S., El-Yousef, M.K., Davis, J.M., et al.: Provocation of schizophrenic symptoms by intravenous administration of methylphenidate. *Arch. Gen. Psychiat.*, 28: 185-191, 1973.
60. Janowsky, D.S., and Davis, J.: Methylphenidate, dextroamphetamine and levamphetamine: Effects on schizophrenic symptoms. *Arch. Gen. Psychiat.*, 33: 304-308, 1976.
61. Van Kammen, D.P., Docherty, J.P., Mordes, S., et al.: Acute amphetamine response predicts antidepressant and antipsychotic response to lithium carbonate in schizophrenic patients. *Psych. Res.*, 4: 313-325, 1981.
62. Janowsky, D.S., and Risch, S.C.: Amphetamine psychosis and psychotic symptoms. *Psychopharmacology*, 65: 73-77, 1979.
63. Bell, D.S.: The experimental reproduction of amphetamine psychosis. *Arch. Gen. Psychiat.*, 29: 35-40, 1973.
64. Connell, P.H.: *Amphetamine Psychosis.* Maudsley Monograph 5. London: Oxford University Press, 1958, p. 75.

65. Ellinwood, E.H., Jr.: Amphetamine psychosis: Descriptions of the individuals and process. *J. Nerv. Ment. Dis.*, 144: 273-283, 1967.

66. Griffith, J.D., Cavanaugh, J.H., and Held, J.: Experimental psychosis induced by the administration of d-amphetamine. In: D. Costa and S. Garattini (Eds.), *Amphetamines and Related Compounds.* New York: Raven Press, 1970.

67. Griffith, J.D., Cavanaugh, J.H., and Oates, J.A.: Psychosis induced by the administration of d-amphetamine to human volunteers. In: D.H. Efron (Ed.), *Psychotomimetic Drugs.* New York: Raven Press, 1970.

68. Griffith, J.D., Cavanaugh, J., and Held, J.: Dextroamphetamine: Evaluation of psychotomimetic properties in man. *Arch. Gen. Psychiat.* 26: 97-100, 1972.

69. Angrist, B., Shopsin, G., and Gershon, S.: Comparative psychotomimetic effects of stereoisomers of amphetamine. *Nature,* 234: 152-153, 1970.

70. Angrist, B.M. and Gershon, S.: The phenomenology of experimentally induced amphetamine psychosis: Preliminary observations. *Biol. Psychiatry,* 2, 95: 107, 1970.

71. Bell, D.S.: A comparison of amphetamine psychosis and schizophrenia. *Brit. J. Psychiat.,* 3: 701-707, 1965.

72. Carpenter, W.T., and Strauss, J.S.: Cross-cultural evaluation of Schneiders's first-rank symptoms of schizophrenia: A report from the international pilot study of schizophrenia. *Am. J. Psychiat.,* 131: 682-687, 1974.

73. Carpenter, W.T., Strauss, J.S., and Mulch, S.: Are there pathognomonic symptoms in schizophrenia? An empiric investigation of Schneider's first-rank symptoms. *Arch. Gen. Psychiat.,* 28: 847-852, 1973.

74. Carpenter, W.J., Jr., Strauss, J.S., and Bartko, J.J.: Flexible system for the diagnosis of schizophrenia: Report from the WHO international study of schizophrenia. *Science,* 182: 1275-1277, 1973.

75. Carpenter, W.T., Jr., Strauss, J.S., and Bartko, J.J.: Use of signs and symptoms for the identification of schizophrenic patients. *Schizophr. Bull.,* 37: 76-81, 1974.

76. Schneider, K., *Clinical Psychopathology.* M.W. Hamilton (trans.). New York: Grune & Stratton, 1959.

77. Janowsky, D.S., El-Yousef, M., Davis, J., et al.: Antagonistic effects of physostigmine and methylphenidate in man. *Am. J. Psychiat.,* 130: 1370-1376, 1973.

78. McCabe, M.S.: Reactive psychosis and schizophrenia with good prognosis. *Arch. Gen. Psychiat.,* 33: 571-576, 1976.

79. Angrist, B.: Toxic manifestations of amphetamine. *Psychiatric Annals,* 8: 9, 1978.

80. Ellinwood, E.H., Jr.: Treatment of reactions of amphetamine-type stimulants. *Current Psychiatric Therapies,* 15: 163-169, 1975.

81. Perry, P., Wilding, D.C., and Juhl, R.P.: Anticholinergic psychosis. *Am. J. Hospital Pharmacy,* 35: 725-728, 1978.

82. Goodwin, F.: Psychiatric side effects of levodopa in man. *JAMA,* 218, 13: 1915-1920, 1971.

83. Yamura-Tobias, J., Diamond, B., and Merlis, S.: The action of L-Dopa on schizophrenic patients (a preliminary report). *Curr. Ther. Res.,* 12: 528-531, 1970.

84. Murphy, D.L., Brodie, H.K.H., Goodwin, F.K., and Bunney, W.E.J.: L-Dopa; Regular induction of hypomania in "bipolar" manic depressive patients. *Nature,* 229: 135, 1971.

85. Klawans, H.L.: Levodopa-induced psychosis. *Psychiatric Annals,* 8, 9: 19-29, 1978.

86. Goolkers, P., and Schein, J.: Psychic effects of ACTH and cortisone. *Journal of Psychosomatic Medicine,* 15: 589-613, 1953.

87. Lidz, T., Carter, J.D., Lewis, B.I., and Surratt, C.: Effects of ACTH and cortisone on mood and mentation. *Psychosomatic Medicine,* 14, 5: 363-377, 1952.

88. Rome, H.P., and Braceland, F.J.: The psychological response to ACTH, cortisone, hydrocortisone and related steroid substances. *Am. J. Psychiat.,* 108: 641-651, 1952.

89. Carpenter, W.T., Stauss, J.S., and Bunney, W.E.: The psychobiology of cortisol metabolism: Clinical and theoretical implications. In: R.I. Shader (Ed.), *Psychiatric Complications of Medical Drugs.* New York: Raven Press, 1972.

90. Crane, G.E.: The psychiatric side effects of iproniazid. *Am. J. Psychiat.*, 112: 494-501, 1956.

91. O'Connor, J.B., Hawlett, K.S., Jr., and Wagner, R.R.: Side effects accompanying the use of iproniazid. *Am. Rev. Tuberc.*, 68: 270-272, 1953.

92. Ferreira, A.J., and Freeman, H.: A clinical trial of marsilid in psychotic depressed patients. *Am. J. Psychiat.*, 114: 933-934, 1958.

93. Lewis, W.C., Calden, G., Thurston, J.R., and Gilson, W.E.: Psychiatric and neurologic reactions to cycloserine in the treatment of tuberculosis. *Dis. Chest*, 32: 172-182, 1957.

94. Herzberg, B.N., and Johnson, A.: Depressive syndromes and oral contraceptives. *BMT*, 4: 142-145, 1970.

95. Kaye, B.M.: Oral contraceptives and depression. *JAMA*, 186: 522, 1963.

96. Moos, R.H.: Psychological aspects of oral contraceptives. *Arch. Gen. Psychiat.*, 19: 87-94, 1968.

97. Glick, I.D., and Bennett, S.E.: Psychiatric effects of progesterone and oral contraceptives. In: R.I. Shader (Ed.), *Psychiatric Effects of Medical Drugs*. New York: Raven Press, 1972.

98. Weissman, M.M., and Slaby, A.E.: Oral contraceptives and psychiatric disturbance: Evidence from research. *Brit. J. Psychiat.*, 123: 513-518, 1973.

99. Leeton, J.: The relationship of oral contraception to depressive symptoms. *Australia-New Zealand J. Obstet. Gynec.*, 13: 115-120, 1973.

100. Kane, F., Treadway, F., et al.: Emotional changes associated with oral contraceptives in female psychiatric patients. *Comprehensive Psychiatry*, 10, 1: 16-30, 1969.

101. Goodwin, F.K., Ebert, M.H., and Bunney, W.E.: Mental effects of reserpine in man: A review. In: R.I. Shader (Ed.), *Psychiatric Effects of Medical Drugs*. New York: Raven Press, 1972.

102. Ayd, F.J.: Drug-induced depression—Fact or fallacy? *New York Journal of Medicine*, 58: 354-356, 1958.

103. Simpson, F.O., and Waal-Manning, H.J.: Hypertension and depression: Interrelated problems in treatment. *J. Royal College of Physicians London*, 6, 1: 14-24, 1971.

104. Lemieux, G., Davignon, A., and Genest, J.: Depressive states during rauwolfia therapy for arterial hypertension. *Canadian Med. Assn. J.*, 74: 522-526, 1956.

105. MacArthur, J.G., and Isaacs, B.: Mental effects of reserpine (letter). *Lancet*, 2: 347, 1955.

106. Quetsch, R.M., Achor, R.W.P., Litin, E.M., and Faucett, R.L.: Depressive reactions in hypertensive patients. *Circulation*, 19: 366-375, 1959.

107. Adler, S., Methyldopa-induced decrease in mental activity. *JAMA*, 10: 1428-1429, 1974.

108. Hamilton, M.D.: Some aspects of the long term treatment of severe hypertension with methyldopa. *Postgraduate Medical Journal*, 44: 66-69, 1968.

109. Gottschalk, L.A., Stone, W.N., and Gleser, G.: Peripheral versus central mechanisms accounting for antianxiety effects of propranolol. *Psychosomatic Medicine*, 36, 1: 47-56, 1974.

110. Ellis, J.G., and Dimond, E.G.: Newer concepts of digitalis. *Amer. J. Cardiol.*, 17: 759, 1966.

111. Lyon, A., and DeGraff, A.: The neurotoxic effects of digitalis. *Am. Heart. J.*, 65: 839, 1963.

112. Greenblatt, D.J., and Shader, R.I.: Digitalis toxicity. In: R.I. Shader (Ed.), *Psychiatric Complications of Medical Drugs*. New York: Raven Press, 1972.

113. Jacobs, G., and Pores, I.: Aprindine psychosis. *American Heart Journal*, 100, 3: 347-348, 1980.

Chapter 7

Transient Psychosis
Related to Alcoholism

*Marc Galanter, M.D.,
and Nicholas Walsh, M.D.*

INTRODUCTION

Psychotic symptomatology in the alcohol dependent and abusing patient has recently received increasing psychiatric attention for two reasons: the nature of these symptoms themselves and their relationship to schizophrenia.

In the first place, psychotic phenomena in the alcoholic patient, whether transient or otherwise, are not always appreciated as entities with specific clinical definition. Many transient psychotic features are viewed simply as points along the clinical continuum toward delirium tremens. Discrete and usually short-lived clinical conditions such as alcoholic hallucinosis, for example, remain unrecognized, poorly managed, and poorly understood. Accordingly, preemptive therapeutic interventions are made, particularly in the presence of hallucinatory and delusional symptoms. Unnecessary administration of neuroleptic agents or extra-large doses of benzodiazepines are often undertaken in these cases. This lack of understanding and use of improper therapeutic technique are found among both physicians and paraprofessional health workers, both of whom play a prominent therapeutic role in the alcoholism treatment field. A better defined approach to conceptualizing alcohol related psychotic symptoms would contribute considerably to clearer understanding and treatment.

The second important reason underlying recent attention to this subject is the diagnostic significance of psychotic symptomatology in the alcoholic patient. Some authors feel that the minority of alcoholics who experience psychotic symptomatology are really suffering from a predisposition to schizophrenia, while others point out that the two disorders are distinct in their mode of onset and that most alcoholics with histories of psychotic symptoms do not go on to demonstrate schizophrenia on follow-up.

This chapter will define the different clinical syndromes associated with psychotic symptoms as they appear in relation to alcoholism. The states which are described are subsumed under the headings of *intoxication, withdrawal,* and *organic states.* A general description will be given for each syndrome, but the main emphasis will be on the nature of the associated psychotic phenomena and the appropriate treatment.

In order to ensure clarity for the reader, time-honored titles are retained in the descriptions, for example, Korsakoff psychosis. Similarly, a final section on organic psychosis is included, even though this refers mainly to the dementia associated with alcoholism and is usually not seen as a transient or reversible process.

CAUSES, DIAGNOSIS, AND TREATMENT OF TRANSIENT PSYCHOSIS

Intoxication States

Pathological intoxication

Uncomplicated acute alcohol intoxication appearing as common drunkenness is well recognized by varying degrees of exhilaration and excitement, loss of restraints, irregularity of behavior, loquacity, slurred speech, irritability and drowsiness (aspects of this condition will be more fully elaborated upon in the following section).

On rare occasions a few individuals show an uncommon variety of this excitatory phase of acute alcohol intoxication, when the characteristics of acute intoxication are superseded by outbursts of aggressive, irrational, and destructive behavior. This is seen to occur after drinking only relatively small amounts of alcohol. This state is known as pathological intoxication (1) or alcohol idiosyncratic syndrome. A sensitive, gentle, and often mild-mannered person may become assaultive, belligerent, and out of contact with others after only one drink (or an amount insufficient to induce intoxication in most people). An older term for this condition is the "alcohol disinhibition syndrome." It should be noted that the abrupt change in behavior actually occurs while the individual is drinking or shortly thereafter. The patient usually then falls into a deep stupor; later, he may have no memory of the incident.

The duration of the behavior is brief, ceasing within a few hours. Initially, the dyscontrol and impulsivity result in violent outbursts directed toward inanimate objects such as furnishings, walls, accessories, etc. This should not cloud the potential that exists for assaultive, homicidal or even suicidal behavior. This angry and excited phase is then followed by a phase of confusion with disorientation and sometimes visual hallucinations. The diagnosis can be made by collateral history or later by the subject himself, when it can be confirmed that an amount of alcohol as small as one ounce of "hard" liquor was consumed and preceded this pathological state (1). Also, another pertinent observation is that the individual will be seen to return to his normal state as the blood alcohol level falls.

This state of pathological intoxication probably represents an inherent or constitutional idiosyncratic reaction to alcohol and is known to recur consistently with intake over prolonged periods of time. Also, this allergic-type reaction to alcohol is seen more often in the borderline or hysterical personality disorder.

A small percentage of these patients has been studied and found to have temporal lobe spikes on the EEG after receiving small amounts of alcohol. These patients are seen by some as having an underlying epileptic predisposition showing seizure equivalent activity.

Another group of patients who have been identified as displaying pathological intoxication are those who have suffered previous brain injury and trauma or who have had encephalitis in the past. Furthermore, persons who are unusually fatigued or have a debilitating physical illness or, indeed, who are just becoming older may also respond inappropriately to small amounts of alcohol.

A similar type of idiosyncratic or intolerant reaction can complicate the administration of barbiturates.

Management of pathological intoxication is more important than that of simple intoxication and the administration of diazepam or even haloperidol (Haldol) 5 mg. IM may be necessary for treatment (2). Repeat administration is rarely required in the acute case. Recognition and awareness of the possibility of the presence of this condition are essential and, since drinking alcohol is clearly related to this disorder, long-term treatment lies in abstention.

Acute intoxication (simple) with hallucinations

Transient hallucinations and delusions have been extensively de-scribed in relation to both acute and long-term withdrawal syndromes. In contrast, similar symptoms accompanying uncomplicated alcohol in-toxication or overdose have not always been recognized (except in the case of pathological intoxication). It is observed, for example, that simple alcohol intoxication or drunkenness can result in irrational behavior and thinking. Other features which accompany it include impaired judgment and attention, perceptual disturbances and distortions, as well as irrit-ability and emotional lability. In responding to these changes, the in-toxicated individual may become disorganized, delusional, or depressed.

It is well-known that an individual's psychological and psychopath-ological traits may be accentuated or altered in the setting of acute alcohol intoxication (3). For example, an individual who tends to be somewhat suspicious may, under the influence of alcohol, become markedly par-anoid. These altered characteristics can be attributed to alcohol on the basis of such physiological correlates as flushed face, unsteady gait, nystagmus, and incoordination.

The recognition of acute alcohol intoxication is based on most of the above-mentioned features, but other factors exist which also determine its appearance. The most important of these are the person's weight, recent food intake, the amount and type of alcoholic beverage taken and how rapidly the alcohol was ingested. Some generalizations can be made, although a wide spectrum exists in the variety and intensity of response to increasing amounts of alcohol.

With the taking of one standard alcoholic drink most people do not feel any differently from normal, although some may become a little more talkative. This corresponds to a blood alcohol concentration (B.A.C.) of 0.03%. With the intake of another drink, the alcohol con-centration rises to 0.05%, and most people feel relaxed, with some low-ering of inhibitions. If no further alcohol intake takes place, this sedating or mildly disinhibiting effect lasts for three to four hours, followed by mild agitation (or minor irritability) for a further six hours. These reac-tions are not often noticed by the individual because of preoccupation with other activities or the onset of normal sleep. However, established alcohol abusers, moderate social drinkers or even occasional drinkers may well experience this fluctuation in affect.

Now, if four or five drinks are taken within an hour or so, a blood alcohol concentration of 0.1% is reached. Most people who are intolerant of alcohol will feel intoxicated at this level, although some will deny intoxication. With six to ten drinks (taken within 1 ½ to 2 hours,) the blood alcohol concentration will reach 0.15% to 0.3%. Irrational and disorganized behavior may then occur. Of course, with higher levels of alcohol—0.35% to 0.4%—the person becomes comatose. This level is considered the LD_{50}—the lethal dose for 50% of the population. Actually, this level can be reached by drinking a quart of whiskey in an hour. Alcohol exerts its fatal effects either by a direct depression of respiration or by aspiration of vomitus.

Simple or uncomplicated intoxication with barbiturates and other sedative-hypnotic compounds may similarly be associated with bizarre or transient psychotic phenomena.

Certain neurological diseases, such as the cerebellar ataxias and multiple sclerosis, may mimic the psychological and physiological features of alcohol intoxication.

Another condition deserving consideration here is "blackouts," which are not true psychotic episodes but refer to a transient phase of amnesia. After the individual becomes sober, he or she cannot recall events that had occurred over the "drunken" period of several hours, even though the state of consciousness (as observed by others) was not altered during this period. If interviewed or tested during the blackout, the individual will contribute past historical facts but be unable to formulate new ideas or discuss ongoing events. The significance of these episodes is unclear. They do not necessarily indicate progression of alcohol addiction, as is generally assumed. Indeed, blackouts seem to occur just as frequently among consistent social drinkers or the occasionally indiscreet infrequent drinker. These episodes of amnesia relate to an acute state of intoxication and are distinct from the more formal alcohol amnestic disorder due to thiamine deficiency associated with prolonged and heavy use of alcohol (see Korsakoff psychosis below).

States of acute (simple) alcohol intoxication can present with various neuropsychiatric symptoms as a result of complications resulting from falls or accidents while drinking. These complications are frequently due to skull fractures and subdural hematomas. Acute alcohol intoxication may also accompany functional or toxic disease states. Many other sequelae of acute alcohol intoxication occur and it is now well established that one-fourth of all suicides, one-half of highway fatalities, and one-half of all murders occur while the individual is acutely intoxicated.

Mild to moderate degrees of alcohol intoxication with or without transient psychotic-type symptoms require no special treatment, and in most cases several hours of sleep will assure resolution of the symptoms with the clearing of the blood alcohol levels. Occasionally, haloperidol 5 mg might be considered during the early phase of alcohol intoxication, when undue "excitement" may occur corresponding to a rising alcohol blood level. This also allows for continued medical monitoring, particularly of the level of consciousness during serial evaluation.

In the uncomplicated case of acute or simple alcohol intoxication, certain folk remedies, such as a cold shower, strong coffee, and forced physical activity, have been recommended. There is no evidence, however, that any of these methods influence the rate of disappearance of the intoxication syndrome.

Increasing or undue somnolence should alert one to the possibility of multiple drug use. Transient psychotic features occurring in an acutely intoxicated patient may also signal the appearance of withdrawal symptoms due to recent reduction in alcohol intake. This may occur even in the context of continuing consumption. This phenomenon, as well as others associated with the emergence of alcohol withdrawal delirium, will be described below.

Psychotic exacerbation of functional states secondary to alcoholism

Many clinicians have observed close links between psychosis and alcohol abuse. As stated previously, the condition of pathological intoxication is seen more often in people with borderline personality disorders. Also, some cases of alcoholic auditory hallucinosis, as we shall see in a later section, may in time come to resemble schizophrenia.

Many patients with formal schizophrenic thought disorder abuse alcohol. These are patients with a premorbid schizoid personality style and often with a family history of schizophrenia. In many of these ongoing cases, alcohol itself in "normal" or excess amounts may lead to a worsening of the symptomatology. This is particularly seen in relation to reality-testing, where greater regression takes place. Clinical observers have noted that some acutely intoxicated schizophrenic patients are less likely to show the early disinhibitory effects of alcohol intake. Some of these patients appear to become sedated more readily and more frequently.

Many subjects who are clinically seen as alcohol-abusing are known to have underlying schizophrenia (4). In these individuals, alcohol masks the schizophrenic process, particularly the underlying sense of isolation and estrangement. These subjects, who may appear to be outgoing, are thought to be putting on a façade, facilitated by alcohol, which thus helps to cover a fragmented, detached, and depressed state.

Patients presenting with alcohol abuse or alcohol-related medical illness show other psychopathological traits, also seen in true schizophrenia. These characteristics include dependency, hostility, and sexual immaturity. Many alcohol-abusing patients remain very much self-oriented and self-involved and often see other people only as need-satisfying objects. These patients are then seen as using alcohol as a substitute for social, sexual, or even parenting functions.

It is now thought that a proportion of diagnosed alcoholic patients who show poor reality-testing are predisposed to temporary psychotic episodes not related to a true schizophrenic diagnosis and independent of the known psychotic symptoms which develop secondarily to withdrawal or abstinent states.

The symptoms of borderline personality disorder are now well-known and include impulsivity and unpredictability, identity disturbance, affective instability, etc., as well as possible predisposition to (micro) psychotic episodes. This later symptom, in particular, may be precipitated by alcohol intoxication, overdose or withdrawal, as well as by other substances and factors. It should be noted that people who abuse alcohol, compared to the general population, have the same, if not a greater, propensity to develop other psychotic conditions. Included in this list are psychotic depression, psychotic forms of manic-depressive illness, schizophrenic psychosis in temporal lobe epilepsy, amphetamine psychosis, puerperal psychosis, and endocrine psychosis.

Thus, it appears now that alcohol can precipitate acute psychotic relapse in well-compensated schizophrenia. This probably occurs more often than is realized. Also, the masking role of alcohol is often overlooked in schizophrenic disease or other psychiatric illness. Either way, it still remains difficult to separate the clinical entities involved and in quite a few cases it is impossible.

Recent work has suggested the possibility of genetic predisposition to alcoholic psychosis (5). Also, it has been found that alcoholic patients who develop psychotic symptoms or whose psychosis is precipitated or unmasked by alcohol have certain behavioral characteristics in common. These include early life developmental and domestic instability, higher levels of adult antisocial behavior, and a significant increase in the use of most illegal drugs.

This close linkage between alcohol abuse and psychotic illness is reflected in the fact that one-third of the patients admitted to psychiatric hospitals with a diagnosis of functional illness have serious drinking problems.

It should be recognized that many well-compensated schizophrenic patients suffer psychotic relapse when alcohol ingestion is commenced and sustained or if severe and continuous alcohol abuse takes place. Even smaller amounts of alcohol or amounts consistent with levels of social drinking can be detrimental to some schizophrenic patients. Such patients should be made aware of the potentially hazardous effects of even moderate amounts of alcohol and should be instructed or directed accordingly. Furthermore, attention should be paid to the possibility that cessation or reduction in alcohol intake may play a strong contributory role in the evolution and presentation of an acute psychotic episode, independent of any psychotic process precipitated specifically by alcohol or its withdrawal. This refers to the emergence of an ongoing schizophrenic state which is unmasked by alcohol withdrawal.

Withdrawal States

Delirium tremens or alcohol withdrawal delirium

This is the most dramatic and serious form of the alcohol withdrawal states, representing its final stage IV. Earlier stages, are still classically represented by tremulousness and anxiety (stage I), hallucinations (stage II), and grand mal seizures (stage III). This end stage point can be reached in a number of different settings. An individual drinking excessively and steadily for many years may be admitted to hospital for an unrelated accident, illness, or operation. With this sudden cessation of alcohol intake, he may present with delirium tremens two to four days after admission. Other individuals may discontinue drinking themselves following a long drinking spree. They may experience several days of tremulousness or suffer one or more seizures. Just as the subject may be recovering from these symptoms, delirium tremens suddenly develops.

This syndrome is characterized by marked autonomic hyperactivity with tachycardia, elevated blood pressure, hyperhidrosis, fever, dilated pupils, tremors and diaphoresis (6). Other features of general hyperactivity that are present include insomnia, itching, cramps, hyperacusis and tinnitus.

The delusions that occur are often paranoid and the hallucinations that are present are more often visual than auditory and are often of a persecutory nature. The hallucinations are usually accompanied by agitated behavior.

Patients then become globally confused and are fully disoriented. This is the hallmark of delirium tremens (7). Early in the confusional state, terrible nightmares or "the horrors" occur; this may be the first clue of impending delirium. It is usual for the confusion to vary over time, but it is generally much worse at night. This fluctuating mental status prevents the patient from directing meaningful attention or from engaging in goal-directed thinking or behavior. The hallucinations often merge with the confusional state, although a lucid interval usually separates the delirious manifestations from the hyper-adrenergic state. Seizures hardly ever occur after the development of the delirium.

In the majority of cases, delirium tremens is benign and short-lived, ending as abruptly as it begins. The subject usually falls into a deep sleep after the relentless activity and wakefulness of several days. Then, after a number of hours, the subject awakens lucid, quiet, and exhausted and with virtually no memory for the events of the delirious period. In just over 70% of cases the condition resolves in less than three days. In approximately 10% the delirium resolves in less than 24 hours.

It should be noted that only 5-6% of those withdrawing from a high intake of alcohol go on to develop delirium tremens, if left untreated. A patient who gives a history of early morning shakiness and nausea that is relieved by alcohol is at a considerably greater risk of eventually developing delirium tremens. These symptoms, when relieved by alcohol, represent some of the features of physical dependence. Furthermore, a patient who gives a past history of delirium tremens has increased risk of its recurrence.

In the classical case, the symptoms of delirium tremens occur on the second or third day after abstinence (or after reduction in alcohol intake.) The symptoms peak at the fourth day and subside during the first week. Less commonly, the delirious state subsides more gradually; more rarely still, there may be one or more relapses, with several distinct episodes of delirium separated by intervals of lucidity. In these unusual cases, the entire process may last for as little as several days or as long as four to five weeks.

Some patients display atypical delirious and hallucinatory states with confusion, which are thought to be partial or less severe forms of the syndrome. These unusual forms of the delirium tremens complex are manifested in some patients by a transient state of quiet confusion, agitation, and peculiar behavior lasting several days or even weeks.

The first episode of alcohol withdrawal delirium, whether manifested classically or otherwise, usually occurs after five to 15 years of heavy drinking. This disorder occurs initially, at least for the most part, in patients in their thirties or forties.

In 5% to 15% of cases of delirium tremens, a fatal outcome occurs, particularly in the presence of underlying medical and surgical illness. Thus, it is essential to search for any underlying disorders. This approach, which is often highlighted only in cases of delirium tremens, should also be considered in other withdrawal and intoxicating states. Certain disorders seem to occur with greater frequency in patients presenting with delirium tremens. Such concomitant conditions include pulmonary disease, hepatic disease, meningitis, subdural hematomas, dehydration, hyperthermia, seizure disorders, and electrolyte abnormalities (particularly hypokalemia and hypomagnesemia) with resultant cardiac rhythm disturbances (8).

The diagnosis can be made quite readily when physically dependent alcoholics develop a violent clinical reaction—acute alcohol withdrawal—upon reduction or cessation of alcohol intake. This reaction usually follows a lengthy bout of heavy drinking lasting for a period of at least one or more weeks. It is also important that other conditions with similar clinical features be considered. Such conditions include intracranial and systemic infection, withdrawal from barbiturates and benzodiazepines, and such metabolic emergencies as thyrotoxicosis and hypoglycemia.

The causes of delirium tremens are not yet fully understood. It is known that hyperirritability of the cerebral cortex occurs and this, along with β-adrenergic discharge from the brain stem, causes increased secretion of sympathicomimetic and other amines. This hypersecretion of amines probably accounts for the hyperactive changes seen, i.e, agitation, vasomotor changes, and tremor. Why this postulated neurochemical disturbance only takes place when blood alcohol levels are falling is not clear. A similar blood alcohol concentration is reached in the early and intermediate stages of intoxication and no similar response is seen.

In severe forms of withdrawal respiratory alkalosis occurs due to hyperventilation. Hypomagnesemia and hypokalemia are also seen. Some authors have suggested a pathophysiological link with fatty acids, prostaglandin E and zinc (9). Also, the production of a specific but as yet unidentified toxin is proposed to account for the protean manifestations in delirium tremens.

Most clinicians agree that the best specific approach to the treatment of patients with serious withdrawal symptoms is the early administration of "replacement" drugs that are cross-tolerant with ethanol (10). These drugs include the benzodiazepines and paraldehyde, although some centers use other drugs, including phenothiazines. General management issues will be addressed initially, and discussion of the individual drug compounds will be undertaken later.

Immediate management involves sympathetic handling, careful observation, and treatment, preferably in the medical ward. As previously noted, other underlying causes or precipitants of the syndrome should be treated if present. Such conditions include head injury, pancreatitis, liver disease, and pneumonia. Actually, it is now recognized that pneumonia is the most common medical condition precipitating delirium tremens. Also, alcoholic patients with this infection usually have multilobar involvement, a high incidence of aspiration pneumonia, and a high incidence of infection due to Klebsiella organisms. In the older alcoholic patient, with any general infection, fever is not always present. The presenting features can be a change in baseline mental status with drowsiness, confusion, and unresponsiveness.

In the general management of delirium tremens, fluid and electrolyte balance should be restored. Severe degrees of agitation and perspiration accompanying withdrawal may require the administration of extra fluids daily.

In some patients, presenting symptoms of bizarre and agitated behavior may well be due to hypoglycemia. In these cases glucose should be administered. High potency vitamin preparations (particularly vitamin B) are also given by injection. This is particularly necessary in hypoglycemic cases when the administration of IV glucose may serve to consume the last available stores of thiamine, thereby precipitating Wernicke's disease. Finally, for the first day or two, additional supplements of 50 ml to 100 ml of potassium should be given in divided doses.

The choice of drug for administration in acute alcohol withdrawal delirium (as well as in other withdrawal and intoxicant states) often depends on the orientation and location of the treatment center, as well as personal preference (11). Actually, over 100 drugs have been tried in the treatment of withdrawal, including, of course, alcohol itself in reducing amounts. Other agents that are used are 100% oxygen or a combination of oxygen and nitrous oxide (12), tiapriadel, trazodone, and injectable lorazepam. The drug of choice generally in the United Kingdom and Ireland is chlormethiazole (Heminevrin) in an initial dose of 500-1500 mg every six hours (13).

In the United States chlordiazepoxide is the recommended drug. This is because of its rapid onset of action when given orally, its gradual buildup of blood levels, its raising of seizure threshold, and a lesser and slower development of tolerance than the barbiturates. Initial doses are 50 mg to 100 mg orally, which can be repeated every 60-90 minutes until the patient experiences a calming effect. At this point, the medication is then usually changed to 50 mg every four hours and then tailed off. With most patients this regimen should permit complete withdrawal in five to seven days. It is important to prevent oversedation during the day.

Another agent receiving reemerging attention in the treatment of severe alcohol withdrawal is paraldehyde, which is a short-acting sedative hypnotic that has cross tolerance with alcohol. The dose usually given is 10 cc orally every four to six hours. Rectal administration is not indicated because of the danger of developing regional proctitis.

Diazepam is also used for withdrawal, given as 10 mg IV initially and repeated at 30-minute intervals. Chlordiazepoxide and diazepam, which are longer-acting than paraldehyde, have pharmacologically active metabolites that are protein-bound. Therefore, the dosage of these drugs, as indicated, must be progressively decreased in order to avoid the toxic effects of drug accumulation, especially in patients with hypoproteinemia. There is also abuse potential with these medications and thus withdrawal problems remain a possibility.

Recently, the use of oxazepam has been advocated in acute withdrawal delirium. This agent, in contrast to the other benzodiazepines (chlordiazepoxide and diazepam), has a shorter half-life and is converted to an inactive metabolite. Thus, toxic accumulation of this drug is much less likely to occur. It should be noted that all these suppress anxiety and prevent convulsions for the most part. If convulsions occur, chlordiazepoxide or diazepam is the drug of choice, since phenytoin does not act quickly enough. Recently, the beta-blocking agent propranolol (Inderal) has been shown to effectively decrease withdrawal tremor when 40 mg per day by mouth is given. This drug does not prevent convulsions or augment the action of the sedatives and caution must be exerted in its administration.

Phenothiazines are not usually given to treat alcohol withdrawal delirium because they lower seizure threshold and may potentiate hypothermia in withdrawal. Antihistamines, often used for their sedative effects, are also contraindicated because they can alter the sensorium. This may cloud the clinical picture by producing hallucinations and delirium. These unusual effects of antihistamines are possibly related to a centrally acting anticholinergic action.

Thus, it is seen that proper management of delirium tremens requires astute clinical skills with an appreciation of the various modes of presentation and the different complications that can arise with this syndrome.

Alcoholic hallucinosis

This condition was previously thought to be part of the spectrum of the acute alcohol withdrawal syndrome, but is now recognized as a distinct clinical entity occurring usually within 48 hours of cessation or reduction in alcohol intake (14). In some cases, the symptoms appear after a period of abstinence lasting from a few hours to a week or ten days. It is important to note that progression to full-blown delirium tremens does not usually occur. Initially, the patient complains of bad dreams, consisting of nightmarish episodes with disturbed sleep, which the patient finds difficult to separate from "real" experience. Sounds and shadows are misinterpreted in the beginning and familiar objects may appear distorted and assume unreal forms. This is why the term "hallucinosis" is used—because these early features are not hallucinations in strict terms. After this illusionary phase, the distinctive feature of the phenomenon arises—in the form of voices. Less commonly, unformed sounds like hissing, buzzing, cackling or mumbling predominate.

In the majority of cases the voices are unpleasant and disturbing, often belonging to a group of people or a gang planning some action against the patient or his family. The voices, often discussing the patient in the third person, can be threatening and force the patient at times to call the police or arm himself against the intruders. Voices may also come from the heating system, radio, and TV. They are not of a command nature. In addition, the patient may experience fleeting visual hallucinations, facilitated perhaps by the auditory hallucinations, of persons hiding outside the window, behind the door, or passing through the room. The visual phenomena may also be animated and comprise various forms of animal or insect life. These visions may occur singly or in panoramas, may be natural in appearance or take on distorted or hideous forms.

The patient commonly has delusions of a persecutory nature corresponding to the auditory hallucinations. He may feel that other people know about him and his problems or even that people may try to record his thoughts. Delusions dealing with supernatural beings, particularly the devil, are not unusual.

Other signs of withdrawal following prolonged intoxication may occur with these patients, including tremulousness and seizure activity. During the illness the patient has no insight into the nature of the hallucinations and delusions, although he usually remains fully oriented. Most frequently, the disorder lasts only a few hours or days, typically less than a week. In about 10% of cases, the symptoms may last several weeks or months or longer.

This condition, then, is diagnosed when vivid auditory hallucinations occur with a clear sensorium shortly (usually within 48 hours) after cessation of or reduction in heavy ingestion of alcohol in an individual who has been alcohol-dependent for a period of months to years. The hallucinations initially may have a formless organic quality like cackling, knocking, whispering, or roaring sounds. In the classic case the patient hears voices which usually talk in derogatory terms to or about the patient and his family. The auditory and accompanying visual hallucinations are rather simple and primitive, lacking the fantastic, illogical, and bizarre character of true schizophrenic hallucinations. Some earlier authors viewed this syndrome as a "schizophrenic" reaction precipitated by alcohol abuse and withdrawal.

The condition can be well differentiated from true or process schizophrenia by several factors. For example, the majority of patients at the time of their first episode of alcohol hallucinosis are in their forties and fifties, usually following 10 to 15 years of heavy drinking. In contrast, schizophrenia rarely presents initially after the age of 40. The onset of symptoms in acute hallucinosis is characteristically acute, not insidious, and clearly and temporally related to cessation or reduction of drinking. The alcoholic patient may have appropriately affective responses, such as perplexity, anxiety, and depression. Also, most of these patients, in contrast to schizophrenics, improve spontaneously over short periods of time, i.e., from days to weeks.

As stated, this condition is still seen by some as part of an alcoholic abstinence syndrome in view of the occurrence of other features of withdrawal, principally tremulousness. Most patients retain a clear sensorium with absent or only mild confusional states, and are usually fully orientated in place and person. Any cognitive or intellectual impairment that occurs is usually attributed to sequelae of chronic alcohol intake.

These patients should be treated initially by support and restraints if necessary. Appropriate benzodiazepines may be administered and then gradually withdrawn. Thiamine and multi-vitamin supplements should also be given for the general dietary deficiency states often found in these patients. In most cases the patient's psychosis will resolve after the withdrawal has been completed. Neuroleptics should be reserved only for the occasional patients who remain psychotic upon completion of the treatment for withdrawal. (This group of patients will be discussed in the following section.)

Thus, any middle-aged patient with a history of alcohol abuse who presents with an acute onset of hallucinations and delusions (as described in this section) should be carefully screened for the possibility of hallucinosis and for other evidence of withdrawal.

Postwithdrawal paranoia with auditory hallucinations (acute)

In the previous description of alcoholic hallucinosis, it was noted that in most cases the symptoms resolve and that a full recovery is characterized by the patient's realization that the hallucinated voices were "imaginary." The patient may also be able to recall with clarity the abnormal thought content of the psychotic episode. In about 8% of cases of alcoholic hallucinosis, however, the clinical picture of illusions, auditory or mixed hallucinations persists for weeks or longer. This category of symptoms may be designated as an acute postwithdrawal paranoia with auditory hallucinations. This designation may be confused with "the alcohol paranoid state," an older term referring to pathological intoxication. This condition of postwithdrawal paranoia with auditory hallucinations generally retains a benign and transient form, despite the continuing hearing of voices, which are usually scathing and critical. These voices may remain present even if the patient is sober. Some patients continue to drink heavily in an attempt to get rid of the voices and such persistent and frequent drinking increases the patient's risk of further episodes of acute alcoholic hallucinosis and the persistence of auditory hallucinations on withdrawal.

This syndrome may require neuroleptic medication for a number of weeks until symptom control has been achieved. Most patients remain symptom-free after drug therapy is terminated. A small number of patients who present initially with acute hallucinosis may go on to develop chronic psychotic symptoms. This is estimated at about 2% and refers to those patients included under the heading of "Non-intoxicated Paranoid State" in the following section.

The physician should be aware of the possibility of the syndrome of postwithdrawal paranoid state with auditory hallucinations (15) and should focus on the alcoholic etiology of the symptoms in the rehabilitation of the patient in order to prevent recurrent psychotic episodes.

Non-intoxicated paranoid state or chronic postwithdrawal (auditory)
hallucinations with paranoia

This state, which initially is indistinguishable from the transitory or
acute form, can be recognized as early as a week after the onset of the
illness. The patient, suffering from acute hallucinosis with auditory hallucinations that are threatening and derogatory, becomes quiet and re-
signed. Ideas of reference and of influence become prominent, as well
as other poorly systematized paranoid delusions. After some time these
patients begin to show some of the symptoms of schizophrenia, with
illogical thinking, vagueness, tangential associations, and inappropriate
and dull affect. In some of these chronic cases the premorbid state and
family history are not suggestive of the presence of an underlying latent
or incipient schizophrenic process.

This remains a controversial area. Some authors suggest that no direct
connection exists linking alcoholism and hallucinosis to functional
schizophrenic illness (16), and that the phenomena described here are
more likely to be representative of an organic or metabolic deficit not
yet elucidated. Others agree that auditory hallucinations persisting
months or years after alcohol withdrawal, with the patient no longer
drinking, represent the presence of a previously unrecognized schizophrenic process masked by alcohol.

There is also some suggestion that repeated attacks of acute alcoholic
(auditory) hallucinosis render the patient more vulnerable to this chronic psychotic state. Some of these apparently rare chronic cases may
require neuroleptic drug therapy indefinitely.

Organic States

Korsakoff's psychosis

In contrast to alcohol intoxication and abstinence syndromes accompanied by psychotic symptoms, a small but important group of similar-
style illnesses can occur in chronic alcoholics due to secondary metabolic
and nutritional deficiencies. Such an acute or chronic state is Wernicke's
disease, which is characterized by neuropsychiatric and neurological
symptoms caused by a deficiency of Vitamin B_1. In its acute state the
main features include ocular disturbances with lateral rectus muscle
palsy and nystagmus, ataxia with a wide-based and uncertain gait, nutritional polyneuropathy, and derangement of mental function. Though
not a true transient psychosis, this state is represented by a global con-

fusional state with profound apathy, listlessness, and disorientation. A small number of the patients may show symptoms of alcohol withdrawal, either delirium tremens or a variant thereof.

Symptoms of apathy, drowsiness, and profound confusion seen in the acute phase gradually recede after administration of thiamine, but a defect in retentive memory and learning stands out more clearly (17). These elements of short-term memory and learning deficit constitute the main features of Korsakoff's psychosis, which is now also known as the alcohol amnestic disorder. It should be noted that in the alcoholic nutritionally deficient patient with Wernicke's disease, Korsakoff's psychosis is the residual psychic component of Wernicke's disease.

Other features accompanying the alcohol amnestic syndrome (or Korsakoff's disease) are cerebellar ataxia and myopathy. The alcohol amnestic disorder usually follows an acute episode of Wernicke's encephalopathy. Complete recovery is seen in 20% or more of these patients. The remaining patients suffer quite severe gaps in memory and are unable to sort out events in their proper temporal sequence.

These patients are unable to retain new material for more than a few minutes, even though registration is temporarily possible. There is always an associated defect in recall and reproduction of memories formed days or months before the onset of the illness. Dislocation of events in time and the fabrication of stories, called confabulation, are generally seen.

Thankfully, this disorder is now apparently rare because of the routine administration of thiamine during detoxification. The administration of 50 mg of thiamine IV or IM to a patient presenting only with ocular and ataxic signs will prevent the development of Korsakoff's psychosis. The thiamine injections are repeated daily until the patient resumes a normal diet.

In untreated or unrecognized cases the incomplete recovery of the memory deficit suggests that the condition is the result of irreversible structural changes, presumably in the limbic system.

Other forms of amnestic syndromes exist, although the form described as Korsakoff's disease is by far the most common. Other pathological processes that may occur more frequently in the alcoholic population can also give rise to amnestic syndromes. These conditions include infarction of the posterior cerebral arteries, herpes simplex encephalitis, hypoxia, head trauma, and surgical intervention.

Delirium tremens also involves memory impairment. In this case the impairment is accompanied by clouding of consciousness. Dementia associated with alcoholism, which will be discussed in the following

section, also has memory impairment accompanying the major intellectual and cognitive deficits.

Finally, several diseases have been described which are found mainly
in the alcoholic population. These neurological conditions may well be
accompanied by amnestic and psychological symptoms and include alcoholic cerebellar degeneration, Marchiafava-Bignami disease (or primary degeneration of the corpus callosum), central pontine myelinolysis,
and alcoholic cerebral atrophy. Indeed, these disorders may simply represent different facets of the same disease process.

Organic psychosis

This section is mainly devoted to dementia associated specifically with
long-term alcohol abuse. This condition is listed as an organic mental
disorder attributed to the ingestion of alcohol. Actually, most of the
other conditions listed and described in this chapter, including alcohol
intoxication, pathological intoxication, alcohol withdrawal syndrome,
alcoholic hallucinosis, and alcohol amnestic disorder, are formally and
strictly categorized as organic mental disorders due to alcoholism.

Dementia associated with alcohol is now a fairly well recognized entity. It is characterized by moderate to severe intellectual deficits associated with prolonged and heavy ingestion of alcohol. Although not
viewed as a transient psychosis, the more severe forms of dementia may
resemble psychotic behavior.

This syndrome rarely begins before the age of 35 and the severe form
appears to be rare. It is well-known that mild and sometimes reversible
intellectual impairment is found commonly among alcohol-dependent
subjects and this finding may represent early cases of the syndrome.
Moderately severe cases are often manifested by social impairment, as
well as disruption of work and grooming habits. The more severe cases
require constant care and are often totally oblivious to their surroundings, with hostile exhibitionism often seen. It is interesting to note that
in established cases the evidence of dementia persists long after the
cessation of alcohol.

It should also be noted that other organic processes occurring specifically in the alcoholic patient can give rise to confusion, disorientation,
and psychotic symptomatology as well. The best example is hepatic
precoma and encephalopathy. In this condition episodic disorders of
consciousness occur with fluctuating mental status as a complication of
advanced liver disease and portal systemic shunts.

Other encephalopathies occurring in the general population, such as pancreatic, hypoglycemic and endocrine encephalopathies, may well present with greater frequency in the alcoholic population.

Antabuse (disulfiram) is best used to protect the episodic and spree drinker from the impulse to drink. When taken with alcohol, acetaldehyde levels rise and nausea, vomiting, and hypotension occur. The drug Antabuse itself has few side effects. Mild polyneuropathy may occur with prolonged use. When Antabuse is administered with other drugs, transient psychotic symptoms have been reported in some cases. These other agents include the anti-fungal agent metronidazole (Flagyl) and the anti-tuberculous agent isoniazid (INH). The mechanism of interaction is believed to be related to changes in the catecholamine metabolic pathways.

CONCLUSION

Alcohol dependence and alcohol abuse have now probably replaced hysteria as the great modern mimic of medicine. In psychiatric medicine, transient psychotic symptoms occur in many conditions, including alcoholism and alcohol-related illness. In these cases auditory and visual hallucinations can occur with delusions and disorientation. The time course and clinical description of the phenomena observed may help to organize a better approach toward understanding and treatment.

The appearance of auditory hallucinations with or without paranoid delusions in a clear sensorium may be due to alcohol-related factors. This can only be established if a clear or confirmed drinking history is suspected or obtained. The development of visual hallucinations with confusion and agitation in any patient should require the pursuit of a drinking history. Thus, acute psychiatric symptoms in any patient presenting to the emergency room should be evaluated in the light of past or present alcohol intake or abstinence. It should be noted that many cases of alcohol-related psychosis clear up in a matter of days or weeks.

There are a number of cases where a clear distinction between alcoholic psychosis and schizophrenia is difficult or impossible to make. Notwithstanding this, every attempt should be made to better understand and treat these cases because of the differences in course and prognosis.

REFERENCES

1. *Diagnostic and Statistical Manual of Mental Disorders, Third Edition. (DSM-III)* Alcohol Organic Mental Disorders, pp. 129-139. Washington, D.C.: American Psychiatric Association, 1980.

2. Galanter M., and Bender, S.: Alcoholism. In: H.F. Kohn (Ed.), *Current Therapy*. Philadelphia: W.B. Saunders, 1982, pp. 875-880.
3. *Diagnostic and Statistical Manual of Mental Disorders, Third Edition. (DSM-III)* Alcohol Abuse, Alcohol Dependence, pp. 169-170. Washington, D.C.: American Psychiatric Association, 1980.
4. Schuckit, M.A.: The history of psychotic symptoms in alcoholics. *J. Clin. Psychiat.*, 63: 53-57, 1982.
5. Hrubec, Z., and Omenn, G.: Evidence of genetic predisposition to alcoholic cirrhosis and psychosis. *Alcoholism: Clin. and Exper. Research*, 5: 207-215, 1981.
6. Victor, M., and Adams, R.D.: Alcohol. In: K. Isselbacher, R.D. Adams, E. Braunwald, R. Petersdorf, and J. Wilson (Eds.), *Harrison's Principles of Internal Medicine*, vol. 1, ed. 9. New York: McGraw-Hill, 1980, pp. 969-977.
7. Lewis, D.C., and Femino, J.: Management of alcohol withdrawal. *Rational Drug Therapy*, 16: 1-5, 1982.
8. Kissin, B.: Alcohol abuse and alcohol related illness. In: J. Wyngarden and L. Smith (Eds.), *Cecil Textbook of Medicine*, vol. 2, ed. 16. Philadelphia: W.B. Saunders, 1982, pp. 2016-2022.
9. Brown. C.G.: The alcohol withdrawal syndrome. *Ann. Emerg. Med.*, 11:276-280, 1982.
10. McNichol, R.W.: *The Treatment of Delirium Tremens and Related States*. Springfield, IL: Charles C Thomas, 1970.
11. Management of alcohol withdrawal symptoms. *Brit. Med. J.*, 282: 502, 1981.
12. Lichtigfeld, F.J., and Gilman, M.A.: The treatment of alcohol withdrawal states with oxygen and nitrous oxide. *S. Afr. Med. J.*, 6, 61 (10): 349-351, 1982.
13. McGrath, S.D.: A controlled trial of chlormethiazole and chlordiazepoxide in the treatment of the acute withdrawal phase of alcoholism. *Brit. J. Addict.*, 70 (Suppl 1): 81-86, 1975.
14. Surawicz, F.G.: Alcoholic hallucinosis: A missed diagnosis: Differential diagnosis and management. *Can. J. Psychiat.*, 25: 57-63, 1980.
15. Victor, M., and Hope, J.: The phenomenon of auditory hallucinations in chronic alcoholism. *J. Nerv. Ment. Dis.*, 126: 451-481, 1958.
16. Schuckit, M.A., and Winokur, G.: Alcoholic hallucinosis and schizophrenia: A negative study. *Brit. J. Psychiat.*, 119: 549-550, 1971.
17. Talland, G.: *Deranged Memory: A Psychonomic Study of the Amnesic Syndrome*. New York: Academic Press, 1965.
18. Victor, M., Adams, R.D., and Collins, G.H.: *Wernicke-Korsakoff Syndrome*. Philadelphia: F.A. Davis Co., 1971.

PART III

Transient Psychoses in Vulnerable Populations

Chapter 8

Transient Psychoses and Personality Disorders

Leo E. Hollister, M.D.

Acute psychotic states occur in several possible contexts: as an exacerbation of chronic schizophrenia; as an acute schizophrenia-like episode in a patient not previously diagnosed; as acutely excited psychotic states of uncertain cause; as an acute manic psychosis; as psychotic symptoms associated with the disturbance often labeled "borderline"; as an acute manifestation of senile brain disease; as a psychosis in previously well-adjusted patients in intensive care units; and as a reaction to the ingestion of, or withdrawal from, various social drugs. We shall consider in this discussion the diagnosis and treatment of each of these types of transient psychoses.

GENERAL PRINCIPLES IN TREATING TRANSIENT PSYCHOSES

Some general guidelines should be followed:

- More specific antipsychotics preferred.
- Do not over-treat; aggressive treatment regimens are not proven.

- Dose and frequency of dosage must be individually determined.
- Maintenance doses should be reduced as patient improves.

EXACERBATION OF CHRONIC SCHIZOPHRENIA

An exacerbation of chronic schizophrenia is usually insidious. Treatment with antipsychotic drugs, which seldom terminate their action immediately upon discontinuation, allows a gradual and attenuated return of symptoms. Patients often can stop taking drugs for prolonged periods with little apparent change; then some acute life stress occurs and a florid psychosis may develop. Symptoms may include the characteristic schizophrenic disturbances of thinking, affect, and behavior. Patients may come to medical attention because of difficulty with their families or involvement with law enforcement agencies, or because they run out of money.

A previous well-documented episode of schizophrenia with a marginal socioeconomic adjustment afterwards usually confirms the diagnosis. It is well to consider other factors that may have triggered the exacerbation, however. Among younger patients, one must always consider the possibility that the use of social drugs precipitated the exacerbation. Intercurrent illness or injury may be a factor in the middle-aged. Any of the multiple disorders that may cause new mental symptoms will evoke symptoms resembling schizophrenia in such patients. Thyrotoxicosis, anoxemia, electrolyte imbalance, or a head injury may be masked by the established repertoire of schizophrenic symptoms. Older patients may lose control due to small strokes, with psychiatric manifestations predominating. It is essential, therefore, to consider the many factors, some remediable, that may have exacerbated a recurrence of schizophrenia.

Treatment of a schizophrenic exacerbation is no different from customary treatment of schizophrenia. Since the patient will probably have tried a variety of antipsychotic drugs, the one producing the most favorable response in the past is the one to use during the current episode. When rapid remission is desired, either to minimize hospitalization or to avoid it completely, large oral or parenteral doses of one of the highly potent antipsychotic drugs, such as thiothixene, haloperidol, and fluphenazine, are sometimes used. Although daily doses of 80 mg or more seem to achieve the desired aims, further experience by the original proponents of high dosage has led to the conclusion that 80 mg of fluphenazine a day is no better than the standard 20 mg, since both produce equivalent benefits and adverse effects (1, 2).

Depot forms of these drugs should not be used for initial treatment; it is essential to have rapid release of the drug and rapid feedback regarding the chosen drug's effectiveness in controlling the patient. Depot preparations should be reserved for maintenance treatment.

Although many crisis centers try to avoid rehospitalizing such patients, a brief return to the hospital may serve several useful purposes: The hospital may offer "asylum" for recovery from untenable life situations; the diagnostic facilities available are better suited for ruling out possible physical changes that might have caused the exacerbation of psychosis; and the response to renewed drug treatment can be better evaluated with the patient under close observation. Moreover, patients' tenuous adjustment outside the hospital may have been irretrievably damaged; they may no longer have people who are willing to care for them until they have been returned to reasonably good condition.

In summary, patients in an exacerbation of schizophrenia need a renewed evaluation of their diagnosis, of their drug treatment, and of their social placement.

Possible Treatment Program for Acute Exacerbation of Schizophrenia

- Haloperidol 10 mg po immediately, with dose repeated every 4 hr until behavioral control is achieved.
- Haloperidol 10 mg bid po, for subsequent treatment.

ACUTE SCHIZOPHRENIA

An episode of schizophrenia-like psychosis in a patient not previously diagnosed may represent the initial stages of a chronic, debilitating life-long infirmity or simply a transient psychosis in someone vulnerable to become schizophrenic under severe life stresses. In any case, the initial treatment of the episode is the same. Antipsychotic drug treatment is recommended in acute schizophrenia, even though some patients may improve spontaneously (3). Good premorbid function, acute onset of the disturbance, and strong social support may indicate the "reactive" or "good prognosis" form of schizophrenia. Subsequent clinical course is the best measure of the situation, however.

A patient who has been functioning well in school or on the job and who suddenly becomes psychotic might justify one of the rapid treatment methods currently in vogue. Unless some useful purpose can be served by quick remission, however, the conservative approach may be in the patient's best interest, since it insures against overtreatment.

A rapid treatment course might be initiated with oral or parenteral doses of 5 to 10 mg of haloperidol repeated at intervals of one to two hours until adequate symptomatic control is achieved. When the parenteral drug is used, the subsequent daily dose of the less bioavailable oral form may have to be somewhat higher, but usually it remains the same as the parenteral dose. There is very little evidence to suggest that the parenteral route produces more satisfactory or expeditious outcomes than the oral. The only unequivocal advantage of parenteral dosage lies in the fact that acutely psychotic patients may not take oral drugs reliably; with injection, the treating physician can be sure the drug enters the body.

The rate of remission determines the way in which doses of the antipsychotic drugs are tapered. Once remission occurs, most patients can be maintained on much smaller doses. Continuation of high initial dosage may confound the picture with a drug-induced depression or a drug-induced akinetic state, either of which may exaggerate the severity of the residual symptoms.

Not only should dosage reduction be attempted, but many authorities also recommend that all patients should be tried on a drug-free program after remission from a first attack of schizophrenia. A minority of such patients may represent the reactive type of schizophrenia, which requires treatment only during acute episodes. On the other hand, those that show definite symptoms of relapse while off drugs may have the "process" type of schizophrenia that will require some amount of sustained drug treatment for life.

Possible Treatment Program for Acute Schizophrenia or Other Excitements

- Haloperidol 5 mg IM; repeat every 1-2 hr until behavioral control is achieved.
- Continue haloperidol orally in 2 divided doses per day, each dose representing one-half of the total amount needed for behavioral control.
- Trial without drug after remission.

ACUTELY EXCITED AND AGITATED PATIENTS

In many clinical situations, the exact cause of a transient psychosis is not known. Treatment must be given as an emergency measure. One study of the use of haloperidol and chlorpromazine in 58 such patients found the former to be preferable—15 of 30 patients who received a single 5 mg injection of haloperidol were controlled and another eight patients were improved. Results with injections of 50 mg of chlorpromazine were less gratifying (Table 1) (4). Although it could be argued that a 10:1 ratio of dose between the two drugs did not equate their potencies, larger doses of chlorpromazine are often associated with postural hypotension or pain and inflammation at the injection site. The better tolerance of patients for the high-potency agents now makes these drugs the preferred agents.

Differences between high potency drugs are small, if existent at all. In a controlled comparison between haloperidol and thiothixene in 30 patients with acute psychosis, using doses of from 4 to 32 mg, findings were equally satisfactory with both drugs (5). Although the small sample—only 15 patients in each group—might have failed to detect a subtle but real difference, the results are credible in the light of clinical experience with such drugs.

Considering the many adverse reactions that are unique to chlor-

TABLE 1

Comparison of Haloperidol and Chlorpromazine in Acutely Excited and Agitated Patients

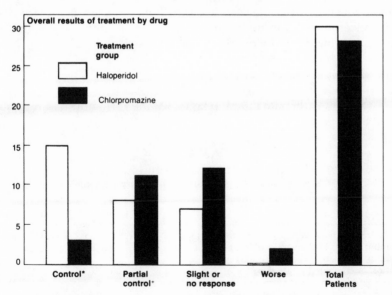

*patient calm, communicative, cooperative. + patient manageable but still very disturbed
Adapted from Baastrup PC, et al.[7]

promazine, some of us have argued that it is now obsolete. Thioridazine is not amenable to emergency use, both because a parenteral form is not available and because the total daily dose must be limited to 800 mg. Thus, the field has been pretty well narrowed down to the high-potency agents.

ACUTE MANIC PSYCHOSES

These psychoses may be difficult to distinguish from those of acute schizophrenia. Many are lumped in the emergency treatment of acutely agitated states with vague diagnoses. Although lithium carbonate is the preferred treatment for milder exacerbations of mania, it is inappropriate as the sole treatment of severely manic patients because of its slow onset of action (6).

Today, clinicians prefer to use a high-potency antipsychotic, despite the reputation of chlorpromazine for having greater sedative effects. The reported interaction between haloperidol and lithium, with severe neurologic sequelae, does not seem to have much substance (Table 2) (7). Nevertheless, the combined action of lithium and antipsychotics may produce more severe extrapyramidal syndromes than those associated with antipsychotics alone. Since lithium treatment should be started simultaneously with antipsychotics, the choice of drug is a matter of some concern. With careful monitoring, however, any of the high-potency drugs, including haloperidol, may be used.

Possible Treatment Program for Acute Mania

- Lithium carbonate 0.5 mEq/kg (a 300 mg dose unit has roughly 8 mEq).

TABLE 2
Concurrent Treatment with Lithium Carbonate and Haloperidol in 425 Patients*

	Median	Range
Maximum lithium carbonate dosage (mg/day)	1,350	300-3,300
Maximum serum lithium concentrations (mEq/liter)	1.0	0.2-2.0+
Maximum haloperidol dosage (mg/day)	9	1-60
Duration of combined treatment (days)	40	1-2, 900

*Number of patients, 425; treatment periods, 759
+A single value 3.7 mEq/liter
Adapted from Baastrup et al. (7).

- Thiothixene 10 mg po; repeat every 4 hr until behavioral control. Continue with oral divided doses as needed.
- Haloperidol could also be used, with any combination of lithium and antipsychotic expect greater extrapyramidal reactions.

"BORDERLINE" PATIENTS

The use of quotes around borderline indicates an uncertainty of its meaning. It is used increasingly for patients whose diagnosis is not at all clear, but who often have mixtures of schizophrenia-like symptoms, neurotic symptoms, affective symptoms, and personality disorders (8). The term borderline may be better than others to designate such patients, but one should derive no more comfort from it than from terms such as idiopathic or essential; simply providing a name does not provide understanding.

The clinical management of borderline patients boils down to deciding which of the several possible categories of symptoms is most prominent and then treating those symptoms. At various times in the course of the borderline syndrome, treatment with antipsychotic or antidepressant drugs may be indicated. Most patients require antipsychotic drugs, either alone or combined with tricyclic antidepressants. Since many of these patients will have been previously treated with psychoactive agents, one can often make the choice based on their most favorable previous response. Again, high-potency drugs are preferable to low-potency drugs.

The episodes of disturbed behavior in borderline patients can usually be brought under symptomatic control with drug treatment. Relapse is frequent, however, especially when patients are confronted with issues of separation or formation of intimate relationships. Thus, some kind of maintenance drug treatment should be planned. As with maintenance in chronic schizophrenia—of which the borderline syndrome may be a mild variant—drug dosage will be less than that required to produce remission.

Possible Treatment for "Borderline" Patients

- Haloperidol 2 mg tid po, adjusting subsequent doses on clinical response.
- If haloperidol poorly tolerated, try diazepam 15 mg tid po.
- If also depressed, amitriptyline or imipramine up to daily dose of 150 mg and reassess.

SENILE BRAIN DISEASE

Patients with senile brain disease (Alzheimer's disease) run a variable course. For reasons that are not always clear,, these patients become acutely disturbed occasionally, which is associated sometimes with some major life change, such as moving, or with an illness or operation. One must be especially observant for physical causes of agitation, such as pain, when a previously quiet, demented patient becomes agitated, when paranoid delusions and visual or auditory hallucinations become evident, or when behavior is bizarre and sleep-wake cycles are profoundly disturbed.

Antipsychotic drugs do not remedy the specific illness but may be useful for symptom control, which is usually necessary since these patients are disruptive.

Thioridazine, which is highly sedative but has little tendency to evoke extrapyramidal reactions, has been the favored drug for treating these patients. This drug has at least three disadvantages, however: strong adrenergic-blocking effects that can lead to postural hypotension; strong anticholinergic effects that might aggravate the mental disorder; and possible cardiotoxicity. Recent studies have shown that high-potency neuroleptics, such as fluphenazine, haloperidol, and thiothixene, are equally effective and well tolerated (9). Most patients will respond to relatively low doses, which should always be used initially; a few will ultimately require fairly high doses before full symptomatic control is reached.

One drug combination used successfully to control "wild wanderers" is haloperidol, 3 mg, combined with lorazepam, 1 mg, three times daily. Antiparkinson drugs are added as needed. Control is rapid and any extrapyramidal syndromes are rapidly reversible (10). For long-term maintenance treatment, it may be advisable to try a depot preparation such as fluphenazine decanoate. Doses of 12.5 mg IM every two weeks have been reported to be safe and effective (11).

Possible Treatment Program for Senile Brain Disease

- Haloperidol 3 mg tid po.
- Diazepam 5 mg at night for sleep.
- When aberrant behavior is controlled, try a 6-month trial with dihydroergotoxine mesylate 6 mg daily.

"INTENSIVE CARE" PSYCHOSIS

The modern technology of medicine is awesome even to those of us close to it. For patients encountering it for the first time, especially when they are in a somewhat confused state—after triple bypass graft, for example—the encounter may be enough to evoke a transient psychotic state. The patient awakens in the intensive care unit only to find tubes in every orifice, including some that previously they did not know existed. Mental confusion with hallucinations can occur in patients who never before had shown the slightest mental abnormality. Similar changes have been seen in patients admitted to coronary care units (12).

One must take pains to rule out physical causes of the psychosis: abnormal electrolytes; silent bleeding; vascular accidents, such as a pulmonary embolus or stroke; various causes of hypoxemia; and drug reactions. Among the drugs to watch for are the atropine-like agents, cimetidine, lidocaine, and theophylline. Alcohol withdrawal also comes especially to mind. If the psychosis persists once these causes have been ruled out, treatment is truly needed,

The traditional sedative drugs, such as the benzodiazepines or barbiturates, make matters worse by increasing confusion. Low-potency antipsychotics, with their attendant strong antiadrenergic and anticholinergic actions, are also often contraindicated. The high-potency antipsychotics have produced the best results, with haloperidol being the one most commonly used.

Haloperidol has mild effects on circulation and respiration. Doses of 1 to 20 mg may be needed initially, depending on the patient's state and the severity of the reaction. Then one-half of the total dose required for control is given at bedtime or whenever agitation returns. Doses are tapered to 1 to 3 mg at night for two to three days after the patient has become completely clear. Then the drug can be discontinued.

DRUG-INDUCED PSYCHOSES

Alcohol

The social drug likely to be associated with emotional disturbance is alcohol, simply because of its widespread use. Some patients may become aggressive and abusive when acutely intoxicated, whereas others may have this response to relatively small amounts of alcohol, a form of pathological intoxication. Sedation is desirable but conventional sedative-hypnotics are usually not very effective—patients may be as tolerant of these drugs as they have become of alcohol. Further, the respiratory depressant effects of these drugs and alcohol, to which tolerance does not develop, may be addictive.

When such patients require sedation, a parenteral dose of a high-potency antipsychotic is generally effective—haloperidol, 5 mg IM, every 30 to 60 minutes until control is achieved. Usually no further treatment is needed once the effects of alcohol have passed.

The most common form of alcohol withdrawal syndrome is delirium tremens (DT). A patient with the full-blown syndrome does not seem to respond specifically to any drug treatment, but in those with incipient DT the conventional sedative-hypnotic drugs often stop its progression. Diazepam, given repeatedly in intravenous boluses of 10 mg followed by 5 mg every five minutes, can be titrated to produce the exact level of sedation desired. Once that level has been attained, the patient can be maintained with oral doses of this drug or some other (13). Milder cases of alcohol withdrawal may be treated with oral doses of sedative-hypnotics.

During withdrawal from alcohol, some patients retain a clear sensorium but have marked hallucinations, the so-called alcoholic hallucinosis. Many authorities believe that this occurs in patients vulnerable to schizophrenia who become psychotic under the stress of alcohol withdrawal or even heavy drinking. Treatment with conventional sedative-hypnotic drugs is not highly effective. Good responses are obtained with high-potency neuroleptics, however. The treatment program might be the same as that for acute alcoholic intoxication. Most patients require drug therapy only temporarily.

Stimulants

Prolonged use of amphetamines or cocaine may produce a paranoid psychosis that closely resembles paranoid schizophrenia. Usually, simple withdrawal of the drug will remedy the situation. If the psychosis is severe, however, antipsychotic drug treatment is warranted. Haloperidol is preferred over chlorpromazine since it does not interfere with the clearance of amphetamines from the brain.

Hallucinogens

Hallucinogens like LSD, mescaline, and psilocybin produce "bad trips" that are best managed by simple sedative-hypnotic drugs. When the sedated patient awakens, the effects of the hallucinogen have disappeared. Long-lasting psychoses associated with this class of hallucinogens are uncommon, and the general feeling is that their occurrence probably reflects incipient schizophrenia provoked by the drug. Thus, treatment would be the same as for any other type of schizophrenia.

Phencyclidine (PCP), currently the favored hallucinogen, is much more likely than other drugs to produce a state closely resembling schizophrenia. Such patients are difficult to control (14). Antipsychotic drugs are useful in the acute treatment of these disorders and may have to be maintained if the psychosis does not remit promptly after the effects of PCP have waned.

Continual gastric suction and acidification of the urine with ammonium chloride in doses of 1 to 2 g four times daily are effective ways to hasten the disappearance of PCP (15). The drug is secreted into the stomach from the blood and then reabsorbed through the enteric tract; gastric suction interferes with this gastroenteric recycling. Because PCP is a basic drug that remains ionized in an acid urine and thus is not reabsorbed by the kidney, its excretion is hastened by urine acidification.

CONCLUSION

Both psychiatric and medical illnesses may engender an acute psychosis with severe agitation that requires emergency treatment. Some of these psychoses are probably self-limited and therefore truly transient, while others need prompt and effective treatment. Antipsychotic drugs are required for most of these situations. Over the years, the advantages of high-potency drugs have reduced the use of the low-potency agents for this purpose, even though the latter are reputed to be more sedative. Now the drugs of choice for the various transient indications, high-potency drugs, such as haloperidol, thiothixene, and fluphenazine, can be safely and effectively given in large doses by either the oral or parenteral route.

REFERENCES

1. Donlon, P. T., and Tupin, J. P.: Rapid "digitalization" of decompensated schizophrenic patients with antipsychotic agents. *Am. J. Psychiat.*, 131: 310-312, 1974.
2. Donlon, P. T., Meadow, A., Tupin, J. P., et al.: High vs. standard dosage fluphenazine HCl in acute schizophrenia. *J. Clin. Psychiat.*, 39: 19-23, 1978.
3. National Institute of Mental Health—Psychopharmacology Service Center Collaborative Study Group: Phenothiazine treatment in acute schizophrenia. *Arch. Gen. Psychiat.*, 10: 246, 1964.

4. Gerstenzang, M. L., and Krulisky, T. V.: Parenteral haloperidol in psychiatric emergencies: Double-blind comparison with chlorpromazine. *Dis. Nerv. System*, 38: 581-583, 1977.
5. Stotsky, B.A.: Relative efficacy of parenteral haloperidol and thiothixene for the emergency treatment of acutely excited and agitated patients. *Dis. Nerv. System*, 38: 967-973, 1977.
6. Prien, R. F., Caffey, E. M., Jr., and Klett, C. J.: Comparison of lithium carbonate and chlorpromazine in the treatment of mania. *Arch. Gen. Psychiat.*, 26: 146-153, 1972.
7. Baastrup, P. C., Hollnagel, P., Sorensen, R., et al.: Adverse reactions in treatment with lithium carbonate and haloperidol. *JAMA*, 236: 2645-2646, 1976.
8. Gunderson, J. G., and Singer, M. T.: Defining borderline patients: An overview. *Am. J. Psychiat.*, 132: 1-10, 1975.
9. Branchey, M. H., Lee, J. H., Amin, R., et al.: High- and low-potency neuroleptics in elderly psychiatric patients. *JAMA*, 239: 1860-1862, 1978.
10. Fine, W., and Walker, D. J.,: Management of the elderly agitated demented patient. *Brit. Med. J.*, 2: 580, 1977.
11. Green, M. F.: Depot tranquillisers for disturbed behavior. *Brit. Med. J.*, 2: 1027, 1977.
12. Cassem, N. H., and Hackett, T. P.: Psychological aspects of a myocardial infarction. *Medical Clinics of North America*, 61: 711-721, 1977.
13. Thompson, W. L., Johnson, A. D., Maddrey, W. L. et al.: Diazepam and paraldehyde for treatment of severe delirium tremens. *Annals of Internal Medicine*, 82: 175-180, 1975.
14. Burns, R. S., Lerner, S.E., Corrado, R., et al.: Phencyclidine—States of acute intoxication and fatalities. *Western Journal of Medicine*, 123: 345-349, 1975.
15. Domino, E. F., and Wilson, A. E.: Effects of urine acidification in plasma and urine phencyclidine levels in overdose. *Clinical Pharmacological Therapy*, 22: 421-424, 1977.

Chapter 9

Transient Psychoses in Children and Adolescents

Gabriel V. Laury, M.D.

INTRODUCTION

Transient psychoses occurring in adults have been described and reported extensively in the medical literature.

In DSM-III (1), one can find the entries of schizophreniform disorder and brief reactive psychosis (both conditions can occur in adolescents). French psychiatrists make frequent use of the diagnosis of "bouffée délirante" (2). In recent articles, Cancro reports that a full and permanent recovery is a possible outcome for the schizophrenic patient (3, 4).

Complete recovery can occur in adolescents suffering from psychiatric disturbances of psychotic proportions. In other instances psychiatric disabilities of adolescence continue to manifest themselves as adult disabilities (5, 6).

Health professionals usually have difficulty accepting the diagnosis of childhood psychosis. They call it, somewhat euphemistically, "pervasive developmental disorders" (7). Cantor, however, deplores the

145

deletion of "childhood schizophrenia" from DSM-III (8). Transient psychoses, also known as prepsychotic states or "cas limités," have been only occasionally described in the literature (9), yet experienced physicians have witnessed normal individuals who had been formally diagnosed as psychotic when younger by respected and competent psychiatrists.

COMMON ERRORS OF DIAGNOSIS

Mental health professionals working with children and adolescents may make two errors when they examine a youngster who shows psychotic symptoms.

The first common error is to consider such symptoms as the first stage of an inexorable lifelong psychosis. The patient will then be labeled as schizophrenic and carry this stigma with him, possibly for the rest of his life (10). This attitude on the part of the therapist often causes a self-fulfilling prophecy. Once aware of the youngster's "final" diagnosis, health professionals, parents, school authorities, and the community at large will consider him/her as disturbed, regardless of his/her actual condition and daily functioning.

The child, too, will behave as "crazy" when everybody considers him or her to be so. In many instances, as he comes out of his psychotic episode, he may become depressed when he realizes that everybody around him is convinced that he will have, sooner or later, another emotional breakdown.

Another common error is to think wishfully that every youngster will someday outgrow his problems and deny available evidence that he is psychotic. It is understandable that a physician may be reluctant to brand forever the child as psychotic. He is right in believing that the condition may be transient, only a "passing phase," and that the youngster should be given another chance. However, when further episodes of decompensation take place, the therapist must be able to correctly diagnose and treat the child.

Physicians who fail to recognize or accept the severity of the young patient's psychopathology may consequently not treat the patient the way he or she should be treated. For instance, they do not prescribe the required antipsychotic medication, which might improve the patient's condition, or recommend a residential setting if this is the choice indicated.

In some instances, the parents do not want to hear that their child is psychotic. They may, however, accept a more innocuous label to characterize their child's symptoms. Thus, the physician may obtain better cooperation from the parents if he calls their psychotic child a "primary behavior disorder" or a "schizoid" or "borderline" personality. The result is that children, "officially" diagnosed as neurotic, are given major tranquilizers. This discrepancy between the official diagnosis and the treatment prescribed could lead the way to legal difficulties for the physician, who could be accused of malpractice if the patient showed adverse side effects from antipsychotic medication.

TRANSIENT PSYCHOSES IN CHILDREN AND ADOLESCENTS

Transient psychosis can occur in children and adolescents. The symptomatology can be quite severe. Yet, to the relief of the youngster, the family, and the physician, such a psychosis is only short-lived. Indeed, well-functioning adults can remember how "crazy" they were at a young age. Some were even able to hide their emotional difficulties from others. Some showed obvious signs of psychosis, but recovery occurred spontaneously or, more frequently, following therapy. Such psychosis can be functional or have an organic background.

FUNCTIONAL TRANSIENT PSYCHOSES

In many instances, the young patient's psychopathology comes to the attention of his physician. The latter, detecting symptoms of psychotic proportions, refers his patient, for confirmation of the diagnosis and treatment, to a psychiatrist in the community or even to a psychiatric institution. In some cases, the child may even be committed—generally at his parents' request—to a mental institution. Often, however, by the time the psychiatrist sees the patient, the symptoms may already have decreased or even disappeared and he or she appears to be normal.

Clinical Case #1

In the following instance, a florid psychotic symptomatology had a sudden onset, and a duration of about three weeks followed by recovery.

> Raoul is a married, 40-year-old lawyer who consults a psychiatrist for marital problems. He recalls that as a young adolescent, he went, on one occasion, through several weeks of disarray. He suddenly broke off with his friends and started fighting with other

children because he thought that they were spying on him. He heard God's voice telling him he was destined to become a prophet and saw a crucifix on the wall at night. He went on shoplifting sprees, stealing useless goods out of stores. He stole money from his parents as well as from their guests. He broke into a shoe repair store at night and took several pairs of boots. He started to drink and smoke. One evening, hearing God's voice and afraid of being detected smoking, he started a fire by hiding a lighted cigarette under a mattress.

He became depressed and convinced that he would end his life in a mental asylum or in a jail. He was getting bad marks in school. Afraid of his parents' reaction should they find out about his poor work, he decided to kill himself. On several occasions, he cut his wrist with a razor blade and bled slightly. However, as he lacked the courage to cut his wrist more deeply, he decided to jump out of the window of his third floor apartment. One foot on a chair, the other on the window sill, he was on the verge of jumping . . . but hesitated at the last moment. After a few weeks, his hallucinatory experiences disappeared and he gradually became his own self once more. Again, he functioned at a high level in all areas of his life and was sociable, pleasant, and respectful of other people's property.

His busy parents, involved in their work and active social life, never noticed any change in their son.

Clinical Case #2

In the following instance a possible cause for decompensation could be found. Psychopathology was severe but cleared after only two months of intensive psychotherapy and pharmacotherapy.

James was a 15-year-old adolescent in junior high school. A few months after his parents' separation, he suddenly began to accuse himself of being the cause of their marital difficulties. He would call his estranged father in the middle of the night to apologize for his behavior. He refused to talk to his former friends, persuaded that they were saying mean things about him behind his back. In school, he was convinced that he was not bright enough to compete with his peers and spent his time daydreaming. He complained that one teacher could read his mind and was aware of his sinful thoughts. At home, he was unable to concentrate on his homework.

One evening, he exposed himself to two women parked in a car. They called the police. When two policemen came to arrest him,

Jim suggested that they, too, should undress as a sign of humility, mortification, and brotherly love. By now, his alarmed parents took him for intensive psychotherapy, which lasted for about two months and was supplemented by psychotropic medication. After a slow start—caused by his initial unwillingness to cooperate with his therapist—he began to improve in all aspects of his functioning. The following term, he was back in school and socializing normally with his peers. Ten years later, James is a well functioning individual and has shown no recurrence of psychotic symptoms.

Differential Diagnosis and Prognosis

The differential diagnosis between long-term and transient psychoses is difficult to establish. In schizophrenia, for instance, one can often find a prepsychotic stage, as well as periods of remission and exacerbations (11). In fact, generally, only the natural history of the disorder will show whether it was transient. The odds are in favor of a psychosis being transient when:

- Its beginning is abrupt.
- It follows a major stress, such as the loss of a loved person, birth of a sibling, separation of parents or school difficulties.
- The youngster earlier has been mentally well-balanced.
- The family history is negative for mental illness.

On the other hand, the following factors are predictive of a severe and chronic psychosis:

- Low IQ.
- Severity of the illness from the very beginning.
- Language deficiency.
- Little or no schooling (12).

Other authors add to this list the presence of stereotypic movements and automutilation (13, 14) and the existence of psychotic signs at an early age (15). The prognosis for a child's emotional illness will also depend in large part on:

- His/her ability to engage meaningfully in a therapeutic relationship.
- His/her parents'—or parental surrogates'—ability to collaborate actively in the treatment process.

    • The treating physician's attitude toward the patient, the illness, and his/her ability to treat him.

Treatment

A psychosis should be treated as such. Psychotherapy and pharmacotherapy will be useful in the vast majority of cases. Whenever feasible, the child should continue to stay with his family.

Telling the Parents

The physician must be extremely careful and tactful in telling the family about their child's diagnosis and prognosis. He should certainly not give them false hopes. On the other hand, it would be highly unfair, if not cruel, to omit mentioning to them the possibility of improvement or even disappearance of their child's florid psychosis. The physician should avoid harboring an attitude of hopelessness and be open to the possibility that things may work out eventually. Otherwise, his/her pessimism may cause the realization of a self-fulfilling prophecy. Indeed, if the physician is convinced that the patient is doomed to a lifelong psychiatric disability, he/she will generally, and unknowingly, convince the child, as well as his/her family, that this is the only outcome.

TRANSIENT PSYCHOTIC DEPRESSION IN CHILDREN AND ADOLESCENTS

Does Depression Exist in Children and Adolescents?

It has been claimed that children's limited development makes it difficult for them to express feelings of major depression (7). Some physicians question the validity of childhood depression as a clinical entity (18), and show marked reluctance to accept such a diagnosis in young patients (17). Parents, too, are often unaware of their child's depression, even when severe. They appear genuinely surprised when the physician brings it to their attention.

Psychiatrists have frequently noticed the existence of depression and suicidal ideations in youngsters (20). These are often precipitated by "psychosocial stressors," e.g., the loss of a love object, feelings of rejection, and the existence of a debilitating condition. Such a traumatic event can be followed by a single short-lived episode of depression with eventual return to the earlier affective state. This condition seems closely related to the DSM-III diagnosis of "major depression, single episode."

Attachment Disorder of Infancy

Spitz was among the first in the U.S. to describe and document (anaclitic) depression (19). Today, the term "attachment disorder of infancy" is favored. In this condition, an infant separated from his mother displays severe symptoms of psychopathology: poverty of play, failure to thrive, regression in language and toilet functions, withdrawal, rocking, thumbsucking, and attempts at self-injury, such as headbanging. The early return of the mother, that is within a few days, will put an end to the above symptoms. When this return is out of the question, optimal substitute maternal care must be provided to avoid a worsening of the infant's condition (20).

Transient Depression in Children and Adolescents

Bowlby, in England, has pointed out the similarities between withdrawn and depressed behavior in young children and the mourning reaction in adults. He has also reported that the timely return of the love object can reverse severe symptoms of depression in the child (21). Anthony and Scott, studying manic-depressive psychosis in childhood, concluded that "it may be transiently manifested during childhood under strong physical or psychological pressure" (22).

Depression is common during adolescence. It may represent a manifestation of age-appropriate adjustment to the realities of growing up or an indication of a disabling psychiatric illness (23). It can be transient or long-lasting. Depression is a major cause of upheaval and problems for the young patient and his/her family. It can interfere with the patient's harmonious functioning, cause him/her to act out, and lead to suicide. Indeed, 12% of all suicide attempts are made by adolescents, and 10% of all people who commit suicide are under the age of 20. Many "accidents" in youngsters can represent a "suicidal equivalent" (24), e.g., a child taking an overdose of drugs from the medicine cabinet or the adolescent involved in a car crash.

Therapeutic Considerations

The physician must take seriously signs of depression, regardless of his patient's age. He will keep in mind that a serious depressive reaction can rapidly disappear, sometimes permanently. The disappearance may be spontaneous or may follow the judicious use of therapy.

The clinician should be careful not to unnecessarily "psychiatrize" his young patients, as they generally possess a strong potential for natural cure of depression. In addition, family intervention, coupled with the lowering of external stresses and demands, is often a major aspect of their treatment. If this therapeutic approach is insufficient, then anti-depressant drugs and psychotherapy are indicated.

TRANSIENT ORGANIC BRAIN SYNDROMES

Delirium can appear at any age, but is particularly frequent in children. In earlier classifications, it was called acute brain syndrome, acute confusional state, or toxic psychosis. It is reversible, and its duration is brief (generally less than a week) as opposed to dementia (chronic brain syndrome).

Its essential features are generally clouding of consciousness and disturbances in sleep/wake patterns. It is also characterized by perceptual disorders (such as hallucinations), an acute onset, and confused thinking. Delirium is also often associated with emotional disturbances.

Etiology

Delirium may be caused by numerous conditions, such as substance intoxication or withdrawal, physical illness, and metabolic disorders. Any febrile illness may, at times, produce a delirious reaction in children.

Substance Intoxication and Withdrawal

In children, mental disorders of psychotic proportions can be caused by numerous substances, such as alcohol, cannabis, amphetamines, phencyclidine (PCP), and volatile organic glues, whether used singly or in combination. Such disorders can occasionally be observed among adolescents in the infirmary of a large campus or in the emergency room of a general hospital. They can occur in an individual taking drugs or at the stage of withdrawal. Psychiatric medications, too, can cause delirious states in susceptible youngsters. Even over-the-counter preparations often found in homes have the potential for producing organic brain disorders when taken to excess (25). The psychotic symptoms frequently abate and disappear with the removal of the causative substance.

Amphetamine psychosis resembles a schizophrenic reaction, paranoid type. Its use occasionally starts as a diet aid, rather than being motivated by a search for a "high." Withdrawal can be associated with marked depression and suicidal thoughts.

Anamnesis, interviews with the patient, his friends or relatives, as well as a complete physical examination and laboratory tests, are helpful in establishing the diagnosis of organic psychosis. The health professional must remember that normal children may show hallucinations in the absence of any intake of drugs and that they should not be labeled ipso facto as psychotics (26-28).

Inhalation of Volatile Organic Glues

Glue sniffing, with its vivid hallucinations, is more common in children of low socioeconomic background. The following statements are from children who sniffed glue and subsequently displayed psychopathology of such magnitude that they were placed in psychiatric hospitals. Most of these children recovered within weeks. Those who returned to the community and resumed glue sniffing started hallucinating again (29).

> "When high on glue, I used to dream about my boyfriend and I also saw and heard the spirits with the ugly faces. I recall one time three of us were sniffing and we saw the same ghosts. I've never seen ghosts before I started sniffing. Once, high on glue, I felt like killing my ex-boyfriend and girlfriend because the voices had told me to do so."

> "When I was sniffing glue, I had visions of Christ and of Bishops and of Mary and of Joseph. Several times I had seen them before. At other times, I have seen these ghosts while on glue and they told me to go and kill my parents."

> "I had sniffed glue and I was going home. A straw duck with a long neck and a big face was chasing me down the block. I started running. I was scared. People were looking at me."

> "When I sniff glue, I start hearing and seeing spirits. They are always the same ones. There are good ones and bad ones. Once they told me to kill my girlfriend with a scissors and I was really thinking about doing it."

Clinical Case #3

> Freddy is an 11-year-old boy who has always functioned normally. One afternoon, he complains of ferocious itching, appears frightened, talks constantly, and refuses to leave his mother. Upon questioning, he tells her that menacing bugs are all around him.

He sees them clearly and describes them in minute detail. Convinced that thousands of bugs are crawling under his skin, he begs her to cut his skin open in order to remove them. That night, he refuses to turn off the light in his room, fearing that the bugs will overwhelm him once he is alone in the dark.

Taken to the emergency room of a prestigious university medical center, he is at first diagnosed as suffering from schizophrenia. An experienced child psychiatrist, however, after a lengthy anamnesis, prolonged questioning, and exhaustive physical examination, discovers that Freddy had surreptitiously taken drugs from the family medicine cabinet. These were anti-Parkinsonian drugs used by his grandfather. The physician reassured child and parents and 48 hours later the whole picture had cleared.

Physical Illness

Mental anomalies accompanying physical illness can be limited to a clouding of consciousness. In other instances, they can mimic a psychosis and be accompanied by regressive behavior. Such psychoses, writes Mayer-Gross, are "often very transient, sometimes lasting only for an hour or two" (30). In other cases, they may persist for days. They usually terminate without any serious sequelae.

In some instances, the child tends to cling to the regression and its advantages. Parents, too, may accpet the extension of secondary gains to the child. They are so glad he or she is doing better that they will spoil him/her a little longer. These regressive patterns are not psychotic in nature. Generally harmless and short-lived, they do not call for the prescription of psychotic medication.

REFERENCES

1. *Diagnostic and Statistical Manual of Mental Disorders, Third Edition. (DSM-III).* Washington, D.C.: American Psychiatric Association, 1980.
2. Kroll, J.: Philosophical foundations of French and U.S. nosology. *Am. J. Psychiat.,* 136: 1135-1138, 1979.
3. Cancro, R.: Overview of schizophrenia. In H.I. Kaplan et al. (Eds.), *Comprehensive Textbook of Psychiatry.* Baltimore: Williams and Wilkins, 1980.
4. Kaplan, H.I., and Sadock, B.: *Modern Synopsis of Psychiatry.* 3rd ed. Baltimore: Williams and Wilkins, 1982.
5. Masterson, J.F.: *The Psychiatric Dilemma of Adolescence.* Boston: Little, Brown, 1967.
6. Offer, D., and Offer, J.: Three developmental routes through normal male adolescence. In: S. Feinstein and P. Giovacchini (Eds.), *Adolescent Psychiatry.* New York: Jason Aronson, 1976.
7. Ambrosini, P., and Puig-Antich, J.: Childhood major depressive disorder. *The Bulletin of the Area II Council of the American Psychiatric Association,* 24, 6: 10, May-June 1982.

8. Cantor, S. et al.: Childhood schizophrenia: Present but not accounted for. *Am. J. Psychiat.*, 139: 758-762, 1982.

9. Bender, L.: Twenty years of clinical research on schizophrenic children. In: C. Caplan (Ed.), *Emotional Problems of Early Childhood.* New York: Basic Books, 1955.

10. Loman, L.A., and Larkin, W.E.: Rejection of the mentally ill: An experiment in labeling. *Sociological Quarterly,* 17, 4: 555-560, 1976.

11. Heuyer, G.: *Introduction à la Psychiatrie Infantile.* Paris: PUF, 1969.

12. Rutter, M. et al.: A five to fifteen year follow-up study of infantile psychosis: II. social and behavioral outcome. *Brit. J. Psychiat.*, 113: 1183-1199, 1967.

13. De Ajuriaguerra, J.: *Manuel de Psychiatrie de l'Enfant.* Paris: Masson, 1970.

14. Bollea, G.: Prognostic des psychoses infantiles, numéro spécial, IV Congrès de Psychiatrie, Sandorama, 1966.

15. Lemay, M.: *Psychopathologie Juvenile.* Paris: Fleurus, 1973.

16. Kashani, J.H. et al.: Current perspectives on childhood depression: An overview. *Am. J. Psychiat.*, 138: 143-153, 1981.

17. Froese, A. P.: Pediatric referrals to psychiatry. III: Is the psychiatrist's opinion heard? *International Journal of Psychiatry in Medicine,* 8, 3: 295-301, 1977-78.

18. Poznanski, E.O.: The clinical phenomenology of childhood depression. *Am. J. Orthopsychiat.*, 52: 308-313, 1982.

19. Spitz, R.A.: Anaclitic depression. *Psychoanalytical Study of the Child,* 2: 313, 1946.

20. Freud, A., and Burlingham, D.: *Infants Without Families.* New York: International Universities Press, 1944.

21. Robertson, B.M., and Bowlby, J.: Responses of young children to separation from their mothers. *Courrier du Centre International de l'Enfance,* 2: 131-142, 1952.

22. Anthony, E. J., and Scott, P.: Manic-depressive psychosis in childhood. *Journal of Child Psychology and Psychiatry and Allied Disciplines,* 1: 53-72, 1960.

23. Easson. W.M.: Depression in adolescence In: S. Feinstein and P. Giovacchini (Eds.), *Adolescent Psychiatry.* Vol. V. New York: Jason Aronson, 1971.

24. Gossner, E.: Depression and suicide in childhood and adolescence. *Carrier Foundation Letter,* 80: 1-4, May 1982.

25. Fauman, M.A.: Drug history essential in emergency room syndrome triage. *Psychiatric News,* April 2, 1982, 18-19.

26. Wilking, V., and Paoli, C.: The hallucinatory experience. *Journal of the Academy of Child Psychiatry,* 5, 3: 431-440, 1966.

27. Bender, L.: Twenty years of clinical research on schizophrenic children. In: C. Caplan (Ed.), *Emotional Problems of Early Childhood.* New York: Basic Books, 1965.

28. Rothstein, A.: Hallucinatory phenomena in childhood: A critique of the literature. *Journal of the American Academy of Child Psychiatry,* 20: 623-635, 1981.

29. Preble, E., and Laury, G.V.: Plastic cement: The ten cent hallucinogen. *International Journal of the Addictions,* 2: 271-281, 1967.

30. Mayer-Gross, W., Slater, E., and Roth, M.: *Clinical Psychiatry.* Baltimore: Williams and Wilkins, 1969.

Chapter 10

Psychoses and Agitated States in the Elderly

Randall Christenson, M.D., and
Dan Blazer, M.D., Ph.D.

INTRODUCTION

Transient psychotic episodes and agitated states are common in the elderly. As the population grows older, the number of elderly persons with these mental disorders will multiply significantly and increasing numbers of mental health workers will be called upon to evaluate and treat these individuals. Fortunately, patients with these disorders usually improve with proper management. However, many clinicians assume that mental disorders in the elderly are chronic and minimally responsive to treatment. This therapeutic nihilism results in treatable disorders being overlooked. Those aged with chronic disorders, such as dementia, may also suffer from a treatable superimposed disorder that aggravates the primary symptoms and increases morbidity. Thus, knowledge of reversible psychiatric disorders in the elderly, along with

156

a high index of clinical suspicion, can result in reduction of symptoms and morbidity in many psychotic and agitated elderly patients.

Although older patients tend to seek psychiatric care less often than younger patients, it is estimated that at least 15% have some degree of psychiatric impairment (1). Several factors play a role in the vulnerability of the elderly to psychiatric disorder. They often suffer from increased loss of loved ones, general decline in their functional ability, and social isolation, all of which heighten their susceptibility to mental disorders. The aging process itself may also play a role in this increased vulnerability.

Delirium, major affective disorders, and paranoid disorders account for the vast majority of transient psychotic episodes and agitated states in the elderly. There is significant overlap between the presenting symptoms of these three conditions, necessitating a thorough and careful evaluation for proper diagnosis and effective therapeutic intervention. For example, a patient presenting with the complaint that his neighbors are harassing him to the point that he must move could be delirious, psychotically depressed, or functionally paranoid. A decline in cognitive function is often seen in depression as well as delirium. The purpose of this chapter is to describe these three disorders and their management. Features in clinical presentation or management that are unique or more common in the elderly are given particular attention.

Before describing the disorders themselves, certain guidelines should be stated that will aid the clinician in overcoming barriers to communication with the elderly during an evaluation. Many elderly patients have a high anxiety level, which is heightened by interacting with the clinician, and this may inhibit the patient's cognitive functioning. Problems with hearing and vision decrease the patient's ability to perceive and may result in distortions of the clinician's questions. Older patients also tend to be cautious and may omit important information. Transference factors may also impede effective communication. The older person may view the clinician as a parent figure, leading to increased dependency, or as a child figure, leading to instruction-giving or a condescending approach. Negative transference reactions often develop when the patient is forced by family members to see the clinician. The clinician must also be aware of his or her own attitudes toward the elderly, such as his or her fear of aging. Countertransference issues around conflict with parents or grandparents and the clinician's lack of understanding about what it means to grow old may also hinder the evaluation and treatment process. (2).

Several techniques are useful in facilitating communication with the elderly. It is important to approach the person with respect. Using last names is preferable to calling the patient by his or her first name or calling him or her grandpa or grandma. Assuming a position near the person and the careful use of touch often facilitate communication, as does speaking clearly and slowly. Inquiry into presenting problems should be actively and systematically sought, and the patient should be given ample time to answer the questions. Elderly patients often need more time to respond than younger ones. Attention to nonverbal behavior provides important clues to understanding the patient that might not be expressed verbally. (2).

DELIRIUM

Delirium is the most common transient psychosis in the elderly and thus it is essential for the mental health worker to recognize the disorder and to secure proper treatment for the patient. This organic disorder, also known as acute confusional state or acute brain syndrome, is characterized by acute or subacute onset of global cognitive dysfunction due to disturbances in brain metabolism. Disturbances in memory, thinking, attention, and perception decrease the patient's ability to comprehend and appropriately act upon environmental cues. The course is marked by fluctuations in level of impairment, which is often worse at night, and results in either complete recovery or progression to some level of irreversible cognitive impairment, such as dementia, or to coma and death.

The Epidemiology of Delirium

The epidemiology of delirium is not well established. Bedford (3), in a study of 5,000 patients at the Oxford Geriatric Unit, a general medical hospital, found that 80% were mentally confused. In a study of all patients over the age of 60 admitted to San Francisco General Hospital, Simon and Cahan (4) found that 13% had an acute brain syndrome in the absence of a chronic brain disorder. Another 40% had both acute and chronic brain disorders. The patients with only acute brain disorders were younger and suffered from alcohol or drug abuse and malnutrition. The mixed group was older and most frequently suffering from cardiovascular disease and malnutrition. Seymour et al. (5) found that 16% of the patients over 70 years old admitted to a general medical unit had an acute confusion state. Titchener et al. (6) studied psychological reactions of geriatric patients to surgery. They observed that about 25% had acute organic psychosis and over half of these progressed to a chronic mental deterioration. From these data it is apparent that the incidence of delirium in elderly patients admitted to the hospital is high.

There are several reasons for the higher prevalence of delirium in the elderly. First, the older person is more likely to develop cerebral pathology and normally has less reserve capacity, which lowers the threshold for development of delirium. Impaired cerebral circulation increases vulnerability to hypoxia. The elderly are also more susceptible to illnesses and thus have a higher incidence of chronic disease, resulting in more episodes of illness that may produce delirium. Elders are also more sensitive to medications that can cause cerebral dysfunction. Unfortunately, many of these medications are often needed to treat the diseases associated with delirium.

The Etiology of Delirium

Several factors, environmental as well as organic, play a role in the development of delirium in the elderly. The organic etiologies are no different in the elderly than in other age groups. However, certain etiological factors are more commonly seen in the geriatric population. Cardiovascular disorders, malnutrition, infection, and alcohol have been shown to be the most common factors associated with delirium in the elderly. Adverse drug reactions are also a common cause of cognitive impairment. Krakowski and Langlais (7) report that admission to a hospital, anesthesia, and surgery are the most common causes of acute psychiatric disturbance among hospitalized elderly. Etiological factors associated with delirium in the aged are listed in Table 1.

Decreased drug metabolism and increased drug sensitivity render the elderly more susceptible to the toxic effects of medications. Benzodiazepines and other sedative hypnotics depress cerebral activity and exacerbate cognitive dysfunction. Medications with anticholinergic properties such as tricyclic antidepressants, antipsychotics, and anti-Parkinsonian drugs can cause an atropine-like psychosis with confusion and hallucinations. Postural hypotension, a side effect of some psychotropic and antihypertensive medications, can contribute to cognitive impairment. Electrolyte disturbances from diuretics and digitalis toxicity may present as confusion. Narcotics, steroids, and L-dopa can cause psychosis. Older persons are more sensitive to the bromides, which continue to be in

TABLE 1
Etiology of Delirium in Late Life

---

1. Drugs: sedatives-hypnotics, antipsychotic agents; tricyclic antidepressants;
   lithium; narcotic analgesics, such as propoxyphene and pentazocine;
   antihypertensives; anticholinergics; diuretics; digitalis; antiparkinsonian drugs; chlorpropamide; cimetidine; steroids; indomethacin; cancer
   chemotherapeutics; L-dopa; bromides.
2. Alcohol intoxication and withdrawal.
3. Dehydration and metabolic disorders: especially electrolyte imbalance; hepatic encephalopathy; renal failure; respiratory failure; endocrinopathies; hypothermia and hyperthermia; hypoglycemia and hyperglycemia.
4. Cardiopulmonary disorders: cardiac failure; arrhythmia; myocardial infarction; pulmonary embolism.
5. Cerebrovascular disorders: stroke; transient ischemic attack; subdural hematoma; cranial arteritis; cerebral vasculitis.
6. Infection, especially pumonary or renal; meningitis and/or encephalitis; bac-
   teremia.
7. Neoplasm: intracranial, extracranial.
8. Nutritional disorders, Vitamin B-complex deficiency.
9. Head trauma, burns.
10. Epilepsy.
11. Surgery.

Adapted from Lipowski, Z. J. (39).

some over-the-counter medications. Many "tonics" contain a significant
amount of alcohol, which either singly or in combination with other
drugs may result in an intoxication and symptoms of delirium.

Typical signs and symptoms of medical disorders may be absent in
the elderly. Instead, these disorders may present as withdrawal, apathy,
or cognitive impairment. Such patients are also susceptible to dehydration and electrolyte disturbances which exacerbate the cerebral dysfunction. Any cardiovascular or pulmonary disorder that causes cerebral
ischemia or hypoxia can cause mental confusion, as can any cerebrovascular disorder. Infections, especially pulmonary or renal, metabolic
disorders, neoplasms, trauma, and malnutrition such as vitamin B complex deficiency are common etiologic factors of delirium.

Environmental factors often exacerbate mental confusion in the elderly. A change in environment, often necessary to provide medical
care, may worsen confusion, especially in individuals already vulnerable
to delirium. Decreased vision and hearing augment disorientation, as
does the anxiety generated by the illness and the patient's difficulty in
processing a new environment.

The Clinical Presentation of Delirium

The clinical presentation of delirium varies considerably. Disturbances in attention, cognition, perception, motor behavior, and the sleep cycle are the main clinical features. There is usually, but not always, a rapid onset of symptoms. A fluctuating clinical course is a hallmark of the disorder, during which certain personality factors are exaggerated.

The patient may complain of mild confusion, lethargy, restlessness, insomnia, or vivid nightmares. These give way to more severe symptoms, which are often first noticed at night. Changes in the level of consciousness occur with either an increase in arousal or, as commonly seen in the elderly, quiet withdrawal. As the clouding of consciousness progresses, the patient's ego defenses break down and he or she may experience anxiety, depression, or paranoia. With further changes in level of consciousness, the thought processes become more disorganized, with a decrease in the ability to interpret correctly and act purposefully on the environment.

A disturbance in orientation is a hallmark of delirium and easily tested clinically. Orientation to time is followed by loss of orientation to place. When the delirium is more severe, patients may misidentify people, although rarely will they not know their own identity. Most patients have lucid intervals during which they are oriented. Patients generally have additional memory problems as well, especially in recent memory. Any preexisting dementia confounds the orientation and memory impairment.

Patients often have difficulty attending to the environment, as evidenced by decreased concentration, increased distractibility, and difficulty fixing attention on relevant stimuli. Thought progression is slowed and irrational; primary process thinking may intrude. Associated are disturbances in perception. Delirious patients also experience illusions and hallucinations. Hallucinations tend to be visual but may affect any sensory modality. The elderly are reported to have fewer hallucinations than younger age groups (4, 8).

Disturbances in motor activity are frequently seen. Psychomotor behavior ranges from extreme hyperactivity with agitated, aggressive, excited behavior to extreme hypoactivity with lethargy, passivity, and general immobility. Within the course of the illness, the patient's activity level may vary considerably. Hyperactivity is more commonly associated with drug withdrawal, while hypoactivity is more common in delirium from other causes (9). Hypoactivity presents less of a behavioral problem and may, therefore, be overlooked.

Speech is also affected. It may be either rapid and pressured or slow and hesitant. Indistinct or slurred speech is common in the elderly. Other symptoms seen more often in the elderly include tremor, usually course and irregular, and urinary incontinence. Asterixis, seen mainly in severe metabolic disturbances, and multifocal myoclonic jerks also occur in delirium.

Sleep cycle changes are almost always present and manifested in several ways. There may be no discernible cycle with the patient napping irregularly or hardly sleeping at all. The cycle may be reversed, with the patient showing drowsiness and sleep during the daytime and insomnia at night.

By definition delirium is a transient disorder. It results in one of three possible outcomes. These are complete recovery, progression, or transition to a nonreversible process or death. Studies of the mortality associated with delirium in the elderly report between 17% and 33% die in the first month (3, 4). Most who recover do so in two to four weeks, although return to a full premorbid level of functioning may take much longer. The rate of progression to a nonreversible disorder is unknown.

The diagnosis of delirium is usually made clinically on the basis of the symptoms described above. The evaluation of delirium includes a history and physical examination to establish the diagnosis and ascertain the underlying cause(s). Mental status exams should assess the patient's attention, affect, orientation, memory, perception, and psychomotor activity. Laboratory tests should include electrolytes, blood gases, liver function tests, appropriate cultures, and drug and alcohol screens when appropriate. The history and physical exam may suggest that other laboratory tests are necessary to establish the etiology. EEG is useful when the diagnosis is in doubt or if a structural disorder is suspected. Slowing of the EEG is the usual finding.

In the elderly the main diagnostic difficulty is separating delirium from dementia. Patients may have a dementia with a delirium superimposed. Simon and Cahan (4) found that 75% of those in their study with acute brain disorders also had a chronic brain disorder. As delirium is reversible with treatment, the differential diagnosis of any global cognitive impairment must include delirium. These clues help differentiate the two disorders: Acute onset, fluctuations in orientation, awareness, attention and perception and disturbances in the sleep-wake cycle all suggest delirium. Dementia tends to have a gradual onset, fewer fluctuations in the course, and fewer sleep-wake cycle disturbances.

There is no evidence that Alzheimer's disease itself can cause delirium. However, some Alzheimer's patients show an increase in confusion at

night, often referred to as "sundowning." Sensory deprivation and sleep
cycle changes have been postulated as etiologic factors in these disturbances.

The Treatment of Delirium

Management of delirium involves a multifaceted approach. First, the
underlying cause must be diagnosed and treated. Gradual withdrawal
of all non-essential medications will reverse many deliriums. Second,
any exacerbating factors, such as hypoxia, dehydration or electrolyte
disturbances, should be corrected. Perhaps most important in reduction
of symptoms is providing good general medical and nursing care. Hospital rooms should be kept quiet and well lighted during the daytime
and dimly lighted at night. A radio or television adds sensory stimulation, which may be especially useful at night. A calendar and clock
improve orientation. Reassurance, careful and repetitive explanations
by personnel of procedures, and reorientation by all the medical staff
are essential to minimize confusion and anxiety. The presence of a relative or friend in the room often provides a sense of familiarity and
security.

Vital signs, careful observations, and serial mental status exams are
essential in monitoring the patient's progress and detecting any sudden
decline in his/her condition. Patients who are agitated, restless or fearful
may need sedation to protect against injury. In the elderly patient, small
doses of haloperidol 0.5 to 2 mg is favored by many because of its low
anticholinergic and hepatotoxic effects. Thioridazine is more sedating
but has higher anticholinergic effects. Physostigmine is the treatment
of choice for anticholinergic delirium and benzodiazepines are used in
hepatic encephalopathy.

AFFECTIVE DISORDERS

Affective disorders, including both major depressive disorders and
bipolar disorders, constitute another major diagnostic category of reversible psychoses seen in the elderly. Since depressive symptoms are
frequently seen in older persons, one must distinguish normal fluctuations in mood (i.e., dysphoria) from the major affective disorders. Affective disorders often present with different manifestations from those
typically seen in younger age groups. Both depression and mania in the
elderly will be described, focusing primarily on those features unique
to the elderly.

The Epidemiology of Late Life Affective Disorders

Depression is one of the most common psychiatric disorders in late life. In a community survey, Blazer and Williams (10) found that nearly 15% of the elderly had significant dysphoric symptoms and about 4% had symptoms of a major depressive disorder. Several studies show that anywhere from 30% to over 50% of patients admitted to psychogeriatric wards have a severe depression (10). The incidence of mania is less certain. The community prevalence of manic disorders is estimated between 1 and 2% in the elderly (11). Post (12) found that between 6.5% and 18% of hospitalized geriatric cases with affective disorders had manic symptoms.

The Etiology of Late Life Affective Disorders

Depression has multiple causes that encompass the biological, psychological, and social dimensions of human existence. Major affective disorders have a genetic predisposition. Some studies suggest that this is a less important factor in the elderly than in younger patients. Functional deficiencies in the amine neurotransmitter system, especially serotonin and norepinephrine, are currently the most accepted biological mechanisms for depressive disorders. An increase in MAO levels in the brain (13) and other changes in the synthesis, activity, and degradation of biogenic amines in the elderly may contribute to the increased incidence in this population (14). Kupfer and Foster (15) have shown that depressed patients show a decreased latency in the onset of REM sleep. Sleep patterns change with aging, although it is not clear what role this plays in the depressed elderly.

Loss plays an essential role in the genesis of depression in the elderly. Loss is ubiquitous in the life of the older person and involves not only loss of loved ones but perhaps more importantly loss of one's function and security, including declining health, decrease in control over one's life, decrease in productivity, and often a decrease in status and/or financial resources. Loss is thought to contribute to depression by decreasing self-esteem (16), by increasing negative cognitions in the depression prone (17), and by facilitating learned helplessness by decreasing one's sense of control over one's life in the environment (18). The recognition of one's weakness and inability to supply necessary needs and drives and defend against threats to security results in a loss of self-esteem, a major psychodynamic in the depressed aged (19). Social factors thought to contribute to depression include social isolation, with decreased social support systems and increases in stressful life events.

The Clinical Presentation of Late Life Affective Disorders

The classical clinical presentation of depression is a pervasive mood of sadness, hopelessness, or irritability, accompanied by a loss of interest in the usual activities and an inability to derive pleasure from life. Disturbances in sleep, appetite with weight changes, sexual drive, concentration, energy levels, and psychomotor activity are typically associated with this disorder. These patients have decreased self-esteem, feel worthless, and have excessive guilt feelings. They feel helpless and hopeless about the future and they may see this as the fate they deserve. Suicidal ideation and behavior are common among severely depressed patients and the risk of the patient's actually committing suicide increases during the early recovering phase, when the patient has more energy to commit the act. Successful suicide is far more common among elderly white males than among any other group in North America. Paranoid delusions, poverty of ideas, and a delusional degree of lowered self-esteem are seen in psychotically depressed patients.

Although depression in the elderly often presents in the same way it does in younger patients, there appears to be a significant number of depressed aged whose depression is manifest in ways different from the younger population. Because of this, many potentially treatable depressive disorders in the elderly are overlooked. Elderly patients demonstrate less guilt and internalized anger and more feelings of emptiness, unwarranted pessimism about the future, self-blame, and increased apathy. In fact, apathy and withdrawal from usual activities may be the only clue that the patient is depressed. Depressed elders tend to be more agitated (12) and more commonly lose weight (20).

Atypical presentations of depression include hypochondriasis, pseudodementia, pain, and the late onset of alcohol abuse. De Alarcon found that 63% of depressed patients in his study showed hypochondriasis (21). For 25% of these patients, hypochondriasis was the dominant symptom. Only 19% of these, however, expressed a lifelong concern about health. Another common atypical presentation is pseudodementia, i.e., the patient presents with symptoms similar to dementia (22). These patients appear to suffer from significant memory loss, but tend to answer "I don't know" to questions during the mental status exam. Demented patients will give more near-miss answers. Most of these patients also exhibit marked dependency for physical care and emotional support. A trial of antidepressants may be necessary to make the diagnosis. Williamson (23) reports that localized pain may be a primary symptom of depression even with denial of depressed mood or other depressive symptoms. These patients are obsessional, careful, self-demanding people whose pain serves as a self-punishment for the inability to achieve unrealistic goals. Recent development of alcoholism or other drug abuse may be an indication of depression as well. One must especially consider this diagnosis in the person who begins drinking excessively for the first time in late life.

As with depression, mania can present in a typical fashion or in an atypical one. The typical symptoms are the mirror image of depressive symptoms and include elation or euphoria, increased self-esteem and confidence, delusions of omnipotence, psychomotor overactivity, overproductive speech, flight of ideas, and increases in appetite, energy, and libido. In the elderly, overactivity is not as pronounced, speech tends to be circumstantial, obsessive thought patterns occur, and paranoid delusions are common. Irritability and anger occur more frequently than euphoria. A mixed presentation of manic and depressive symptoms is not uncommon. Shulman and Post (24) have noted a higher incidence of cerebral organic disorders in males who have manic episodes after 60 years of age.

The Diagnosis of Late Life Affective Disorders and Differential Diagnosis

The diagnosis of affective disorders is based on the history and mental status examination, with emphasis on the assessment of the potential for suicide. A medication history is also important, as many medications, including several nondiuretic antihypertensives, L-dopa, and steroids, can cause depression. Laboratory diagnostic aids are currently being developed. Thus far the one most useful clinically is dexamethasone-suppression test (25).

Sleep EEG studies and urinary amine metabolites, MHPG, and 5-HIAA may have clinical utility as well in the future. In addition to major depressive disorders, late life bereavement, dysthymic disorders, and depressive neurosis produce depressive symptomatology.

Differential diagnosis for depression includes organic affective disorder secondary to hypothyroidism, Cushing's disease, occult malignancy, vitamin deficiency syndrome or mass lesions of the brain, somatoform disorders (hypochondriasis), paranoid disorders, dementia, and sleep disorders. It is possible to have a major affective disorder in addition to one of these as well. For example, depression is fairly common in mild to moderate dementia (26). A differential for mania includes agitated depression, organic mental disorders (dementia and delirium), drug-induced psychosis, hyperthyroidism, schizoaffective disorders, catatonic excitement, and the hypomanic phase of the cyclothymic disorder.

The clinical course of the major affective disorder is typically one of recurrent episodes. Patients experiencing a depressive disorder when younger may have a recurrence of depression or a first manic episode 10 to 20 years later, not infrequently in late life (24). Episodes of affective psychosis tend to become more frequent, more severe, and more protracted with increasing age (12). In two studies of elderly depressed patients, Post (12, 27) found that less than one-third had lasting recovery at either three- or six-year follow-up. In his later study, 37% had further attacks with good recoveries, 25% had some degree of depressive invalidism, usually with further attacks, and 12% were continuously ill.

The Treatment of Late Life Affective Disorders

For the severely depressed patient, management involves multiple therapeutic interventions, including psychotherapy and some somatic therapy. Generally, the severely depressed patient responds best to an empathic supportive therapy that focuses on the here and now, in which the clinician emphasizes concern and understanding, while assuring control of the situation and the hope for improvement. More insight-oriented individual, group, or family therapies that address the psychological factors involved in the development of the depression can be initiated after the patient has sufficiently improved to benefit from them. Enhancement of self-esteem and working-through of loss are important issues for psychotherapy. Social interventions aimed at decreasing social isolation and increasing the patient's activity level in the community are often helpful once the patient has recovered enough to carry out these activities.

The mainstay of somatic treatments for depression is the tricyclic antidepressants (TCA). Those patients with "biological signs" (sleep, appetite, and psychomotor disturbances), pervasive dysphoria, clear onset, a history of previous improvement or family history of response are those most likely to respond. Depressive symptoms integral to another psychiatric disorder, chronic depressive symptoms, previous multiple drug failures, or prominent hysterical features tend to be less responsive (28). The tertiary amines appear best for agitated depressions and the secondary amines are more useful for retarded depression, though further research is needed to confirm this impression. Clinicians should start with low doses, often one-third to one-half that given to younger patients, and build up slowly. The aged are more sensitive to the many side effects of TCAs. Anticholinergic effects can result in aggravation of glaucoma, urinary retention (especially in males with benign prostatic hypertrophy), constipation, confusion, blurred vision, and dry mouth.

Cardiac side effects due to alpha adrenergic blockade and a quinidine-like effect result in postural hypotension, widened QRS complexes on the EKG, and arrhythmias. Great caution must be exercised when using these medications in those particularly susceptible, that is, those with cardiac disease, narrow angle glaucoma and benign prostatic hypertrophy. For cases unresponsive to TCAs, or when TCAs are contraindicated, or when rapid improvement due to a high suicide potential is needed, electroconvulsive therapy is indicated. With modern anesthesia and muscle relaxation, this treatment is safe and effective. Reversible memory deficits, however, frequently accompany the treatment. Monoamine oxidase (MAO) inhibitors are also effective in treating depression, although usually reserved for use if TCAs have been ineffective. Patients taking MAO inhibitors must be on a special tyramine free diet to avoid the possibility of a hypertensive crisis.

The somatic treatment of manic patients involves the use of antipsychotics and lithium carbonate. Antipsychotic agents control the acute manic symptoms, and lithium carbonate prevents the recurrence of manic symptoms. After screening with a 24-hour creatinine clearance, the medication can be started in low doses and gradually increased to the target blood levels of .5 to .8 mEq/liter, keeping the blood level less than 1.0 mEq/liter. 450 to 600 mg of lithium carbonate per day is a usual dose in the very old. The daily maximum is 900 mg per day (29).

PARANOID DISORDERS

Paranoid symptoms and behavior are fairly common in the elderly. These symptoms, which range from mild suspiciousness to psychotic delusional symptoms, cause considerable problems for those who must relate to and provide care for the elderly. Generally the patients are brought for an evaluation only when their symptoms are severe enough to arouse the concern of family, neighbors, or nursing home personnel. Those who are just suspicious generally do not come to the attention of the medical health worker.

The Epidemiology of Late Life Paranoid Disorders

Suspiciousness and paranoid ideation are thought to occur frequently among the elderly, although definite epidemiological data are lacking at this time. Lowenthal (30), in a study of 530 patients admitted for psychiatric screening at a San Francisco general hospital, found that 205 patients had suspiciousness by history. However, only six were predominantly characterized as suspicious and 14 were diagnosed as having a functional paranoid disorder. Several European studies indicate that around 10% of the first psychiatric geriatric admissions are for functional paranoid disorders (31).

The Etiology and Clinical Presentation of Late Life Paranoid Disorders

Persecutory ideas and delusions are symptoms and not a disorder per se. The symptoms can arise from affective disorders (both depressed and manic), delirium, and dementia, as well as from various paranoid disorders. Although there is currently no consensus about classification of paranoid disorders in the elderly, four subtypes, based primarily on Post's work, will be presented. The mildest is suspiciousness, in which the patients have vague complaints about external forces controlling their lives. Paranoid hallucinosis, which tends to be a transient paranoid reaction, involves a more focused complaint and often is accompanied by hallucinations. Paraphrenia or schizophreniform illness is a more severe form in which the patients have persectory beliefs, such as ideas of observation, in addition to hallucinations and disordered thinking. Paranoid schizophrenia is the most severe paranoid disorder, in which first-rank Schneiderian symptoms (ideas of reference, influence phenomena, etc.) are manifest, as well as delusions and hallucinations. There is debate as to whether this disorder, when it first develops in the elderly, is the same as seen in younger patients. This section will focus on the transient paranoid reactions and briefly touch on organic causes of paranoia.

Although paranoid reactions are seen throughout the life cycle, there is some evidence that they are more common in the elderly (32). Several factors appear to be associated with this increased vulnerability. Social isolation, increased loss in interpersonal relationships, sensory loss (especially in hearing), decreases in a sense of security, medical illness, and the aging process itself are all believed to increase susceptibility to paranoid ideation. Many of these factors which decrease the patient's control over the environment are not controllable by the individual. The older person, in an attempt to explain the losses, may regress to more primitive defenses and externalize the fault as belonging to others rather than to self. Busse and Pfeiffer (33) indicate that projection may be used more frequently by the elderly, as the more complex and highly focused defenses are no longer available to them. Projection may also serve a reconstructive function in those with decreased vision or hearing.

According to Post (34), the most common paranoid symptomatology in the elderly is paranoid hallucinosis. The paranoid thinking is narrow, well focused and often directed toward persons or situations geographically or emotionally close to the individual. Common examples include delusions that someone has stolen or rearranged the individual's personal possessions or that the neighbors are harassing him. Those with hearing impairment may perceive interfering voices from next door. These may be accompanied by visual or, more commonly, auditory hallucinations. There usually is no evidence of other thought disorder or of a more complex delusional system, such as an organized plot against the patient. These symptoms, which are quite disturbing to the patient and those around him or her, can often be understood in terms of the patient's personality and life situation. Social isolation, which is often increased by these symptoms, is a frequent precipitant of paranoid reactions, especially when combined with physical impairment or sensory loss. Other stresses, such as a loss of spouse or job and any failure that decreases self-esteem and increases insecurity, may precipitate a paranoid reaction. Schapira (35) believes that many older people suffering from paranoid reactions have lifelong abnormal personality traits. Paranoid personalities are characterized by oversensitivity, suspiciousness, poor self-esteem, hostility, eccentricity, and rigidity. Their object relations tend to be poor and they use projection as a defense mechanism.

Paranoid ideation and paranoid hallucinosis can be associated with delirium and other medical illnesses. Any of the etiological factors associated with delirium can cause paranoid symptoms. Neurological disorders including temporal lobe epilepsy, endocrine disorders including Addison's disease, hyperparathyroidism, hyperthyroidism, and infectious disease can cause paranoid reactions. Alcohol and drug abuse, including bromides and barbiturates, may result in paranoid symptoms. Amphetamine-like compounds found in decongestants, phenylpropanolamine, and propylhexedrine have been associated with paranoid symptoms (36). Anticholinergic medications, levodopa, and steroids are also known to cause paranoid reactions.

When a patient presents with acute persecutory ideas or suspiciousness, one first must determine whether the patient's complaints are paranoid or whether they are accurate. Given the frequent bias against the elderly, the individual's suspicions may be in reaction to a realistic assessment of the situation. Once it has been determined that the suspiciousness and persecutory thinking are pathological, one needs to determine the cause. Organic causes must be ruled out by a careful history, physical examination, and laboratory tests. Affective disorders also must be considered in the workup. The diagnosis of the functional paranoid disorders is made on the basis of history, which usually must be obtained from or clarified by others, and a mental status examination. A history of social isolation, sensory deficits, losses, or a premorbid paranoid personality assists in making the diagnosis.

The Treatment of Late Life Paranoid Disorders

Treatment for the acute paranoid disorders should reduce symptoms and ameliorate the underlying causes. As a patient's symptoms tend to alienate family and care providers necessary to the patient, quick reduction of these symptoms is important. Changes in environment, particularly to a more structured and safe one, often decrease anxiety and alleviate the symptoms. Antipsychotic medications in small doses are useful. Haloperidol 0.5 mg bid, thioridazine 10 mg po bid, or thiothixene 1 mg bid are preferred by many geriatric psychiatrists. In treating the underlying causes, social stressors should be reduced and social isolation decreased whenever possible. Proper corrective eyeglasses and hearing aids should be obtained for those with visual or hearing loss. Any organic cause must be treated.

Psychotherapeutic interventions directed to increasing self-esteem and exploring alternative interpretations of the situation are helpful (33). Carstensen and Fremou (37) have found that behavioral approaches utilizing nursing home personnel can be helpful. Regardless of the approach taken, it is important for the therapist to be nonthreatening, empathic, and scrupulously honest to establish an alliance with the patient (38). All interventions, such as discussions with the family regarding the patient, and treatment decisions should be carefully explained to the patient, including what will occur and the rationale behind it. These approaches singly or in combination are often effective in relieving paranoid symptoms. For some, the delusions disappear and for others the delusions remain but are tolerated. Relapses are not unusual. Generally, discontinuation of antipsychotic medication is advisable after the patient is stable for six to nine months, although some will need to be maintained for a longer period of time.

REFERENCES

1. Blazer, D.G.: The epidemiology of mental illness in late life. In: E.W. Busse and D. G. Blazer (Eds.), Handbook of Geriatric Psychiatry. New York: Van Nostrand Reinhold, 1980.
2. Blazer, D.G.: Depression in Late Life. St Louis: C.V. Mosby, 1982.

3. Bedford, P.D.: General medical aspects of confusional states in elderly people. *Brit. J. Psychiat.*, 2: 185-188, 1959.
4. Simon, A., and Cahan, R.B.: The acute brain syndrome in geriatric patients. *Psychiatry Research Reports*, 16: 8-21, 1963.
5. Seymour, D.G., et al.: Acute confusional states and dementia in the elderly: The role of dehydration/volume depletion, physical illness and age. *Age and Aging*, 9, 3: 137-146, 1980.
6. Titchener, J.F., et al.: Psychological reactions of aged to surgery. *Archives of Neurology and Psychiatry*, 79: 63, 1958.
7. Krakowski, A.J., and Langlais, L.M.: Acute psychiatric emergencies in a geriatric hospital. *Psychosomatics*, 15: 72-75, 1974.
8. Robinson, G.W.: The toxic deliriums of old age. In: O.J. Kaplan (Ed.), *Mental Disorders in Late Life*. Stanford: Stanford University Press, 1956, pp. 227-255.
9. Posner, J.: Delirium and exogenous metabolic brain disease. In: P.B. Beeson, W. McDermott, and J.B. Wyngarden (Eds.), *Cecil's Textbook of Medicine, 15th Edition*. Philadelphia: W.B. Saunders, 1979, pp. 644-650.
10. Blazer, D.G., and Williams, C.D.: Epidemiology of dysphoria and depression in an elderly population. *Am. J. Psychiat.*, 137, 4: 439-444, 1980.
11. Kay, D.W.K., Beamish, P., and Roth, M.: Old age mental disorders in Newcastle-Upon-Tyne. *Brit. J. Psychiat.*, 110: 146, 1964.
12. Post, F.: The factor of aging in affective illness. In: A. Coppen, and A. Walk (Eds.), *Recent Developments in Affective Disorders. Brit. J. Psychiat.*, Supplement No. 2, 1968.
13. Robinson, D.S., et al.: Aging, monoamines, and monoamine oxidase. *Lancet*, 1: 290, 1972.
14. Lipton, M.A., and Nemeroff, C.B.: The biology of aging and its role in depression. In G. Usdin, and C.K. Hofling (Eds.), *Aging: The Process and the People*. New York: Brunner/Mazel, 1978, pp. 47-95.
15. Kupfer, D.J., and Foster, F.G.: Interval between onset of sleep and rapid-eye-movement sleep as an indication of depression. *Lancet*, 2: 684-686, 1972.
16. Bibring, E.: The mechanism of depression. In: P. Greenacre (Ed.), *Affective Disorders*. New York: International Universities Press, 1953, pp. 13-48.
17. Beck, A.T.: *Depression: Causes and Treatment*. Philadelphia: University of Pennsylvania Press, 1967.
18. Seligman, M.E.P.: Depression and learned helplessness. In: R.J. Friedman, and M.M. Katz (Eds.), *The Psychology of Depression: Contemporary Theory and Research*. Washington, D.C.: V.H. Winston, 1974.
19. Busse, E.W., Barnes, R.H., and Silverman, A.J.: Studies in the process of aging: Factors that influence the psyche of elderly persons. *Am. J. Psychiat.*, 111: 896, 1955.
20. Winokur, G., Behan, D., and Schlesser, M.: Clinical and biological aspects of depression in the elderly. In: J.O. Cole and J.E. Barrett (Eds.), *Psychopathology in the Aged*. New York: Raven Press, 1980, pp. 145-153.
21. De Alarcon, R.: Hypochondriasis and depression in the aged. *Gerontology Clinics*, 6: 266-277, 1964.
22. Wells, C.E.: Pseudodementia. *Am. J. Psychiat.*, 136, 7: 895-899, 1979.
23. Williamson, J.: Depression in the elderly. *Age and Aging*, 7: 35-40, 1978.
24. Shulman, K., and Post, F.: Bipolar affective disorder in old age. *Brit. J. Psychiat.*, 136: 26-32, 1980.
25. Carrol, B.J., Feinberg, M., Greden, J.F., Tarika, J., Albala, A.A., and Haskett, R.F.: A specific laboratory test for the diagnosis of melancholia. *Arch. Gen. Psychiat.*, 38: 15-23, 1981.
26. Reifler, B.V., Larsen, E., and Hanley, R.: Coexistence of cognitive impairment and depression in geriatric outpatients. *Am. J. Psychiat.*, 139, 5: 923-926, 1982.
27. Post, F.: The management and nature of depressive illness in late life: A follow-through study. *Brit. J. Psychiat.*, 121: 393-404, 1972.

28. Goodwin, F.K.: Drug treatment of affective disorders: General principles. In: M.E. Jarvik (Ed.), *Psychopharmacology in the Practice of Medicine*. New York: Appleton-Century-Crofts, 1977, pp. 241-253.

29. Foster, J.R., Gershell, W.J., and Goldfarb, A.J.: Lithium treatment in the elderly. *Journal of Gerontology*, 32: 299, 1977.

30. Lowenthal, M.F.: *Lives in Distress*. New York: Basic Books, 1964.

31. Bridge, T.P., and Wyatt, R.J.: Paraphrenia: Paranoid states of late life. II. American research. *Journal of American Geriatrics Society*, 28, 5: 201-205, 1980.

32. Fish, F.: Senile paranoid states. *Gerontologia Clinica*, 1: 127-131, 1959.

33. Busse, E.W., and Pfeiffer, E.: *Behavior and Adaptation in Late Life*. Boston: Little, Brown, 1969.

34. Post, F.: Paranoid disorders in the elderly. *Postgraduate Medicine*, 53, 4: 52-56, 1973.

35. Schapira, K.: Paranoid personality. *Practitioner*, 210: 38-43, 1973.

36. Manschreck, T.C., and Petri, M.: The paranoid syndrome. *Lancet*, 2: 251-253, 1978.

37. Carstensen, L.L., and Fremou, W.: The demonstration of a behavioral intervention for late life paranoia. *Gerontologist*, 21, 3: 329-333, 1981.

38. Swanson, D.W., Bohnert, P.J., and Smith, J.A.: *The Paranoid*. Boston: Little, Brown, 1970.

39. Lipowski, Z.J.: *Delirium: Acute Brain Failure in Man*. Springfield, IL: Charles C Thomas, 1980.

PART IV

Evaluation and Management of Transient Psychoses

Chapter 11

Transient Psychosis in the Emergency Room

Menachem Melinek, M.D., and Uriel Halbreich, M.D.

INTRODUCTION

The acutely psychotic patient usually comes to professional attention first in the emergency room. For the psychotic patient, the evaluation and treatment decisions made during the emergency room visit can determine subsequent treatment and may even determine the course of illness, at times determining whether the illness will have a transient course.

Transient psychosis presents in the emergency room as an acute picture. Although the transient nature of the acute psychotic state cannot usually be determined upon the immediate presentation in the emergency room, in many cases the initial evaluation may enable the physician to predict the course of illness. Transient psychosis is, of course, usually a "post facto" diagnosis, since one cannot know its transient character until recovery.

The initial evaluation takes place in the emergency room, which is often not only the first but the only place where the relevant history can be obtained. Physical and neurological assessments are an integral part of the initial evaluation, along with the social and psychiatric. All of these evaluations take place in a "charged" atmosphere, given the limitations of time and space and the need to arrive at a rapid decision on diagnosis, treatment, and disposition to home, hospital, or outpatient facility.

Acute onset psychosis is a common presentation in the general hospital emergency room and requires rapid, effective management. It is a medical emergency because these patients may act on their distorted reality in ways that may result in injury or death; moreover, somatic therapies can effect a rapid remission.

Table 1 summarizes some of the factors that may affect the physician's

TABLE 1
Some Factors Influencing Evaluation, Decision-making Process and Disposition in the Psychiatric Emergency Room

1. Pressure of time.
2. Patients convey a sense of emergency (2).
3. Rapid assessment is given a high premium.
4. Impersonal and transient nature of emergency room situation.
5. "On call" coverage by busy residents and interns reinforces the therapist's wish to return to what he or she was doing as soon as possible (3).
6. "Not taking a chance" attitude by the therapist because of a combination of factors, such as legal issues, potential for violence, and concern for personal safety (4).
7. Frequently negative attitude of the emergency room medical staff towards mental patients.
8. Rapid disposition encouraged to produce available space, since emergency room space is usually limited (1).
9. Therapist tendency to focus on disposition indicators (like overt symptoms) rather than on dynamic and social issues or on the possibility for rapid treatment in the emergency room.
10. Therapist knowledge about community resources.
11. Unavailability of inpatient beds (5).
12. The likelihood of hospitalization as a disposition has been shown to be higher for patients who are mute and who have past psychiatric history and poor physical appearance (6).
13. Increased likelihood of hospitalization with advanced age (7).
14. Single, divorced or widowed patients are more likely to be hospitalized.
15. Men are more likely than women to be hospitalized when they display identical symptoms (8).
16. There is evidence of social class and racial bias in diagnostic and dispositional decisions (9, 10).

judgment and action in the emergency setting. It is not surprising to find that more than half of psychiatric patients seen in a large metropolitan hospital emergency room had disposition decisions made in less than 15 minutes (1).

The evaluation of the acutely psychotic patient, as well as the disposition for that patient, depends many times on how transient the psychosis is. Finding that a psychosis originally thought to be acute is actually transient significantly alters that disposition. Thus, diagnosis is an important determinant of disposition; when a diagnosis of transient psychosis is made, there is a tendency for rapid treatment and an effort to avoid hospitalization.

A SYSTEMATIC APPROACH TO THE DIAGNOSIS OF TRANSIENT PSYCHOSIS IN THE EMERGENCY ROOM

Transient psychosis in the emergency setting often has two characteristics that may assist the clinician in the process of differential diagnosis and management: 1) acute onset; and 2) brief duration.

Table 2 presents a schema for differential diagnosis that the clinician can consider when faced with an acute psychosis with a possible short course. This scheme follows some of the guidelines for the differential diagnosis of psychotic features presented in DSM-III (11, p. 200) and the management of acute psychosis presented by Anderson and Kuehnle (12).

The baseline description of transient psychosis presented here refers to rapid development—usually over days or weeks—of perceptual distortions; disturbances in thought, affect or reality-testing; marked loosening of associations; poverty of thought content; markedly illogical thinking; and bizarre, disorganized, or catatonic behavior lasting a few weeks, usually less than two. While the DSM-III sets an arbitrary figure of up to two weeks' duration for its definition of "brief reactive psychosis," we feel that the diagnosis of transient psychosis cannot rest upon such an absolute time frame and that a more flexible delineation, such as "duration of less than a few weeks," leaving the ultimate decision to the clinician, is more appropriate. We prefer to call psychoses lasting longer than those few weeks "extended psychosis." If the clinician obtains a history of extended psychosis with sufficient data to imply that the present acutely psychotic state is part of an overall chronic picture, the situation warrants the diagnosis of an acute exacerbation of an extended psychosis.

To make the differentiation between an extended and a transient psychosis, the emergency room physician should pay careful attention to

TABLE 2
Decision Tree for Transient Psychosis
[Modification of DSM-III (11)]

Rapid development (usually over days or weeks) of disturbances of perception, thought, affect or reality-testing, including: hallucinations, delusions, incoherence, marked loosening of associations, poverty of content of thought, markedly illogical thinking, and bizarre, disorganized or catatonic behavior.

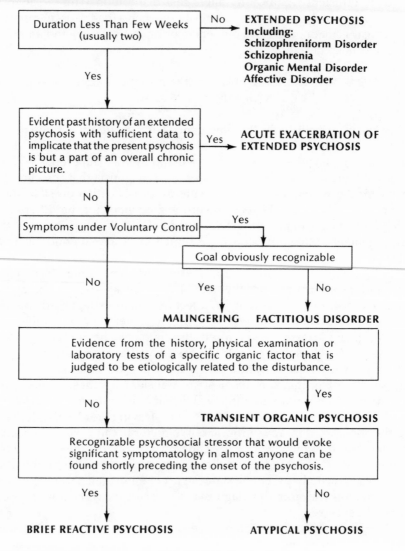

Duration Less Than Few Weeks (usually two) — No → **EXTENDED PSYCHOSIS Including: Schizophreniform Disorder Schizophrenia Organic Mental Disorder Affective Disorder**

Yes

Evident past history of an extended psychosis with sufficient data to implicate that the present psychosis is but a part of an overall chronic picture. — Yes → **ACUTE EXACERBATION OF EXTENDED PSYCHOSIS**

No

Symptoms under Voluntary Control — Yes → Goal obviously recognizable

No   Yes   No

MALINGERING   FACTITIOUS DISORDER

Evidence from the history, physical examination or laboratory tests of a specific organic factor that is judged to be etiologically related to the disturbance.

No   Yes

TRANSIENT ORGANIC PSYCHOSIS

Recognizable psychosocial stressor that would evoke significant symptomatology in almost anyone can be found shortly preceding the onset of the psychosis.

Yes   No

BRIEF REACTIVE PSYCHOSIS   **ATYPICAL PSYCHOSIS**

history-taking, since the psychiatric history can be the most important single factor in arriving at an accurate diagnosis and formulating an appropriate treatment plan. Patients can be poor informants and their mental state may preclude comprehensive interviewing; therefore, other sources of material should be utilized as well, including family, friends, police or ambulance attendants and, if the patient has been in treatment before, the patient's therapist or family doctor. The emergency room may be the only place that information from people other than the patient himself can be obtained.

Table 3 presents relevant historical questions that can assist the evaluating emergency room clinician in determining the longitudinal picture. The term "extended psychosis" refers here to the following clinical entities: schizophreniform psychosis, schizophrenia, affective disorders, and organic mental syndrome. A typical example of an acute exacerbation of an extended psychosis is the patient suffering from schizophrenia who has been stabilized on psychotropic medication and who, when he stops taking his medication, decompensates.

TABLE 3

Psychiatric History in Emergency Room Setting Geared Towards Evaluation of Psychosis of Acute Onset

1. *Symptoms History*—When did they begin? What is their nature: Constant? Increased? Fluctuated in intensity? How does the patient describe them? Circumstances when symptoms began:
    A. Recent loss or death, divorce, separation, loss of body function
    B. Injury, illness
    C. Drug use
2. *Somatic Functioning History*—Has there been any somatic change? Sleep disturbances? Weight or Appetite changes? Gastrointestinal changes (constipation)? Any pains? Cardiovascular, respiratory, excretory or neurological changes?
3. *Mental Status History*—During the illness course has the patient felt or has the informer witnessed signs of a change in patient mental status? Any hallucinations (auditory, visual, gustatory, olfactory, other)? Paranoid ideations? Ideas of reference? Delusions (grandeur, persecution, somatic)? Thought disturbances (racing thoughts, making no sense, bizarre content, blocking, etc.)? Obsessions? Compulsions? Ritualistic, disorganized, catatonic or bizarre behavior? Hypochondriasis? Feeling of anxiety (free-floating, overwhelming)? Depression? Elated mood? Intense anger or fear? Identity or sexual confusion? Homicidal or suicidal ideations or acts?
4. *Past Psychiatric History*—Any psychiatric history? Any psychiatric hospitalizations (if yes, when? how long? where? why?)? Has patient seen a ther-

apist, psychiatrist or a G.P. for emotional problems? (If yes, get identifying data.) Has patient received ECT in the past? Has he been on any medication? (Cite psychiatric medications.) Has he been taking it? What medications and how much? Any difficulties with the law? Any incarceration (where? what for? how long?)? Any psychiatric diagnosis given in the past?

5. *Dangerousness*—Is patient suicidal or homicidal? Any plans (suicidal or homicidal)? Any possession of lethal weapon? Any previous attempts? How many times? Has he given away any possessions? Any command hallucinations?

6. *Drug History*—Any medication taken or discontinued recently? Can it explain present symptoms? Drug use (marijuana, LSD, DMT, STP, amphetamines, mescaline, other hallucinogens, PCP, heroin, methadone, glue sniffing, cocaine, others)? How many times? When? How long? Any sedatives? Minor tranquilizers? If patient is on major tranquilizers, did he stop taking them recently?

7. *Alcohol History*—If positive, how much? How many days per week? Alone? Period of the day? Any episodes of delirium tremens? Attended Alcoholics Anonymous? Hospitalized for detoxification or intoxication?

8. *School and Work History*—When did patient graduate? School problems? Could patient hold a job? How many? For how long?

9. *Social History*—Where does patient live? With whom? Interpersonal relationships? Religion?

10. *Medical History*—Any medical disease? Operations? Could any medical illness explain his symptoms? Medical hospitalizations? Accidents? Any somatic treatment at the present?

11. *Family History*—Any history of mental problems in family? Suicide, depression, alcoholism, dementia, mania, schizophrenia, anybody saw or sees a psychiatrist or was hospitalized for mental condition? Epilepsy?

If the psychotic symptoms seem to be under voluntary control, with a clearly recognizable goal, the diagnosis of malingering is warranted. The emergency room is the most frequent setting for making this determination. This is a common phenomenon in urban emergency rooms, especially during the winter months when patients who have no place to stay and no food come to the hospital simulating psychotic behavior and requesting admission.

Many drug abusers and chronic alcoholics know that bizarre and belligerent behavior or suicidal threats will get them hospitalized. Phrases such as "the voices are telling me to kill myself" will alarm even the most experienced physician. The diagnosis of factitious disorder may be made when the goal of the behavior cannot be clearly recognized.

It is important to consider three other principal diagnostic categories: transient organic psychosis, brief reactive psychosis, and atypical psychosis.

Transient Organic Psychosis

All patients presenting with an acute psychotic picture, and especially those demonstrating a brief course, should be screened for the possibility of an organic psychosis: evidence from history, physical examination or laboratory tests of a specific organic factor. In a large-scale study, Hall and co-workers (13) found that an organic illness was the absolute or presumed cause of the psychiatric syndrome in 9.1% of the patients. Twenty-eight percent were diagnosed as being functionally psychotic and 20% experienced visual hallucinations or distortions, while only 0.5% of nonmedically impaired psychiatric patients presented these symptoms.

Medical history-taking, with careful systems review, biochemical and laboratory screening, and attentive physical examination, is a must in most psychiatric patients who are evaluated in the emergency room. The presence of visual hallucinations, distortions or illusions should alert the examining physician to rule out carefully any underlying medical disorder, since prompt recognition of an underlying medical disorder lessens the probability of progression of the disease and irreversible damage. It can also prevent needless treatment with psychotropics and long-term psychiatric hospitalization with all its legal and moral implications, including the affixing of an unnecessary label to a medically ill patient, which may reduce chances for improvement and impose a needless liability.

In studying the practices of psychiatric residents in the emergency services, it was found that 59% of residents failed to perform physicals; when physical examinations were done, the results proved useful in 92% of cases (14). The physician in the emergency room can call on specialists from virtually every branch of medicine, thus enhancing his or her ability to arrive at a timely diagnosis and begin proper care.

At times, physical examinations are not performed on the acutely psychotic patient because of an actual or assumed lack of cooperation. A sympathetic but firm and unambiguous approach to the patient can gain cooperation in most cases. Sometimes one has to use a high potency antipsychotic (Haldol 5-10mg IM) or restraints because of uncontrollable agitation. Reliable vital signs should always be obtained. A careful neurological examination is of extreme value, with special attention to subtle signs of cortical dysfunction, cranial nerves, cerebellum and motor systems. Careful attention to extrapyramidal and autonomic symptoms is important.

Laboratory findings help to define the probability of a medical etiology in cases where such a disorder exsits (13). Tests include SMA-18, white count and differential, hemoglobin, hematocrit and, when anemia is suspected, red cell indices. Toxicologic screening, EKG, urinalysis including microscopic analysis of sediment, and chest and skull x-rays should also be considered.

Such behavioral emergencies as acute psychosis should be viewed as having an underlying organic etiology until proven otherwise. A tentative diagnosis of organic psychosis should be made if evidence or suspicion of a specific organic factor exists (based on history, physical examination or laboratory tests) and is judged to be etiologically related to the psychotic picture.

An expanded discussion of medical disorders that can cause organic psychosis is presented in Chapter 4 of this book. Here we will examine the transient organic psychosis by syndromes.

1) Transient delirium

Delirium is a medical emergency and demands prompt evaluation and treatment. The onset of delirium is usually acute (hours or days) and the clinical picture can fluctuate, thus giving the appearance of a transient psychosis. At times, one may observe a completely lucid clinical picture alternating with a period of frank psychosis. Since it is by definition a reversible organic brain syndrome, delirium can be mistakenly treated as a functional disorder and is frequently unrecognized (13). Early identification and prompt determination of the underlying etiology are essential for recovery.

Delirium is associated with disorderd function of all the highest cerebral centers. There is a major failure of recognition, integration and control, resulting in disordered thought and behavior and in clouding of consciousness, with diminished capacity to move or to center on and maintain attention to environmental stimuli. The clinical picture can include such perceptual disturbances as misinterpretations, illusions or hallucinations, incoherent speech, disturbances of sleep, and psychomotor agitation or retardation. If memory is testable, major disturbance or disorientation is a common finding.

Table 4 enumerates an extensive list of etiological factors in delirium (14-18). The common categories of causative factors include toxemia, respiratory and metabolic changes, central nervous system infections, non-infective cerebral disease, cerebral anemia, drug and environmental toxins, endogenous intoxication, and heatstroke.

TABLE 4
Etiological Factors of Delirium

I. *Toxemia*
1. General infection is obvious, e.g., septicemia, typhus.
2. Evidence of infection is slight (especially in debilitated or alcoholic subjects), e.g., pneumonia, influenza, pyelitis, pezinephris abscess.

II. *Respiratory and Metabolic Changes*
1. Respiratory alkalosis ($\downarrow$ blood CO_2), e.g., hyperventilation, hepatic insufficiency, anoxia, hyperpyrexia (hypothalamic involvement or infections), gramobacteremia.
2. Respiratory acidosis ($\uparrow$ blood CO_2), e.g., cardiopulmonary diseases (emphysema, CHF, asthma), injury or toxic paralysis of respiratory center, asphyxia, hypokalemia with respiratory muscle weakness.
3. Metabolic alkalosis ($\uparrow$ biocarbonate, $\downarrow$ CL), e.g., chronic nephritis, hypercortisonism, dehydration (from any cause), diuretic-induced potassium depletion, laxatives, steroids, prolonged vomiting with potassium chloride depletion associated with gastric acid loss. Extensive burns, prolonged I.V. therapy with dextrose and water.
4. Metabolic acidosis (only in rare cases can cause delirium).

III. *CNS Infections*
1. Encephalitis (acute or chronic)
2. Meningitis (bacteria, viral, fungi, parasites, any other organism)
3. Cerebral abscess
4. Encephalomyelitis
5. Rabies
6. Cerebral syphilis
7. Trypanosomiasis
8. Polio-encephalitis
9. Cerebral malaria
10. Sydenham's chorea

IV. *Non-infective Cerebral Disease*
1. Cerebral vascular disorder—hemorrhage, subarachnoid thrombosis, embolism, arteriosclerotic cerebral degeneration.
2. Raised intracranial pressure
3. Acute head injury—extradural or subdural hematomas
4. Intracranial neoplasma—skull tumors, meningiomas, cranial nerve tumors, connective tissue tumors, ductless gland tumors, congenital tumors, granulomatous, metastatic
5. Neurofibromatos (Von Reckhinghausen's disease)
6. Tuberous sclerosis (Bournville's disease)
7. Multiple sclerosis
8. Primary degeneration of corpus callosum (Marchiafava disease)
9. Chronic progressive chorea (Huntington's chorea)
10. Pellagra
11. Wernicke's encephalopathy
12. Amyotrophic lateral sclerosis
13. Psychomotor epilepsy, postictal psychosis

V.   *Cerebral Anemia*
     1. Acute blood loss
     2. CO_2 poisoning
     3. Severe primary anemia: pernicious anemia, aplastic
     4. Severe secondary anemia
     5. C.H.F.
VI. *Drugs and Environmental Toxins*
     1. Delirium tremens (alcohol withdrawal delirium)
     2. Barbiturates or similarly acting sedative or hypnotics, withdrawal de-
        lirium.
     3. Amphetamine or similarly acting sympathomimetics
     4. Phencyclidine (PCP) or similarly acting arycyclohexylamine
     5. Colchicin
     6. Salicylate
     7. Diphenylhydantoin and congeners
     8. Digitalis and cardiac glycosides
     9. Quinine and cinchona derivatives
    10. Insect bites
    11. Mushroom poisoning
VII. *Endogenous Intoxication*
     1. Uremia
     2. Diabetic ketosis
     3. Cholemia
     4. Porphyria (acute, intermittent)
     5. Adrenal cortical hypofunction
     6. Pituitary hypofunction
     7. Myxedema
     8. Hyperthyroidism
     9. Hypocalcemia
    10. Hepatolenticular degeneration (Wilson's disease)
    11. Hepatic encephalopathy
    12. Hypomagne-siumemia
VIII. *Heat*
     Heatstroke

---

2) Transient dementia

Transient dementia can be considered in the differential diagnosis of transient psychosis. Memory impairment, disturbances of higher cortical function, impaired judgment, and impairment of abstract thinking can all coexist with a recognizable loss of intellectual ability of sufficient severity to interfere with social and occupational functioning (11, p. 107-112). Dementia can be either acute or insidious in onset, depending on the etiology. The emergency room physician should be aware of the syndrome since it is often reversible (19). We refer the reader to an excellent etiological list by Cummings et al. (20).

3) Transient organic delusional syndrome

This refers to patients who, while in a normal state of consciousness, present delusions, especially those of a persecutory nature. Other types of delusions can be found, including depressive delusions, grandiose delusions, somatic delusions, and Capgras' phenomenon. Conditions capable of bringing about these symptoms are listed in Table 5.

4) Transient organic hallucinations

Hallucinations occur frequently as a symptom of medical illness. All types of hallucination may be found in organic hallucinosis, as well as in functional or toxic disorders. The mode and content of the hallucinatory phenomena may give the clinician clues as to the nature and cause.

Visual hallucinations in the absence of auditory hallucinations should make one suspect an organic syndrome (24). In delirium tremens, the typical hallucinations are of spiders, rats, and insects and are very frightening in nature. Lines, dots, or flashes of light are simple hallucinations that might appear in hallucinogenic drug intoxication, epilepsy, migraine, temporal arteritis, advanced syphilis, and retinal disease. Lilliputian hallucinations can be found in several organic and toxic states, especially anticholinergic and cocaine psychoses (25, 26). In temporal lobe epilepsy, visual hallucinations are usually accompanied by auditory hallucinations of a religious content and appear as scenes or panoramas.

Auditory hallucinations. Simple sounds such as buzzing or bells are commonly reported in salicylism, diseases of the middle ear, auditory nerve injury and deafness, acoustic neuroma, or any organic psychosis. If voices are heard in a state of clouded sensorium, the common etiology is toxic or organic psychosis. If the sensorium is clear, the diagnosis is usually that of a functional psychosis.

Gustatory or olfactory hallucinations are reported more often in organic or toxic conditions such as temporal lobe epilepsy, in which an unpleasant odor is the most frequent perception. It is often also perceived in migraine. *Somatic hallucinations of pain* can also be experienced in temporal lobe epilepsy or migraine, along with an epigastric discomfort. Toxic states are also known to produce *tactile zoopathy* (cocaine bugs);

TABLE 5
Differential Diagnosis of Transient Organic Delusional Syndrome

I. *Transient persecutory delusions* (21)
   A. *Primary CNS pathology*
      1. Temporal lobe epilepsy
      2. Systemic lupus erythematosus
      3. Normal pressure hydrocephalus
      4. Encephalitis
      5. Meningitis (22)
      6. Marchiafava-Bignami Disease
      7. Neurosyphilis
      8. Cerebral malaria
      9. Subacute bacterial endocarditis
     10. Trichinosis
   B. *Endocrinopathies and metabolic disorders*
      1. Myxedema
      2. Hyperthyroidism
      3. Cushing's syndrome
      4. Addison's disease
      5. Hyperparathyroidism
      6. Hypoparathyroidism
      7. Vitamin B_{12} deficiency
      8. Sodium depletion
   C. *Drug induced*
      1. Amphetamine
      2. Levodopa
      3. Tetracycline (23)
      4. LSD
      5. Cannabis
      6. PCP
II. *Depressive, grandiose or somatic delusions*
      1. Cushing's syndrome
      2. Addison's disease
      3. Hyperthyroidism
      4. Hypothyroidism
      5. Systemic lupus erythematosus
      6. Neurosyphilis
      7. B_{12} deficiency
      8. Bromide intoxication
      9. Pentazocine intoxication (somatic delusions)
III. *Capgras' phenomenon* (False belief that a close person is an imposter; Reported in various brain disorders.)

other organic states can also produce a feeling of body infestation with insects (27).

5) Drug intoxication and withdrawal—induced transient psychosis

Over the past 20 years, we have witnessed a sharp increase in emergency room visits and in the utilization of psychiatric emergency services, far exceeding the increase in the use of emergency medical and surgical services (28, 29). This change is partially due to a greater increase in drug-related problems requiring emergency intervention (5). A study at Massachusetts General Hospital noted a 118% increase in emergency department treatment of suicide attempts by drug overdose between 1964 and 1972 (30).

Transient psychosis due to drug intoxication or drug withdrawal should be one of the first considerations in the evaluation of acute psychosis in the emergency room setting. The chance that an acute psychosis might be related to drug use or withdrawal is supported by the following, roughly estimated annual figures for the United States in the last several years: 100 million people drink alcohol. Twenty million are alcoholics. Seven and a half million people use sedative hypnotics and over 400,000 people are narcotic addicts. Ninety percent of drug overdoses are mixed (31). The differential diagnosis of drug-induced psychiatric syndromes is presented in Chapter 6 of this book (Drug-induced Psychoses). We will, therefore, limit ourselves to a review of the symptoms in the section on emergency treatment.

6) Intermittent recurring organic psychosis

Several illnesses deserve special note under this heading. Patients with these disorders can show up in the emergency room with brief but acutely psychotic behavioral problems as part of the recurrent and intermittent course of these illnesses. Multiple sclerosis (MS) is typically episodic in nature. It may strike suddenly and there are no typical signs and symptoms. Labile emotionality, depression, brief acute psychotic episodes and explosive emotional dyscontrol may occur (32). Acute intermittent porphyria, a hereditary (autosomal dominant) disease of young adulthood resulting from a deficiency of the enzyme required for complete porphyrin metabolism, causing a toxic accumulation of porphyrin analogues, may first be presented to the psychiatrist. The psychiatric manifestations may range from anxiety states to an acute schizophreniform psychosis, usually of brief duration. A history of recurrent acute abdominal pain should alert the clinician to the possibility of this disorder. Attacks can be precipitated by giving barbiturates or griseofulvin. Psychiatric symptoms and abdominal pain respond favorably to phenothiazines and are often refractory to opiates (33).

Systemic lupus erythematosus (SLE) is another chronic intermittent illness that can present as an acute, brief schizophreniform psychotic picture with clear sensorium (34). Other organ systems are also commonly involved. Such indications as joint and muscle pains, fever, skin rash, and symptoms pointing to myocardial, kidney, pulmonary, and CNS involvement usually alert the clinician to the possibility of this disorder. Serum of SLE patients contains antinucleoprotein antibodies and may contain anti-DNA antibodies. Some of the acute psychotic states associated with SLE may be steroid-induced in patients who are treated with these hormones.

Pheochromocytoma, also a disease of young people, is characterized by paroxysmal release of pressor amines produced by a catecholamine-producing tumor. The symptoms range from anxiety states to acute, brief psychotic episodes. The most common physical symptoms are hypertension, pallor, sweating and tachycardia. Administrations of a test dose of Regitin and biochemical assay of elevated catecholamines by 24-hour urine collection can aid in the diagnosis (33).

Acute, often brief, hallucinatory psychosis can be the only presenting symptom of pancreatitis. Fever, abdominal pain, and a positive alcoholic history should raise the index of suspicion (34). Some convulsive disorders may be manifested by psychotic behavioral equivalents. Episodic dyscontrol syndrome belongs to this category and is characterized by intermittent violent behavior, at times accompanied by an aura and abnormal EEG (temporal focus) (35). Patients may present with minimal seizure activity but with a prolonged transient psychotic episode (interictal psychosis) (36).

7) Transient organic catatonic and mutism states

Transient catatonia and mutism may appear in various medical as well as psychiatric illnesses. Table 6 (after Gelenberg [36]) summarizes the various conditions that may present at onset with catatonic signs and symptoms.

Catatonia or mutism does not always signify schizophrenia. There is some evidence, in fact, that this presentation may be seen more frequently in affective disorders (37, 38). The catatonic syndrome may at

TABLE 6*
Disorders in Which Catatonic Signs and Symptoms Have Been Reported at Onset

Psychiatric Conditions
   Schizophrenia
   Affective disorders
   Conversion disorders
   Dissociative disorders
   Reactive psychosis
Neurologic Conditions
   Basal ganglia disorders (arteriosclerotic parkinsonism, focal lesions of the pallidum)
   Disorders of the limbic system and temporal lobes (viral encephalitis, vascular lesions of the temporal lobes, tumors of the septum pellucidum)
   Diencephalon disorders (tumors, hemorrhage in the third ventricle, focal thalamic lesions)
   Other lesions and disturbances (frontal lobe tumors, anterior cerebral artery aneurysms, arteriovenous malformations, diffuse brain trauma, diffuse encephalomalcia, petit mal epilepsy, postictal states, tuberous sclerosis, Wernicke's encephalopathy, narcolepsy, intracranial hemorrhage, cerebral cortex infarctions, subdural hematomas)
Metabolic Conditions
   Diabetic ketoacidosis
   Hypercalcemia
   Pellagra
   Intermittent acute porphyria
   Homocystinuria
   Hepatic encephalopathy
   Hypothyroidism
Toxic Agents
   Organic fluorides
   Illuminating gases
   Mescaline
   Ethanol
   Phencyclidine (PCP)
   Neuroleptics (neuroleptic malignant syndrome, neuroleptic-induced catatonia)

*After Gelenberg (36) and others.

times be produced by the effects of the major tranquilizers on the hypothalamus, leading to a condition known as malignant neuroleptic syndrome. The main symptom picture includes hypertonicity, dyskinesia, stupor, hyperthermia, pallor, and pulmonary findings (39). Another catatonic syndrome may follow overly aggressive antipsychotic treatment. Iatrogenic catatonia is an extreme form of dystonia which is relieved by the withdrawal of the neuroleptic and institution of anti-cholinergic therapy.

A high incidence of psychotic catatonic symptoms is reported in cases of viral encephalitis—especially in encephalitis due to herpes simplex (40). An erroneous assumption that a patient has functional catatonia can lead to disastrous outcome.

The evaluation of the mute/catatonic patient in the emergency room is best done when the physician poses and attempts to answer the following questions:

1) Is the patient deaf?
2) What is the patient's mother tongue?
3) Does the patient suffer from aphasia?
4) Does the patient suffer from dysarthria?
5) Is there any evidence for organicity?
6) Are there any accompanying neurological signs?
7) Are there fluctuations in level of consciousness?
8) Are there any abnormal physical or laboratory findings?

Glicksman (41) suggests five points that can help to differentiate be-tween organic and functional states of catatonic stupor:

1) *Age*—The older the patient, the more likely that there is organ-icity; *sex*—hysterical stupor, usually of a few hours' duration, almost always occurs in women under the age of 30; *legal sta-tus*—this is important in the differential diagnosis of malingering in patients who are in legal difficulty.
2) *Appearance of being asleep*—In functional catatonic stupor one does not observe decreased muscle tone and respiratory changes that accompany organic states.
3) *Sodium amytal interview*—This has been recommended to differ-entiate organic from functional catatonic states. Patients with organic etiology tend to become progressively confused and their level of consciousness drops under IV amytal. The patient who has a functional state might become more talkative. Neu-roleptic-induced akinesia and mutism will yield to amytal; the patient will wake up and begin talking. Patients with the so-called malignant neuroleptic syndrome will respond to aman-tadine but not to other anti-parkinsonian agents.
4) *EEG*—Almost always normal in patients with functional states.
5) *Caloric stimulation*—In functionally ill patients this will elicit a nystagmus with slow component toward the irrigated ear (last-

ing two to three minutes) and in organic stupor there will be a tonic deviation toward the irrigated ear.

Transient Functional Psychosis

The new DSM-III (11, pp. 200-202) diagnostic entity, brief reactive psychosis, assumes the following essential features:

1) *Psychosocial stressor*—"The psychotic symptoms appear immediately following a recognizable psychosocial stressor that would evoke significant symptoms of distress in almost anyone."
2) *Acute psychotic picture*—"The clinical picture involves emotional turmoil and at least one of the following psychotic symptoms: incoherence, or loosening of associations, delusions, hallucinations, behavior that is grossly disorganized or catatonic."
3) *Transient nature*—The psychotic symptoms last more than a few hours but less than two weeks and there is an eventual return to the premorbid level of functioning.
4) *Premorbid psychopathology*—No period of increasing psychopathology preceded the psychosocial stressor.
5) *No other mental disorder* is responsible for the clinical syndrome.

If no psychosocial stressor of the nature described above is found, it suggests an alternate diagnosis of atypical psychosis. This diagnosis is a "residual" category, used when the clinical picture does not allow for specific categorization.

There is no clear consensus in the literature on the adequacy of transient functional psychosis as a classification. Hollender and Hirsch (42) looked into the syndrome called "hysterical psychosis" and considered these transient psychoses to be manifestations of the disruption of ego functions under stress. The condition is not restricted to those with histrionic personalities. Weiss and Rhoads (37) suggest the existence of a continuum of vulnerability to this phenomenon in various personality types: "The psychosis will be manifested in responses to an emotional stress which is specific for an individual, related to the intensity of the stress, degree of ego strength and the extent of support within the environment." DSM-III mentions as predisposing factors the existence of personality pathology, including paranoid, histrionic, narcissistic, schizotypal, or borderline personality disorders. The relationship between borderline personality disorder and transient psychosis is explored extensively in other chapters in this volume.

The emergency room physician should be familiar with the culture or subculture of the population served by his specific emergency room, since social responses can differ from culture to culture (43). This may also be an important influence on course of illness after the first episode. During psychotic episodes, the behavior appears to be stereotyped and learned, since it is shaped by a particular culture. We have had extensive experience with brief psychotic episodes in the Puerto Rican population of the Bronx. Transient psychotic behavior in this culture, labeled as *"attake,"* has a dramatic presentation and usually brings many family members to the emergency room. It often lasts a few hours to a few days and relates to a stressful event, most often aggressive in nature. The psychotic phenomena may vary from hallucinations, delusions, and de-personalization to acute catatonia and mutism. There is a strongly vol-atile affective component which may recede as suddenly and dramatically as it began. One also observes a common belief in spiritual involvement. The many reports in the literature of "culture-shock"-induced transient psychosis (44) underline the importance of cultural factors in brief re-active psychoses of this kind, such as those in Caribbean (45) and East African patients (46), the Puerto Rican Syndrome (47), the Bena Bena hysterical psychotic attack (48), and many others.

The term "reactive psychosis" has been used by some investigators to describe a psychotic decompensation of brief duration (days or weeks) in vulnerable individuals subjected to overwhelming emotional trauma (49). The psychoses are characterized by acute onset and preservation of emotional contact. Longitudinal research indicates that they may be differentiated from both schizophrenia and manic-depressive psychoses on the basis of symptomatology and course. Scandinavian investigators have also used the term "psychogenic psychoses" for these syndromes and have suggested that, when carefully diagnosed, these "reactive psychoses" stand for a clinically selected cluster of patients who are genetically sufficiently distinct to be considered as a specific diagnostic category (50).

Different psychosocial stressors have been reported. It is important to note that some therapeutic interventions can bring about the devel-opment of an acute transient psychosis. Encounter groups and T-groups are reported to be associated with precipitation of transient, acute psy-chosis in vulnerable individuals (51). Prevention of therapeutically in-duced acute psychotic episodes depends on the therapist's skill in identifying the patient's vulnerability and his ability to make timely and important decisions. Emotionally loaded therapeutic methods, such as those which promote intense feelings through powerful encounters, implosion, and emotional flooding, have been reported to induce psychotic episodes, which have also been reported with relatively safe procedures (52). Other therapeutic approaches, such as those which promote deeply-felt emotional relationships between patient and therapist, which may last for years and dominate the patient's emotional life, primal states, altered states of (un)consciousness, emotional catharsis, and massive transference reactions, are also implicated in precipitation of acute psychotic episodes (53). "Cinematic" psychoses have been reported following horror movies. For example, the film *The Exorcist* has been noted for its traumatic influence on previously unidentified psychiatric patients (54).

"Homosexual panic" is a form of transient psychosis characterized by delusions and hallucinations that "blame" the patient, in scornful and derisive terms, of diverse homosexual acts. Patients with schizoid personality who have effectively sheltered themselves in the past from physical intimacy are typically susceptible to this form of transient psychosis, especially in settings that promote same-sex intimacy, such as military barracks and college dormitories (55).

Combat Shock

Combat shock may manifest with psychotic symptoms. It is not a routine emergency room diagnosis but can only be made when one is presented with casualties of belligerent activities. In Freud's words, the acute stress leading to the combat syndrome is "an experience which, within a short time, presents the mind with an increase in stimulus too powerful to be dealt with or worked through in a normal way" (56).

The best treatment for the syndrome is prevention, the elimination of environmental and situational factors contributing to increased vulnerability. Among these factors are: 1) a long, *passive* waiting for something to happen; 2) imminent changes or a threat which continues for a long time; 3) lack of motor activity and active response; 4) chronic tiredness or weariness; 5) isolation or lack of group identity; 6) doubts about the justification of the war and mistrust in the leadership and command structure; 7) many casualties in the unit, bad physical conditions, and symptoms of exhaustion in other soldiers.

The most prevalent symptoms of combat shock states are neurotic, mostly seen as conversion states such as paralysis, aphonia or tremors; anterograde or retrograde amnesia (or both); affective symptoms such as depression, tearfulness; apathy and irritation with a low threshold; hyperventilation, sweatiness or tachycardia; dissociative states or stupor; twilight levels of consciousness or confusion.

Psychotic symptoms may be present with any of the above and one should differentiate between the "neurotic" or "pseudopsychotic" confusional state and a genuine acute psychosis. The diagnosis of psychosis is reserved for those patients who show obvious signs of psychosis, such as impairment of reality-testing and disturbances of thinking processes or thought, sensory deprivation, etc.

If a soldier suffering from combat shock arrives in the emergency room, it is either a mistake or a bad prognostic sign or both. Treatment should take place as close as possible to the time and place of combat. Delay of treatment or transfer to a centralized hospital increases the possibility of chronicity. If the patient is manageable and not extremely agitated, treatment in the emergency room is limited to rest before admission to a specialized unit. Tranquilizers are sometimes needed before the transfer. Additional procedures are not recommended in the emergency room: They should be performed in the combat zone or be delayed until the patient reaches the unit.

Strategies for Treatment of Transient Psychosis in the Emergency Room

Transient psychosis is a "retrospective" entity in that in most cases the transient nature of the psychosis is not evident before the resolution of the episode. The best therapeutic approach is that which gives the most expeditious relief of the acute psychosis. The acutely psychotic patient may be persistently at risk for an abrupt, aggressive discharge that can result in suicide, homicide, or lesser injury to self and others. The psychotic disintegration is extremely distressing for the patient: One hears such statements as "I would rather have physical pain than this emotional pain." Although the issue is still speculative, it is felt that postponement of treatment may lead to chronicity (12).

A systematic and structured approach to the patient with a possible transient psychosis may prove to be extremely helpful, especially in the pressured environment of the emergency room. Table 7 presents a General Management Algorithm. The treatment approach depends on information from the history and from the physical and psychiatric examinations given to the patient during the initial assessments in the emergency room. As the first step, the clinician should determine whether the situation is life-threatening. If this is the case, the first goal is the control of the airway, assuring adequate ventilation and oxygenation. The physician should then proceed to stabilize vital signs. Blood pressure, rectal temperature, and pulse should be closely monitored and oxygen supplementation should follow immediately. An IV line with a continuous infusion of saline or lactated Ringer's solution should be installed, especially in hypotensive patients. In normotensive or hypertensive patients, one should "keep the vein open" using 5% dextrose in water (D5W) (57). Blood should be drawn for serum glucose and, if time allows, for CBC, BUN, electrolytes and toxicological screening. This should be done before the IV lines are put in and should be sent for immediate analysis. A comatose patient should be given a 100 cc bolus

TABLE 7*

Initial Evaluation and Management of
Acute Psychosis in the Emergency Room

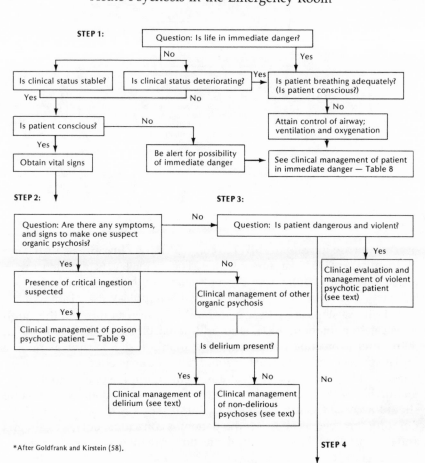

*After Goldfrank and Kirstein (58).

TABLE 7 (Continued)

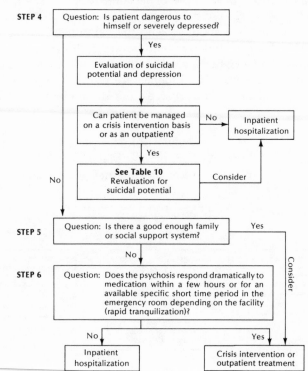

of 50% glucose in water (D50W) to correct for hypoglycemia and 100 mg of thiamine HCl IM to assure adequate coenzyme levels in patients with possible thiamine deficits. A dose of naloxone (Narcan), a narcotic antagonist, should be given also (2mg IV—5 ampules). (See Table 8.)

After these steps are taken, one should perform a quick but thorough physical examination, EKG, and additional blood studies as needed; then, after protecting the airway, one should install an orogastric line for lavage, activated charcoal or ionic cathartic as needed. If there is no question about the disposition at this point, admit the patient to the ICU for further care. If the patient's life is not in immediate danger, one should ascertain that the patient's clinical status is stable. If it is deteriorating, proceed as above. If the patient is conscious, obtain vital signs and then ask the following critical question: Are there signs and/or symptoms suggestive of organic psychosis?

TABLE 8*
Clinical Management of the Patient in Immediate Danger

Check blood pressure, pulse rate (strength and regularity) and rectal temperature. Immediately stabilize abnormal vital signs.

Administer
1. Supplemental oxygen and suction secretions.
2. Normal saline and lactated Ringer's solution if patient is hypotensive and D5W (5% dextrose in water) if patient is hypertensive. Keep intravenous line open.
3. 100 cc of 50% dextrose in water (D50W)—100 mg thiamine chloride (HCl) and 2 mg (5 ampules of naloxone [Narcan])

Perform
1. Quick but thorough physical examination—lungs, heart, abdomen, nervous system.
2. 12 lead EKG. Draw bloods for additional tests if not already obtained.
3. Passage of orogastric hose (protecting airway if this is not already secured) and introduce lavage, activated charcoal and ionic cathartic as indicated.

Admit
1. Admit patient to Intensive Care Unit.

*After Goldfrank (59, p. 5) and others.

If organic etiology is considered, the presence of critical ingestion has to be ruled out. If there is any suspicion of drug/poison-induced psychosis, one should follow the general managment outlines delineated in Table 7 (after Goldfrank and Kirstein [58]) and the guidelines for the clinical management of the poiscned patient in Table 9. One should always be aware of the suicidal risk (see Table 10).

Several agents produce a specific psychiatric and physiological picture and require some specific antidote (such as physostigmine). The reader is referred to the specific algorithms for the following drug presentations:

1) Acute agitated transient psychosis with parasympathetic shut-down—Table 11 (60-62);
2) Acute transient psychosis with signs of hallucinogen ingestion—Table 12 (29);
3) Acute transient psychosis with signs of sympathetic excess—Table 13 (29);
4) Acute phencyclidine-induced transient psychosis—Table 14 (29, 63-65).

Where there is a question of other organic etiology, the physician should ask himself about the possibility of delirium. The treatment of

TABLE 9*
Clinical Management of Poisoned Psychotic Patient

1. *Conservatism*—Be cautious; drug-related psychoses are not usually fatal.
2. *Cardiorespiratory*—Stabilization.
3. *Identify agent*—How much, when and how was the substance taken (only partly reliable)?
4. *Specific antidote*—Administer if indicated (such as physostigmine or Narcan).
5. *Nonspecific Antidote*—Try to avoid.
6. *Verbal contact*—Should be kept with the patient. Support and reassurance, orientation and a non-challenging communication are needed.
7. *Environment control*—Patient should be in a quiet room with few people.
8. *Patient control*—Pharmacological and physical restraints should be avoided if possible. Avoid phenothiazines. If patient is extremely psychotic, give haloperidol 5 mg T.I.D. supplemented by a minor tranquilizer, preferably lorazepam (Ativan) up to 10 mg per day.
9. *Hospitalization*—Always should be the rule when patient is withdrawing from amphetamines, barbiturates, alcohol or polydrug dependency, or psychosis does not remit in emergency room within reasonable short time (according to facility available), or patient is dangerous to himself and/or others.

*After Goldfrank (59, p. 121) and others.

TABLE 10
Reevaluation for Suicidal Potential

Reexamine:
1. Social presence of support system (living alone, family available, marital status)
2. Command hallucinations
3. Severity of depression
4. Previous attempts at suicide
5. Alcohol or drug abuse
6. Major recent loss
7. Availability of firearms
8. Existence of a plan for suicide
9. Age, sex, religion, race factors
10. Impulsivity—can patient make a contract to come to the emergency room rather than act out?

↓

> Crisis Intervention or
> Outpatient Treatment

TABLE 11
Specific Management Algorithms for Drug-induced Psychosis—The Major Presentations

ACUTE AGITATED PSYCHOSIS
WITH PARASYMPATHETIC SHUTDOWN

(Drugs such as: antihistamines, antiparkinsonian drugs, antipsychotics, antispasmodics, belladona alkaloids and synthetic relatives, over-the-counter medications, tricyclic anti-depressants)
Look for central and peripheral signs of anticholinergic toxicity.

Central Signs	Peripheral Signs
Anxious presentation	Arrhythmias
Agitation	Atrial or ventricular tachycardia
Amnesia	Decreased salivation (dry mouth)
Aphasia	Decreased sweating (dry skin)
Confusion	Decreased bronchial and nasal secretions
Coma	Decreased GI motility
Circulatory collapse	Dysphagia
Choreoathetoid movements	Edema of vulva, glottis, lips
Delirium	Flush
Dysarthria	Hyperpyrexia
Disorientation	Hypertension
Excitement	Hypotension
Euphoria	Mydriasis
Hallucinations (Lilliputian)	Vasodilation
Hyperactivity	
Lethargy, somnolence	
Myoclonus	
Nausea and vomiting	
Respiratory failure	
Tremor	
Seizures	

Identify agent responsible by hx. or lab. exam, but do not wait for results to initiate treatment.

BASIC CARE
Assure open airway: Prevent respiratory failure, prevent aspiration.
Start intravenous line: Prevent hypotension (normal saline or Ringers lactate).
Induce emesis or lavage: According to level of consciousness (and time lapsing from ingestion).
Monitor cardiac function.

ADVANCED CARE
Physostigmine indications: Delirium, severe hypertension, life-threatening dysrhythmias, coma, seizures, extreme agitation, hallucinations and stupor.
Administration: When any one of the above plus peripheral signs of anticholinergic toxicity 1-2 mg IV over two minutes slowly—if response occurs, may be repeated every 30 minutes as needed.
Lidocaine: 1 mg per Kg IV with continuous maintenance infusion—for life-threatening Ventricular arrhythmias.

NaHCO₃: For arrythmis that do not respond to physostigmine 1-2 mg per Kg IV.
Phenytoin: For ventricular arrythmias if the three above did not help and for seizures 50 mg per minute IV up to 1 gm loading dose and up to 300 mg IV per day.
Cardiac pacing: If arrythmia is refractory to drug treatment.
Hypotension: IV fluids, if no response—norepinephrine 2-4 microgram per minutes as needed.
Diazepam: For seizures refractory to physostigmine, 5-10 mg IV.
Hypothermia or Hyperthermia: External warming or cooling as needed.
Admit to ICU: Do not discharge if patient is not stable for 24 hours.

TABLE 12
Acute Psychosis With Signs and Symptoms of Hallucinogen Intoxication

1. Identify the agent.
2.   Is there a sympathetic excess?

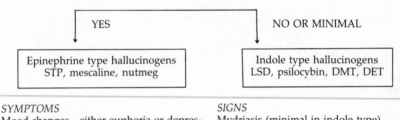

YES	NO OR MINIMAL
Epinephrine type hallucinogens STP, mescaline, nutmeg	Indole type hallucinogens LSD, psilocybin, DMT, DET

SYMPTOMS
Mood changes—either euphoria or depression
Perceptual changes including increased vividness, distortions, illusions, synesthesia, pseudohallucinations, distortions of body image
Confusion, impaired judgment
Anxiety, panic, fear of losing control (LSD)
Increased distractibility
Depersonalization and derealization
Paranoid delusions

SIGNS
Mydriasis (minimal in indole type)
Hyperthermia (minimal in indole type)
Tachycardia
Hypertension (minimal in indole type)
Sweating
Psychomotor agitation or withdrawal behavior
Hyperreflexia (LSD)
Paresthesias (LSD)

TREATMENT
1. *Environment control*: Patient in quiet room, minimum of light, noise and distraction.
2. *Patient control*: Talking down, reassurance.
3. *Medication*: Only if needed. Minor tranquilizer (Lorazepam, Valium) or haloperidol up to 30 mg daily. Avoid phenothiazines.
4. *Restraints*: Only if needed (when patient is dangerous to himself and others).
5. *Hospitalization*: If psychosis does not remit within a reasonable time period (according to available facility). If patient is dangerous to himself and others.
6. *Observation and follow-up for flashbacks.*

TABLE 13

Acute Psychosis with Signs and Symptoms
of Sympathetic Excess

1. Identify agent: amphetamine, cocaine.
2. Look for the following signs and symptoms.

SYMPTOMS	SIGNS
Florid paranoid psychosis with clear sensorium	Tachypnea
	Mydriasis with normal light reflex
Loose associations	Dry mouth
Euphoria, elation, depression, emotional lability	Tachycardia
	Hypertension
Ideas of reference	Psychomotor agitation
Visual and auditory hallucinations (vivid, frightening or criticizing and commanding)	Hyperactive reflexes
	Malnutrition (in chronic users)
	Needle marks
Restlessness, wakefulness, decreased sleep, hyperalertness	Hyperthermia
	Sweating
Irritability, hostility and aggressiveness	Tremulousness
Talkativeness (manic-like pressured speech)	Seizures
Severe abdominal pain (mimicking an acute abdomen—amphetamine)	Stereotypic behavior such as lip biting, skin picking, bruxism
Tactile hallucinations of small animals (cocaine bugs)	

TREATMENT

Controlled quiet environment.
Acidify urine below pH 6.6.
Control: Hyperpyrexia
    Seizures (diazepam—5-10 mg IV).
    Psychosis (haloperidol—begin with 5 mg TID and increase or decrease according to needs).
Observation and follow-up for violent behavior and "crashing."

the patient with delirium depends strongly on the specific cause of that delirium. For specific etiological considerations, the reader is directed to Table 4. The general treatment approach is offered here in step-by-step structure:

1) Identify the cause of the delirium.
2) Until this is done and the delirium is treated, maintain the electrolyte balance with IV fluids and a patent IV.
3) Provide appropriate diet for the patient; make sure he/she eats and drinks.
4) Monitor blood pressure, rectal temperature and heart rate.
5) Promptly treat infection, hyperthermia, and impending circulatory collapse.

TABLE 14
Acute Psychosis Following Phencyclidine (PCP) Ingestion

1. Identify agent.
2. Diagnose level of intoxication according to symptomatology.

Relatively Low Doses	*Relatively Moderate Doses*	*Relatively High Doses*
(on the order of 5 mg in the adult leading to an estimated serum level of 20-30 ng/ml)	(approximately 5-10 mg leading in the adult to 30-100 ng/ml serum level)	(over 10 mg leading in the adult to serum levels of 100 ng/ml and higher)
agitation and excitement gross incoordination blank stare appearance catatonic rigidity catalepsy inability to speak horizontal or vertical nystagmus loss of response to pinprick flushing diaphoresis hyperacousis	coma or stupor eyes remain open pupils in midposition and reactive nystagmus vomiting hypersalivation repetitive motor movements myoclonus (shivering) muscle rigidity on stimulation flushing diaphoresis fever decreased peripheral sensations (pain, touch, and position)	prolonged coma (from 12 hours to days) eyes closed variable pupil size, but reactive hypertension opisthotonic posturing decerebrate positioning repetitive motor movements muscular rigidity convulsions (at doses of 0.5 to 1 mg/kg) absent peripheral sensation decreased or absent gag and corneal reflexes diaphoresis hypersalivation flushing fever

Psychologically the patient may have the following subjective responses: changes in body image, estrangement, disorganization of thought, feelings of inebriation, drowsiness and apathy. The patient may show marked negativism and hostility as well as bizarre behavior. Later, the patient may be amnesic for the drug episode.

PHENCYCLIDINE PSYCHOSIS
Usually the onset is acute, even few days after ingestion. The psychosis is of several days' to a few weeks' duration, clinical presentation ranges from catatonic and mute state to bizarre and violent behavior. There is a history of insomnia, confusion, paranoia and periods of withdrawal alternating with aggressive, unpredictable behavior. Auditory hallucinations, incoherent speech, delusions of paranoid persecution of unsystematized nature. A clinical picture that is non-distinguishable from acute paranoid schizophrenia.

TREATMENT
Depends on the different phases corresponding to the time course of actions of the drug.
1. *Respiratory depression*—External respiratory assistance.
2. *Hyperthermia*—External cooling.

3. *Hypertension*—Treatment with diazoxide (Hyperstat) or hydralazine-HCL (Apresoline).
4. *Convulsions*—IV diazepam (Valium) with constant attention to maintenance of open airway.
5. *Isolation*—The patient is placed in a calm environment with limited sensory input minimizing the phase of excitability and agitation. Do not attempt to talk the patient down at this stage. Set firm control and structure. Continue monitoring of vital signs.
6. *Unmanageable patient*—Restraints.
7. *Medication*—Do not use phenothiazines during the acute stage because of possible anticholinergic potentiation with PCP; use haloperidol (Haldol) repeated hourly 5 mg IM up to 30-40 mg per 24 hours. If the patient is still not under control one can use benzodiazepines which are not metabolized via oxidative pathway, i.e., oxazepam and Lorazepam since diazepam prolongs half-life time of PCP. At the present time a reliable injectable form of Lorazepam is available but is not approved yet by the FDA for the treatment of behavioral problems.
8. *Acidification of urine*—Do not use ascorbic acid since it does not effectively acidify urine. The pH goal of urine is less than 5.5. Urine acidification can be achieved by using IV ammonium chloride 2-3 Meq/Kg every six (6) hours and PCP clearance is increased 100-fold. Monitor blood pH, blood gases, BUN, blood ammonia level and electrolytes.
9. *Gastric lavage*—PCP is poorly absorbed in the stomach and a possible enterohepatic circulation mechanism exists; aggressive gastric lavage can have a major role in getting rid of the toxin.

---

6) If the patient is alert, reassure him/her and orient him to the environment, explaining carefully his/her medical condition and the treatment procedures involved in treating it.
7) Maintain a stable environment. Keep a small light on; try to have one nurse take care of the patient as much as possible. See Table 8 for the treatment of the patient whose life is in immediate danger.

Reversible dementia, as noted above, can mimic the presentation of transient psychosis in the emergency room. The physician should be alert to those forms of dementia which are treatable and can present with signs of psychosis. These etiological entities include: anoxia due to chronic respiratory and cardiac insufficiency, cerebral abscess, tumor, angioma, infection, aneurysm, subdural hematoma, electrolyte imbalance, Addison's disease, normal-pressure hydrocephalus, hypothyroidism, hepatic or renal failure, and hypoglycemia. Hypoglycemia deserves a special note, as we have found it to be one of the most common contributors, other than drug ingestion, to the clinical picture of transient psychosis. Every patient with an acute or sudden psychotic picture should have an immediate evaluation for blood glucose, in addition to other tests. If the results indicate hypoglycemia, the patient should be given an immediate dose of intravenous 50% glucose in water (100 cc).

An open line should be maintained until the basis of the hypoglycemia is found and treated.

The next step is to assess whether or not the acutely psychotic patient is violent and dangerous (Step 3, Table 7). We feel that this aspect of transient psychosis deserves attention because of the association of violence with many forms of transient psychotic disease.

TREATMENT APPROACH TO THE ACUTELY PSYCHOTIC, VIOLENT PATIENT IN THE EMERGENCY ROOM

The emergency room is viewed by many as the "front line." It is the entrance to the hospital milieu and often serves as a stage for violent behavior. Medical personnel in emergency rooms get hurt more frequently than any other medical staff members. The patient is not known to the physician and many times the examination there is the first medical contact for the patient. Acute phases of many conditions are most often seen there and it is at this acute phase that the potential for violence is highest.

Physicians should carefully scrutinize any interaction with a violent patient to clarify whether they are functioning as caretakers or as agents of the law, whether they are the agent of the patient or the agent of society. It also helps to ask oneself whether one is going to be able to discover the underlying causes of the violence when one has evaluated and treated the patient.

Some of the factors that are associated with violent behavior are as follows (66):

1) A past history of violent behavior
2) Drug or alcohol abuse
3) Family instability
4) History of violence in the home by the parents
5) Sociocultural characteristics
6) Childhood violence
7) The presence of psychological factors associated with violence—underlying doubts about manhood or gender identity, homosexual fears, overcontrol (leading to unexpected explosions of violence) paranoia, impulsiveness, lowered self-esteem, and/or depression
8) Age—80% of violent acts are perpetrated by those under 50 years of age
9) Impulsive sexual behavior, including sexual assaults
10) Availability of weapons, including firearms

Warning Signs Indicating Imminent Assault During Examination or Interview

Be alert for abrupt changes in gross behavior.

1) Change in body posture
2) Change in tone of voice (from usually loud to suddenly quiet)
3) Change in motor activity—sudden grinning, masseter sign (a sudden tightening of the masseters), pacing faster than usual, especially at the exits, eye contact (direct staring), advancing and retreating, startled response
4) Change to being contentious and the onset of heavier respiration
5) Atypical demandingness
6) Verbal threats
7) Potentially assaultive delusions or command hallucinations
8) Possession of a weapon
9) Your own intuition is the most important warning. If you are uncomfortable and feel you might be assaulted, be careful!

Organic Psychotic Conditions With Known Association With Violence

1) Acute organic mental syndrome (OMS)—delirium (multiple etiologies)
2) Anticholinergic psychosis
3) Alcoholic brain syndromes—intoxication, hallucinations or withdrawal delirium
4) Pathological alcohol intoxication syndrome
5) Hallucinogen-induced psychosis
6) Sedative or hypnotic intoxication or withdrawal (due to a general disinhibiting effect)
7) Sundowner's syndrome—fluctuating acute OMS
8) Temporal lobe epilepsy
9) Structural lesions—temporal lobes, frontal lobes or limbic system
10) Epilepsy—aggressive discharge especially during premonitory aura or postictal phases
11) Phencyclidine psychosis
12) Encephalitis
13) Amphetamine psychosis—paranoid or delirious
14) Paradoxical agitation and assaultiveness in response to psychoactive medications

Functional Psychotic Conditions Associated With Aggression

1) Acute transient manic state—elevated, expansive or irritable mood with high activity level. Excessive involvement in activi-

ties without recognition of painful consequences for self or others
2) Acute brief reactive psychosis
3) Acute psychosis of any type associated with command assaultive auditory hallucinations
4) Homosexual panic

Certain treatment principles are of utmost importance, since there is
not enough time to "think" when violence occurs. Becoming familiar
with these principles can save lives. Whenever possible the aim of intervention should be therapeutic, to treat the underlying disorder if it
is known or suspected. Patients with violent tendencies should be
trained to come to the emergency room whenever they feel themselves
in danger of going out of control. The physician who treats such a patient
should encourage the patient to "come into the emergency room when
you feel you're going to lash out," assuring the patient that the emergency room staff will help him control such impulses. The physician
should acknowledge the patient's anger but continually emphasize the
self-destructiveness of violence. Such physicians should be familiar with
treatment approaches to violent behavior and thus protect both themselves and the patient. Treatment should be geared to the level of urgency of threat (67).

A. Warning Signs Only

1) Treat verbally (no restraints or medication).
2) Get information from patient or others about what is so upsetting to the patient.
3) Get information from patient or others about what has been
helpful in the past in retaining controls.

Clinical illustration

Dan, a tall and heavy 28-year-old man, was interviewed in the
morning by the attending psychiatrist in the emergency room. He
had been brought in acutely psychotic by the police the night before
after assaulting a bartender who would not serve him free beer.
He was not psychotic when interviewed the next morning and felt
guilty about his behavior. "I am very impulsive," he said, "I strike
out easily, especially when I get crazy, mad and paranoid." The

psychiatrist asked him what helps him to calm down when he is mad. "You know," said Dan, "the only thing that calms me down is when I say to myself what my mother tells me when I am mad—'Dan, stop acting stupid. Be a mensch [Yiddish for man].' " Dan has been living with his mother, does not have close friends and has been drinking on and off. He cannot stay alone; he feels that he lives in a shell, as if he lives someone else's life. He claims there is no substance to him and that he goes "bananas" whenever he doesn't get his own way. Toward the end of the interview, one of the security guards entered the evaluation room to ask about Dan's disposition (he had been restrained when psychotic). "Get out of here," Dan said, "I'm not a psycho." "Okay," the guard responded, "but you are a psych patient and I have to know the disposition." An argument was soon underway and Dan was angry and prepared to punch the security man. The psychiatrist said, "Dan, stop acting stupid. Be a mensch." Dan calmed down.

4) Help patient to clarify and recognize his angry feelings and to verbalize them. This should be accompanied by verbal reassurance that the staff will act in every possible way to prevent him from losing control (67). Many psychotic patients are not aware that they are angry. Teaching the patient to recognize his anger is a major aim of the interaction with this kind of patient. Questions such as "How do you feel when you are angry?" or "Do your muscles tense when you feel anger?" are helpful in alerting the patient to the refinements of various emotional states. Many impulsive people lack the ability to fantasize action prior to initiating it. Questions like "If you are apprehended, are you prepared for trial, conviction, jail, etc.?" help the patient reality test and predict the consequences of violence.

5) If other people in the room seem to be provoking the patient (staff, guards, family members, police, etc.) they should be asked, politely but firmly, to leave.

6) The interviewer must not exhibit excessive anxiety and must project confidence in his own skill. Anxiety on his part may confirm to the patient that there are no controls (68).

7) Others (staff, guards, family, etc.) should be alerted to the possibility of violence and at times should become involved in the consultation. The evaluator should not stay alone with the patient if he feels uncomfortable about it. This increases the chance of an assault.

8) Do not take a chance: If you suspect that a patient might be armed, have the patient searched by a trained security officer.

9) When homosexual panic seems to be contributing to the pa-

tient's turmoil and violence, he should be treated and evaluated by a staff member of the opposite sex

B. Violence, Although Not Yet Occurring, Is Imminent: The Severely Agitated Patient

Treat the situation according to the guidelines above if there is still hope of gaining cooperation.

C. The Actively Violent Patient Who May Be Dangerous to Himself or Others

1) A trial of verbal interaction, though usually unsuccessful, should be tried first. The patient's anger must be acknowledged and he must be told that he will be protected from acting on his impulses. Medication should be offered but most of the time it will be necessary to restrain the patient before administering medication.
2) A sufficient show of force will many times enable the violent patient to give up his aggressive behavior, especially if there are many staff members and security officers available at the scene (69).
3) Do not demand that the patient surrender his weapon. If the patient is threatening you with a dangerous weapon (gun, knife, etc.), it is best to ask the patient to put the weapon in a neutral place, such as in the drawer, in the sink, etc. The patient needs assurance that the evaluator will not be in a position to grab the weapon and use it against him. Never ask the patient to give you the gun!
4) Physical restraints are meaningful to patients who are losing control. Restraining a patient safely requires a number of individuals who are trained carefully ahead of time. They should be briefed about the violent individual. If the patient is barricaded in a room, he should preferably be approached by three people, defending themselves by placing a mattress in front of themselves, who can corner him and restrain him. A useful plan is to assign one person to each of the extremities and one for the head. *The combative individual must be restrained as quickly as possible and as humanely as possible* (68, 70).
5) You must know how to protect yourself, avoid an assault, and handle violence when it occurs. It is difficult to instruct an individual on how to behave under conditions of extreme stress and alarm. One tends to react spontaneously and there is little

or no time for tactical thinking. It is for this very reason that familiarity with these techniques is so important, allowing the endangered clinician to adopt and adapt as the situation requires. These tips must be used selectively and carefully: They may work on one patient and escalate the situation with another.

(a) Counterthreatening is very effective at times (using such phrases as "If you do not control yourself, I am not going to treat you," may be very effective with a regressed individual). If you are big and the patient is very small and unarmed, you can *consider* defending yourself physically.

(b) Escape may be a wise move if the patient is unarmed. This will enable you to call for help.

(c) Another tactic some people find useful is total compliance, doing whatever the patient wants you to do.

(d) If you can take over the helpless, sick role, you might become a nonthreatening object and inspire the violent patient to stop and take care of you. A classical example is that of a patient who was threatening the evaluating clinician with a gun. The physician became nauseated and vomited. The patient put the gun away and hurried to the aid of the sick physician. The expression of helplessness and fear may have the same calming effect.

(e) Feeding the patient, offering food, drink (non-alcoholic) and cigarettes, has a calming and nurturing effect. The message conveyed is, "I care about you."

(f) If there is an alarm system, don't hesitate to use it. The timing is very important: The people who come to help do not have any idea what is happening in the interview room.

6) Medication should be prepared, if possible, before the restraint is applied (67, 71). The best route is IV, enabling good control and rapid high blood levels of medication. Absorption of oral and IM medications cannot be predicted. Since it is likely that the patient might resist the administration of the medication, IM might be the only way to give it.

7) There are some general principles to keep in mind when medicating a violent patient.

(a) When the etiology of the violence (or the psychosis) is in doubt, observe before acting.

(b) Behavioral interactions should precede pharmacological ones.

(c) When the diagnosis is unclear but medication is necessary, give the most benign medication.

(d) Use the drug's side effects (e.g., sedation) to enhance clinical efficacy.

The most useful medications for acute, crisis situations are discussed below.

The barbiturates (especially the short-acting ones) can be given either IM or IV with caution. Amobarbital is effective in doses of 200-500 mg.

Benzodiazepines can be given IV, IM or PO. Diazepam (5-10 mg) is very effective when given slowly IV. The patient should be observed very closely for signs of respiratory depression. Because the route lacks severe side effects, oral administration is preferred. The drug given orally has excellent absorption and a long half-life of 20 to 50 hours. Uncooperativeness can rule this out, however. In a restrained patient who is uncooperative, IM administration may be needed, although here, too, blood levels cannot be predicted. Short-to-intermediate-acting benzodiazepines are now also available (lorazepam [Ativan] and Oxazepam [Serax]) which may be more suitable for emergency room use. An IM form of lorazepam is currently available but its use is restricted to preoperative anesthetic use by the FDA. The IM form of the drug seems to give predictable blood levels and can thus be very useful in a crisis situation.

Phenothiazines and other antipsychotics can be administered orally in liquid (concentrate) and tablet forms. In agitated, combative patients, the IM route is preferred. Thorazine, which is relatively low in potency, has a high index of sedation, making it particularly suitable for this kind of situation. Loxapine (Loxitane) is a useful liquid medication (dose: 40-60mg over 24 hours), which has no taste given orally. Haloperidol (Haldol) is the most popular choice. Five to 10 mg can be given IM on an hourly basis to a maximum of 60 mg over 24 hours. Haloperidol may help control the psychotic symptomatology and behavior with minimal hypotensive side effects and with strong antipsychotic effect. It is important to note that phenothiazines lower the seizure threshold and thus should be used with caution when a convulsive disorder is suspected.

Prediction of Dangerousness and Alternatives to Hospitalization (72)

No one has yet developed a reliable method for predicting dangerousness. Such predictions are usually unreliable (73). Physicians are usually no better at predicting which patients will be dangerous than laymen. A past history of mental illness is in no way a predictor of violence.

If the patient has a good enough social support system and is not acutely dangerous to himself or others, one may consider making a "contract" with him or her. The patient is asked whether he/she could walk into the emergency room and speak with the clinician on duty whenever he/she feels that controls are slipping. Being able to make this contract is usually a positive prognostic sign and may avoid unnecessary hospitalizations. One should offer the patient "crisis intervention" (frequent visits to the emergency room or a crisis team on a limited basis) or a referral to an outside agency which can offer this service to the patient.

Once it has been determined that the acutely psychotic patient is not dangerous to himself or others and is not violent, the next step is to determine that the patient is not severely depressed or acutely suicidal. (The reader is referred to the DSM-III for a description of major depression [11, pp. 210-215].) A major depression can be part of the clinical presentation of transient psychosis. It is important to determine whether the depressed patient can be managed on an outpatient basis or with crisis intervention. If the physician's clinical impression is that the risk should not be tolerated, inpatient hospitalization must be considered. If it is unclear, the suicidal potential should be carefully reevaluated (see Table 10).

The first step in the evaluation of an acutely psychotic suicidal patient should be the evaluation of the patient's immediate dangerousness to himself. The evaluation involves gathering information from the patient, relatives, medical staff, and police accompanying patient, assessing the degree of lethality if there has been a suicide attempt, and taking responsibility to insure the patient's safety so that a more thorough and careful assessment can take place. This can take the form of one of any number of possible suicide precautions, depending on the availability of hospital resources (physical plant, nurses, security staff, aids, housestaff, family, etc.), lethality of attempt, and the presence of a secured quiet room in the emergency room or in a psychiatric unit. The physician must keep in mind that an unsupervised moment can result in the patient's bolting from the hospital and going through a window or injuring himself with a dangerous instrument (IV line, broken bottle, sharp instrument).

The patient's immediate survival is the primary consideration but this is a goal which of necessity emphasizes safety at the expense of independence, autonomy, freedom, responsibility, and at times even dignity (74). The patient's reaction to this restraint should be taken into consideration, since many people will react strongly and possibly aggressively when their freedom is restricted.

After securing the patient's safety, one must consider the patient's family and support systems. If there is sufficient social support, one can consider outpatient treatment or a crisis intervention approach in the emergency room setting. The patient should be medicated and observed closely for a period of time in the emergency room if the facility makes that possible. High-potency drugs such as haloperidol or fluphenazine HCL have an advantage in an emergency setting over the low potency medications such as chlorpromazine. The high potency medications are also less likely to promote hypotension in the same doses (75).

The sedative effect of antipsychotic drugs is unnecessary and may be counterproductive in the treatment of acute psychosis, since most of these patients are afraid of losing control and the "zombie" effect of the drugs can lead them to feel that they've lost control of their bodies. The IM route is preferable (or alternatively liquid concentrate), since many patients do not cooperate or can spit or cheek pill medications. The most popular medication is haloperidol. There is considerable evidence on the effectiveness and lack of complications from IV haloperidol, but this has not yet received FDA approval. Dudley, Rowlett and Loebel (76) have reported successful experience with IV haloperidol and make the following recommendations: the upper limit for rate of administration is 5 mg per 30 seconds or 10 mg per minute. No extrapyramidal side effects were noted with this route. Haloperidol is a safe and effective adjunct in the treatment of acute delirium and seems superior to diazepam. The issue of dosage and so-called rapid tranquilization is still being debated. The underlying logic is similar to that used in medical emergencies when loading doses of digoxin or heparin are given. If one loads the brain receptors quickly, a critical level can be reached in a day or two with faster antipsychotic response. The several authors who have examined this hypothesis have failed to demonstrate any long- or short-term gain from the uses of doses of antipsychotics in dose equivalents greater than 300 mg of chlorpromazine per day (77).

Anderson and Kuehnle (12) have suggested starting with an initial dose of 5-10 mg of haloperidol, depending on age, weight and severity of symptoms. This dose can be repeated hourly until adequate improvement is seen, the patient sleeps, or the maximum cumulative dose of 60 mg has been reached for the 24-hour period. The patient should be kept in a quiet environment and accompanied by a staff member. Major side effects may occur, including dystonia and extrapyramidal side effects, and patients should be informed of this in advance, since patients who are not prepared may become noncompliant. Side effects, especially dystonia, may be treated with Benadryl IM (25-50mg) or IV. This may be repeated after half an hour if the side effect does not resolve.

To summarize, the goal of initial therapy is to produce a therapeutic baseline from which the patient can continue treatment either on a crisis intervention or an outpatient basis. If no adequate baseline can be achieved, the patient should be admitted to the inpatient service.

REFERENCES

1. Mankoff, L.D., Mischorr, M.T., Tomlinson, K.E., et al.: A program of crisis intervention in the emergency medical setting, *Am. J. Psychiat.*, 131: 47-50, 1974.
2. Miller, W.B.: A psychiatric emergency service and some treatment concepts. *Am. J. Psychiat.*, 124: 924-933, 1968.
3. Wood, E.: Resident psychiatrist in the admitting office. *Arch. Gen. Psychiat.*, 13: 54-61, 1964.
4. Gersons, B.E.: Psychiatric emergencies: An overview. *Am. J. Psychiat.*, 137: 1-11, 1980.
5. Spitz, L.: The evolution of psychiatric emergency crisis intervention services in a medical emergency room service. *Comp. Psychiat.*, 17: 99-113, 1976.
6. Krystal, H.: Discussion of Baxter, S., Chodorkoff, B., Underhill, R., Psychiatric emergencies: Dispositional determinants and validity of the decision to admit. *Am. J. Psychiat.*, 124: 1546-1548, 1968.
7. Schwartz, M., and Errera, P.: Psychiatric care in a general hospital emergency room. II: Diagnostic features. *Arch. Gen. Psychiat.*, 9: 113-121, 1963.
8. Boverman, I., Vogel, S., and Boverman, L.: Sex-role stereotypes and clinical judgments of mental health. *J. Consult. Clin. Psych.*, 34: 1-7, 1970.
9. Hanson, G., and Babigian, H.: Reasons for hospitalization from the psychiatric emergency service. *Psychiatric Quart.*, 3: 336-351, 1974.
10. Yamamoto, J., and Goin, M.: Social class factors relevant to psychiatric treatment. *J. Nerv. Ment. Dis.*, 142: 332-339, 1966.
11. *Diagnostic and Statistical Manual of Mental Disorders, Third Edition.* (DSM-III). Washington, D.C.: American Psychiatric Association, 1980.
12. Anderson, H.W., and Kuehnle, C.J.: Strategies for the treatment of acute psychosis. *JAMA*, 229: 14, 1974.
13. Hall, R.C.W., Popkin, M.K., DeVaul, R., Faillale, L.A., and Stickney, S.K.: Physical illness presenting as a psychiatric disease. *Arch. Gen. Psychiat.*, 35, 11: 1315-1320, 1978.
14. McIntyre, J.S., and Romano, J.: Is there a stethoscope in the house (and is it used)? *Arch. Gen. Psychiat.*, 34: 1147-1151, 1977.
15. *The Merck Manual of Diagnosis and Treatment.* 14th Edition. Chapter 121: Neuropsychiatric syndromes in organic cerebral disease, pp. 1302-1308. Robert Berkow (Ed.), New Jersey: Merck Laboratories, 1982.
16. Walker, S., III: *Psychiatric Signs and Symptoms Due to Medical Problems.* Springfield, IL: Charles C Thomas, 1967.
17. MacKenzie, I.C.K.: Delirium. In: F.D. Hart (Ed.), *French Index of Differential Diagnosis.* Second Edition. Bristol: Wright and Sons, Ltd., 1979.
18. Kaufman, M.R.: Management of the acute psychotic episode in a general hospital. *Hospital Medicine*, 1, 11: 1-8, 1965.
19. DeVaul, R.A., and Zisook, S.: Reversible organic brain syndrome clues to quick recognition. *Medical Times*, 105: 9-15, 1980.

20. Cummings, J., Benson, D.F., LoVerme, S. Jr.: Reversible dementia. *JAMA*, 243, 23: 2434-2439, 1980.
21. Freedman, A.M., III: Delusions, depersonalization and unusual psychopathological symptoms. In: R.C.W. Hall (Ed.), *Psychiatric Presentations of Medical Illness*. New York: Spectrum, 1980, pp. 75-80.
22. Walker, S., III: Infectious diseases which present as psychological disorders. In: Walker, S., III (Eds), *Psychiatric Signs and Symptoms Due to Medical Problems*. Springfield, IL: Charles C Thomas, 1967, pp. 46-71.
23. Finland, M., Grigsby, M.E., and Haight, T.H.: Efficacy and toxicity of oxytetracycline and chlortetracycline. *Arch. Internal Med.*, 93: 23-43, 1954.
24. Jones, R.O.: Delirium. In: R.D. Pasnau (Ed.), *Consultation and Liaison Psychiatry*. New York: Grune & Stratton, 1975, pp. 219-226.
25. Goldfrank, L.R., and Melinek, M.: Locoweed and other anticholinergics. In: L. Goldfrank (Ed.), *Toxicologic Emergencies*. New York: Appleton-Century-Crofts, 1982, pp. 75-84.
26. Cohen, S.: Gift of the sun gold or the third scourge of mankind? *Drug Abuse and Alcoholism Letter*, Vista Hill Foundation, 10: 7, 1981.
27. Seigel, R.K., and Jaryik, M.E.: Drug induced hallucinations in animals and man; and West, L.J.: A clinical and theoretical overview of hallucinatory phenomena. In: R.K. Seigel, and L.J. West (Eds.), *Hallucinations: Behavior, Experience and Theory*. New York: John Wiley and Sons, 1975.
28. Bluestone, H., and Melinek, M.: Effects of the urban crisis on the community general hospital. *Hospital and Community Psychiatry*, 32,6: 477-480, 1982.
29. DiSclifani, A., Hall, R.C.W., and Gardner, E.R.: Drug induced psychosis: Emergency diagnosis and management. *Psychosomatics*, 22, 10: 845-855. 1981.
30. O'Brien, J.: Increase in suicide attempts by drug ingestion. *Arch. Gen. Psychiat.*, 34, 10: 1165-1169, 1977.
31. Goldfrank, L.: General perspective. In: L. Goldfrank (Ed.), *Toxicological Emergencies*, Second Edition. New York: Appleton-Century-Crofts, 1982.
32. Newman, G.: Intermittent recurring psychoses. In: R.C.W. Hall (Ed.), *Psychiatric Presentations of Medical Illness, Somatopsychic Disorders*. New York: Spectrum, 1980.
33. Becker, D.M., and Cramer, S.: The neurological manifestations of porphyria: A review. *Med.*, 56: 411-423, 1977.
34. Guze, S.B.: The occurrence of psychiatric illness in systematic lupus erythematosus. *Am. J. Psychiat.*, 123: 1562-1570, 1967.
35. Meletzky, B.M.: The episodic dyscontrol syndrome. *J. Dis. Nerv. System*, 34: 178-185, 1973.
36. Gelenberg, A.J.: The catatonic syndrome. *Lancet*, 1: 1339-1341, 1976.
37. Weiss, J.R., and Rhoads, J.M.: Brief reactive psychosis: A psychodynamic interpretation. *J. Clin. Psychiat.*, 40: 440-443, 1979.
38. Abrams, M.A.: Catatonia: Prediction of response to somatic treatments. *Am. J. Psychiat.*, 134: 78-80, 1977.
39. Stoudemire, A.: The differential diagnosis of catatonic states. *Psychosomatics*, 23, 3: 245-252, 1982.
40. Raskin, D.E., and Frank, S.W.: Herpes encephalitis with catatonic stupor. *Arch. Gen. Psychiat.*, 31: 544-546, 1974.
41. Glicksman, L.S.: *Psychiatric Consultation in the General Hospital*. New York and Basel: Marcel Dekker, 1980.
42. Hollender, M.H., and Hirsch, S.J.: Hysterical psychosis. *Am. J. Psychiat.*, 120: 1066-1074, 1964.
43. Langners, L.L.: Hysterical psychosis: The cross cultural evidence. *Am. J. Psychiat.*, 124, 2: 143-151, 1967.
44. Krieger, M.J., and Zussman, M.: The importance of cultural factors in brief reactive psychosis. *J. Clin. Psychiat.*, 42, 6: 248-249, 1981.
45. Littlewood, R., and Lipsedge, M.: Acute psychotic reactions in Caribbean-born patients. *Psychological Medicine*, 11, 2: 303-318, 1981.

46. Harris, B.: A case of brain fag in East Africa. *Brit. J. Psychiat.*, 139: 162-163, 1981.
47. Fernandez-Marina, R.: The Puerto Rican Syndrome: Its dynamics and cultural determinants. *Psychiatry*, 4: 47-82, 1961.
48. Langness, L.L.: Hysterical psychosis in the New Guinea highlands: A Bena Bena example. *Psychiatry*, 28: 258-277, 1965.
49. Kapur, R.L., and Pandurang, A.K.: A comparative study of reactive psychosis and acute psychosis without precipitating stress. *Brit. J. Psychiat.*, 135: 544-550, 1979.
50. McCabe, M.S., and Stromgren, E.: Reactive psychoses. *Arch. Gen. Psychiat.*, 32: 447-454, 1975.
51. Sale, I., Budtz-Olsen, I., Craig, G., and Kalucy, R.: Acute psychosis precipitated by the encounter group experience. *Med. J. Australia*, 1, 4: 157-158, 1980.
52. Shipley, R.H., and Bondewyns, P.A.: Flooding and implosive therapy: Are they harmful? *Behavior Therapy*, 11, 4: 503-508, 1980.
53. Mahrer, A.R.: Value decisions in therapeutically induced acute psychotic episodes. *Psychotherapy: Theory, Research and Practice*, 17, 4: 454-458, 1980.
54. Bozzuto, J.C.: Cinematic neurosis following "The Exorcist." *J. Nerv. Ment. Dis.*, 161, 1: 43-48, 1975.
55. Linn, L.: Other psychiatric emergencies In: A.M. Freedman, H.I. Kaplan, and B.J. Sadock (Eds.), *Comprehensive Textbook of Psychiatry*. Baltimore: Williams and Wilkins, 1975, pp. 1788-1789.
56. Freud, S.: Introductory lectures. *Standard Edition*, Volume XVI. London: Hogarth, 1955, pp. 274-275.
57. Goldfrank, L.R., Flomebaum, N.E., and Weissman, R.S.: General management of the poisoned and overdosed patient. In: L. Goldfrank (Ed.), *Toxicological Emergencies*. New York: Appleton-Century-Crofts, 1982, pp. 3-18.
58. Goldfrank, L.R., and Kirstein, R.: Amphetamines. In: L.R. Goldfrank (Ed.), *Toxicological Emergencies*. New York: Appleton-Century-Crofts, 1982, pp. 118-121.
59. Goldfrank, L.R.: *Toxicological Emergencies*, New York: Appleton-Century-Crofts, 1982.
60. Hall, R.C.W., Feinsilver, D.L., and Holt, R.E.: Anticholinergic psychosis: Differential diagnosis and management. *Psychosomatics*, 22, 7: 581-587, 1981.
61. Granacher, R.P., Baldessarini, R.J., and Messner, E.: Physostigmine treatment of delirium induced by anticholinergics. *American Family Physician*, 13, 5: 99-103, 1976.
62. Sullivan, J.B., Jr., Rumack, B.H., and Peterson, R.G.: Management of tricyclic antidepressant toxicity. In: M.J. Bayer and B.H. Rumack, (Eds.), *Topics in Internal Medicine—Poisoning and Overdosage*. Vol. 1: 3. New York: Aspen, 1979, pp. 65-71.
63. Hamilton, R., and Garnett, E.: Phencyclidine overdose. *Annals of Internal Medicine*, 9, 3: 173-174, 1980.
64. Allen, R.M., and Young, S.J.: Phencyclidine induced psychosis; *Am. J. Psychiat.*, 135, 9: 1081-1083, 1978.
65. Cohen, S.: P.C.P. (Angel Dust): New trends in treatment. *Drug Abuse and Alcoholism Newsletter*, VII, 6: 1-3, Vista Hill Foundation, 1978.
66. Melinek, M., and Gilner, S.: The violent patient. *Physician Assistant and the Health Practitioner*, 72-75, September 1981.
67. Tupin, J.P.: Management of violent patient. In: R.J. Shader (Ed.), *Manual of Psychiatric Therapeutics*. Boston: Little, Brown, 1977, pp. 125-136.
68. Lion, R.J., Levenberg, L.B., and Strange, R.E.: Restraining the violent patient. *J. Psychiatric Nursing and Mental Health Services*, 10: 9-11, March-April 1972.
69. Hackett, T.P.: Disruptive states. In: T.P. Hackett and N. Cassem (Eds.), *Handbook of General Hospital Psychiatry*. St. Louis: C.V. Mosby, 1978, pp. 246-251.
70. Rosen, H., and DiGiacomo, J.: The role of physical restraint in the treatment of psychiatric illness. *J. Clin. Psychiat.*, 39: 228-232, 1978.
71. Weintraub, M., and Barry, D.: Managing the acutely agitated, aggressive patient. *Drug Therapy* (Hospital Edition), pp. 61-68, April 1970.
72. Farnsworth, D.L.: Dangerousness. *Psychiatric Annals*, 51, 7: 304-309, 1977.

73. American Psychiatric Association Task Force (Chairpersons Lion, J.R. and Kenefick, D.P.). What Can We Predict? Washington D.C.: APA Publications, 1974, pp. 23-30.
74. Litman, R. E.: The assessment of suicidality. In: R.O. Pasnau (Ed.), *Consultation and Liaison Psychiatry*. New York: Grune & Stratton, 1975, pp. 227-236.
75. Anderson, W. H., Kuehnle, J.C., and Catanzano, D.M.: Rapid treatment of an acute psychosis. *Am. J. Psychiat.*, 133, 9: 1076-1078, 1976.
76. Dudley, D.L., Rowlett, D.B., and Loebel, P.J.: Emergency use of intravenous haloperidol. *General Hospital Psychiatry*, 1: 240-246, 1979.
77. Linden, R., Davis, J.M., and Rubinstein, J.: High versus low dose treatment with antipsychotic agents. *Psychiatric Annals*, 12, 8: 769-781, 1982.

Chapter 12

Transient Psychosis:
When to Consult a Psychiatrist

Daniel S.P. Schubert, M.D., Ph.D.,
and Uriel Halbreich, M.D.

As a general rule of thumb, we believe that every patient with acute psychotic manifestations should be seen by a psychiatrist. Transient psychoses are no exception to this rule. For a variety of reasons, however, this is not the case in actual practice. In the following chapter, we will describe what seems to be the present situation in the field and will review some of the reasons for this far-from-optimal state of affairs. We will also cover some indications for referral to a psychiatrist and, finally, what might reasonably be expected from the psychiatrist after the patient has been referred.

GENERAL INDICATIONS FOR PSYCHIATRIC CONSULTATION

Two situations most often lead nonpsychiatric medical specialists to seek psychiatric consultation. The first of these is some difficulty in the ward management of a patient during diagnosis and treatment of a nonpsychiatric condition. The second occurs when there is no medical basis found for the physical complaint. In addition, psychiatric consultations are usually requested for patients with a history of schizophrenia, treatment with antipsychotic medications, hospitalizations in psychiatric services, and presentations with delusions and/or hallucinations.

Certainly psychiatrists should be consulted in these cases, but there are many other areas where psychopathology exists, even though these patients are far less likely to have the benefit of consultation. For example, the quiet and compliant medical patient, although suffering from nervousness, depression, confusion and many other psychiatric symptoms, may not be referred to psychiatry. In general, wherever there is a question of psychiatric pathology, that question should be resolved by a request for psychiatric consultation. That this consultation is necessary is not always sufficiently understood. The issue is influenced by the caretaker's general attitude toward psychiatry.

In studying why medical students do not go into psychiatry, Nielson and Eaton (1) have found that their sampled medical school students, as well as their nonpsychiatric instructors, have developed an attitude that psychiatrists are ineffective in their treatment, unscientific, and tend to over-diagnose psychiatric problems. This has implications for referral practices from medicine to psychiatry and may explain, at least in part, a low referral rate.

It is regrettable that many physicians, both general practitioners and specialists, are not well-versed in modern psychiatry. This lack is reflected in the quality of the diagnosis and treatment of psychiatric problems in their patients. All too frequently they proceed from a layman's point of view or from "commonsense," giving advice in a parental way and at times throwing a barrage of psychotropic medications at the patient. Even in academic settings, this approach is ill-advised and ineffective. Given the high percentage of patients who will continue to be treated for their psychiatric problems by primary care physicians (2), it is surprising that more nonpsychiatrists are not asking for and receiving better training in such management. Unfortunately, even when joint responsibility or a collaborative approach to treating the patient is offered, most nonpsychiatric physicians tend not to accept it (3).

The higher incidence of psychiatric disorders among patients with physical disorders has been documented (4). All too often, the nonpsychiatrist is concerned only with diagnosis and treatment in his/her own area and does not view the patient holistically (5). Depression is frequent on nonpsychiatric wards, but only a small portion of these patients is referred to a psychiatrist for consultation. Studies cited by

Lipowski (6) suggest that perhaps 40% of patients on nonpsychiatric services and 60% of outpatients in medical and surgical clinics have some psychiatric problem. Although estimates vary and referral rates differ from place to place in the United States, usually only about 10% of such patients are referred for psychiatric consultation. Too often the general practitioner acts as an overly restraining filter between the patient and the psychiatrist (7).

Even when a psychiatric diagnosis is made, it is often not followed by appropriate referral: The rate of referral for psychiatric patients diagnosed by general practitioners is between 5% and 25% (8, 9, 10, 11). Sometimes general practitioners will try to treat the acutely ill psychiatric patient while referring chronic patients. Many patients are referred to a psychiatrist only when they fail to respond to the treatment offered by the family doctor.

SPECIFIC REASONS FOR PSYCHIATRIC REFERRAL OF PATIENTS WITH TRANSIENT PSYCHOSES

In general, the nonpsychiatrist will contact the consultant about psychotic behavior arising from the patient's medical condition or treatment. Usually the rule is to call for psychiatric referral if the patient's physical condition or treatment does not adequately explain the transient psychosis. If a patient on steroids reacts with psychosis, for example, it is not surprising. If, however, no transient psychotic reaction is expected, either from the nature of the disease process or from the treatment, the psychiatrist should be consulted. This implies an understanding of the physical and pharmacological bases of psychiatric problems. The book edited by Hall (12) is a helpful guide. In any doubt, one should call a psychiatrist, even to the extreme of calling a specialist in every case of transient psychosis.

The differential diagnosis of transient psychosis is described in other chapters of this book. Therefore, only some specific examples will be given here. Ramani and associates (13) have described the diagnosis of hysterical seizures in epileptic patients. Drug-induced schizophrenia-like syndromes as described by Stone (14) are another area of interest. Psychiatrists have usually been trained in the treatment of medication-induced psychotic syndromes and thus consultation is in order here. People addicted to or withdrawing from barbiturates require specific detoxification programs which may or may not be related to specific psychiatric programs in a given area.

Pseudodementia is described by Wells (15) and Kiloh (16). Wells indicates that there are a number of psychiatric symptoms which can present to the neurologist or internist that mimic or caricature dementia. Kiloh emphasizes that the presence of depression in patients considered demented should suggest a reevaluation in terms of pseudodementia. The history of a prior psychotic episode should also arouse suspicion. He emphasizes the importance of course, in that intermittent episodes and a short course with sudden onset are both unusual in dementia. Josephson and MacKenzie (17) reported on cases of mania that were induced by giving thyroid replacement to hypothyroid patients. Pies (18) reports a case of persistent bipolar illness after steroid administration. In all of these types of cases, psychiatric consultation is warranted even before the medical situation has been stablizied.

Kellner (19) wrote an overall review of psychiatric illness following physical illness. Petty and Noyes (20) reviewed depression secondary to cancer. Probably the greatest number of patients who incur a psychiatric illness after a medical illness will fall into the category of adjustment reactions. Transient psychosis can also occur, however, and again deserves prompt psychiatric consultation.

Studies of life crises have become very valuable in an overall understanding of increased frequency of illness. There is a significant positive correlation between frequency of illness and critical life events. The situation is complicated, since serious illnesses, either physical or mental, are themselves a source of life crises; therefore, one could expect a higher rate of psychiatric problems, including transient psychoses, following severe physical illness.

SCREENING FOR TRANSIENT PSYCHOSIS

No screening instrument is sufficient by itself. Screening instruments are like laboratory tests—each should be an aid to a thorough clinical evaluation. When questions remain, a psychiatric evaluation is indicated.

DePaulo and Folstein (21, 22) have recommended the use of psychiatric screening instruments, particularly on the neurological service. They used the Mini Mental State (23) for cognitive disturbance and the General Health Questionnaire (24). On neurological wards they found that 67% of the patients had either cognitive defects or emotional disturbance—or both. In 30% of their patients, psychiatric disturbance was not recognized by the physician. The majority of these disturbances persisted at discharge.

Another self-administered personality inventory is the Minnesota

Multiphasic Personality Inventory (MMPI). Although longer, it takes little time on the part of the physician, requiring only introduction and explanation; also, it can be mechanically scored. It can indicate psychiatric difficulties in a patient who has not been so identified. For non-psychiatrists who feel uncomfortable referring patients for evaluation when symptoms are not clearly psychiatric, the presence of abnormal scores on a screening questionnaire or test can be useful in clarifying and supporting the need for referral. In the case of transient psychoses, the paranoia and schizophrenia scales of the MMPI would be elevated 2-3 standard deviations above the mean for the normal population (T scores above 70-80). Such elevations of MMPI scales may, however, also occur in psychiatric disorders other than transient psychosis.

A popular screening instrument for psychiatric disorders is the SCL-90, which is simple and self-rating (25). Even simpler are such screening questions as: 1) "Do people bother you or irritate you?" followed by samples of positive responses to this question; 2) "Have you had some strange or unusual experiences?" which can be followed up by "Have you had any experiences which you can't explain?" These should be followed by asking for examples if the answer is positive. These enable the physician to tap possible delusions and other thought disorders and hallucinations. Where positive answers are followed by possible delusional or hallucinatory answers, referral for psychiatric consultation is warranted.

WHEN PSYCHOLOGISTS AND SOCIAL WORKERS SHOULD CONSULT A PSYCHIATRIST

Psychologists, social workers, and other mental health professionals should most often consult with a psychiatrist when a mood and/or behavioral problem exists which indicates the possible need for hospitalization. The first and most obvious of such indications is the acutely or actively suicidal patient. Patients with psychoses or nonpsychotic major depressive disorders are natural referrals to a psychiatrist because of the potential for biological treatment of these disorders, on either an inpatient or outpatient basis.

Hospitalization of the acutely suicidal patient prevents him from self-injury or suicide. A closed inpatient ward exerts a good deal of control over a patient's actions, making it preferable to an outpatient setting in such situations. The homicidal or destructive patient presents a corollary to the suicidal individual. In the case of the psychotic patient, treatment should always include biological approaches, supplemented by psy-

chotherapy and milieu interventions. Biological treatment is also frequently helpful in major depressive disorders. Psychotherapy should
continue concomitant with the administration of medication (26). It may
be added that where the slightest suspicion exists of such disorders as
indicated above, psychiatrists may usefully be consulted by nonmedical
mental health workers for an initial, biologically oriented screening of
the patient. Psychiatrists have long worked in fruitful collaboration with
psychologists, social workers and other professionals on both the evaluation and management of patients who may respond to biological approaches.

Some type of medical contact is essential if the psychologist or other
professional is seeing a patient who may have physical illness as a basis
for the psychiatric syndrome. Hall (12) has provided a useful outline to
use in this area. Psychologists and other primary nonmedical therapists
should urge their patients to have annual physical examinations. The
psychiatrist is usually more aware of the psychiatric presentations of
physical illness than the primary care physician and can be useful in this
regard.

WHAT CAN BE EXPECTED OF THE PSYCHIATRIST

When the psychiatrist receives a request for consultation from either
a nonpsychiatric physician or a nonmedical mental health practitioner,
he or she should be expected to make full use of the information given
by the referring source as well as by the patient's medical record. The
psychiatrist is expected to do a full psychiatric examination, including
a mental status examination. At times he will have to obtain further
historical material, if not available. The nonmedical professional would
be unlikely to have medical records from prior physical examinations,
for example, and the psychiatrist will have to obtain them so that he/she
can review the patient's medical history. He/she may also have to gather
further history from friends or relatives of the patient to reach a secure
diagnosis. This often requires collaboration with the referring professional and others involved with the patient.

After examination of the patient, the psychiatrist needs to formulate
a complete differential diagnosis, from both medical and psychiatric
points of reference, taking into account both physical conditions present
and nonpsychiatric medications being taken. The Diagnostic and Statistical Manual of the American Psychiatric Association (DSM-III) suggests
that it is also useful to look at life crises and social stressors over the
two prior years.

The formulation the psychiatrist reaches then permits him or her to suggest the optimal treatment plan. When working with nonpsychiatrists, the psychiatrist must show an orderly approach to the formulation of a diagnosis, which is possible using DSM-III or another structured diagnostic system. He or she must also educate the referring source on the effectiveness of psychiatric treatment. (Some examples of papers showing the effectiveness of psychopharmacology and psychotherapy are cited in references 1, 26, 28, 29, 30, 31.)

If the patient is hospitalized for medical/surgical illness, the psychiatrist should work collaboratively with the surgeon or internist to provide necessary treatment. At discharge, or if the patient is not in the hospital, the psychiatrist should either assume primary responsibility or make an appropriate referral of the patient. As indicated above, the psychiatrist is the best person to manage the biological treatment of emotional illness. If the psychiatrist is not in charge of the case, he/she should assume a collaborative role on the treatment team, assisting the nonpsychiatrist with the difficulties that arise when a clinician is not specifically oriented to a particular type of treatment or medication. The psychiatrist may take a similar stance with the nonphysician therapist. The psychiatrist's involvement should be ongoing and he/she should be able to assume temporary responsibility for the patient or be available for frequent consultation.

THE PSYCHIATRIST AS CONSULTANT

The consulting psychiatrist will be called upon to assume different roles as a function of the various consultation sources. He will assume or emphasize different things when he is called upon by a nonpsychiatric physician than when he is called upon by a nonphysician. A number of role features are common to working with both types of referring sources. Aside from being available for ongoing consultation (3), the psychiatrist will be called upon to do the same examination, assessment and treatment planning as he would for his own patients, including history and differential diagnosis. He will have to specify more clearly and in greater detail what the differential diagnosis includes and his reasons for various diagnoses than he would for a psychiatrist who is consulting with him. He cannot assume, for example, that the nonpsychiatrist is familiar with the criteria for the DSM-III diagnoses (27). His management plan should also be specified clearly, as should recommendations for further evaluation. He should also encourage consultation along the course of the treatment.

The psychiatrist should take the initiative in further evaluation of the patient, especially where the diagnosis is unclear, pursuing the case to his own satisfaction and communicating the results to the referring source. If the treatment plan calls for a therapeutic trial of psychoactive medication, the psychiatrist should indicate when results should be seen and ask for a further consultation, perhaps after one month, when the medication will have had a chance to work. At that time, if there has been no improvement, the psychiatrist will be able to recommend alternative management strategies in addition to any he might have indicated in his original assessment and plan.

The psychiatrist as consultant should also be aware of the interface between his area of expertise and that of the consultee. This has been discussed in the previous section. If, for example, one is consulted by a nonpsychiatric physician, one should be aware of the psychiatric presentations of medical illness and take this into account in one's evaluation. Likewise, the interactions between medications given by the primary physician and psychiatric medications must be a consideration and should be shared with the referring source. Finally, the psychiatrist must take into account the interaction of the ward milieu with the patient's individual dynamics.

COLLABORATION BETWEEN PSYCHIATRIST AND PRIMARY CAREGIVER AFTER THE CONSULTATION

We have presented some of the general areas of collaboration between psychiatrist and primary caregiver. To recapitulate briefly, the psychiatrist should take responsibility for ongoing evaluation of care and management of the patient and for further differential diagnosis as necessary. This is relatively easy in an inpatient setting but requires further effort with outpatients. The psychiatrist should be in contact with the primary caregiver within several weeks after discharge to learn whether further information involved in the evaluation is available. He should also determine if the initial trial of psychiatric treatment and/or medication has been successful. Most often the detailed recommendations for further management will bear repeating at this time. The patient may need to be reevaluated for further diagnosis and treatment planning.

Ideally, the collaboration is a mutual effort between psychiatrist and referring source (3). This is not always the case. The optimal situation finds psychiatrist and nonpsychiatrist in the same environment at least weekly. This allows for "curbstone consultation," ongoing evaluation, easy communication and collaboration between the two caregivers. In the absence of such a situation, it is sometimes difficult to enter into a collaborative treatment.

The psychiatrist is often called upon to coordinate medical care, particularly in an academic setting. This is not to say that the psychiatrist will give the care but that he or she will be responsible for making sure that the patients are referred to appropriate personnel. The psychiatrist should not hesitate to assume such a role, as it makes his usefulness as consultant greater in the long run, enabling him to see consultation from both sides. He can then see that difficulties met in dealing with nonpsychiatric personnel may be those he is producing in his own responses. Aside from the self-corrective effect this may have, he can also get to know personally people with whom he consults and who consult with him (32).

Such collaboration should be the norm rather than the exception. It is unfortunate that health care providers in specialty and subspecialty areas tend to focus on their own areas of expertise and not on the interface with other disciplines. In the area of primary care, conversely, health providers tend to take on responsibility for problems they are not equipped by training or experience to handle. As a consultant, therefore, one is faced with the subspecialist who is unaware of the problems of the patient that do not intersect his own area of expertise. At other times, one may encounter an overzealous primary physician who is ignoring his own lack of expertise in special areas.

A greater reliance on consultation and the development of one's own network of medical referrals and consultants will improve both of these unfortunate situations. Consultants should encourage this by availability and collaboration and should refer their own patients to other physicians as it becomes appropriate. Consultation is usually not *overdone* but *underdone*, both to psychiatry and to other areas of health care.

While this is not the place to offer models of health care, it is possible that in the future an interconnecting network of health care providers may provide not only the most complete but also the most effective and least expensive health care possible. Consultation in psychiatry may, hopefully, help by working toward this end.

REFERENCES

1. Nielson, A.C., and Eaton, J.S.: Medical students' attitudes about psychiatry. *Arch. Gen. Psychiat.*, 38: 1144-1154, 1981.
2. Houpt, J.L., Orleans, C.S., George, L.K., and Brodie, H.K.H.: The role of psychiatric and behavioral factors in the practice of medicine. *Am. J. Psychiat.*, 137: 37-47, 1980.

3. Schubert, D.S.P.: Shared responsibilities: A psychiatrist's thoughts on problems with psychiatric consultations to internal medicine. *Psychosomatics*, 23: 833, 839, 843, 1982.
4. Eastwood, M.R., and Trevelyan, M.H.: Relationship between physical and mental disorder. *Psychological Medicine*, 2: 263-272, 1972.
5. Lipowski, Z.J.: Holistic medical foundations of American psychiatry. *Am. J. Psychiat.*, 138: 888-895, 1981.
6. Lipowski, Z.J.: Review of consultation psychiatry and psychosomatic medicine: Clinical aspects. *Psychosomatic Medicine*, 29: 201-224, 1967.
7. Goldberg, D., and Huxley, P.: *Mental Health in the Community: The Pathway to Psychiatric Care*. London and New York: Tavistock, 1981.
8. Fisch, R., Shapiro, S., and Goldensohn, S.S.: Family physician referrals for psychiatric consultation and patient initiative in seeking care. *Soc. Sci. Med.*, 4: 273-291, 1970.
9. Schein, 1976. Cited in Goldberg and Huxley, No. 7.
10. Shepherd, M., Cooper, A., Brown, A., et al.: *Psychiatric Illness in General Practice*. New York: Oxford University Press, 1966.
11. Lucke, Krantz, and Kramer. Cited in Goldberg and Huxley, No. 7.
12. Hall, R.C.W.: *Psychiatric Presentation of Medical Illness: Somatopsychic Disorders*. New York: SP Medical and Scientific Books, 1980.
13. Ramani, S.V., Quesney, L.F., Olson, D., and Gumnit, R.J.: Diagnosis of hysterical seizures in epileptic patients. *Am. J. Psychiat.*, 137: 705-709, 1980.
14. Stone, M.H.: Drug related schizophrenic syndromes. *Int. J. Psychiat.*, 13: 391-441, 1973.
15. Wells, C.E.: Pseudodementia. *Am. J. Psychiat.*, 136: 895-900, 1979.
16. Kiloh, L.G.: Pseudodementia. *Acta Psychiatrica Scandinavica*, 37: 336-351, 1961.
17. Josephson, A.M., and MacKenzie, T.B.: Thyroid-induced mania in hypothyroid patients. *Brit. J. Psychiatr.*, 137: 222-228, 1980.
18. Pies, R.: Persistent bipolar illness after steroid administration. *Arch. Int. Med.*, 141: 1087, 1981.
19. Kellner, R.: Psychiatric ill health following physical illness. *Brit. J. Psychiat.*, 112: 71-73, 1966.
20. Petty, F., and Noyes, R.: Depression secondary to cancer. *Biological Psychiatry*, 16: 1203-1220, 1981.
21. DePaulo, J.R., and Folstein, M.F.: Psychiatric disturbance in neurological patients: Detection, recognition and hospital course. *Annals of Neurology*, 4: 225-228, 1978.
22. DePaulo, J.R., Folstein, M.F., and Gordon, B.: Psychiatric screening on a neurological ward. *Psychological Medicine*, 10: 125-132, 1980.
23. Folstein, M.F., Folstein, S.E., and McHugh, P.R.: "Mini-mental state," A practical method for grading the cognitive state of patients for clinicians. *Journal of Psychiatric Research*, 12: 189-198, 1975.
24. Goldberg, D.P.: The detection of psychiatric illness by questionnaire. London: Oxford University Press, 1972.
25. Derogatis, L.R., Lipman, R.S., and Covi, L.: The SCL-90. In: G. Williams (Ed.), *E.C.V.E.U. Assessment Manual for Psychopharmacology*. United States Department of Health, Education and Welfare, Rockville, MD, 1976.
26. DiMascio, A., Weissman, M.M., Prusoff, B.A., et al.: Differential symptom reduction by drugs and psychotherapy in acute depression. *Arch. Gen. Psychiat.*, 36: 1450-1456, 1979.
27. *Diagnostic and Statistical Manual of Mental Disorders, Third Edition*. Washington, D.C.: (DSM-III) American Psychiatric Association, 1980.
28. Davis, J.M.: Overview: Maintenance therapy in psychiatry: I. Schizophrenia. *Am. J. Psychiat.*, 132: 1237-1245, 1975.
29. Davis, J.M.: Overview: Maintenance therapy in psychiatry: II. Affective disorders. *Am. J. Psychiat.*, 133: 1-11, 1976.

30. Bergin, A.E., and Lambert, M.J.: The evaluation of therapeutic outcomes. In: A.E. Bergin and S.L. Garfield (Eds.), *Handbook of Psychotherapy and Behavior Change: An Empirical Analysis, Second Edition.* New York: John Wiley and Sons, 1978, pp. 139-189.
31. Smith, M.L., Glass, G.V., and Miller, T.I.: *The Benefits of Psychotherapy.* Baltimore: Johns Hopkins University Press, 1980.
32. Schubert, D.S.: Obstacles to effective psychiatric liaison. *Psychosomatics,* 19: 283-285, 1978.

Chapter 13

Forensic Aspects of
Transient Psychoses

*Harvey Bluestone, M.D.,
and John Melella, M.S.W.*

INTRODUCTION

Transient psychosis is an extremely broad and potentially vague clinical entity. Despite the ubiquitous nature of the phenomenon, there is virtually no legal reference to it as a discrete psychiatric entity. There are probably several reasons for this. One reason is that the terminology is too new and has not as yet made its way into the reported legal cases and other legal publications. A second reason is that transient psychosis includes a very broad category of disorders, encompassing many smaller, discrete categories, which are often classified by their etiology (1). A third reason for the lack of specific reference to transient psychosis is that the law tends to look at psychiatric concepts differently from the way physicians look at them.

CONCEPTUAL ISSUES

Problems With Terminology

With regard to terminology, a term or concept may only be reported in the legal literature after it has been at issue in a specific legal case. The term "transient psychosis" is not commonly used by psychiatrists and therefore has not appeared in reported cases. Only after psychiatric experts use the terminology in their capacity as experts in a reported case will that issue be specifically addressed. Terms that are more frequently used, which are more or less synonymous, are: temporary insanity, delirium, brief reactive psychosis, and acute drug reaction.

Problems of Vagueness

The scope of the clinical entity called transient psychosis is so broad as to include psychoses due to physical illness and acute exacerbations of schizophrenia. These are situation-oriented cases that in law are looked at more often on a case by case basis. The only general consensus about transient psychoses applies to their temporal aspects. This makes them difficult to categorize from a legal standpoint. The law is not sensitive to categorization on this basis.

Problems of Perspective

Where psychiatrists view their patients' illnesses from a diagnostic or descriptive point of view, the courts tend to view situations from a mental competency-disability point of view. Thus, the courts tend to deal with situations that arise from the patient's having or lacking certain mental capacities, rather than discerning why these capacities, on the part of the patient, do or do not exist. This leaves questions about the nature of the particular mental illness more properly in the hands of the mental health experts.

CONCEPTUAL LEGAL ASPECTS

Given the absence of legal cases having to do specifically with transient psychosis, an attempt will be made to discuss the more general legal aspects of short-term psychosis. Wherever it is possible, attempts will be made to make connections to the transient aspects of psychoses. At the same time, we will attempt to give helpful, practical suggestions about avoiding potential legal liability in areas where it is most likely to arise.

Professional Validation

Because of the relatively rapid recovery time associated with transient psychotic states, the phenomenon does not always lend itself to professional verification. From a legal standpoint, a transient psychosis may give rise to legal implications, where the mental status of the patient at the time an event occurred might be purely speculative. The most visible example of this problem is often seen in criminal insanity defenses. Other more benign but common examples where professional verification is legally important occurs where an individual's competency to marry, to enter into a contract, or to make a will is called into question. The inherent difficulty in reconstructing the mental status of a person suffering from a brief psychotic reaction in the past is self-evident.

Obviously, the number of situations in which transient psychosis can occur is also limitless. Therefore, the present discussion will be confined to situations where the psychosis is directly observable by practitioners. The places where it is most likely to be observed are the psychiatric emergency room, medical wards of a hospital, and the therapist's office or outpatient clinic. Here, where the direct observation of a psychotic state is first encountered, the practitioner becomes inextricably involved in the clinical assessment and appropriate treatment and/or disposition of the patient. In so doing, he or she becomes legally responsible for the consequences of his/her actions or failure to act.

The Emergency Nature of Transient Psychoses

Every clinician knows of cases where patients were substantially out of contact with reality. During this time it is difficult to predict what actions (if any) the patient may take. Any sudden psychotic break with concomitant perceptual distortions, paranoid ideation, depression, and possible dissociative episodes may render that patient unpredictable and perhaps even dangerous. This makes any transient psychosis a potential emergency.

In the event of a potential emergency resulting from psychosis, the practitioner must make a decision as to whether immediate hospitalization is required. The clinician must quickly evaluate the mental status of the patient, available hospital resources, and alternative methods of handling the emergency. The presence of concerned family members may make it possible to treat the patient at home. If hospitalization is needed and the hospital at which the patient appears does not have space for him/her, then suitable transfer must be arranged.

If the clinical judgment is that immediate hospitalization is required, consideration must be given to the form of that admission. If the patient meets the criteria for voluntary admission and is willing to enter the hospital voluntarily, this form of admission is to be preferred. However, it may be necessary to invoke the emergency procedure for hospitalization. This is generally established by law, which requires that the patient, if not confined, will pose an imminent danger to himself or others (2).

In New York State, for example, a patient can be held for 48 hours against his/her will in a facility approved and equipped to provide for such emergencies, and up to 15 days after having been given notice of his/her rights and legal status and after confirmation by a second psychiatrist. We have chosen New York for our example since it is generally considered to be an acceptable model statute. It deals with the necessary concerns of enabling rapid hospitalization when required, as well as protecting patient rights in difficult situations—goals which we agree to be essential in such statutes. It is probable that other state statutes also address these concerns, although we are not as familiar with them as with our own state laws concerning emergency admissions. The appropriate N.Y. State Statute is included in the Appendix (3).

Generally, following such statutory procedures will provide immunity from liability. However, a wrongful commitment could give rise to legal actions on various grounds, including defamation, false imprisonment, or malicious prosecution.

ISSUES GIVING RISE TO CIVIL LIABILITY

Malpractice

Malpractice suits are filed against psychiatrists and other mental health professionals less frequently than against other physicians. However, the frequency of these suits appears to be increasing. Not only is the number of lawsuits against mental health professionals increasing, but the focus and theories of the actions are multiplying (4). Early lawsuits were brought under a fraud theory, i.e., the patient had been promised a miracle cure or the therapist tricked the patient under the guise of treatment. The most notorious of these cases involved having sexual relations with the patient (5). Today a lawsuit is most likely to be brought in negligence for either improper treatment or failure to act. The majority of these suits pertains to wrongful involuntary commitments, drug therapy, and negligence in the management of the patient. Liability will occur only if the treating professional fails to conform to a certain standard of care. The standard of care defines the legal responsibility for the practitioner.

Standard of Care

Any professional is held to a duty "to possess and apply the knowledge and to use the care and skill that is ordinarily used by reasonably well qualified professionals of the same field. Therefore, a physician will be held to the standard of care of the reasonably qualified physician" (6). A psychiatrist will be expected to possess and apply the knowledge and skill of the reasonably qualified psychiatrist. Liability will only be found when the practitioner has deviated from this standard of care. The law does not require that one give the best possible treatment. More importantly, the law does not impose liability for an error in professional judgment unless the error resulted from a failure to follow an established procedure.

Wrongful Commitment

It is conceivable that a patient in an acute psychotic state could meet the criteria for emergency involuntary commitment and then quickly, after being admitted, reconstitute to his prepsychotic condition without any awareness of his apparent need for hospitalization. In such a case there is always the possibility that the patient may believe that he was wrongfully committed and sue the admitting psychiatrist. In most cases involving wrongful commitment, the patients have alleged that the psychiatrist was negligent because he could not prove that the patient was mentally ill and dangerous "beyond a reasonable doubt." The duty of the psychiatrist to the individual to assure that the patient meets commitment criteria is not "beyond a reasonable doubt" but the lower standard of "clear and convincing evidence." This standard was established by a U.S. Supreme Court decision in *Addington v. Texas* in 1979 (7). In *Addington* a patient was committed to Austin State Hospital in Texas on the basis of "clear, unequivocal and convincing evidence" of mental illness and dangerousness: He appealed his commitment, requesting application of the higher standard of proof used in criminal cases—proof "beyond a reasonable doubt." This view has been espoused by many who feel that the mental patient is entitled to all the protections of the criminal justice system (8). The less stringent standard espoused in *Addington* allows the psychiatrist more flexibility or broader interpretation of an emergency.

The Supreme Court rejected *Addington's* contention and noted that "given the lack of uncertainty and fallibility of psychiatric diagnosis, there is a serious question whether or not the state could ever prove beyond a reasonable doubt that an individual is both mentally ill and dangerous." The case supports a distinction between civil commitment and criminal procedures, while recognizing that the individual rights of a patient requiring treatment might need to be temporarily restricted. Although it applied to a long-term commitment, from a legal standpoint the *Addington* decision provides a reasonable standard by which the psychiatrist will be judged in any civil action brought for wrongful commitment (5).

Drug Therapy

Some of the more serious legal problems in recent years have arisen out of the use of drug therapy. Many of the cases now in the courts are based on allegations of misdiagnosis and the wrongful use of drugs (9).

Modern psychiatric treatment relies heavily on the use of antipsychotic medication. This use of drugs can be particularly problematic when treating an acute psychotic reaction, for a variety of reasons. Often the etiology of the psychosis is not known. It might be a reaction to street drugs or to drugs prescribed by other physicians, or the result of some physical ailment.

Sometimes transient psychotic episodes result from experimental trials with new drugs, dosages, or drug combinations. Unfamiliarity with immediate and long-range side effects of drug combinations may induce a temporary psychosis. Failure to recognize symptoms, allergic reactions, and a host of other unforeseen effects in a timely fashion, particularly in the elderly, have all led to litigation. Contributing factors which have led to litigation in these circumstances have been failure to conduct proper physical examinations and laboratory tests, poor supervision and case management, failure to consult specialists, and failure to obtain informed consent from the patient or his/her family (9).

Most malpractice suits brought against psychiatrists involving the use of drugs are based on a theory of negligence. In order to be found liable, the court must find that the psychiatrist deviated from acceptable standards of care and practice. This means that a psychiatrist will generally be held to the same standards of professional competency wherever he practices. The old defense of "Community Standards" has been rejected by many decisions, where the courts have upheld the proposition that professional custom no longer determines the standard of care (10).

In examining standards of care the courts accord considerable weight to scientific literature. The courts will also weigh the risk-benefit ratio of using a particular drug regimen, but not always from a medical viewpoint. Juries are seldom sympathetic to physicians about risk-benefit issues, when an obviously damaged patient appears in front of them in the courtroom. The psychiatrist might also be liable if he or she fails to monitor patients carefully and does not react promptly to recognizable symptoms or side effects resulting from the drugs. He/she should also be sure to explain to the patient what drug is being prescribed and the possible risks involved as soon as the patient is able to appreciate this information. Failure to properly inform the patient about risk-benefit issues can lead to liability.

Informed Consent

One of the most serious problems facing the psychiatrist from a legal standpoint is the issue of informed consent. What the courts mean by informed consent is that the patient has a right to communicate with those responsible for his care and to receive from them adequate information concerning the nature and extent of the medical problem, the alternatives, if any, the treatment plan, the risks involved with it, and the prognosis. A widely used court definition of consent liability is: "A physician violates his duty to his patient and subjects himself to liability if he withholds any facts which are necessary to form the basis of an intelligent consent" (11). Under informed consent every adult* patient (or, in the case of a minor, parent or guardian) has a fundamental right to know and understand, in a general way, what is medically wrong with him/her, what the therapist plans to do about it, what the risks of a potential treatment are, what alternatives exist, and, finally, the probable outcome of the treatment.

When a patient is in a psychotic state and is therefore irrational, eliciting consent can become an insuperable problem. According to Twardy, in such cases it is almost imperative that the consent be obtained from

---

*The definition of "adult" varies with different legal jurisdictions and for different medical procedures.

the patient's parents, spouse, or, if necessary, a court appointed guardian (9). Finally, it must be remembered that the patient's psychotic state at the time of the consent might have been so severe as to make him incapable of consenting; any consent given under these circumstances would be invalid on that ground (12, 13). In an emergency situation where the patient is in no condition to exercise judgment, Tancredi suggests that it is necessary where possible to involve the next of kin or other family members in the decision-making process (14).

In attempting to obtain consent from the family of an acutely psychotic patient, one must be careful not to violate the patient's right to privacy. It is conceivable that information transmitted to family members might be detrimental to other aspects of the patient's life. This may give rise to later causes of action against the practitioner for breaching a confidential relationship. If the hospital-based practitioner is uncertain about what to do, he/she should seek advice from the hospital's attorney.

Right to Refuse Treatment

Recent cases in New Jersey and Massachusetts have held that involuntary patients may have a right to refuse medication and other treatment. In *Rennie v. Klein* (15) an action was brought by patients for injunctive relief against a hospital and staff with regard to the administration of certain drugs. On appeal the court held that under New Jersey Law a voluntary patient has an absolute right to refuse treatment, and once the consent is withdrawn he/she cannot be medicated in a non-emergency situation. The court went on to say that involuntary patients have a limited right to refusal, which can only be overridden if due process safeguards are followed. The court indicated that these safeguards would be served through review by a psychiatrist, so long as the psychiatrist was not a member of the treatment team involved with the patient.

In a similar Massachusetts case, *Rogers v. Okin* (16), the court again held that a patient can refuse antipsychotic drugs in a non-emergency situation. The court went on to say that certain constitutional rights cannot be abrogated in non-emergency situations in the absence of the use of proper procedural safeguards. Violation of these rights will give rise to civil liability on the part of the practitioner.

In *Rennie* an emergency was narrowly defined as ". . . a sudden, significant change in the patient's condition which creates danger to the patient himself or to others in the hospital. Medication may then be forcibly administered for 72 hours. Certification by the medical director of the hospital may extend that period for another 72 hours if threat to life and limb continues. . . ."

In *Rogers* the defendants, who were the psychiatric staff of a state hospital, asked that the court allow a broader definition of "psychiatric emergency." They asked that forced medication be justifiably given in any of the following situations: 1) suicidal behavior, seriously meant or gesture; 2) assaultiveness; 3) property destruction; 4) extreme anxiety and panic; 5) bizarre behavior; 6) acute or chronic emotional disturbance interfering with patient's daily functioning; 7) immediate medical response to prevent the likelihood of further clinical deterioration. The court held that the defendants' definition was too broad, unwieldy, and subjective. Therefore, a committed patient could only be medicated in an emergency situation, against his will, in which "a failure to do so would result in a substantial likelihood of physical harm to that patient, other patients, or to staff members of the institution."

There seems to be no disagreement on the narrow definition of what constitutes an emergency. However, courts have not yet agreed on how far the parameters of a psychiatric emergency should extend.

Liability for Patient's Suicide

Rarely are malpractice cases brought against individuals for the suicide of a patient. Most of the lawsuits involving suicide have focused on failure of a hospital in which the patient is confined to observe and to properly protect the patient (17).

The general rule is that a hospital must exercise such care in protecting a patient as the circumstances require. This includes known mental conditions. Failure to exercise the necessary degree of care will give rise to a negligence action (18). Liability will not be imposed where the suicide was unforseeable and where the patient gave the careprovider no reason to anticipate it (19). As with other negligence cases an error in judgment will not create liability for a patient's suicide.

In *Katy v. State* (20), a patient was admitted to the hospital and diagnosed by a psychiatrist as having a neurotic depression. His wife informed the hospital staff that the patient had previously attempted suicide. The staff made a judgment, however, that the patient was not a suicidal risk at the present time. The patient was placed in a semi-open ward and later committed suicide by jumping in front of a train following his escape from the ward. The court held that there was no evidence that the doctors had been negligent in their diagnosis and that a mere failure in judgment alone was not sufficient to impose liability on the hospital.

The standard of care for suicide cases will be judged as the standard of care for any negligence case, i.e., whether that physician exercised that degree of care which would have been exercised by a reasonable individual under similar circumstances. If there is reason to believe that the patient might take his/her life, the doctor will be expected to make an informed reasonable assessment of the suicidal patient and then make a judgment about how to treat him/her. The decision to hospitalize will be judged by the standard of the average practitioner under similar circumstances. When the patient experiencing a transient psychosis represents a suicidal risk, an immediate judgment must be made as to whether this individual requires hospitalization.

LIABILITY TO THIRD PARTIES—RELEASE OF MENTAL PATIENTS

One of the most difficult and controversial questions dealing with the legal aspects of transient psychosis is delineating the duty owed by mental health professionals to third parties. A common but frequently overlooked scenario involves the harm caused by the recently released hospital patient into the community.

> Take for example John Doe, who has a long history of assaultive behavior. John is perceived as having an underlying character disorder with antisocial and explosive features. He is also prone to acute psychotic episodes. One evening after nearly beating his wife to death, John is brought to the psychiatric emergency room by the police; he is admitted on an emergency basis as having a brief reactive psychosis. He is treated as an inpatient. Three days later his psychotic symptoms remit to the point where he no longer requires hospitalization.
>
> In the meantime, his wife, Jane, informs you that this is the thirty-seventh such incident in the past two years. As a matter of fact, she tells you that John is an extremely violent person even when not psychotic and that as soon as he is released from the hospital he is likely to beat her again for calling the police in the first place. John, now without psychosis, confirms Jane's concerns by telling you that he will get even with her for causing him to be hospitalized. Do you release him? If you do, and he does what you expect him to do, i.e., beat up Jane again, are you liable if Jane sues you for negligent release?

As a general rule, the usual negligence standard will apply and the psychiatrist will not be liable for a nonnegligent discharge of a patient who subsequently harms another person (21). Specifically, in releasing a confined mental patient, neither a physician nor his employer will be held liable for the doctor's honest errors of professional judgment.

The majority of the cases with regard to negligent release have taken place in California and New York. Both states' courts have basically made public policy decisions comparing the rights of the public to the patient's needs. In both states, in determining whether a patient's release accorded with a proper measure of care owed both the public and the patient, the courts have frequently emphasized the duty of the public to accept certain facts. These include the facts that the treatment of mental illness is not an exact science; that rehabilitative visits outside the institution are desirable therapeutic goals; that given the often erratic behavior of mental patients certain risks to the public are inherent in the release of any such person; and that such risks must often be counterbalanced with the needs of the patient, if he or she is ever to be cured or reenter society (21). These cases generally have involved the release of patients from state psychiatric hospitals.

Duty to Warn Third Parties of Possible Danger

As yet there are few guidelines as to when the confidentiality privilege will be waived in favor of protecting parties outside of the therapeutic relationship. Medical ethics have long provided that confidentiality must give way where "it becomes necessary in order to protect the welfare of the individual or the community" (23).

Recently there have been cases where courts have imposed liability on a psychotherapist, finding an affirmative duty to use reasonable care to protect a third party. This duty was first imposed by a California Supreme Court in *Tarasoff v. Regents of The University of California* (23). In *Tarasoff*, a student of the University of California confided to a clinical psychologist that he intended to kill his girlfriend, later identified as Tatania Tarasoff. The psychologist requested the campus police to detain him. The police did detain the student, but released him when he appeared rational. The psychologist's supervisor subsequently directed that no further action be taken to detain the student. The student discontinued contact with the psychologist and killed Ms. Tarasoff two months later. Neither she nor her family had prior warning.

The woman's parents filed suit against all parties involved for failure to confine the patient or to warn Ms. Tarasoff of the danger to her life. On appeal the California Supreme Court held, in part, that the psychotherapist who determines or should have determined that a patient presents a danger to a third party has a duty to warn that third party.

Furthermore, the court held that this duty could be discharged in one or more of the following ways: 1) by warning the victim or others likely to apprise the victim of danger; 2) by notifying the police; or 3) by taking whatever other steps are reasonably necessary under the circumstances.

Tarasoff established the duty of a therapist to protect third parties from violent ourbursts of their patients. However, the court did not address other significant issues, such as the potential for self-inflicted harm or property damage, or liability when the specific victim has not been identified. Subsequent court decisions that have addressed these issues may provide some guidance to practitioners.

The issue of the duty to warn in instances of potential self-inflicted harm was addressed in *Bellah v. Greenson* in 1977 (24), wherein the parents of a daughter who had committed suicide filed suit against her psychiatrist. The parents alleged that the psychiatrist should have warned them of their daughter's suicidal tendencies.

Although the psychiatrist was aware of this patient's suicidal inclinations, the court held that the duty to warn a third party did not extend to self-inflicted harm or where the danger consisted of property damage. The court interpreting *Tarasoff* did not require that a therapist disclose confidential information unless the strong interest in confidentiality is counterbalanced by an even stronger public interest, namely, safety from violent assault.

Courts have also since considered whether there is a duty when there is no identifiable victim. In 1980, in *Thompson v. The County of Alameda* (25), the California court held that there is no duty to warn where the victim might be a member of a large public group of potential targets.

However, a federal court has upheld the opposing viewpoint. In *Lipari v. Sears & Roebuck Co.*, 1980 (26), the Federal trial court ruled that it is not necessary to know the identity of the intended victim but only that the therapist, under the circumstances, could have foreseen an unreasonable risk of harm to the injured party or class of persons of which the injured party was a member. *Lipari* represents an expansion of a therapist's duty to act to prevent danger to third parties. The court went on to say that it was not unfair to require a psychotherapist to take those precautions that would be taken by a reasonable psychotherapist under similar circumstances.

Some states will provide immunity from liability based on strong statutory confidentiality laws. A Maryland appellate court agreed with a psychiatrist that no duty to warn third parties existed in that state. In *Shaw v. Glickman*, 1980 (27), a suit was brought against all the members of a psychiatric team by a woman's lover, who was wounded by gunshots after the patient, the woman's husband, discovered him in bed with his wife. The victim based his argument on the team's alleged negligence in failing to warn him of the husband's unstable, violent condition and the foreseeable danger it presented to him. The Maryland Court concluded that no duty to warn was owed, because the patient disclosed no intent to injure the victim and because, under Maryland law, disclosure of the patient's violent proclivities would have been a violation of the psychiatrist/psychologist privilege statute.

Although there is now some case law to provide guidance to practitioners faced with the dilemma of determining what circumstances warrant violations of the interest in protecting confidentiality, there are still many unanswered questions about the duty owed the third parties.

Admittedly, simple and authoritative responses to these questions have not been formulated. However, Cooper (28) makes the following suggestions to aid the therapist in making such a determination. First, the therapist should evaluate the patient's previous behavior. Has the patient followed through with other threats made in the past or initiated any specific activity that would further the realization of the threatened activity? Second, how would the patient respond to direct confrontation by the therapist seeking to impose external control on his behavior? In summary, a therapist should be able to demonstrate that he acted on a reasonable belief that the patient's behavior warrants warning a third party. Finally, the therapist should seek to limit such disclosures to those reasonably necessary to avert possible danger. To minimize the negative impact on the therapist-patient relationship, the therapist should discuss frankly with the patient the therapist's duty and position on this aspect of their relationship.

> Given these guidelines, perhaps it will be somewhat easier to determine how to handle the hypothetical John and Jane Doe situation referred to at the beginning of this section. John has a long and consistent history of violently assaulting his wife. He has also told you that he intends to do it again after his release. Since there is no medical reason to keep him hospitalized, because his transient psychosis has remitted, you will probably have to release him. Before releasing him however, you should make every effort to talk him out of retaliating against his wife, and tell him that you will have to notify Jane and the police about the violent intentions.
>
> Finally, under the circumstances, you will probably be on fairly safe legal ground if you do notify both his wife, a potential foreseeable victim, and the police that you are releasing a patient who

is very likely to do violence to Jane. Since you are not a jailor there is little more that can be done.

CONCLUSION

Twardy, an attorney, writing on malpractice in *Medical Trial Techniques Quarterly* (9), makes the following general suggestions about how to avoid potential psychiatric malpractice liability. Given what is known about potential emergency situations resulting from a sudden onset of psychosis, these suggestions should be modified to take into account psychiatric emergencies. Remember, in a narrowly defined emergency situation one can do whatever is necessary to avoid danger to life and limb. But as soon as the imminence of the danger subsides and the emergency no longer exists, the practitioner will be held to the standards of non-emergency situations. These are, according to Twardy:

1) Make sure that the patient understands the nature of his/her problems and gives informed consent to any treatment. If the patient is unable to give explicit and informed consent, consult with parents or spouse or, if necessary, get a court order. Do not administer drugs against a patient's will unless you can convince a court that it was really an emergency.

2) Remember that a court may require that extremely extensive information be given to the patient in order to be satisfied that the consent is indeed informed. It may be necessary to describe every possible side effect regarding antipsychotic medication, with degree of risk, level of severity, and alternatives, which may include prognosis if no medication is used.

3) Keep abreast of new developments in the field through continuous psychiatric education, new textbooks, and the reading of professional journals.

4) Know your drugs, their efficacy, indications and contraindications, shortcomings, side effects and synergistic effects. Be sure of what you prescribe.

5) Except for unusual circumstances in a research institution, with proper legal advice, safeguards and informed consent, do not experiment. Stick to accepted psychiatric standards.

6) Read carefully drug literature and manufacturers' recommendations.

7) Prescribe as few drugs as possible. Exclude those that are not absolutely necessary, and take every step to insure that the drugs are not likely to be ingested with alcohol or in excessive dosages.

8) Be sure to find out what other medication outpatients are getting from other doctors or are buying over the counter. Make
sure they are compatible with your prescription.

9) Monitor the progress of patients, be alert for the appearance
of side effects, and deal promptly with problems.

10) In hospital situations, avoid "standing orders." Write new orders whenever necessary.

11) Unless you are absolutely sure of your diagnosis and treatment,
get a second opinion.

12) Maintain a friendly and informative rapport with the patient.
Patients who like their doctors seldom sue.

13) Never promise or guarantee a cure to either the patient or his
family; you may be making a legally binding contract.

14) Keep good medical records.

15) Watch everything you say because anything you say may be
used against you in court.

16) Don't be too hasty in releasing suicidal or homicidal patients
from inpatient or outpatient status. When you do release them,
be sure that suicidal or homicidal trends are, if not totally resolved, at least minimally active, that the patients continue
medications, and that they are supervised optimally at home.

17) If a patient appears to be litigiously inclined, refer him or her
politely to someone else. You have a right to refuse to treat a
patient and so do the others.

18) Except in an emergency, be sure that the referral to other competent psychiatrists is made politely, and that the patient has
enough time to find another psychiatrist. Don't abandon the
patient.

19) Make sure that you know a lawyer who is familiar with psychiatric issues, so that when in doubt you can seek legal advice.

In the final analysis, the psychiatrist frequently is confronted with
decisions involving conflicting values and even conflicting laws. Whether
the patient is admitted or released, whether a family or potential victim
is warned—such issues bring these conflicts into play. Unfortunately,
no court decisions and no law books can make this decision for the
doctor; his or her judgments must be based upon his/her best professional opinion—and frequently these judgments have to be made with
insufficient information.

APPENDIX

EMERGENCY ADMISSIONS FOR IMMEDIATE OBSERVATION, CARE, AND
TREATMENT—ARTICLE 939 N.Y. STATE MENTAL HYGIENE LAW (1978) (3)

(a) The director of any hospital maintaining adequate staff and facilities for the observation, examination, care, and treatment of persons alleged to be mentally ill and approved by the commissioner to receive and retain patients pursuant to this section may receive and retain therein as a patient for a period of fifteen days any person alleged to have a mental illness for which immediate observation, care, and treatment in a hospital is appropriate and which is likely to result in serious harm to himself or others. "Likelihood to result in serious harm" as used in this article shall mean:

1) Substantial risk of physical harm to himself as manifested by threats of or attempts at suicide or serious bodily harm or other conduct demonstrating that he is dangerous to himself, or

2) A substantial risk of physical harm to other persons as manifested by homicidal or other violent behavior by which others are placed in reasonable fear of serious physical harm.

The director shall cause to be entered upon the hospital records the name of the person or persons, if any, who have brought such person to the hospital and the details of the circumstances leading to the hospitalization of such person.

The director shall admit such person pursuant to the provisions of this section only if a staff physician of the hospital upon examination of such person finds that such person qualifies under the requirements of this section. Such person shall not be retained for a period of more than forty-eight hours unless within such period such finding is confirmed after examination by another physician who shall be a member of the psychiatric staff of the hospital. Such person shall be served, at the time of admission, with written notice of his status and rights as a patient under the section. Such notice shall contain the patient's name. At the same time, such notice shall also be given to the mental health information service and personally or by mail to such person or persons, not to exceed three in number, as may be designated in writing to receive such notice by the person alleged to be mentally ill. If at any time after admission, the patient, any relative, or friend, or the mental health information service gives notice to the director in writing of request for court hearing on the question or need for immediate observation, care, and treatment, a hearing shall be held as herein provided as soon as practicable but in any event not more than five days after such request is received, except that the commencement of such hearing may be adjourned at the request of the patient. It shall be the duty of the director upon receiving such notice of such request for hearing to forward forthwith a copy of such notice or a record of the patient to the supreme court or county court in the county where such hospital is located. A copy of such notice and record shall also be given the mental health information service. The court which receives such notice shall fix the date of such hearing and cause the patient or other person requesting the hearing, the director, the mental health information service and such other persons as the court may determine to be advised of such date. Upon such date, or upon such other date to which the proceeding may be adjourned, the court shall hear testimony and examine the person alleged to be mentally ill, if it be deemed advisable in or out of court, and shall render a decision in writing that there is reasonable cause to believe that the patient has a mental illness for which immediate inpatient care and treatment in a hospital is appropriate and which is likely to result in serious harm to himself or others. If it be determined that there is such reasonable cause, the court shall forthwith issue an order authorizing the retention of such patient for any such purposes in the hospital for a period not to exceed fifteen days from the date of admission. Any such order entered by the court shall not be deemed to be an adjudication that the patient is mentally ill, but only a determination that there is reasonable cause to retain the patient for the purposes of this section.

(b) Within the fifteen days of arrival at the hospital if a determination is made that the person is not in need of involuntary care and treatment, he shall be discharged unless he agrees to remain as a voluntary or informal patient. If he is in need of involuntary care and treatment and does not agree to remain as a voluntary or informal patient, he may be retained beyond such fifteen day period only by admission to such hospital or another appropriate hospital pursuant to the provisions governing involuntary admission on application supported by medical certification and subject to the provisions for notice, hearing, review, and judicial approval of retention or transfer and retention governing such admissions, provided that, for the purposes of such provisions, the date of admission of the patient shall be deemed to be the date when the patient was first received under this section. If a hearing has been requested pursuant to the provisions of subdivision (a), the filing of an application for voluntary admission on medical certification shall not delay or prevent the holding of the hearing.

(c) If a person is examined and determined to be mentally ill the fact that such person suffers from alcohol or substance abuse shall not preclude commitment under this section.

REFERENCES

1. Hollister, L.E.: Transient psychoses and personality disorders. In: J. Tupin (Ed.), *Transient Psychosis: Diagnosis and Management.* Ft. Washington, PA: McNeil Labs, 1980, pp. 20-26.
2. *Lessard v. Schmidt,* 349 F. Supp. 1078 (E.D. Wis. 1972).
3. Mental Hygiene Law, Vol. 34A, Section 9.39, *McKinney's Consolidated Laws of New York Annotated,* West St. Paul, MN, 1978.
4. *Annot.,* "Malpractice Liability with Respect to Diagnosis and Treatment of Mental Disease," 99 A.L.R. 2d 599, 1965.
5. Horan, D.J., and Guerrine, M.E.: Developing legal trends in psychiatry and the law. *The Journal of Psychiatry and the Law,* 9, 1: 65-89, 1981.
6. For example, Illinois Pattern Jury Instructions (Civil), Section 105.01 (2d. ed. 1971).
7. *Addington v. Texas,* 47 U.S.L.W. 4473. (1979).
8. Ennis B., and Emery, R.: *The Right of Mental Patients.* An American Civil Liberties Handbook. New York: Avon, 1978.
9. Twardy, S.: The issue of malpractice in psychiatry. *Medical Trial Techniques Quarterly,* Annual, 161-176, 1979.
10. *Helling V. Carey,* 83. Wash. 2d 514, 52d 981 (1974).
11. *Salgo v. Leland Standford, Jr. University Board of Trustees,* 154 Cal. app. 650, 317, p. 2d 170 (1957).

12. Louisell, D.W., and Williams, H.: *Medical Malpractice* at 594.43-594.64, Matthew Bender (1974); See also Walty and Sheuneman, Informed consent to therapy, 64 *Nw U.L. Rev.* 628 (1970).
13. *Annot.*, Medical competency of patient to consent to surgical operation as medical treatment. 25 A.L.R. 3d 1439 (1969).
14. Tancredi, L.R.: Emergency psychiatry and crisis intervention: Some legal and ethical issues. *Psychiatric Annals*, 12, 8: 804, 1982.
15. *Rennie v. Klein*, 476 F. Supp. (Dist. N.J. 1979).
16. *Rogers v. Okin*, 478 F. Supp. 1342 (D.C. Mass. 1979).
17. *Annot.*, Liability of hospital or sanitorium for injury or death of patient as a result of his escape or attempted escape. 70 A.L.R. 2d 347 (1960).
18. *Annot.*, Civil liability for death, suicide. A.L.R. 2d 571 (1950).
19. *Weglary v. State*, 31 App. Div. 595, 295, N.Y.S. 2d 152 (1968).
20. *Katy v. State*, 46 Misc. 2d 61, 285 N.Y.S. 2d 912 (1965).
21. *Annot.*, Negligence—Release of mental patient. A.L.R. 3d 699 (1971).
22. A.M.A., Medical Ethics, Section 9.
23. *Tarasoff v. Regents of the University of California*, 551 p. 2d 334 (Cal. 1976).
24. *Bellah v. Greenson*, 141 Cal. Rptr. p. 2 (Cal. 1977).
25. *Thompson v. The County of Alameda*. 167 Cal. Restr. 70 (Cal. 1980).
26. *Lipari v. Sears & Roebuck Co.*, 497 F. Supp. 185 (D. Neb. 1980).
27. *Shaw v. Glickman*, 415 A 2d 625 (Md. App. 1980).
28. Cooper, A.E.: Duty to warn third parties. *JAMA*, 248,4: July 23/30, 1982.

Chapter 14

Management Problems of Borderline and Transient Psychotic Patients

Alberta J. Nassi, Ph.D.,
Joe P. Tupin, M.D., and
Deborah Y. Muth, M.S.W.

Leonardo's (Da Vinci) drawings of hair and water give a good idea of what turbulence "looks like." Mental turbulence, whether one's own or that of the community in which one lives, is much more difficult to depict; its existence and significance cannot be understood if the turbulence is not observed. Today almost any newspaper displays signs of turbulence; it exists in areas which have hitherto been regarded as civilized. If turbulence is demonstrated, the reply is likely to be, "What about it? We all know this." . . . (I)t is hard to penetrate what we "all know" and to suggest that there may be something that has not yet emerged from the turbulence, just as there may be something—we do not know what—that led to the turbulence. Are we then to inhibit the turbulence? Or are we to investigate it? (1, p. 11).

It was no accident that Bion (1) invoked the image of emotional turbulence to characterize borderline pathology. Several of the most influential articles in the literature on the borderline personality emphasize the prevalence of intense affect, a history of impulsive behavior and chaotic interpersonal relationships (2). Likewise, the diagnostic criteria employed in DSM-III identify mood instability with inappropriate, intense anger, impulsive and potentially self-damaging behavior, and intense, unstable interpersonal relationships (3).

Grinker, Werble, and Drye (4) observed that "anger seems to constitute the main or only affect that the borderline patient experiences" (p. 90). Kernberg (5) proposed that "excessive pregenital aggression" is the primary etiological factor in the borderline condition. While there is general agreement about the prominence of anger in the diagnostic picture, there is considerable controversy about the instinctual versus defensive nature of the aggression (6, 7). The spectrum of angry behaviors may include "hostility, rage reactions, acting-out, self-destructiveness, detachment, mutism, and demandingness" (2).

The impairment of ego functions presents additional problems in the treatment of borderline patients. The inability to tolerate anxiety, the lack of impulse control, the tendency to revert to primary process thinking, the weakness of the synthetic and integrative functions, and the use of primitive defenses including splitting and projective identification all complicate the treatment process (5). Kernberg (8) and Eisenstein (9) underscored inadequate impulse control as the dominant ego defect in borderlines. Indeed, a history of impulsivity and self-destructiveness is "(t)he characteristic most frequently ascribed to the behavior of borderline patients" (2). Moreover, comparative studies have suggested that impulsive behavior discriminates borderline from schizophrenic, neurotic, or characterologically-disordered populations (10, 11). A considerable range of acting-out behaviors has been reported, including self-destructive acts, destructive acts toward others, antisocial behavior, and substance abuse. While no particular impulse pattern is predominant, self-destructive behavior is more frequent than violence to others (10). The repertoire of self-damaging acts includes repeated overdoses, suicide threats and gestures, self-mutilation, usually by slashing and burning, and sexual promiscuity and perversions.

Still another essential feature of the therapeutic problems with borderline patients is the premature activation in the transference of primitive, conflict-laden object relationships. The defensive strategies characteristic of borderline patients cultivate predominantly negative transference reactions—a crucial factor in the differential diagnosis of the condition (7, 12). Therapeutic relationships are marred by clinging dependency, demandingness, devaluation, and manipulation (2). The prospect of the development of transference psychosis further threatens to subvert the treatment process. Indeed, the precipitous breakdown of the therapeutic bond has prompted Adler (13) to challenge the appropriateness of the alliance concept in the treatment of borderline patients.

Literature devoted to the treatment of borderline conditions has focused primarily on general therapeutic approaches and techniques, the behavior of borderline patients in psychoanalysis and psychoanalytic psychotherapy, and the vicissitudes of transference and countertransference reactions. Given the pervasiveness of management difficulties in the treatment of borderlines, the relative absence of writings that address specific behavioral manifestations and appropriate therapeutic responses is striking. While there are notable exceptions, including discussions of suicide gestures and threats (14, 15, 16), medication problems (17), self-mutilation (18), and psychotic regressions (5, 19), articles pertaining to violence, substance abuse, sexual acting-out and rage reactions among this population are strikingly absent. This chapter will explore the dynamics underlying the notorious management problems of the borderline patient, describe specific behavioral manifestations, and attempt to apply general treatment principles to each management issue.

MANAGEMENT PROBLEMS IN THE CONTEXT OF OBJECT RELATIONS THEORY

The impaired ego development, object relationships, and lack of cohesive self characteristic of patients with borderline personality structure provide the backdrop for complex problems in psychotherapy. Adler (20, 21) describes the unfolding of the borderline dilemma in which feelings of aloneness and abandonment emerge as components of intense rage when primitive longings are frustrated by others. The precipitants of borderline regression typically involve the actual or symbolic loss of a relationship that once fostered a sense of cohesion and containment. The loss may indeed be the result of insatiable demands for nurturance and support, or the borderline patient's perception that such supplicants would be inadequate even if they realistically could be granted. In the context of therapy, the limitations of the therapeutic situation may be sufficient to evoke infantile rage akin to the strivings of a small child who demands feeding, holding, touching, warmth and comfort to survive, but does not see it forthcoming (22).

In describing the dynamics of transference regression, Kernberg (5) pinpoints the patient's intensified use of primitive defenses such as splitting and projective identification as the "crucial decompensating force." The incapacity to synthesize aggressively determined and libidinally determined self- and object images constitutes the major defect in the borderline individual's development. Maintaining split "all good" and "all bad" internal object representations averts the experience of guilt, depression, and concern for others, which Kernberg regards as a major goal of development and treatment.

The projective identificatory features of patients with borderline organization function mainly to externalize all-bad, aggressive self- and object images. As a consequence, borderline patients experience persons in their object world as dangerous and retaliatory, which necessitates mobilization against the fantasied harm (23). This process is manifested in the transference as an intense distrust and fear of the therapist, who is perceived as attacking and destroying the patient. Consequently, sadistic attempts to control and overpower the therapist are justified in order to fend off the therapist's aggression: "It is as if the patient's life depended on his keeping the therapist under control" (5, p. 80). The patient's aggression inevitably evokes a surge of counter-aggressive feelings in the therapist.

These projections do not constitute pure aggression, but rather represent self-object images tied to aggressive drives (5). Primitive self- and object representations are linked together in borderline patients, who unpredictably vacillate between both. It is as though the patient is at once separate and interchangeable with the therapist. Kernberg (5) cites an example of how the therapist may embody the sadistic mother figure in the transference to correspond to the patient's self-representation as the terrified, attacked child. The roles may then be precipitously reversed—the patient identifying with the sadistic mother and casting the therapist into the position of the guilty, frightened, rebellious child. There is an inherent threat that aspects of the treatment relationship may dangerously approach a recapitulation of the early pathological object relationships. A vicious cycle may ensue in which the patient projects aggression onto the therapist and then reintrojects a severely distorted image of the therapist. At the extreme, transference psychosis may be precipitated, when the patient can no longer distinguish the transference objects from the therapist as a real person and loss of reality-testing is further reflected in delusions and hallucinations.

The treatment process of borderline individuals is further complicated by the presence of cognitive and perceptual disturbances. Clinical experience reveals a failure of evocative memory or object permanence—that is, an inability to summon up internal representations of others (24). The capacity to evoke sustaining images of nurturing figures, which is usually achieved around 18 months of age, is transiently lost in borderline patients—in short, "out of sight, out of mind."

This perceptual impairment plagues the psychotherapeutic process, where the patient's inability to retain an inner image of the therapist between sessions severely limits the continuity of therapy, attenuates the impact of confrontation, clarification, and interpretation, and contributes to reliance on primitive defenses (24). In the height of a regressed state, the borderline patient may be unable to distinguish the previously valued aspects of the therapist even if he or she is in the same room.

Psychotherapy with borderline patients is never immune to the emergence of their essential vulnerability, regardless of therapeutic approach or orientation. Kernberg (5) has advanced the position that empathic and supportive treatment settings do not deter the inevitable negative therapeutic reactions and may actually encourage the ventilation of aggression outside of the treatment realm. Brandchaft and Stolorow (6), however, drawing on Kohut's contributions, have recently challenged the assumption of excessive pregenital aggression as an etiological bedrock and maintain that manifest psychopathology is always co-determined by the patient's self disorder and the therapist's ability to understand it. They suggest that the emergence of pervasive rage in the treatment signals iatrogenic reactions to "the therapist's consistent inability to comprehend the developmental meaning of the patient's archaic states and of the archaic bond that the patient needs to establish" (6, p. 26). Masterson (25) endorses a more moderate position in which he cites the experience of abandonment depression as the key feature in the borderline's notorious reputation for rage reactions, but notes that intense countertransference may prolong these episodes.

CLINICAL MANIFESTATIONS OF MANAGEMENT PROBLEMS

Suicidal Gestures and Threats

Kernberg (15) has identified "malignant narcissism" as a major factor in chronic self-destructive behavior with suicidal potential. In addressing himself to the chronic self-destructive syndrome, Kernberg characterized this subset of borderline patients as predominantly aloof and uninvolved with others. When their grandiosity is challenged, they experience intense humiliation, and rageful attacks and depressive episodes often follow. Their ability to remain calm in the face of their suicidal potential, amidst the pleading efforts of others, serves to enhance damaged self-esteem. Grandiose strivings may be gratified by a sense of triumph over death and pain and the experience of control over death—so feared by others.

Kernberg (15) elucidates the tyrannical sense of power inherent in suicidal behavior and other forms of self-destructiveness. The patient embodies victim and victimizer and experiences freedom from fear, as well as a "sense of triumph" over the therapist, who is likely to appear concerned, fearful, and impotent when faced with the patient's suicidal potential.

Suicidal gestures represent not only triumph over the therapist and the external world, but also release from fear by identification with the aggressor (15). In order to escape persecution by internal, projected primitive object representations, the patient has to attack and persecute in return. The therapist's forbearance and reliability in the face of aggression reflects the search for a "remnant good object relation." Interpretation of suicidal wishes as an attack on the therapist may relieve some of the suicidal pressure and provide a forum to explore intense rage toward the therapist within the parameters of the treatment.

Practically, the most urgent task is to limit the suicidal risk sufficiently in order to proceed with psychotherapeutic intervention. Interpretation of the underlying rage may precipitate another suicidal attempt to demonstrate how damaging the therapist is to the patient. A precondition for psychological exploration of chronically suicidal behavior is implementation of protective environmental controls to insure that the patient will not act on self-destructive impulses. Preventive strategies may range from extracting a firm commitment from the patient to instituting sufficient external controls via family supervision or hospitalization.

When antisocial tendencies such as dishonesty further cloud the clinical picture, suicidal risk cannot be adequately assessed (15). Suicidal behavior may occur at any point and constitutes a chronic threat in the therapeutic endeavor. Recognition by the therapist that the patient may die, as well as discussion of the lethal potential with the patient and relatives, may undermine the vicious cycle of tyranny and secondary gain and permit therapy to proceed.

Jensen and Petty (14) described the rescue fantasies implicit in suicide attempts. Among borderline patients the designation of the rescuer and the opportunity presented may be so veiled in symbolism and obscurity that the fantasy is almost imperceptible. The aggression directed against the object or potential rescuer passively threatens to transform the rescuer into a murderer if the rescue fantasy is not carried out in reality.

On the other hand, the rescue attempt may be facilitated or even orchestrated by the individual. For example, one of our suicidal borderline patients went to extremes to successfully elude the psychotherapist and police as to her whereabouts, but eventually returned to the clinic site in order to be caught.

The importance of the active, unequivocal role of the rescuer, who is likely to be the psychotherapist, needs to be underscored (14). The awesome responsibility implicit in the recognition of rescue fantasies may encourage denial or minimization of threat. However, active intervention is usually demanded, since interpretation rarely suffices. Moreover, the therapist has to be prepared to intervene continuously. Resorting to therapeutic neutrality or passivity to avoid the responsibilities of the rescuer or the inherent manipulation are expressions of countertransference hate that can be disastrous for the patient (16).

Maltsberger and Buie (16) sensitively observed that it is impossible to treat borderline suicidal patients without the manifestation of countertransference hatred. The suicidal patient's repetition compulsion to participate in relationships characterized by malice and aversion is reactivated in the therapist's countertransference reaction. Eventually, the patient can be shown how such behavior leads to an attacking or rejecting response in others. However, the discharge of such feelings in the therapeutic relationship can be fatal to the patient. The therapist's repression, self-flagellation, reaction formation, projection, and denial of countertransference increase the likelihood of suicide. Acknowledgment, acceptance, and ultimately containment of countertransference rage are the only prophylaxis to antitherapeutic acting-out.

Substance Abuse

While it has been argued that a definitive diagnosis of borderline personality organization ultimately rests on the underlying ego pathology rather than symptomatology, impulse neurosis and addictions are often suggestive pathognomonic signs (5). Nonetheless, strikingly little attention has been devoted to the treatment implications of substance abuse and the borderline patient. The relative neglect of addiction problems may emanate in part from the assumption that abuse diminishes with treatment of the underlying psychological problems (26). However, the tendency to compartmentalize alcoholism and drug addiction on the part of the therapist may represent a collusion with the patient to "split off" problematic aspects of daily living from the treatment proper. In a similar fashion, drug intake fosters an illusion of well-being and good-ness in the patient that activates the split-off "all good" self- and object images and encourages the denial of "all bad" internalized object relations by providing a temporary escape from intolerable guilt or internal persecution. While borderline patients may occasionally "confess" their self-destructive and antisocial acts to the therapist, they frequently resume such behavior once pardoned by their "honest" communication from the burden of responsibility for future actions (15). Thus, the therapist may be seen as sanctioning addictive behavior by silence or otherwise being responsible for disrupting it.

Hellman (26) maintains with regard to alcoholism and borderline conditions that abstinence is an absolute precursor to progress in psychotherapy. He argues that effective treatment of the alcohol-abusing borderline patient demands recognition of two distinct pathological processes. From this standpoint, therapy best proceeds when the importance of alcoholism is integrated into the overall treatment approach: "It is important for the therapist to actively explore and work with alcohol-related issues rather than to simply make a referral to an alcohol education program or AA in an attempt to move to deeper, 'psychological' issues, which hold more interest . . ." (26, p. 316).

The prognosis for borderline patients suffering from alcoholism and drug addiction depends in part on their capacity for impulse control and the potential for replacing the patient's inability to suppress the addictive symptom with a temporary external structure (5). Prognosis improves to the extent that the patient has sufficient impulse control to prevent the symptom from interfering with therapy or if a protective environment is available in the form of hospitalization or day treatment. In some cases, psychotherapy may best begin with an initial period of prolonged hospitalization.

Additional parameters of technique may be necessary to prevent and predict episodes of uncontrollable acting-out. That is, setting limits should be introduced early in the treatment before intense transference distortions arise to complicate such prohibitions. Patients ought to be warned initially that it is likely in the course of treatment that addictive urges may recur and become very intense. The therapist needs to communicate explicitly the expectation that such impulses must be discussed in the therapy and that the patient assumes responsibility for not acting on them or for eliciting help from the therapist to provide external controls. The therapist has to consistently impart the expectation that the patient express himself or herself verbally rather than in action.

Self-mutilation

Dissociative episodes are accompanied by nihilistic fears that may give rise to self-mutilation to cause pain as a means of confirming the borderline patient's existence (19). Simpson (18) characterizes the "art of cutting" as a self-prescribed treatment inasmuch as it represents an attempt toward achieving reintegration and repersonalization. Suicidal ideation is not typically associated with the act, which is inimical to suicide to the extent that it represents relief from "a state of dead unreality to reality and life" (18, p. 44). In fact, cutting is often characterized by patients as similar to orgasmic pleasure, in that following mounting tension, relief is experienced as the blood flows.

Simpson has described the function of blood as a transitional object:

> Blood is a permanently available, efficiently stored and readily released, transitional object used by those borderline patients who cut themselves. It is a hidden, potential security blanket carried about within oneself; capable of giving a comforting, warm, brilliant envelopment (18, p. 44).

Indeed, one of our borderline patients derived comfort, relief, and a sense of control from drawing blood and storing it in a vial that could be carried at all times and periodically inspected.

The act of self-mutilation in borderline patients provides a reliable escape from the defense of depersonalization—"releasing blood to serve as a transitional object in mediating the recathexis of porous ego boundaries and tenous body image" (18, p. 46). The patient's sense of insignificance, unreality, and failure to take purposive action is temporarily challenged. The act represents retaliation against frustration and deflects the rage from objects less likely to survive a direct and an overt attack. As in the case of suicidal gestures, self-mutilators experience triumph over the therapist or primary object and the external world, but also diminished fear by identification with the aggressor (15). That is, to escape persecution by internal, projected object images, the patient attacks and persecutes in return. For example, one of our patients, in the course of hospitalization for self-mutilation, requested to be placed in restraints and then proceeded to struggle and fight against them. The patient simultaneously embodied victimizer and victim—aggressor and aggressed.

As in the case of suicide potential, the most urgent treatment task is to limit the self-mutilating actions, which not only threaten the patient and the therapy, but may in themselves provide primitive gratification that effectively halts any progress (15). Acts of self-mutilation need to be sufficiently controlled for the therapist to have a free field for psychotherapeutic intervention. Therefore, a precondition for psychological exploration is adequate environmental control, either in the form of a verbal commitment or through the use of auxiliary structures such as family supervision, day treatment, or hospitalization. Rather than ordering the patient to renounce such behavior, the therapist needs to discuss the reasons for effective restraints and for the therapist to be assured of the patient's safety. Only when these precautions are insufficient should cessation of self-mutilating acts be a precondition for continuing the treatment.

Kernberg (15) has suggested that it is essential to confront the sadistic component of self-mutilation, though it may be outwardly presented as a manifestation of depression and suffering. The fact that the patient's objective endangerment may force the therapist into a fearful, impotent and solicitous role may reinforce the patient's unconscious omnipotence. As in the case of suicidal threats, the interpretation of the sadistic elements of self-mutilation may precipitate a demonstration.

Preventive strategies in the form of setting limits ahead of time, as suggested for substance abuse, are also indicated (5). That is, patients with a history of cutting themselves should be informed that such impulses will be activated during intense stages in the treatment. Recognition and direct acknowledgment of the chronic risk with the patient and relatives may diffuse the potentially vicious cycle of omnipotent control focused upon self-destructive acts (15). The therapist also has to make explicit the expectation that the patient will candidly discuss such impulses and assume responsibility for not acting on them or elicit help from the therapist in the form of external controls. Thus, the therapist communicates the assumption that the patient will express himself or herself in words rather than actions. The ability to communicate discomfort is a critical variable in determining whether a slash, for example, will occur (27).

Basic to the psychotherapy is the foundation of a working therapeutic alliance between patient and therapist. The patient needs to identify and interact with the therapist, who must be a real and not a detached figure. Self-mutilating behavior frequently triggers retaliatory and sadistic impulses in the therapist. It is critical that the patient's need for limit-setting not be confused with the therapist's guilt over sadistic and retaliatory punitive responses. The therapist needs to be aware of his or her own aggressive impulses, acknowledge them, and perhaps view them as an understandable response to the patient's behavior.

Within the hospital setting, Grunebaum and Klerman (27) have suggested that treatment of self-mutilation proceed in three phases. In the first phase, it should be demonstrated to the patient that his or her welfare is the direct and nonsadistic concern of the staff. The second phase should move toward encouraging the patient to assume responsibility for his or her own life. Finally, as termination approaches, planning for return to the community should be actively combined with provisions for continued psychotherapy.

Psychotic Regression

Transient psychotic episodes may develop in patients with borderline personality organization when they are under heightened emotional stress, under the influence of drugs or alcohol, or in the course of severe transference regression. Indeed, several authors suggest that the presence of brief, ego-dystonic, psychotic experiences is partly diagnostic of the borderline syndrome (5, 19). Several symptoms associated with these psychotic experiences include: sustained beliefs of worthlessness and preoccupation with hopelessness, depersonalization and derealization, visual and auditory perceptual distortions, paranoid beliefs, and self-boundary confusion (19).

Psychotic regression is typically precipitated by the real or imagined loss of a primary object. Gunderson (19) interprets psychotic phenomena in borderline patients as efforts to ward off the subjective experience of aloneness. The psychotic experience represents an intrapsychic attempt to restore the lost object. For example, visual and auditory perceptual distortions frequently involve the voice or image of the lost other. Dissociative episodes temporarily detach the patient from the reality of bodily discomfort and from the environment that evoked intolerable distress. Ideas of reference not only render protection from unacceptable self-evaluations, but also create a pseudocommunity to sustain involvement with others when no primary object exists.

Transference Psychosis

Kernberg (5) reserves the term transference psychosis for the loss of reality-testing and the appearance of delusional material within the transference that does not noticeably affect the patient's functioning outside of psychotherapy. He traces transference regression to the intensified use of projective identification:

> Rapidly alternating projection of self-images, and object-images, representing early pathological internalized object relationships,

produces confusion of what is "inside" and "outside" in the patient's experience of his interactions with the therapist. . . . It is this loss of reality-testing in the transference which most powerfully interferes with the patient's capacity to distinguish fantasy from reality, and past from present in the transference, and also interferes with his capacity to distinguish his projected transference objects from the therapist as a real person (pp. 83-84).

Thus, the therapist and the transference object become indistinguishable. For example, one of our patients in the course of a psychotic episode perceived her therapist to be her feared mother and attempted to run her over in a car. At other times, the therapist may be identified with a projected dissociated self-representation, such as the patient described by Kernberg who believed his analyst was having an affair with the patient's mother and consequently threatened to kill him. Manifestations of developing transference regression in the therapeutic process include: gradual ineffectiveness of interpretations and the therapist's own feelings that words are no longer meaningful, dramatic acting-out, and communication of a general sense of urgency. The patient's incapacity to listen or interact by means of verbal communication may coincide with a total loss of what previously appeared as a good capacity for introspection and insight.

While hospitalization may be required, as in the case of our assaultive patient, it is often possible to resolve the transference psychosis within the psychotherapy. Kernberg (12) emphasizes aspects of the "holding" function of the therapist, as described by Winnicott (30), during such regressed periods. First of all, the therapist's consistent refusal to give up on the patient and insistence that work proceed, however slowly, offers the patient hope and faith in the possibility of change. In addition to ongoing emotional availability, the therapist attempts to provide an auxiliary ego to help integrate confusing and contradictory verbalizations and behavior. Interpretations have a holding effect inasmuch as cognitive efforts to understand the patient promote ego consolidation.

Hospital Management

Hospitalization is indicated for psychotic episodes that occur during periods of excessive emotional turmoil, under the effects of drugs or alcohol, or in the course of a transference psychosis that cannot be resolved on an outpatient basis. Successful hospitalization is facilitated by early diagnosis, clear definition of the goals, limits, and expectations of inpatient treatment and staff awareness of the countertransference dynamics (28). A well-structured hospital milieu program provides "an average expectable environment," which communicates the expectation that the patient be responsible and relinquish the option of acting on impulses for immediate relief. The treatment strategy should combine limit-setting and interpretative psychotherapeutic approaches (5, 13, 20). Short-term hospitalization is generally indicated.

The capacity to set limits empathically without punishing the patient is a major requirement, since much of the work of the treatment team is directed toward limiting the "total gratification fantasy" of these patients (20). Excessive limit-setting obscures the patient's dynamics and fosters infantilization. On the other hand, if limits are lax, permitting unchallenged regression to occur, conflicts may be acted out within the hospital setting that gratify primitive pathological needs. A regressive spiral is frequently activated in treatment settings that are primarily supportive and protective. The covert control and implicit threat of engulfment accelerate angry and self-destructive behaviors in the patient, which in turn command tighter restrictions (19).

It is virtually impossible to treat borderline patients without manifestation of intense countertransference reactions. In order not to discharge such feelings in the treatment, the hospital staff needs to acknowledge countertransference danger signals and have opportunities to explore such issues in staff meetings. In spite of the maturity of the staff, regressive group phenomena with borderline patients are inevitable. To the extent that the hospital setting temporarily takes on the role of primary object, psychotic phenomena may occur as discharge approaches (19). If such behavior is viewed only as a manipulative ploy, staff may insist upon immediate discharge, which invariably precipitates self-destructive actions or intensified psychosis. Assurance about the ongoing availability of the hospital staff can help to end the psychotic episode and permit successful transition. The capacity of the institution to serve as a transitional object facilitates termination and transfer.

SUMMARY AND CONCLUSIONS

The intense affect, impulsivity, and interpersonal volatility characteristic of persons with underlying borderline personality organization challenge the psychotherapeutic enterprise. The impaired ego development, impoverished object relationships, and lack of cohesive self in these patients all contribute to pervasive management difficulties. Psychotherapy is especially complicated by the borderline's developmental failure to achieve object permanence. The countertransference contributions to notorious negative therapeutic reactions also needs to be considered in light of recent controversy.

Consideration of the management problems inherent in the treatment of borderline patients demands certain caveats lest all treatment dilemmas be ascribed to the "intractable" or "untreatable" nature of this population. In our flight from frustration, ignorance, and painful self-awareness, there is always the temptation to merely quell, objectify and project the emotional turbulence of the borderline individual. We are confronted with the eternal dilemma described by Bion (1)—whether to simply inhibit the turmoil or to explore it in all its facets. Searles (cited in Levene) likewise cautions that:

> (E)ven the patient's most severe psychopathology has some counterpart, perhaps relatively small by comparison but by no means insignificant, in (our) own *real* personality functioning. . . . (I)nner refusal to perceive any reality basis in . . . the patient's projection-laden, transference-linked images . . . inevitably boomerangs (29, pp. 30-31).

Failure to acknowledge these countertransference components is to ultimately embody our own characterizations of the patient as essentially nonhuman, incapable of caring, or incurably sadistic.

REFERENCES

1. Bion, W.R.: Emotional turbulence. In: P. Hartocollis (Ed.), *Borderline Personality Disorders: The Concept, the Syndrome, the Patient.* New York: International Universities Press, 1977.
2. Gunderson, J.G., and Singer, M.T.: Defining borderline patients: An overview. *Am. J. Psychiat.*, 132: 1-10, 1975.
3. *Diagnostic and Statistical Manual of Mental Disorders, Third Edition. (DSM-III).* Washington, D.C.: American Psychiatric Association, 1980.
4. Grinker, R.R., Werble, B., and Drye, R.: *The Borderline Syndrome: A Behavioral Study of Ego Functions.* New York: Basic Books, 1968.
5. Kernberg, O.: *Borderline Conditions and Pathological Narcissism.* New York: Jason Aronson, 1975.
6. Brandchaft, R., and Stolorow, R.: A current perspective on difficult patients. Paper presented at UCLA Symposium on Narcissistic and Borderline Disorders: Current Perspectives, Los Angeles, October 1982.
7. Modell, A.: Primitive object relations and the predisposition to schizophrenia. *International Journal of Psycho-analysis*, 44: 282-292, 1963.
8. Kernberg, O.: A psychoanalytic classification of character pathology. *Journal of American Psychoanalytic Association*, 18: 800-802, 1970.
9. Eisenstein, V.W.: Differential psychotherapy of borderline states. *Psychiatric Quart.*, 25: 379-401, 1951.

10. Gunderson, J.G.: Characteristics of borderlines. In: P. Hartocollis (Ed.), *Borderline Personality Disorders: The Concept, the Syndrome, the Patient.* New York: International Universities Press, 1977.
11. Goldstein, W.N.: A study of impulse control in the borderline patient. *Psychiatria Clinica,* 44: 81-87, 1981.
12. Kernberg, O.F.: The structural diagnosis of borderline personality organization. In: P. Hartocollis (Ed.), *Borderline Personality Disorders: The Concept, the Syndrome, the Patient.* New York: International Universities Press, 1977.
13. Adler, G.: Hospital management of borderline patients and its relation to psychotherapy. In: P. Hartocollis (Ed.), *Borderline Personality Disorders: The Concept, the Syndrome, the Patient.* New York: International Universities Press, 1977.
14. Jensen, V.W., and Petty, T.A.: The fantasy of being rescued in suicide. *Psychoanalytic Quart.,* 27: 327-339, 1958.
15. Kernberg, O.F.: Paranoid regression, sadistic control and dishonesty in the transference. Paper presented at UCLA Symposium on Narcissistic and Borderline Disorders: Current Perspectives, Los Angeles, October 1982.
16. Maltsberger, J.T., and Buie, D.H.: Countertransference hate in the treatment of suicidal patients. *Arch. Gen. Psychiat.,* 30: 625-633, 1974.
17. Havens, L.: Some difficulties in giving schizophrenic and borderline patients medication. *Psychiatry,* 31: 44-50, 1968.
18. Simpson, M.A.: Self-mutilation and the borderline syndrome. *Dynamische Psychiatrie,* 10: 42-48, 1977.
19. Gunderson, J.G.: Psychotic regressions in borderline patients. In: J. Tupin (Ed.), *Transient Psychosis: Diagnosis and Management.* Fort Washington, PA: McNeil Laboratories, 1980.
20. Adler, G.: Hospital treatment of borderline patients. *Am. J. Psychiat.,* 130: 32-35, 1973.
21. Adler, G.: The myth of the alliance with borderline patients. *Am. J. Psychiat.,* 136: 642-645, 1979.
22. Adler, G.: The usefulness of the "borderline" concept in psychotherapy. In: J.E. Mack (Ed.), *Borderline States in Psychiatry.* New York: Grune & Stratton, 1975.
23. Chessick, R.D.: Externalization and existential anguish in the borderline patient. *Arch. Gen. Psychiat.,* 27: 764-770, 1972.
24. Rinsley, D.B.: Object constancy, object permanency and personality disorder. Paper presented at UCLA Symposium on Narcissistic and Borderline Disorders: Current Perspectives, Los Angeles, October 1982.
25. Masterson, J.F.: The borderline and narcissistic disorders: An integrated developmental approach. Paper presented at UCLA Symposium on Narcissistic and Borderline Disorders: Current Perspectives, Los Angeles, October 1982.
26. Hellman, J.M.: Alcohol abuse and the borderline patient. *Psychiatry,* 44: 307-317, 1981.
27. Grunebaum, H.V., and Klerman, G.O.: Wrist slashing. *Am. J. Psychiat.,* 124: 527-534, 1967.
28. Wishnie, H.A.: Inpatient therapy with borderline patients. In: J.E. Mack (Ed.), *Borderline States in Psychiatry.* New York: Grune & Stratton, 1975.
29. Levene, H.I.: The borderline syndrome: A critique and response to recent literature on its etiology, dynamics and treatment. *San Francisco Jung Institute Library Journal,* 3: 22-32, 1982.
30. Winnicott, D.W.: *The Maturational Processes and the Facilitating Environment. Studies in the Theory of Emotional Development.* New York: International Universities Press, 1965.

Chapter 15

Assessment and Treatment
of the Catatonic Patient

Charles B. Schaffer, M.D.,
Ronald Campbell, M.D.,
and Joe P. Tupin, M.D.

INTRODUCTION

Until recently, the term catatonia has been synonymous with schizo-phrenia. During the past decade, there has been a rekindling of interest in this clinical entity as a result of research discoveries in the areas of clinical phenomenology, neuroendocrinology, and psychopharmacol-ogy. These discoveries have resulted in the recognition that catatonia is more than just a subtype of schizophrenia.

Three important factors have necessitated a different approach in the evaluation and treatment of the catatonic patient. First of all, rather than a subtype of schizophrenia, catatonia should be considered a nonspecific syndrome (constellation of signs and symptoms) which can be associated with a wide variety of both medical and psychiatric disorders. Indeed, most patients presenting with catatonic features are more likely to be suffering from a major affective disorder than schizophrenia (1). Second, catatonia is not rare. On the contrary, there is a great likelihood of encountering the syndrome, and this fact makes it imperative that clinicians of all disciplines be aware of the differential diagnosis and special management problems associated with the catatonic patient. Third, catatonia can be a life-threatening condition, either as a result of undiagnosed medical problems or complications of the catatonic state itself. This risk is another argument for an aggressive diagnostic workup and thorough familiarity with the likely causes and complications of the catatonic state.

EPIDEMIOLOGY

The incidence of the catatonic syndrome has been said to be declining. However, some investigators have reported a significant incidence of the syndrome. Guggenheim and Haroutun (2), in an epidemiologic study of Monroe County, New York, found an incidence of 5% among newly diagnosed cases of schizophrenia and 10% among the total schizophrenic cohort. Taylor and Abrams (3) found that 28% of 123 acutely ill manic patients manifested signs of catatonia. These two studies show that the syndrome is not uncommon.

RECOGNITION OF THE SYNDROME

There are no pathognomonic signs or symptoms of catatonia. Most experts in this field suggest that the diagnosis be made by the presence of one or more of the following signs: mutism, posturing, rigidity, stereotypic motor activity, automatic obedience, negativism, waxy flexibility, catalepsy, and stupor. Other signs often associated with catatonia may include grimacing, echolalia, echopraxia, motor and thought blocking, staring, impulsiveness, combativeness, nudism, excitement, or retardation. Catatonia can be either retarded or excited, depending on the predominant level of motor activity. These signs and their definition are listed in Table 1.

HISTORY

Catatonia was first described by Kahlbaum in 1874 (4). He described a group of patients manifesting negativism, catalepsy, mutism, stereotypy, and verbigeration.

TABLE 1
Signs Associated with Catatonia

Mutism—Refusing to speak

Rigidity—Stiffness; refusing to bend extremities

Posturing—Assuming unusual postures or exaggerated normal posture for an abnormally long period of time

Negativism—Oppositional behavior in response to requests

Stereotypy—The persistent repetition of postures, acts, or words

Waxy Flexibility—A partial resistance to passive movement, especially seen when upper extremities are placed in an upward position and remain that way even when not supported.

Staring—Looking at an object or into space for prolonged periods of time

Stupor—Inactivity in conjunction with lack of response to environmental stimuli

Echolalia—Repeating what is said by others

Echopraxia—Repeating actions or mannerisms made by others

Automatic Obedience—Instructions carried out in an obedient, robot-like manner; includes echolalia and echopraxia in some studies

Verbigeration—Repetition of meaningless words and phrases

Catalepsy—A condition characterized by waxy rigidity of the muscles so that the patient tends to remain in any position in which he is placed

Kraepelin (5) included excited and retarded forms of catatonia as subtypes of dementia praecox, although he recognized that the syndrome was seen in other illness. Bleuler (6) later coined the term "schizophrenia" and included catatonia as a subtype. He also recognized that catatonia was seen in other conditions.

Over the years, catatonia came to be regarded as a form of schizophrenia. This may well have reflected the tendency of American psychiatrists to both overdiagnose schizophrenia and overemphasize the so-called schizophrenic symptoms on the mental status examination. Recently, however, there has been more attention to the "non-schizophrenic" disorders associated with catatonia, both medical and psychiatric in origin.

MEDICAL DISORDERS ASSOCIATED WITH CATATONIA

The medical literature is now replete with case reports of catatonia associated with major medical conditions. This literature is well summarized by Gelenberg (7) and others. Table 2 lists the medical illnesses which have presented with catatonic symptoms. Although most of these reports are based on isolated case studies, catatonia is not uncommonly

TABLE 2
Medical Disorders Associated with Catatonia

Neurological Conditions	Toxic Agents
Basal Ganglia Disorders	Organic Fluorides
Limbic System and Temporal Lobe Disorders	Illuminating Gas
	Mescaline
Diencephalic Disorders	Phencyclidine
Frontal Lobe Disorders	Amphetamines
Cerebral Vascular Disorders	Pharmacologic Agents
Diffuse Brain Disorders	Neuroleptics
Central Nervous System Infections	Glutethimide (withdrawal)
Epilepsy	Disulfiram
Head Trauma	Morphine (epidural administration)
Wernicke's Encephalopathy	Steroids
Subdural Hematoma	Aspirin
Narcolepsy	Infections
Subarachnoid Hemorrhage	Malaria
Metabolic and Endocrine Conditions	Encephalitis
Diabetic Ketoacidosis	Pneumonia
Hypercalcemia	Other
Pellagra	Membranous Glomerulonephritis
Intermittent Acute Porphyria	Systemic Lupus Erythematosus
Hepatic Encephalopathy	Pulmonary Emboli
Uremia	Thrombophlebitis
Homocystinuria	

seen in association with neurologic disorders, toxic reactions to medications or illicit drugs, metabolic imbalances, severe infections, and, most recently, adverse reactions to antipsychotic medication, especially long-acting depot phenothiazines. It is unclear whether medical conditions are actually the cause of catatonia or whether certain patients are predisposed to becoming catatonic when suffering from any severe physiological insult.

PSYCHIATRIC DISORDERS ASSOCIATED WITH CATATONIA

The psychiatric disorders which have been reported in association with catatonia are listed in Table 3. Abrams and Taylor (1), in the only known prospective study of catatonia, found only 4 of 55 (7%) patients with catatonic symptoms met research criteria for schizophrenia. Thirty-four (62%) met criteria for mania and another 5 (9%) met the research criteria for depression. Nine (16%) had coarse brain disease, including epilepsy, toxic psychosis, encephalitis, alcoholic degeneration, and drug-induced psychosis. The remaining 3 (5%) met criteria for "reactive

TABLE 3
Psychiatric Disorders Associated With Catatonia

Manic-Depressive Disorder
Major Depressive Episodes
Schizophrenia
Conversion Disorder
Dissociative States

psychosis." These investigators also noted that the distribution of catatonic symptoms was homogenous across different diagnostic groups. These results are comparable to those of prior investigators using retrospective methods (8, 9).

ASSESSMENT OF THE CATATONIC PATIENT

Exclusion of an underlying medical disorder is the first priority in the evaluation of the catatonic patient. An exhaustive medical and psychiatric history is mandatory. This should include a review of systems, both for medical and psychiatric symptoms, a thorough review of past medical and psychiatric disorders, a history of medication use, a history of alcohol and drug use, and a family history of psychiatric and medical illnesses. Understandably, many catatonic patients will be unable to provide detailed information; therefore, one should not overlook the possibility that family, friends, or prior therapists can provide key information.

A careful physical examination, including a complete neurological examination, is also indicated. A thorough mental status examination is also of great importance. The amytal interview can be useful as a diagnostic tool (10). This procedure consists of intravenous infusion of a short-acting barbiturate, amobarbital, which often produces a dramatic return to a lucid mental state in patients suffering from underlying psychiatric disorders. The test is also useful for catatonic patients with medical illnesses, for the response is usually one of increased cognitive impairment or somnolence rather than improvement in the mental states.

Laboratory examinations should include toxicologic studies, serology, complete blood count with differential, thyroid function tests, electrolytes, liver function tests, calcium, urinalysis, and arterial blood gasses to test for pulmonary function. An EEG can be of great value in ruling out epileptic conditions, encephalitis, and any diffuse encephalopathy.

A lumbar puncture may be indicated in the presence of fever or localizing neurological signs. A chest x-ray may be helpful in ruling out a pulmonary infection.

Recent investigators have found the dexamethasone suppression test (DST) to be helpful in assessing catatonic patients (11). This test, which is often positive in patients with severe major depressions, can facilitate diagnosis of an affective disorder if positive in a catatonic patient. It should be noted that severe weight loss, certain underlying medical conditions and recent drug or alcohol ingestion can result in a false positive DST result.

Medical consultation should be requested early on in the evaluation of the catatonic patient. Such assistance is usually helpful in the diagnostic workup as well as in ongoing management if the catatonic state is so severe as to predispose the patient to medical complications.

MEDICAL MANAGEMENT OF THE CATATONIC PATIENT

No matter the cause, catatonia should be considered a medical emergency. Careful medical monitoring is mandatory regardless of the diagnosis. Since these patients often refuse food and remain immobile for long periods of time, possible complications include fluid and electrolyte imbalance, dehydration, urinary retention, and pulmonary infection. Inactivity also places the patient at risk for both decubitus ulcers and thromboembolism. Nasogastric tube feeding may be necessary to maintain proper hydration and nutrition until the catatonic patient resumes eating. Continuous close nursing observation and restraints of the extremities are also often part of the care of the catatonic patient, since many of these patients can display sudden, unpredictable, bizarre, or self-destructive behavior.

TREATMENT OF THE CATATONIC PATIENT

There are no double-blind control studies addressing the issue of treatment of catatonia. Once medical problems have been ruled out, most clinicians use antipsychotic medications to bring the patient out of the catatonic state by decreasing the severe symptoms. Aggressive parenteral use of potent neuroleptics is warranted during the first 24 hours, and this intervention usually resolves the most extreme catatonic symptoms. During this initial period, the patient must be reevaluated on a frequent basis, since these same antipsychotic medications can cause a catatonic condition. Deterioration or lack of improvement in the face of antipsychotic use would suggest either a drug reaction or a failure to diagnose an underlying medical disorder.

As described above, the amytal interview has been used as a way of differentiating "organic" from "functional" catatonia. After administration of amytal, the functional catatonic is able to relax and converse, in contrast to the organic catatonic who would tend to become more confused with amytal. It should be stressed that this intervention is more diagnostic than therapeutic, since even when catatonic symptoms are reversed with amytal, the improvement is short-lived and catatonia returns when this short-acting barbiturate is eliminated.

Electroconvulsive therapy (ECT) has also been used in severe states when quick results are mandatory. This intervention has been supplanted by the use of antipsychotic medications and should only be used when the condition is unresponsive to medications or severely life-threatening, and when an affective disorder is suspected to be the underlying problem. Antidepressant therapy or lithium may be used effectively for patients suffering from underlying affective disorders. These drugs are usually not effective during the acute states of catatonia and may even prove hazardous to catatonic patients because of their precarious medical condition. Most clinicians start these medications when the catatonic patient has been stabilized with antipsychotic drugs and is in a more cooperative clinical state.

CONCLUSIONS

The catatonic presents a significant diagnostic and treatment challenge to the mental health clinician. Prompt recognition is imperative, because these patients usually require hospitalization and a vigorous evaluation to rule out serious underlying medical disorders and to prevent the often life-threatening medical complications. Such an aggressive approach is worth the effort since many catatonic patients suffer from an underlying affective disorder and thus have a good prognosis with proper treatment. For this reason, it behooves mental health workers to be aware of the presenting signs and symptoms of catatonia and to immediately triage catatonic patients to the nearest medical facility in order to begin the workup and management of the catatonic patient.

REFERENCES

1. Abrams, R., and Taylor, M.A.: Catatonia: A prospective clinical study. *Arch. Gen. Psychiat.*, 33: 579-581, 1976.

2. Guggenheim, F.G., and Haroutun, M.B.: Catatonic schizophrenia: Epidemiology and clinical course. A 7-year register study of 798 cases. *J. Nerv. Ment. Dis.*, 158: 291-305, 1974.
3. Taylor, M.A., and Abrams, R.: Catatonia: Prevalence and importance in the manic phase of manic-depressive illness. *Arch. Gen. Psychiat.*, 34: 1223-1225, 1977.
4. Kahlbaum, K.: *Die Katatonie.* Berlin: Kirschwald, 1874.
5. Kraepelin, E.: *Dementia Praecox and Paraphrenia.* Huntington, N.Y.: Robert E. Krieger, 1971.
6. Bleuler, E.: Dementia praecox oder Gruppe de Schizophrenien. In: G. Aschaffenburg (Ed.), *Handbuch der Psychiatrie.* Leipzig: Deuticke, 1911, p. 230.
7. Gelenberg, A.J.: The catatonic syndrome. *Lancet*, 1: 1339-1341, 1976.
8. Morrison, J.R.: Catatonia: Retarded and excited types. *Arch. Gen. Psychiat.*, 28: 39-42, 1973.
9. Hearst, E.D., Munoz, R.A., and Tuason, V.B.: Catatonia: Its diagnostic validity. *Dis. Nerv. Syst.*, 32: 453-456, 1971.
10. Perry, J.C., and Jacobs, D.: Overview: Clinical applications of the amytal interview in psychiatric emergency settings. *Am. J. Psychiat.*, 138: 552-599, 1982.
11. Greden, J.F., and Carroll, B.J.: The dexamethasone suppression test as a diagnostic aid in catatonia. *Am. J. Psychiat.*, 136: 1199-1200, 1979.

Chapter 16

Special Pharmacologic Management Problems

Patrick T. Donlon, M.D.

Psychotropic agents can be highly effective in reducing distressing signs and symptoms for the borderline patient. Nonetheless, psychopharmacologic management problems are common. There are six important reasons for this.

1) The patient population is a highly heterogeneous one, making it difficult to establish precise guidelines for agent selection and dosage schedule.
2) Personality defects and symptoms may be so pervasive that the patient continues to be distressed by residual symptoms despite a highly effective and well-tolerated agent.
3) The long-term treatment of choice for most borderline patients is psychotherapy, with drug treatment predominantly adjunctive. Drug management concerns should not overshadow the development of the therapeutic alliance or lead to deterioration in the doctor-patient relationship. Given good rapport, the patient will usually continue treatment until further drug trials provide greater relief.

4) Poor tolerance for subjective distress is characteristic of the borderline patient; thus, if the desired results are not imminent or adverse effects occur, drug compliance and follow-up visits may be jeopardized.
5) Motivation for treatment may be lacking. This is especially true if symptoms are remitting and therapy is considered a stress.
6) The physician must carefully weigh and reweigh his or her attitude toward the borderline patient.

Borderline patients present many situations conducive to the development of negative attitudes, which are outlined in Table 1. Steps must be taken to minimize such feelings, however, since they can adversely affect proper assessment and treatment.

This presentation will review briefly the course and clinical phenomena of the borderline patient population and provide psychopharmacologic and clinical guidelines for long-term management.

OVERVIEW OF THE PATIENT POPULATION

Despite its diverse psychopharmacologic requirements, this mixed clinical population shares many features, including course, phenomena, and need for a comprehensive treatment approach.

Course

Borderline patients frequently have a history of a highly disorganized and stressful childhood. Parenting is often inconsistent, intermittently

TABLE 1
Origins of Negative Attitudes Toward Patient

Patient elicits attitude of rejection and criticism.
Physician seldom positively identifies with patient.
Patient presents mostly during periods of crisis and demands immediate services.
Lack of motivation for follow-up care.
Inability to provide a concise and reliable history.
Assessment and treatment often complicated by poor cooperation.
Patients often do not gratify needs of therapists.
Negative comments from peers about patient's management and progress.
Delayed response to therapy.
Unable or unwilling to meet fee for services.

absent, and associated with many pathologic features. Acting-out and maladaptive behaviors are common in the patient's adolescent years. As adults, the patient may manifest impairment in all areas of functioning—social, occupational, sexual, and psychologic. Alcohol and substance abuses are common, as are civil offenses.

Social relationships are often highly impaired, leading to criticism and rejections by others. A healthy social support is often absent, though desperately needed. The individual commonly drifts into, and is negatively influenced by, an immature, defiant, and unsettled subculture. He or she has poorly developed coping and adaptational skills, with resultant symptom exacerbation or acting-out behavior associated with stress. Despite all of this, the borderline personality is a stable personality type and is not prodromal for psychotic disorders.

Phenomena

The syndrome is often characterized by a stormy life-style, a plethora of symptoms that may present in various and changeable forms, and a cognitive presentation suggestive of mild schizophrenia. It is not surprising that the borderline presentation leads to a low diagnostic reliability, conflicting treatment plans, and varied staff attitudes.

It is advantageous to separate the clinical phenomena into periods of relative remission and acute exacerbation. During remission, compromised socioeconomic functioning, identity ambiguity, anhedonia, amorphous sexuality, a sense of aloneness, poor tolerance for distressing affects, and poor sociability are characteristic. During periods of symptom exacerbation, affects are much more prominent and a wide range of features may present, including micropsychotic episodes, rage reactions, self-destructive behavior, severe dysphoria, and paranoid ideation. Splitting may be highly apparent as the individual is more pressed to communicate. The micropsychotic and other acute signs and symptoms are typically brief in duration (hours) and remit spontaneously.

Need for Comprehensive Treatment

As a rule, patients first present for treatment during a crisis when psychopathologic features are most marked. Such treatment is often provided at public psychiatric emergency centers since immediate assessment is required and patient funding is lacking. The demands for assistance are often intense and exaggerated, as are the patient's symptoms. At this juncture, psychotropic agents, especially neuroleptics and sedative-hypnotics, may be indicated to control catastrophic features, including belligerence, although improvement may be rapid even without drug treatment. For continued treatment, psychotherapy is often the treatment of choice for the motivated patient, with psychotropic agents, when indicated, as adjunctives. Patients often respond best to a therapist who is enthusiastic about treatment and responds in a warm and supportive way, as well as to a milieu that provides structure, support, and consistency.

ASSESSMENT AND INITIAL TREATMENT OF THE SYMPTOMATIC PATIENT

The newly presenting symptomatic patient requires very careful assessment and monitoring. Civil charges may be pending and he or she may be experiencing toxic effects from abused substances, biologic disorders, or trauma. For the cooperative and rational patient the evaluation may be rapid and uncomplicated. For many patients, however, assessment cannot be completed until data have been obtained from other sources (family, peers, medical records, etc.) and the patient has been carefully evaluated for several hours. Information to be included in the workup is listed in Table 2. It is also helpful to document carefully the circumstances that prompted the exacerbation of symptoms.

In general, it is best to withhold medication until the physical examination, historic review, and mental status exam are completed and a presumptive diagnosis is made. This helps to rule out contraindications

TABLE 2
Evaluation of the Symptomatic Borderline Patient

History (from patient, peers, records, etc.)
Course and phenomena
Past response to psychiatric treatment, including drug trials
Social, occupational, civil, etc.
Drug and alcohol abuse
Family
Trauma
Impulse disorders (violence, bodily harm, etc.)

Assessment
Mental status
Physical and neurologic exams
Laboratory data including toxicology
Monitor vital signs
Monitor behavior

---

to drug therapy and to identify patients at greater risk. Severely ill patients should be considered psychiatric emergencies and steps should be taken to reduce risk of injury and provide rapid relief. For the more belligerent and acutely disorganized patient, seclusion, restraining, and hospitalization may all be indicated. Injectable neuroleptics, such as haloperidol, 2.5 to 7.5 mg IM every 30 to 60 minutes, will rapidly reduce catastrophic signs and symptoms in most patients within minutes.

GUIDELINES FOR ADMINISTERING PSYCHOTROPICS

Precise guidelines for separating borderline patients into subgroups that respond optimally to a class of psychotropic agents are not now available. Nonetheless, there are some helpful general guidelines for agent and dosage selection (Table 3).

TABLE 3
Guidelines for Administering Psychotropic Drugs

- Except for highly symptomatic patients, drug therapy is predominantly adjunctive. Doctor-patient relationship is paramount.
- Carefully assess patient before administering drugs.
- There must be definite indications for drug administration.

Drug selection can be simplified by:
- Identification of treatable target symptoms
- Obtaining detailed information on:
  - a) course and phenomena
  - b) past response to psychotropics
  - c) family history profile on mental illness and response to psychotropics
  - d) substance abuse
  - e) biologic parameters (appetite, sleep, vital signs, etc.)
  - f) impulse disturbances
- Explain potential adverse side effects and take steps to minimize or prevent them.
- Parenteral neuroleptics are highly effective for rapidly controlling symptoms.
- Best to initiate treatment with conservative dosages:
  Because dosage requirements cannot be predicted
  To minimize adverse effects
- Give an agent or dosage a chance to work before switching or increasing dosage.
- Maintenance medication may not be required.
- Some patients do well on prn medication.
- In general, antianxiety and sedative-hypnotic agents are not recommended for maintenance because of their higher risk for abuse.

Drugs should be administered only when definitely indicated and after careful assessment to rule out contraindications and establish risk. Drug selection depends on identifying treatable target symptoms and appraising their severity, as well as a careful historical review. Neuroleptics are indicated for psychotic symptoms—hallucinations, idiosyncratic thinking, cognitive disorganization, etc.—and for severe dysphoric states, for example. Historical review can provide information on the presence or absence of past target symptoms; the patient's response to treatment; familial forms of mental illness and response to treatment; possible rationale for and residual effects of past substance abuse; and risk of acting-out behavior.

Parenteral neuroleptics are highly effective for the rapid control of acute psychotic or dysphoric states. Initial dosages of both parenteral and oral preparations should be conservative, since it is difficult to predict dosage requirements. It is important to give an agent or dosage time to work, however, before switching to another or increasing the dose. Explanation by the prescribing physician of a drug's potential adverse side effects will prevent the patient's confusing the drug with psychopathology and will assure better compliance.

As gross symptom presentations may be very brief, it is helpful to discontinue medication after acute treatment until further need can be established. Dosage requirements may vary immensely in patients who require maintenance medication, which should be prescribed in the least amount necessary to provide optimal response. Moreover, dosage should be reduced slowly to nothing over time, in order to establish whether or not continued treatment is necessary. Some patients who require maintenance medication will comply poorly for several reasons, including adverse side effects, lack of insight, poor motivation, suspiciousness, lack of social support system, lack of rapport with physician, and concern over interactional effects with substance abuse. Some cooperative patients do well on prn medication. Finally, since borderline patients are at greater risk for abusing psychotropics, antianxiety and sedative-hypnotic agents should be prescribed only for short periods.

COMPREHENSIVE MANAGEMENT OF THE BORDERLINE PATIENT

The borderline patient may be among the most difficult to manage. Comprehensive treatment and long-term care are essential. Here are nine key items we have found to be essential for the successful management of these patients:

1) *Essential services:* A wide variety of services is necessary, including emergency, hospital, day treatment, and halfway house services.
2) *Proper diagnosis:* Incorrect diagnosis leads to improper treatment in many patients. In younger patients, the differential diagnosis may be problematic. An initial diagnosis of borderline syndrome, for example, may later be more correctly labeled affective disorder or schizophrenia and require different treatment strategies.
3) *Proper treatment:* Treatment requirements vary considerably and must be highly individualized.
4) *Integrated treatment plans:* Patients are often followed by several agencies concurrently. It is important, therefore, that all the treatment plans be consolidated to reduce redundancy and conflicting goals.
5) *Motivated therapist:* Some therapists possess definite skills in working with borderline patients and find their work rewarding. Therapists who lack enthusiasm should refer patients elsewhere.
6) *Receptive treatment setting:* A positive attitude toward patients and their purposes, on the part of all involved personnel, is vital to the success of the treatment as well as to patients' motivation to pursue it.
7) *Appreciation of unique needs, anxieties, and aspirations:* The treatment approach must be unique to each patient, preferably with patient participation in establishing realistic treatment goals for himself or herself.
8) *Availability of a social support system:* A healthy social support system is a requirement for successful rehabilitation. Such a system can be created through socialization activities and through placement in a workshop, halfway house, etc. Family meetings or therapy may help build up family support.
9) *Continuity of care:* It is essential that the same therapist provide care over the long term. This not only facilitates therapeutic progression but ensures immediate intervention should acute symptoms arise.

Chapter 17

Coadministration of Neuroleptics and Antidepressants in Borderline Patients

Faruk S. Abuzzahab, Sr., M.D., Ph.D.

The concomitant use of more than one psychotropic agent in the control of patients with borderline symptoms or transient psychoses requires an understanding of both the underlying clinical condition and the pharmacologic principles involved. Several authors have described the borderline state in excellent recent reviews (1-5), which will not be repeated in this chapter. There is also a need to overcome the criticism of purists who have labeled such a practice as "polypharmacy," with the implication that it is detrimental to the patient. Several diseases, such as tuberculosis and hypertension, have been successfully treated with more than one pharmacologic agent. Moreover, experience has shown the value of coadministering antidepressants and neuroleptics

The author would like to acknowledge the assistance of C. Stonnington and M. Sherman in preparation of the manuscript.

in borderline states, especially when neuroleptics alone have failed to produce symptomatic relief.

In borderline states, as well as in many psychiatric conditions amenable to psychopharmacologic treatment, the clinician should delineate the disturbing symptoms to be controlled before beginning any drug therapy. Although psychotropic agents are known to be symptom rather than disease specific, this simple principle is often ignored by psychiatrists who become mired in diagnostic labels. On the other side of the coin is the tendency to speculate about the etiology of a psychiatric disorder solely on the basis of therapeutic success or failure. The successful application of imipramine in a subgroup of pseudoneurotic schizophrenics led Klein (6) to propose that the borderline personality is a variant of affective disorders rather than of neurosis or schizophrenia. Since all drugs have several mechanisms of action, which are not fully understood, it is very possible that one drug can help alleviate the symptoms of two etiologically divergent conditions. Although neuroleptics, such as haloperidol, can control emesis and schizophrenic symptoms through dopamine blockade, nobody has proposed that vomiting is a schizophrenic disorder!

Another important principle to keep in mind is the possibility that the borderline patient's presenting symptoms may change after the initiation of treatment. An agitated patient may become withdrawn and depressed, for example, or a patient with minor symptoms on admission may become flagrantly psychotic. Both of these states have been associated with the administration of a neuroleptic agent, with some psychotic episodes reported as "psychosis induced by neuroleptics." Closer scrutiny might reveal that the patient had been heading towards a florid psychotic state that merely coincided with neuroleptic administration. Increased dosage or parenteral administration of the neuroleptic with continuous reassessment of the patient's condition invariably brings this exacerbation of symptoms under control.

CHOICE OF NEUROLEPTIC

In managing patients with borderline state or transient psychoses, the first step is to control the looseness of association, paranoid delusions, impaired reality, anger, and anxiety with a neuroleptic agent. Brinkley (7) has illustrated the successful use of low-dose neuroleptic regimens in five borderline patients. Table 1 classifies the neuroleptics according to major chemical subgroups, which usually produce similar clinical effects. Thus, if a patient fails to respond to one agent, another from a

TABLE 1
Classification of Neuroleptics
(Major Tranquilizers, Antipsychotics, Psychostatics)

Tricyclic Neuroleptics
6-6-6 Tricyclic neuroleptics

Phenothiazines
N-aliphatic side chain, propyldimethylan-
ine series:
nonhalogenated group
• promazine HCl (Hyzine, Sparine)
• methoxypromazine (Tentone)
• promethazine HCl (Phenergan, various
mfr)
halogenated group
• chlorpromazine HCl (Thorazine, various
mfr)
•triflupromazine HCl (Vesprin)
N-aromatic side chain, piperidine series:
ethylpiperidyl
• thioridazine HCl (Mellaril)
• mesoridazine besylate (Serentil)
propylpiperidyl
• piperacetazine (Quide)
N-aromatic side chain, propylpiperazine
series:
non-halogenated group
• thiethylperazine maleate (Torecan)
• acetophenazine maleate (Tindal)
• carphenazine maleate (Proketazine)
• butaperazine maleate (Repoise)
halogenated group, oral preparations
• thiopropazate HCl (Danal)
• prochlorperazine (Compazine)
• trifluoperazine HCl (Stelazine)
• perphenazine (Trilafon)
• fluphenazine HCl (Prolixin)

halogenated group, depot preparations
• fluphenazine enanthate (Prolixin Enanthate)
• fluphenazine decanoate (Prolixin Decanoate)

Thioxanthines
Aliphatic side chain:
• chlorprothixene HCl (Taractan)

Aromatic side chain, propylpiperazine:
• thiothixene HCl (Navane)

6-7-6 Tricyclic neuroleptics

Dibenzoxazepine
• loxapine succinate—HCl (Daxolin, Loxitane)

Indole derivatives

Rauwolfia alkaloids
• reserpine (Serpasil, various mfr)

Dihydroindolone
• molindone HCl (Lidone, Moban)

Butyrophenones

Substituted piperidine
• haloperidol (Haldol)

dissimilar class would be more likely to produce results than one from the same subgroup.

Table 2 subdivides the neuroleptics into two clinical psychopharma-cologic groups. The drug's sedating protentials actually form a spectrum (8), but for simplicity they are broadly categorized here as sedating or nonsedating. In borderline patients, the nonsedating agents should be tried first. Only if these fail, or if presenting symptoms include significant

TABLE 2
Clinical Psychopharmacological Profiles of Neuroleptics

Neuroleptics	Sedative-Hypotensive Group	Non-Sedative, Non-Hypotensive Group
6-6-6 Tricyclic Neuroleptics Phenothiazines	**Aliphatic,** e.g., chlorpro-mazine (Thorazine, etc.)	**Piperazine,** e.g., fluphenazine (Prolixin)
	Piperidine, e.g., thiorida-zine (Mellaril)	
Thioxanthines	**Aliphatic,** e.g., chlorpro-thixene (Taractan)	**Piperazine,** e.g., thiothixene (Navane)
6-7-6 Tricyclic Neuroleptics		**Dibenzoxazepine,** e.g., loxapine succinate (Loxitane, Daxolin)
Indole Containing Neuroleptics	**Rauwolfia Alkaloids** e.g., reserpine (Serpasil, etc.)	**Dihydroindolone,** e.g., molindone (Moban, Lidone)
Butyrophenones		e.g., haloperidol (Haldol)
Hypotension	+ + +	0 to +
Tissue deposition above recommended dose*	+	0
Extrapyramidal symptoms	0 to +	+ + to + + +
Sedation	+ +	0 to +
Cholestatic jaundice*	+	0 to +
Bone marrow depression*	+	0 to +
Duration of treatment above recommended dose	acute episodes	acute and chronic episodes

*does not apply to rauwolfia alkaloids

insomnia, anxiety, and agitation, should the sedating group be considered. The nonsedating, nonhypotensive neuroleptics have the added advantage of greater safety when combined with an antidepressant since they have a lower incidence of EKG changes.

A detailed psychiatric history of the patient, with special emphasis on dose, duration, and general response to psychoactive drugs, is of paramount importance in selecting the right neuroleptic for that patient. Since there is a tendency for borderline patients to be involved in self-medication with social drugs, special note should be made of their experience with tobacco, alcohol, and marijuana, all of which induce liver microsomes, thus leading to active breakdown of neuroleptics. This effect may be partially corrected by administering a higher dose of neuroleptic.

Since almost all neuroleptic agents have a long half-life, they may be administered in one dose at bedtime (9), a schedule that tends to increase patient compliance and minimize sedation. With bedtime administration there is usually less need for antiparkinson medications.

CHOICE OF ANTIDEPRESSANT

Klein has identified a subgroup of pseudoneurotic schizophrenic patients who responded to imipramine hydrochloride rather than chlorpromazine on a double-blind basis (10). His patients exhibited massive anxiety, obsessive-compulsive adaptations, somatic preoccupations, anhedonia, and frequent agitation. Hedberg et al. (11) have reported a double-blind crossover study that showed that a significantly higher percentage of pseudoneurotic schizophrenics responded to tranylcypromine alone versus trifluoperazine alone and in combination. Patients in both of these studies fall within the same category as borderline states.

In spite of these two reports, most clinicians are hesitant to initiate treatment with antidepressants in borderline patients, especially when psychotic symptomatology is prominent, because antidepressants have a tendency to exacerbate any underlying psychoses. It would seem more judicious, therefore, to initiate treatment with neuroleptics and to add an antidepressant if dysphoria, despondency, and depressive symptoms prevail.

The antidepressants are easily divided into two subgroups: the monoamine oxidase inhibitors and the tricyclic antidepressants (Table 3). They may also be viewed as covering a spectrum from the most sedating to the most activating. All three of the monoamine oxidase inhibitors tend to have activating properties, with tranylcypromine the most activating. Of the tricyclics, the most sedating are doxepin hydrochloride, amitrip-

TABLE 3
Classification of Antidepressant Drugs

Monoamine oxidase inhibitors
Hydrazine
• phenelzine sulfate (Nardil)
• isocarboxazid (Marplan)

Nonhydrazine
• tranylcypromine (Parnate)

Bicyclic compounds
Triazolopyrridine
• trazodone (Desyrel)

Tricyclic compounds
Iminodibenzyls
• imipramine HCl (Tofranil, various mfr)
• imipramine pamoate (Tofranil-PM)
• desipramine HCl (Norpramin, Penofrane)
• trimipramine maleate (Surmontil)

Dibenzocycloheptenes
• amitriptyline HCl (Amitril, Elavil, Endep)
• nortriptyline HCl (Aventyl)
• protriptyline HCl (Vivactil)

Dibenzoxepine
• doxepin HCl (Sinequan, Adapin)

Dibenzoxazepine
• amoxapine (Asendin)

Tetracyclic compounds
Dibenzobicyclooctadiene
• maprotiline HCl (Ludiomil)

tyline hydrochloride, and nortriptyline hydrochloride (Table 4), and the more activating are imipramine hydrochloride, imipramine pamoate, desipramine hydrochloride, trimipramine maleate, and protriptyline hydrochloride. The latter is the most activating.

Since tricyclic antidepressants are generally the most widely prescribed, they are the agents commonly coadministered with neuroleptics. Patients who are significantly agitated and anxious benefit from the sedating type of antidepressant, while those with anhedonia and lack of energy and drive benefit from the activating group.

In a double-blind, placebo-controlled study, Chouinard et al. (12) divided 96 schizophrenic patients into four treatment groups: placebo; amitriptyline hydrochloride, 125 mg/day; perphenazine, 20 mg/day; and

TABLE 4
Clinical Psychopharmacological Profile of Antidepressants

SEDATING

Sedating Heterocyclic Antidepressants
doxepin HCl (Sinequan, Adapin)
maprotiline HCl (Ludiomil)
amitripytline HCl (Elavil, etc)
nortriptyline HCl (Aventyl, Pamelor)
trazodone (Desyrel)
trimipramine maleate (Surmontil)
amoxapine (Asendin)

Activating Tricyclic Antidepressants
imipramine HCl & pamoate (Tofranil, etc)
desipramine HCl (Pertofrane, Norpramine)
protriptyline HCl (Vivactil)

Monoamine Oxidase Inhibitors
isocarboxazid (Marplan)
phenelzine sulfate (Nardil)
tranylcypromine (Parnate)

ACTIVATING

amitriptyline hydrochloride plus perphenazine. After 12 weeks of treatment, there was no evidence to indicate the superiority of amitriptyline plus perphenazine over perphenazine alone. Since the patients that received amitriptyline alone did not differ from those on placebo, one would argue that 125 mg of amitriptyline might be an ineffective dose in this population. Furthermore, these patients were not selected on the basis of having depressive symptomatology.

In another double-blind, placebo-controlled trial by Prusoff et al. (13), 35 schizophrenics with depressive symptoms were given either amitriptyline hydrochloride, 100 to 200 mg, plus perphenazine, 16 to 48 mg/day, or perphenazine alone. Although the combined drugs were found to be more effective than the neuroleptic agent alone in reducing symptoms of depression after four months of treatment, they were less effective in reducing thought disorder. This failure may be the result of tricyclic antidepressant activation of the underlying psychoses, a situation that may require a readjustment of neuroleptic dosage.

Since monoamine oxidase inhibitors require that patients be on tyramine-free diets, they are reserved for patients who fail to respond to tricyclic antidepressants.

Patients taking the tricyclic antidepressant-neuroleptic combination must discontinue anticholinergic antiparkinson medication (Table 5) since all tricyclics have potent anticholinergic properties.

TABLE 5
Classification of Antiparkinson Drugs

Drugs with atropine side effects

Belladonna alkaloids (natural alkaloids)
• dl-hyoscyamine sulfate (Atropine)
• hyoscine hydrobromide (Scopolamine)

Atropine-like agents
• trihexyphenidyl HCl (Artane, Pipanol, Tremin, Hexyphen)
• biperiden HCl and lactate (Akineton)
• cycrimine HCl (Pagitane)
• procyclidine HCl (Kemadrin)
• caramiphen HCl (Panparnit)

Mixed type
• benztropine mesylate (Cogentin)

Phenothiazines
• ethopropazine (Persidol)
• diethazine (Diparcol)

Antihistamine congeners
• diphenhydramine (Benadryl, various mfr)
• orphenadrine (Disipal, Ventromil)
• orphenadrine citrate (Flexon, Myotran, Norflex)
• chlorphenoxamine (Phenoxene)

Drugs without atropine side effects

Dopamine enhancers
• amantadine HCl (Symmetrel)
• levodopa (Levodopa, various mfr)
• levodopa plus carbidopa (Sinemet)
• carbidopa (Lodosyn)
• bromocriptine mesylate (Parlodel)

PHARMACOLOGIC CONSIDERATIONS

In a review of antidepressant-neuroleptic interaction, Extein and Bowers (14) concluded that the agents do not cancel each other's effect because neuroleptics mainly block dopamine receptors while antidepressants prevent reuptake of norepinephrine and serotonin (see figure).

The coadministration of a neuroleptic and an antidepressant does lead to interactions, however. Perphenazine has been shown to inhibit the N-demethylation of two dimethyl tricyclics, imipramine and amitriptyline, *in vitro* in the rat liver microsomal enzyme system (15). Since there is justification for using the combination in a subgroup of depressives,

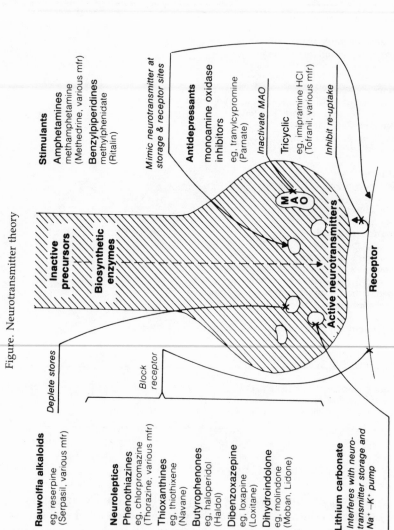

Figure. Neurotransmitter theory

however, it is suggested that use of the monomethyl tricyclics, such as desipramine and nortriptyline, in combination with phenothiazines may be more clinically effective.

Another study showed that after oral or intravenous administration of imipramine ^{14}C, total urinary excretion of radioactivity was decreased in patients with perphenazine, haloperidol, or chlorpromazine (16). The same authors reported that perphenazine treatment decreased nortriptyline ^{14}C urinary excretion, decreased plasma level of nortriptyline metabolites, and increased the plasma level of unchanged nortriptyline. Thus, neuroleptics do inhibit the metabolism of tricyclic antidepressants in man.

In schizophrenic patients assigned to three treatment groups —amitriptyline, 150 mg/day; perphenazine, 20 mg/day; or amitriptyline plus perphenazine—perphenazine significantly increased the steady-state nortriptyline plasma levels, probably through inhibition of the hydroxylation biotransformation pathway (17). Perphenazine had no effect on amitriptyline plasma levels, however, indicating that perphenazine has no influence on the desmethylation pathway or, alternatively, on the hydroxylation of amitriptyline.

CHOICE OF LITHIUM

In patients with emotional lability, hostility, and periodicity, lithium salts are indicated. Rifkin et al. (18) have demonstrated the usefulness of lithium in emotionally unstable character disorders, which would fit the borderline states. Small et al. (19) and Biederman et al. (20) have shown that lithium carbonate added to neuroleptics helped to control nonaffective symptoms in schizophrenics. The initial report of Cohen and Cohen (21) that haloperidol and lithium together produced irreversible brain damage has not been substantiated by other investigators.

CONCLUSION

In borderline patients with transient psychoses, initial treatment should be with a neuroleptic agent, preferably of the nonsedative type. If this fails to control the symptom clusters of depression, a tricyclic antidepressant may be coadministered. Neuroleptics tend to inhibit the metabolism of tricyclic antidepressants in man. The monoamine oxidase inhibitors are reserved for the subgroup of patients who fail to respond to tricyclic antidepressants. Lithium added to neuroleptic treatment may have some value in controlling the nonaffective symptoms of psychoses.

REFERENCES

1. Kernberg, O. F.: Two reviews of the literature on borderlines: An assessment. *Schizophrenia Bulletin,* 5: 53-58, 1979.
2. Liebowitz, M. R.: Is borderline a distinct entity? *Schizophrenia Bulletin,* 5: 23, 1979.
3. Sarwer-Foner, G. J. Borderline personality disorder. In: *Syllabus of Psychiatric Knowledge and Skills Self-Assessment Program.* Washington, D.C.: American Psychiatric Association, 1979, pp. 47-51.
4. Gunderson, J. G., and Kolb, J. E.: Discriminating features of borderline patients. *Am. J. Psychiat.,* 135: 792-796, 1978.
5. Perry, J. C., and Klerman, G. L.: The borderline patient. *Arch. Gen. Psychiat.,* 35: 141-150, 1978.
6. Klein, D. F.: Psychopharmacological treatment and delineation of borderline disorders. In: P. Hartocollis (Ed.), *Borderline Personality Disorders: The Concept, the Syndrome, the Patient.* New York: International Universities Press, 1977, pp. 365-383.
7. Brinkley, J. R.: Low dose of neuroleptic regimens in the treatment of borderline patients. *Arch. Gen. Psychiat.,* 36: 319, 1979.
8. Gerbino, L., and Gershon, S.: Psychopharmacology. In: *Syllabus of Psychiatric Knowledge and Skills Self-Assessment Program.* Washington, D.C.: American Psychiatric Association, 1979, pp. 150-169.
9. Abuzzahab, F. S. Sr.: Obstacles in implementation of higher unit dosage of psychotropic drugs. *Pharmakopsychiatry-Neuropsychopharmakology,* 8: 348-357, 1975.
10. Klein, D. F.: Psychiatric diagnosis and a typology of clinical drug effects. *Psychopharmacologia,* 13: 359-386, 1968.
11. Hedberg, D. L., Houck, J. H., and Glueck, B. C.: Tranylcypromine-trifluoperazine combination in the treatment of schizophrenia. *Am. J. Psychiat.,* 127: 1141-1146, 1971.
12. Chouinard, G., Annable, L., Serrano, M., et al.: Amitriptyline-perphenazine interaction in ambulatory schizophrenic patients. *Arch. Gen. Psychiat.,* 32: 1295-1307, 1975.
13. Prusoff, B. A., Williams, D. H., Weissman, M. M., et al.: Treatment of secondary depression in schizophrenia. *Arch. Gen. Psychiat.,* 36: 569-575, 1979.
14. Extein, I., and Bowers, M. B., Jr.: The pharmacologic meaning of successful antipsychotic-antidepressant combinations. *Comprehensive Psychiatry,* 16: 427-434, 1975.
15. Chittal, S. M., Abuzzahab, F. S., Sr., and Mannering, G. J.: Inhibition of the *in vitro* N-demethylation of imipramine and amitryptyline by chlorpromazine and perphenazine. *The Pharmacologist,* 11: 251, 1969.
16. Gram, L. F., and Overo, K. F.: Drug interaction: Inhibitory effect of neuroleptics on metabolism of tricyclic antidepressants in man. *Brit. Med. J.,* 1: 463-465, 1972.
17. Cooper, S. F., Dugal, R., Elie, R., et al.: Metabolic interaction between amitriptyline and perphenazine in psychiatric patients. *Progress in Neuropsychopharmacology,* 3: 369-376, 1979.
18. Rifkin, A., Quitkin, F., Carrillo, C., et al.: Lithium carbonate in emotionally unstable character disorder. *Arch. Gen. Psychiat.,* 27: 519-523, 1972.
19. Small, J. G., Kellams, J. J., Milstein, V., et al.: A placebo-controlled study of lithium combined with neuroleptics in chronic schizophrenic patients. *Am. J. Psychiat.,* 123: 1315-1317, 1975.
20. Biederman, J., Lerner, Y., and Belmaker, R. H.: Combination of lithium carbonate and haloperidol in schizoaffective disorder. *Arch. Gen. Psychiat.,* 36: 327-333, 1979.
21. Cohen, W. J., and Cohen, N. H.: Lithium carbonate, haloperidol and irreversible brain damage. *JAMA,* 230: 1283-1287, 1974.

Chapter 18

A Role for
Antianxiety Agents

Alan J. Gelenberg, M.D.

Anxiety—the awful sense of impending disaster, that something terrible, unnamed, and unpredictable is about to happen—has plagued our species since we climbed down from trees and up the ladder of civilization. And all the while, mankind has been searching for an ideal tranquilizer. Before Valium there was meprobamate, before that bromides and other sedatives, and on back through alcohol and probably unrecorded roots, leaves, and berries.

Anxiety is ubiquitous; benzodiazepine drugs are particularly effective counteragents. Therefore, benzodiazepines have become the most widely used prescription compounds in the world. What distinguishes these compounds from other psychotropic agents—antipsychotics, antidepressants, lithium—is that they are capable of producing a nonspecific and universal alleviation of the symptoms of anxiety—regardless of circumstance, diagnosis, or etiology. Tricyclic antidepressants, by contrast, can reverse specific types of depression; they are not across-the-board mood elevators. But we are brothers and sisters in alcohol and

Librium: Take one at the end of a hard day, and you will relax. The benzodiazepines have outdistanced other antianxiety compounds—such as meprobamate, barbiturates, and certain antihistamines—in popularity, but these other agents still find occasional use today. In addition, the beta-adrenergic blocking drug propranolol (Inderal) has also been used experimentally for the alleviation of anxiety and related symptoms.

Is there a role for antianxiety drugs in the treatment of individuals with chaotic personalities and transient psychosis? This chapter will explore that question, first by looking at the drugs, then by focusing on their use in these patients.

THE BENZODIAZEPINES

Table 1 lists the compounds currently available by prescription in the United States for the treatment of anxiety and insomnia. (Only flurazepam carries the insomnia indication, but probably any benzodiazepine can promote and maintain sleep.) In general, the benzodiazepines are highly effective for the relief of symptomatic anxiety. Response varies from patient to patient, however, and for some patients a dose insufficient to quiet anxiety produces unacceptable side effects.

Benzodiazepines are known for their wide margin of safety: It is almost impossible to commit suicide by overdose—in the absence of other drugs or alcohol (1, 2). These compounds also tend to produce fewer side effects and have a lower potential for creating tolerance and addiction than other sedative-hypnotic compounds. In addition, they have fewer pharmacokinetic interactions with other drugs, although they do potentiate the central nervous system (CNS)-depressing action of alcohol and other sedatives (3).

Drowsiness and ataxia, the most commonly reported side effects of the benzodiazepine group, are related to CNS depression. Some patients, particularly the elderly and those on other CNS-depressing drugs, are more vulnerable to these reactions. Tolerance to the sedation does seem to develop over time (4). Whether or not tolerance develops to the benzodiazepines' antianxiety effect remains unclear.

A greater tendency to express hostility in a small-group setting has been reported in patients taking certain benzodiazepines (5). Long-term use of these drugs has also been associated with depression, apathy, and physical dependence. Withdrawal symptoms—generally in patients taking doses higher than those recommended—include rebound anxiety and insomnia, headache, dizziness, gastric upset, tremulousness, and, at very high doses, grand mal seizures (6). Such symptoms are best

TABLE 1
Benzodiazepines*

	Non-proprietary name	Trade name(s)	Usual dose range (mg/day)	Comments
Long-acting (half-life generally > 12 hr)	chlordiazepoxide	Librium and others	15-100	Poorly absorbed by intramuscular route
	clorazepate	Azene, Tranxene	15-60	May be partially inactivated in alkaline stomach medium
	diazepam	Valium	4-40	Poorly absorbed by intramuscular route
	flurazepam	Dalmane	15-30 (at bedtime)	Generally used only as a nighttime hypnotic
	prazepam	Verstran	10-16	
Short-acting (half-life generally < 12 hr)	lorazepam	Ativan	1-10	Good intramuscular absorption, but parenteral preparation not yet available in the U.S.
	oxazepam	Serax	20-120	

*One other benzodiazepine, clonazepam (Clonopin), is also marketed in the U.S., but is approved only for the treatment of seizure disorders.

treated by reinstituting the initial amount of drug, if known, or, if not, administering enough to reverse withdrawal symptoms and then tapering off gradually. Benzodiazepines share a cross-tolerance with each other, barbiturates, meprobamate, and alcohol; in other words, tolerance to one produces tolerance to another, and substitution of one can reverse withdrawal symptoms from another.

Benzodiazepines taken in early pregnancy may increase the risk of cleft lip and cleft palate in the infant (7). Taken toward the end of pregnancy, a benzodiazepine might cause the newborn to be "floppy" (8).

How benzodiazepines work remains a mystery, although research evidence suggests that they may affect neurotransmission involving gamma-aminobutyric acid (GABA) (9). The recent discovery of benzodiazepine receptors in the brain promises to shed new light on the neuropharmacology of these agents (10).

Although all of the benzodiazepines are comparable in efficacy, they differ in milligram potency: Lorazepam is approximately five times as potent as diazepam, while oxazepam has about one-fifth of the potency of diazepam. Metabolic pathways also differ. Clorazepate and prazepam are actually pro-drugs, transformed in the stomach to an active antianxiety substance—desmethyldiazepam (DMDZ). In the case of clorazepate, this transformation is impaired by an alkaline stomach pH; thus, clorazepate should not be taken with an antacid (11). DMDZ is also a major active metabolite of diazepam and a minor metabolite of chlordiazepoxide. Oxazepam and lorazepam, on the other hand, have no active metabolites; they simply undergo glucuronide conjugation in the liver and are excreted by the kidney—a simple metabolic pathway that may make them the anxiety agents of choice for patients with impaired hepatic function (12).

Intramuscular injection of chlordiazepoxide or diazepam frequently results in erratic and often unsatisfactory blood levels. Intramuscular lorazepam, by contrast, appears to produce more reliable and useful plasma concentrations (13).

The long-lasting benzodiazepines, including flurazepam, have half-lives that can stretch to several days or longer, and their longevity may be further magnified by the presence of active metabolites (14). Therefore, one daily dose will be effective for most patients. Elderly patients should be observed for a gradually developing lethargy that may reflect drug accumulation. The long half-lives also mean that interactions with alcohol and other drugs are still possible a day or more after the last dose (15). Moreover, a patient on a chronic night-time dosing schedule may not be fit to drive in the morning.

The short-acting benzodiazepines, lorazepam and oxazepam, are less likely to accumulate in the body over time. Thus, they may be preferable for use in the elderly (16). They also tend not to produce a morning-after "hangover." When the short-acting agents are used chronically to promote sleep, however, discontinuation can lead to a period of rebound insomnia (17). Like all drugs with short half-lives, lorazepam and oxazepam should be taken several times daily. Increased interpersonal hostility, reported with some benzodiazepines, may be less of a problem with oxazepam (18).

OTHER ANTIANXIETY DRUGS

Table 2 lists other agents that have been used for the treatment of anxiety. Before the introduction of the benzodiazepine anxiolytics, meprobamate and barbiturates were widely prescribed for tranquilization and sedation. Although meprobamate (and the less well-known carbamate derivative, tybamate) and the barbiturates are effective for these indications, they are generally less effective than the benzodiazepines. Moreover, they tend to promote tolerance and addiction, are associated with serious withdrawal complications, and are more likely to cause cardiorespiratory arrest in overdose. Finally, unlike benzodiazepines, meprobamate and barbiturates induce hepatic microsomal enzymes that can alter the metabolism of other drugs (19).

Sedating antihistamine drugs, such as hydroxyzine and diphenhydramine, are used occasionally to relieve anxiety. Although less effective than the benzodiazepines, antihistamines do not appear to encourage dependence, and this may make them attractive for individuals prone to substance abuse. These compounds tend to be more sedating than the benzodiazepines, however, and they lower the seizure threshold, whereas all of the previously mentioned drugs have anticonvulsant activity (20).

The beta-adrenergic receptor blocker, propranolol, has also been used for the treatment of anxiety, as well as for other psychiatric syndromes. Propanolol seems to suppress some of the somatic symptoms of anxiety, such as tremor and tachycardia, and it may actually alleviate psychic anxiety in some patients (21). Evidence regarding the drug's role in the clinical management of anxiety remains inconclusive, however, and its FDA-approved labeling does not include this indication. Because of the

TABLE 2
Other Antianxiety Agents

	Non-proprietary name	Trade names	Usual dose range (mg/day)
Propanediols	meprobamate	Equanil, Miltown and others	1,200-2,400
	tybamate	Tybatran	750-2,000
Barbiturates	butabarbital	Butisol and others	50-120
	phenobarbital	Luminal and others	30-120
Antihistamines	diphenhydramine	Benadryl	50-200
	hydroxyzine	Atarax, Vistaril	200-400
Beta-adrenergic blocker	propranolol*	Inderal	40-360

*Not approved by the FDA for this indication

potential for serious toxicity, particularly in individuals with cardiore-spiratory problems or diabetes, propranolol should be prescribed only by physicians familiar with this class of agents.

MANAGEMENT OF PATIENTS WITH SEVERE PERSONALITY DISTURBANCES

Before any therapy is prescribed, a differential diagnosis is called for. When anxiety is the problem, medical disorders that can cause or mimic anxiety, such as cardiovascular and endocrine disturbances, must be ruled out. Next on the differential list are exogenous substances, such as caffeine and stimulant drugs, that may heighten anxiety and promote insomnia (22). Finally, the clinician considers psychiatric diagnoses with more specific treatments. For example, anxiety associated with a schizo-phrenic psychosis may be alleviated by the judicious use of an anti-psychotic agent, or the panic attacks associated with agoraphobia often respond to an antidepressant. Analogously, individuals who meet the criteria for "emotionally unstable character disorder" may benefit from lithium therapy (23).

The role of anxiolytic drugs in the management of patients with serious character pathology is at best an adjunctive one. For the so-called bor-derline patients, either supportive or insight-oriented psychotherapy —depending on the individual's ego strengths—should be the primary approach. Relaxation training or other behavioral techniques may be used to supplement the more traditional one-to-one format. In some situations, however, the magnitude of the symptoms, the depth of the emotional pain, or the requests and demands of a patient may call for a prescription for a psychoactive drug.

Patients diagnosed as borderline often complain of longstanding, se-verely disabling anxiety. A brief course of benzodiazepine therapy may be helpful in alleviating an acute upsurge in anxiety or insomnia resulting from an environmental stress or intense transference reaction in such patients. Used prudently, the drug will not diminish the patient's mo-tivation for continued psychological work; rather, the decrease in anxiety can increase the patient's involvement and may further cement the ther-apeutic alliance. Long-term use of anxiolytics, however, should be dis-couraged. The drugs may lose efficacy with prolonged administration, and chronic behavioral side effects, such as apathy and diminished im-pulse control, may outweigh the benefits. For patients prone to drug dependency, benzodiazepines, meprobamate, or barbiturates should be prescribed with caution. A sedating antihistamine or propranolol might be considered instead. Borderline patients sometimes suffer from anxiety of such magnitude that a benzodiazepine will be ineffective unless the dose is raised to a level that would produce excessive adverse effects. In such circumstances, an antipsychotic drug might be prescribed, preferably for a brief period.

Whenever any physician prescribes any drug for any patient, the resultant interpersonal and intrapsychic interactions go beyond the mere pharmacologic manipulation of molecules. This is particularly true for patients with immature, emotionally labile personalities, who are especially vulnerable to transference reactions in all forms of treatment, including drug therapy. In prescribing an antianxiety drug requested by the patient, the physician may become the good mother, providing oral nurturance. In different circumstances, he might become the bad father, seeking to invade and control the patient's body. Other personality variables also come into play. For instance, a patient who is vigilant and constantly scanning his surroundings may find the effects of anxiolytic drugs dysphoric: They dull his perception and lower his guard. The only way around these therapeutic sand traps is to discuss the patient's fantasies and wishes regarding a medication, as well as its potential side effects, before initiating therapy.

Antianxiety agents are also useful for treating the transient psychoses of "psychedelic" drug abuse, when anxiety is a primary symptom. Benzodiazepines, administered orally or parenterally, have three major advantages over antipsychotic drugs in treating these reactions: They do not generally produce hypotension; they raise rather than lower the seizure threshold; and they do not add complicating anticholinergic effects.

The clinician should be cautious about prescribing benzodiazepines and other anxiolytics for patients with impulsive or explosive personalities. Because of the risk of lowering the threshold for aggressive or antisocial acts, antipsychotic drugs may be preferable.

SUMMARY

Antianxiety agents will seldom be the therapy of first choice for patients with transient psychoses. Psychotherapy and other drugs will play the primary therapeutic role, with benzodiazepines or other anxiolytic compounds best serving as temporary, adjunctive treatment. Nevertheless, used prudently and conservatively, antianxiety drugs may allow enough symptomatic relief to both facilitate further progress in psychotherapy and improve interpersonal functioning.

REFERENCES

1. Finkle, B. S., McCloskey, K. L., and Goodman, L. S.: Diazepam and drug-associated deaths: A survey in the United States and Canada. *JAMA*, 242: 429-434, 1979.
2. Jatlow, P., Dobular, K., and Bailey, D.: Serum diazepam concentrations in overdose: Their significance. *Am. J. Clin. Pathology*, 72: 571-577, 1979.
3. Gelenberg, A. J.: Ethanol and psychotropics. *MGH Biology Therapy Psychiatry News*, 2: 47-48, 1979.
4. Palva, E. S., Linnoila, M., Saario, I., and Mattila, M. J.: Acute and subacute effects of diazepam on psychomotor skills: Interactions with alcohol. *Acta Pharmacologica et Toxicologica*, 45: 257-264, 1979.
5. Covi, L., and Litman, R. S.: Diazepam-induced hostility and depression. Paper presented at the American Psychiatric Association Annual Meeting, Toronto, Canada, May 1977.
6. Benzodiazepine withdrawal. Editorial, *Lancet*, 1: 196, 1979.
7. Nahas, C., and Goujard, J.: Phenothiazines, benzodiazepines, and the fetus. In: E. M. Scarpelli and E. V. Coxmi (Ed.), *Reviews in Perinatal Medicine*. New York: Raven Press, 1978, pp. 243-280.
8. Gillberg, C.: "Floppy infant syndrome" and maternal diazepam. *Lancet*, 2: 244, 1977.
9. Haefely, W. E.: Central actions of benzodiazepines: General introduction. *Brit. J. Psychiat.*, 133: 231-238, 1978.
10. Braestrup, C., and Squires, R. F.: Brain specific benzodiazepine receptors. *Brit. J. Psychiat.*, 133: 249-260, 1978.
11. Shader, R. I., Georgotas, A., Greenblatt, D. J., et al.: Impaired absorption of desmethyldiazepam from clorazepate by magnesium aluminum hydroxide. *Clinical Pharmacological Therapy*, 24: 308-315, 1978.
12. Sellers, E.M., Greenblatt, D. J., and Giles, M. H.: Chlordiazepoxide and oxazepam disposition in cirrhosis. *Clinical Pharmacological Therapy*, 26: 240-246, 1979.
13. Greenblatt, D. J., Shader, R. I., Franke, K., et al.: Pharmacokinetics and bioavailability of intravenous, intramuscular, and oral lorazepam in humans. *Journal of Pharmacological Science*, 68: 57-63, 1979.
14. Shader, R. I., and Greenblatt, D. J.: Clinical implications of benzodiazepine pharmacokinetics. *Am. J. Psychiat.*, 134: 652-656, 1977.
15. Solomon, F., White, C. C., Parron, D. L., et al.: Sleeping pills, insomnia, and medical practice. *New Eng. J. Med.*, 300: 803-808, 1979.
16. Greenblatt, D. J., Allen, M. D., Locniskar, A., et al: Lorazepam kinetics in the elderly. *Clinical Pharmacological Therapy*, 26: 103-113, 1979.
17. Kales, A., Scharf, M. B., and Kales, J. D.: Rebound insomnia: A new clinical syndrome. *Science*, 201: 1039-1041, 1978.
18. Kochansky, G. E., Salzman, C., and Shader, R. I.,: The differential effects of chlordiazepoxide and oxazepam on hostility in a small-group setting. *Am. J. Psychiat.*, 132: 861-863, 1975.
19. Baldessarini, R. J.: *Chemotherapy in Psychiatry*. Cambridge: Harvard University Press, 1977, pp. 126-146.
20. Barranco, S. F., and Bridger, W.: Treatment of anxiety with oral hydroxyzine: An overview. *Current Therapy Research*, 22: 217-227, 1977.
21. Cole, J. O., Altesman, R. I., and Weingarten, C. H.: Beta-blocking drugs in psychiatry. *McLean Hospital Journal*, 4: 40-68, 1979.
22. Rosenbaum, J. F.: Anxiety. In: A. Lazare (Ed.), *Outpatient Psychiatry: Diagnosis and Treatment, First Edition*. Baltimore: Williams & Wilkins, 1979, pp. 252-256.
23. Quitkin, F. M., Rifkin, A., and Klein, D. F.: Lithium in other psychiatric disorders. In: S. Gershon and B. Shopsin (Eds.), *Lithium: Its Role in Psychiatric Research and Treatment*. New York: Plenum Press, 1976, pp. 295-315.

Name Index

Subject Index

ACTH (adrenocorticotropic hormone), 66-68, 103-104
Acute brain syndrome *see* Delirium
Acutely excited and agitated patients, 136-138
Acute manic psychosis, 138-139
Acute psychosis, 49, 55, 63
Addison's disease, 67, 170, 206
Adenomatosis, multiple, 69-70
Adjustment reactions, 222
Adolescents
  borderline, 18-19
  depression and, 151
  puberty and, 70
  transient psychosis in, 145-154
Adrenal insufficiency, acute, 50
Adrenergic delirium, 50-51
Affective disorders
  atypical, 17-18, 24
  catatonia and, 264, 269
  in the elderly patient, 163-168
  following a major psychosocial stressor, 36-37
  genetic loading for, 23
  thyrotoxicosis and, 63
Alcohol
  borderline patients and, 20, 113, 117, 255, 282
  catatonia and, 266
  delirium in the elderly and, 159-160
  late onset of abuse of, 165-166
  paranoid symptoms and, 114, 125-126, 170
  transient psychosis and, 111-129, 141-142, 152
  violent behavior and, 207
  withdrawal and adrenergic delirium, 51
  see also Delirium tremens (DTs); Drugs, induced mental disturbances
Alcoholic hallucinosis, 111, 123-125, 142
Alcohol idiosyncratic syndrome, 113-114

Alprenolol, 105
Alzheimer's disease, 49, 140, 162-163
Amantadine, 192
Amitriptyline, 139, 283-284, 287
Amnestic syndrome, alcoholic, 127-128
Amobarbital, 192, 212, 267, 269
Amok, 32
Amphetamines, 94-96, 98-99
  paranoid symptoms and, 142, 152, 170
  psychotogenic effects of, 101
  toxicity, 51
  treatment of transient psychosis due to, 203
  violent behavior and, 208
Amytal *see* Amobarbital
Anemia, 56
Angel dust *see* Phencyclidine (PCP)
Anoxia, 206
Antabuse, 129
Antianxiety agents, 289-295; *see also* Specific agents, i.e. Diazepam
Anticholinergic agents, 99-102, 201, 284
Anticholinergic delirium, 52
Antidepressants, 152
  adverse reactions to, 101, 159, 167-168
  affective disorders and, 17, 167
  anticholinergic properties of, 52, 100
  borderline patients and, 139, 279, 282-287
  catatonia and, 269
  corticosteroid psychosis and, 104
  LSD psychosis and, 87
  see also Depression
Antihistamines, 52, 122, 293-294
Antihypertensive agents, 105
Anti-Parkinsonian agents, 100, 140, 284-285
  adverse reactions to, 159
  see also Parkinson's disease
Antipsychotic drugs, 99, 134-143
  adverse reactions to, 159, 266

299